1998

Speaking the Other Self

Speaking the Other Self

American Women Writers

EDITED BY JEANNE CAMPBELL REESMAN

The University of Georgia Press   Athens and London

© 1997 by the University of Georgia Press

Athens, Georgia 30602

All rights reserved

Designed by Kathi Dailey Morgan

Set in Electra by G & S Typesetters, Inc.

Printed and bound by Braun-Brumfield, Inc.

The paper in this book meets the guidelines for permanence
and durability of the Committee on Production Guidelines for
Book Longevity of the Council on Library Resources.

Printed in the United States of America

01 00 99 98 97 C 5 4 3 2 1

01 00 99 98 97 P 5 4 3 2 1

LIBRARY OF CONGRESS CATALOGING IN PUBLICATION DATA

Speaking the other self : American women writers / edited by
    Jeanne Campbell Reesman.
        p. cm.
    Includes bibliographical references and index.
    ISBN 0-8203-1903-1 (alk. paper). — ISBN 0-8203-1909-0 (pbk. : alk. paper)
    1. American literature—Women authors—History and criticism.
2. Feminism and literature—United States—History.   3. Women and
literature—United States—History.   4. Authorship—Sex differences.
5. Women in literature.   6. Self in literature.   7. Canon (Literature)
I. Reesman, Jeanne Campbell.
PS147.S69   1997
810.9'9287—dc21   96-48850

BRITISH LIBRARY CATALOGING IN PUBLICATION DATA AVAILABLE

For My Sister

Janet Denise Campbell Mott

Contents

ix   Foreword / *Linda Wagner-Martin*

xi   Acknowledgments

xiii   Introduction

Part 1. Voice Engendered

3   "Masculinity" in *Uncle Tom's Cabin* / *Cynthia Griffin Wolff*

27   The *Jouissant* Politics of Helen Hunt Jackson's *Ramona*:
The Ground That Is "Mother's Lap" / *Daneen Wardrop*

39   Class and Sexuality in a Mexican Landscape: Katherine Anne
Porter's Marginalia on D. H. Lawrence / *Rae M. Carlton Colley*

54   Mirror, Mirror, on the Wall: Gazing in Edith Wharton's
"Looking Glass" / *Susan Elizabeth Sweeney*

Part 2. Race, Culture, and Diversity

79   The Chronicles of Panchita Villa: A Chicana Guerrillera
Literary Critic / *Tey Diana Rebolledo*

90   What Women? What Canon? African American Women and
the Canon / *Trudier Harris*

96   Said But Not Spoken: Elision and the Representation of Rape,
Race, and Gender in Harriet E. Wilson's *Our Nig*
Ronna C. Johnson

117   "Of One Blood": Reimagining American Genealogy in
Pauline Hopkins's *Contending Forces* / *Lisa Marcus*

144   Nationalism and Korean American Women's Writing: Theresa Hak
Kyung Cha's *Dictee* / *Shu-mei Shih*

Part 3. Form and Shape: Technique

165 Gender and First-Person Narration in Willa Cather's Fiction
Elsa Nettels

176 The "Real Lives" of Sophie Treadwell: Expressionism and the
Feminist Aesthetic in *Machinal* and *For Saxophone* / *Jerry Dickey*

185 Selves and "Other Shadows": Grace Paley's Ironic Fictions
Victoria Aarons

198 From Warrior to Womanist: The Development of June Jordan's
Poetry / *Jacqueline Vaught Brogan*

Part 4. Revising Tradition

213 Lost Boundaries: The Use of the Carnivalesque in Tabitha Tenney's
Female Quixotism / *Sharon M. Harris*

229 Engendered Nature/Denatured History: "The Yares of Black
Mountain" by Rebecca Harding Davis / *Jean Pfaelzer*

246 Whitman, Wharton, and the Sexuality in *Summer*
Abby H. P. Werlock

263 Rewriting the "Rose and Lavender Pages": *Ethan Frome* and
Women's Local Color Fiction / *Donna M. Campbell*

278 Fairy Tales and Opera: The Fate of the Heroine in the Work of
Sandra Cisneros / *Laura Gutierrez Spencer*

288 Amy Lowell and Cultural Borders / *Paul Lauter*

297 Contributors

301 Index

Foreword

Pat Mora writes in *Nepantla: Essays from the Land in the Middle* that a reader's needs can be met, and satisfied, only "when cultural and linguistic barriers are removed." Emphasizing that the world of letters needs "more voices, and more varied voices," Mora foreshadowed the kinds of interchanges that took place at the 1993 San Antonio American Women Writers Conference, an American Literature Association meeting. In voices that ranged from soothing to impassioned to angry, many mesmerizing dialogues between critic and audience, poet and listener, and performer and viewer played themselves out. And we participants were changed in the process.

One of the first academic conferences to focus on the writing of American women and its criticism, the San Antonio meeting was also unique in its geographic location, being itself a kind of "nepantla," or borderland, between Mexico and the States. The conference organizers drew on the vibrant resources of the area: one evening was given over to a reading by three excellent poets, a reading well attended by students and members of the community, Spanish speakers as well as Anglos. Chicana poet Pat Mora read her bilingual poems to enthusiastic response, but that same audience was equally excited by the work of Naomi Shihab Nye and Wendy Barker, neither of whom is Chicana. Somehow, in the crowded auditorium in San Antonio, those "cultural and linguistic barriers" disappeared.

On another day, performances were given by the San Antonio Mujeres Grandes group, a talented ensemble of women poets, playwrights, and performance artists who spoke, sang, danced, and recited for each other and for us, their enthusiastic audience. Although some of their work was presented in Spanish, even the non–Spanish speakers listened eagerly. It was a magical afternoon.

But the real importance of this fusion of Spanish and English was not the literal melding of languages. It was, rather, the spirit warming the 250 participants, as if their sheer will to attend to speakers could break through existing language barriers. They were struggling to hear what was being voiced, even though some of the speakers continued to use standard academic discourse.

Many of the excellent critical essays were also infused with this spirit of the borderland, as if discussing writing by women provided a space that needed mapping. Exploring. Inhabiting. Outstanding scholars both young and mature worked at redefining "sentimentality," while other sessions focused on the way themes probe ethnicity in relation to history and gender; other innovative topics included considerations of autobiography in contemporary women's poetry, methods of transgressing the cultural group boundary, and current experimental women writers. Among those writers reaccessed were Emily Dickinson, Louise Erdrich, Pauline Hopkins, Willa Cather, Toni Morrison, Edith Wharton, June Jordan, Amy Lowell, Kate Chopin, Elizabeth Bishop, Sandra Cisneros, Harriet E. Wilson, and Eudora Welty. But it was also the variety of the critical approaches that made the sessions so informative: new historicism set against psychoanalytic readings, manuscript studies, and feminist interrogation.

Whatever their topic or approach, few of the participants were passive. These women and men had not traveled to San Antonio merely to put in three days of their professional lives; they were engaged—better, they were committed, both to being heard and to listening. They believed in the genuine interchange of ideas. Accordingly, after some papers, there was discussion, correction, and even argument. And dialogue continued after sessions ended, spilling out into corridors and coffee gatherings, art exhibits and meals.

Those of us who were part of the San Antonio conference must thank Jeanne Campbell Reesman for her innovative, human-centered program, a format—and a forum—that allowed us to participate, contribute, and come away with fresh ideas and revitalized responses. These excellent essays extend the life of that meeting and allow readers who were not there to experience at least some of the vigor of the time.

Linda Wagner-Martin
University of North Carolina, Chapel Hill

Acknowledgments

The American Literature Association Symposium on American Women Writers was, as far as I know, the first conference ever held on the subject. For proposing this groundbreaking meeting and for asking me to direct it I warmly thank Alfred Bendixen, under whose leadership the American Literature Association has dramatically expanded possibilities for the presentation of research in American literature. I am also grateful to Alan Craven, Dean of the College of Fine Arts and Humanities at the University of Texas at San Antonio, to Raymond T. Garza, Provost at the University of Texas at San Antonio, and to Peter Balbert, Chair, Department of English, Trinity University, for their support of the symposium. Gail Jones, Nancy Membrez, Judith Fisher, Nina Baym, Trudier Harris, Tey Diana Rebolledo, Linda Wagner-Martin, Wendy Barker, Naomi Nye, Pat Mora, Enedina and Arturo Vasquez, and the Mujeres Grandes shared the commitment to exploring and explaining our subject. I am most indebted to the 250 participants the meeting drew. Their diverse new approaches to American women writers are represented by the selections in these pages.

I would like to thank my colleague Linda Woodson for her perceptive suggestions concerning my definition of "self" through a rhetorical model, and I am grateful to Elizabeth Ammons as well for her early encouragement of this volume. The director of the University of Georgia Press, Karen Orchard, has been part of the project from the beginning, and I am grateful to Cisley Owen, Kristine Blakeslee, and Mark Pentecost for their timely aid.

Grateful acknowledgment is given to the estate of Katherine Anne Porter and to Barbara Thompson Davis, Trustee, for permission to quote from Porter's materials cited in Rae M. Carlton Colley's "Class and Sexuality in a Mexican Landscape: Katherine Anne Porter's Marginalia on D. H. Lawrence."

The quotation from Mildred Bennett's letter to Dorothy C. Fisher cited in Elsa Nettels's "Gender and First-Person Narration in Willa Cather's Fiction" is used by permission of Special Collections, the University of Vermont Library. Nettels's essay appears in slightly different form in her book *Language and Gender in American Fiction* and is reprinted with permission of the University Press of Virginia.

The rights to Sophie Treadwell's works, cited by Jerry Dickey in "The

'Real Lives' of Sophie Treadwell: Expressionism and the Feminist Aesthetic in *Machinal* and *For Saxophone*," are owned by the Roman Catholic Church of the Diocese of Tucson: A Corporation Sole, from whom production rights must be obtained. These excerpts are reprinted by permission of the Diocese of Tucson. Proceeds from the printing or production of Sophie Treadwell's works are used for the aid and benefit of Native American children in Arizona.

Excerpts from June Jordan's *Living Room/Naming Our Destiny*, copyright 1984/1989 by June Jordan, in Jacqueline Vaught Brogan's "From Warrior to Womanist: The Development of June Jordan's Poetry" are used by permission of the publisher, Thunder's Mouth Press, and the author. Quotations from *Civil Wars*, copyright 1981 by June Jordan, are reprinted by permission of the publisher, Beacon Press, and the author. Excerpts from *An Atlas of the Difficult World: Poems 1988–1991* by Adrienne Rich, copyright 1991 by Adrienne Rich, are reprinted by permission of the author and W. W. Norton and Company.

"Mirror, Mirror, on the Wall: Gazing in Edith Wharton's 'Looking Glass,'" copyright by Ohio State University, *Narrative* 3.2 (May 1995), is reprinted here by permission; all rights reserved. Cynthia Griffin Wolff's "'Masculinity' in *Uncle Tom's Cabin*," copyright by the Johns Hopkins University Press, appears in a slightly different version in *American Quarterly* 47.4 (May 1995) and is reprinted here by permission.

"Rewriting the 'Rose and Lavender Pages': *Ethan Frome* and Women's Local Color Fiction," by Donna M. Campbell, was first published in *Resisting Regionalism: Gender and Naturalism in American Fiction, 1885–1915* (Athens: Ohio University Press, 1997).

Introduction

The dramatic and celebrated growth in the teaching and study of American women writers has been the most promising development on the American literary scene in the last twenty years. Reviewing one's own syllabi over that period is a startling and illuminating exercise. Whereas in 1977, say, one might find in an introductory American literature course a lonely Emily Dickinson, perhaps accompanied by newly rediscovered Kate Chopin or still-emerging Edith Wharton, today the choices far exceed the possibilities of even the most crowded syllabus, evidence that perhaps American literature courses need a few extra semesters. This book offers a representative sampling of the exciting new scholarship being pursued in this burgeoning field. Intended for literary scholars, historians, teachers, and students, it offers a feminist, historicized set of readings of both widely recognized and emerging writers from the eighteenth century to the present by scholars emphasizing a variety of concerns and approaching their subjects from positions derived from cultural studies, new historicism, narratology, dialogics, French feminism, psychoanalysis, and gaze theory. The writers under study make up a field full of stimulation and surprises; the essays accordingly respond to the simultaneous diversity and interrelatedness that characterize American women writers. Yet to call our subject a "field" is less accurate, I believe, than to describe it as a set of forces being continuously played out and renewed.

Criticism on many of these writers—these new forces—is accelerating quickly. Scholarship on better-established figures such as Harriet Beecher Stowe, Willa Cather, and Edith Wharton is expanding in many new directions and at last receiving the level of attention their work demands—and it is worth remembering that they have not always been "better established" at all. Wharton's literary reputation has grown steadily over the years, and Cather is at last emerging from the margins of literary respectability among scholars. (Neither has ever hurt for readers.) Stowe's importance has become increasingly emphasized. Even a cursory glance at recent works on these writers reveals the scope of critical treatments.[1] At the same time, many of the nineteenth- and early twentieth-century figures discussed here have virtually been ignored by critics until now. Perhaps the clearest case is Rebecca Harding Davis, who, though appearing more regularly in critical discussions, is still dramatically underrepresented in scholarship; for example, the 1994 *MLA Bibliography* lists sixty-five entries for Emily Dickinson, while only one appears for Davis.[2] Readers of the present volume may wonder at Dickinson's absence here, along with newly prominent figures such as Zora Neale Hurston or Toni Morrison, but the choice is deliberate: these writers either have always received or are now receiving a great deal of attention, and I felt that this book needed to address some less-represented voices. Other figures from the past who have until recently been largely overlooked by critics include Tabitha Tenney, Harriet E. Wilson, Helen Hunt Jackson, Pauline Hopkins, Sophie Treadwell, and Amy Lowell. Katherine Anne Porter is an interesting case, since she is routinely taught, but scholarship has not built up the kind of depth—yet— that one would expect.[3] As far as contemporary writers go, anthologies are starting to reflect these women's significance by including more selections (and more diverse selections), but scholarly publication has not caught up.[4]

The nineteen essays collected here furnish a wealth of illustration for the multiple selves created and addressed in American women's writing. When a given essay is ostensibly about race, it is also about gender and class. When it is an analysis of narrative style, it is a politicized statement, too. When it is about historical influence, it is about what is new. Indeed, not one of these essays can be reduced to a unidirectional thesis, and I have found myself wondering at their intersections. I have arranged them to bring out their inter- relations as much as possible, but they will generate their own patterns for readers. In her essay, Shu-mei Shih describes the Korean American woman's identity as an interrogation of her being simultaneously inside and outside multiple orders, while herself also embodying those orders. In Theresa Hak Kyung Cha's work, "borders both form and coalesce, contest and yield, hence there is no set 'in-between' or 'interstitial' location. As borders shift in time and space, so does the location of the subject." She does not occupy interstitial space, nor does she merely articulate an aesthetics of the interstice; she em- bodies the interstice, and both the inside and outside of the borders that out- line that interstice. This model also describes the many insterstitial selves pres- ent in this collection, and their reverberations from one to another. It is a rhetoric of the Self from selves.

These essays seek to embody a particularly and peculiarly American femi- nine rhetoric of the Self. It is engendered, othered without loss of connection to others and communalized without loss of individuality. I call it "peculiarly American" because of its unique multiethnicity: in treating white, Native American, Latina, African American, and Asian American subjects, it ad- dresses the binaries of Old World/New World, freedom/slavery, colonizer/ colonized, mainstream/margins, individual/collective, us/them, self/other as it also interacts with the binary male/female. But it refuses such binarism at the same time; it is about borders and it is about moving in and through borders. This rhetoric is about language and its borderings and embroiderings, the conflation of "meaning" with its edges. I wish to turn to some theoretical ways of describing this arena of female language, identity, and creativity and to offer some discussion of the multicultural web of relations that characterize the feminine rhetoric of this volume. But first I am drawn to a different kind of description of what it means to "speak the other self."

San Antonio artist and poet Enedina Casarez Vasquez, together with her husband, Arturo Vasquez, paints women "speaking themselves," large canvases and ideographs that present stylized Latina women uttering the Aztec symbol for thought, the voice scroll. But she also has become quite well-known for her *nichos*, iconic devotional boxes anywhere from four inches to five feet in height. They are open at the front and portray inside the Blessed Virgin or local saints, whether San Antonio de Padua or Frida Kahlo. As with her paintings, the brightly painted *nichos* have inscribed around their front edges (or frames) poems that give voice to the images contained within: sometimes they are prayers, sometimes descriptions, sometimes just poems.

These jewel-like windows into the artist's spirit well represent the unusual juxtapositions of inner and outer, speaking and hearing, center and frame in women's writing in America. The "self" portrayed inside the box is the subject, the ego, the I, but because it is framed by the language of the border it finds its way into the world around it through that frame, contextualizing, problematizing, complicating. The border of words constitutes an othering of the image at the same time as it furnishes the connection to the viewer/listener. This framing function gives us the "other self," the one that accompanies and continues the realm of the Self. If the words on the frame are a poem addressed to the saint depicted, then are we the speaker? If the words are one of Kahlo's poems, then is she? If the words are Enedina Vasquez's, then who is speaking? The entire realm of distinctions is deliberately blurred and crossed over in the *nicho*. This is a very different version of the "other," for it leads inward and outward to the multiplicities of the world and all the other others in it; one does not want to be spoken for, even by oneself, or to be "othered" by an "other"—especially along lines of race, class, or gender. Even harder to overcome at times is the muffling of one's own voices by an overriding ego determined to control, organize, and restrict contigencies. But like the *nichos*, the American women writers addressed in this book enact again and again a Self that is constantly surprising in its variability, renewability, permeability, adaptability, in its endless capacity for continuing its story. Self and other are not separate, but joined; the framing box that holds the figure, like the material body, is both an invitation to see in and an avenue outward into discourse with the world. (See the appendix to this essay, "Reading the Nicho.")

Dialogic language is described in literary theory by such figures as Lev Vygotsky and Mikhail Bakhtin. Their work definitively explores the essentially social and semiotic nature of the self, its multifaceted existence through the communal, its fluidity and continual development, as well as the addressivity of the word and the fundamental connection between speaker and hearer.[5] More recently, the cultural psychologist Jerome Bruner has defined the self as developing through narrative. We do not acquire language as spectators of it, but through use. Selves are not "isolated nuclei of consciousness"; rather, they are "distributed interpersonally," and "the lives and selves we construct are the outcomes of [a] process of meaning construction." He speaks of the "transactional self" as a way of describing the relationship between speaker and other, agreeing with Bakhtin that the self is "dialogue-dependent." It is a "way of framing one's consciousness, one's position, one's identity, one's commitment with respect to another."[6] As a specialist in developmental psychology, Bruner urges that "the future needs to create in children an appreciation of the fact that many worlds are possible, that meaning and reality are created and not discovered, that negotiation is the process of constructing new meanings by which individuals can regulate their relations with each other." This will allow us "the power to create reality, to reinvent culture."[7] This power to create or reinvent culture has been an especially vexing one for women writers, since even to address it has been daunting for so many of them: to imagine an audience at all, even a limited one, in the case of Harriet E. Wilson or Pauline Hopkins, was an act of imagining affirmation, imagining interconnectedness, engaging a tentative and tenuous "I" with an unseen other, recognizing and using their own "otherness" in the service of selfhood and community. They consciously and unconsciously had to depend on the "I-self" and the "I-other," both internalized, as existing out there somewhere at the same time.

The most helpful theoretical perspective on rhetoric of the feminine self is provided by Julia Kristeva, throughout whose multivalent career we return again and again to what Toril Moi calls her version of "the subject in process," the "healthy subject" who is "free to construct imaginary fantasies to produce new language."[8] This view of selfhood is found in many of Kristeva's works. In "Stabat Mater," a prose poem meditation on her experience with maternity accompanied by an essay on the cult of the Virgin Mary and its implications for understanding motherhood, Kristeva makes the succinct but enormously significant observation that "A mother is a continuous separation, a division of the very flesh." Her own experience of giving birth was of "My removed marrow, which nevertheless acts as a graft, which wounds but increases me. Paradox: deprivation and benefit of childbirth. But calm finally hovers over pain, over the terror of this dried branch that comes back to life, cut off, wounded, deprived of its sparkling bark. The calm of another life, the life of that other who wends his way while I remain henceforth like a framework. Still life. There is him, however, his own flesh, which was mine yesterday. Death, then, how could I yield to it?"[9]

Elsewhere in her work marginality also "inaugurates the dialogic," as Suzanne Clark remarks: Kristeva "advocates a notion of cultural and personal identity which recognizes that the strangeness of the other is a strangeness within. At the level of the state, this implies the acceptance of foreigners. At the level of the individual, this implies the recognition of the unconscious. Identity, then, must be seen as provisional rather than exclusive, constructed as an effect of the heterogeneous processes of discourses." Poetic language is revolutionary, according to Kristeva, not because it advocates a particular politics but because, as Clark emphasizes, it changes "the very forms of discourse," liberating the "semiotic" and rupturing the constraints of the "symbolic." The subject in process in this disruption is "the unsettling and nonlogical life of the body." These interpretations of Kristeva lead Clark to a "relational, collaborative view of rhetoric," for Kristeva is most interested in "a kind of knowledge that can only be rhetorical, the product of an exchange between speaking subjects." Because "we are, in fact, all strangers, without and within," we must acknowledge "the constructedness and fragility of individual and community identities. The ego, like the nation, should not be defended against otherness by paranoid exclusions; it should rather be conceived as a set of processes." Clark's rhetoric would allow "the inclusion of the foreign, the strange, the unconscious—the woman," for "woman unsettles the repressive identity-making work of the language that would deny process." Thus for Kristeva and for Clark reading Kristeva, the dialogic sphere is a feminine one, and furthermore, it is not "an intersubjectivity of absolutely autonomous identities, but an *intertextuality that is dependent on bodies.*"[10] The conjunction of the new rhetoric, the new feminine, and the new set of (inter)national cultures playing off one another makes Kristeva's work especially suggestive for critics of American women writers. Kristeva's name does not appear often in the essays of this volume, but I find her thought to be a helpful framework (albeit one of many) for reading them.

One of Kristeva's best-known works is the essay "Women's Time," in which she asks the question especially pertinent to *Speaking the Other Self*: "women are writing, and the air is heavy with expectation: What will they write that is new?"[11] In "Women's Time" she demonstrates how humankind's essential and shared separation is transmuted into a dual "I"—ego and other—in women's writing in particular. Kristeva defines feminism politically by examining women's relations to time and representations of history. She begins by contrasting Nietzsche's "cursive" (or linear) time with his notion of "monumental" (or epochal) time, arguing that women are associated with cyclic or repetitive time more akin to monumental than to cursive time. Here her Freudian notion of separation is critical: while both sexes must undergo separation from an undifferentiated mother-infant totality in order to enter into a social order based on the recognition of differences, they undergo it differently. As Patricia Bizzell and Bruce Herteberg note in their analysis of Kristeva's essay, "Men exaggerate the pain of separation and fear to be separated from everything, including the sign of their superior difference, the penis. Women deny the pain of separation and long for wholeness, a longing expressed by longing for the sign this culture treats as the mark of a whole person—namely, the penis." But, they continue, "in Kristeva's view, Western society is founded on the separation or sacrifice of women, who accept their relegation to a subordinate role to aid in differentiating a superior role for men. To remedy this situation, Kristeva suggests that women be brought to consciousness of their oppression," whether through feminist theory and research or by "writing the body." Though women have trouble defining their relation to political (and hence linguistic) power, Kristeva sees the efforts both of early feminists and of many contemporary ones as "terroristic" if they reject the social contract in favor of women-only "counter-societies" or if they adopt the present contract and rule as if they were men. Kristeva takes the risky step of arguing that a "preferable way to reunite with the mother is to become a mother, and she endorses second-generation feminists' return to motherhood as an acceptable vocation," hoping that this will create new feminist models for separation of mother and child, "one that is," as Bizell and Herteberg stress, "not traumatic but . . . still productive of linguistic abilities." Kristeva hopes that "feminists' use of their linguistic abilities—that is, their writing—will also suggest new paths to wholeness." In this sense, Kristeva calls for a third generation of feminists who can understand difference as "irreducible and meaningful" and who will through language, especially women's non-unitary discourse, convey the facts that "many voices are always speaking, and that each individual can have many voices."[12]

We desperately need this new feminist rhetoric, Kristeva muses, this "multiplicity of female expressions and preoccupations," in order to foster an intersection of differences from which "there might arise . . . the real *fundamental difference* between the two sexes: a difference that feminism has the enormous merit of rendering painful, that is, productive of surprises and of symbolic life in a civilization which, outside of the stock exchange and wars, is bored to death" (193). Kristeva connects motherhood as a model for psychic health, language, and specifically literature as the practices that will develop her "utopian" vision, as she calls it. Why motherhood? Because

> Pregnancy seems to be experienced as the radical ordeal of the splitting of the subject: redoubling up of the body, separation and coexistence of the self and an other, of nature and consciousness, of physiology and speech. This fundamental challenge to identity is then accompanied by a fantasy of totality—narcissistic completeness—a sort of instituted, socialized, natural psychosis. The arrival of the child, on the other hand, leads the mother into the labyrinths of an experience that, without the child, she would only rarely encounter: love for an other. Not for herself, nor for an identical being, and still less for another person with whom "I" fuse (love or sexual passion). But the slow, difficult and delightful apprenticeship in attentiveness, gentleness, forgetting oneself. The ability to succeed in this path without masochism and without annihilating one's affective, intellectual and professional personality—such would seem to be the stakes to be won through guiltless maternity. (206–7)

"On the other hand," she continues, "it is in the aspiration towards artistic and, in particular, literary creation that woman's desire for affirmation now manifests itself." Thus, "Why literature?" (207). Because

> What discourse, if not that of a religion, would be able to support this adventure which surfaces as a real possibility, after both the achievements and the impasses of the present ideological reworkings, in which feminism has participated? It seems to me that the role of what is usually called "aesthetic practices" must increase not only to counterbalance the storage and uniformity of information by present-day mass media, data-bank systems and, in particular, modern communications technology, but also to demystify the identity of the symbolic bond itself, to demystify, therefore, the *community* of language as a universal and unifying tool, one which totalizes and equalizes. In order to bring out—along with the *singularity* of each person and, even more, along with the multiplicity of every person's possible identifications (with atoms, e.g., stretching from the family to the stars)—the *relativity of his/her symbolic as well as biological existence*, according to the variation in his/her specific symbolic capacities. (210)

I noted earlier that the feminine rhetoric under discussion here is especially relevant to American literature because of the multiethnic character and particular multiethnic history of women in America. This fact is revealed in such poststructuralist characters as Sula and Sethe in Toni Morrison's novels or in the critics' postmodern devotion to process, as when African American feminist Barbara Christian identifies the idea of process as a critical aspect of an evolving feminist approach—"that is, a resistance to art as artifact, to ideas as fixed, and a commitment to open-endedness, possibility, fluidity—to change." Elsewhere, Christian notes that "in every society where there is the denigrated other . . . the other struggles to declare the truth and therefore create the truth in forms that exist for her or him." [13] A novelist like Morrison, then, as Barbara Waxman observes, may "reinterpret a traditional genre such as the slave narrative or create a new one using postmodern psychoanalytic ideas or through what Henry Louis Gates Jr., has called 'formal signifying': structurally parodic commentary on or protest against earlier texts and styles, especially those of the patriarchy, but also those of earlier black writers." [14] Similarly, among Latina authors there is the Self that dares to speak out, that dares to have an identity, but also the accompanying sense of speaking within and to and out of a community that itself needs to be constantly reinvented: breaking of taboos is characteristic of Chicana writers in particular, as in Sandra Cisneros's poem "Down There" and other works involving her own sense of "guerrilla" creativity. As Tey Diana Rebolledo and Eliana S. Rivero surmise, the self-reflexive and self-conscious features of Chicana writing express a "longing for the ability to say, to paint the world as seen through the eyes of the creator, to play with words and their mysterious power," to write in a way that "knows no restraints, no boundaries." Chicanas write out of a sense of the magical and the mundane together, they write in the ancestral tongues: in Spanish, the language of family culture, and in English, the "thick words" Mexican immigrants must learn to help their children in school. These multiple codes underscore the resistance the Latina self encounters in projecting her voice and both locating and freeing it from its "cultural" context, locating and freeing and relocating the self. [15]

More and more multicultural anthologies are appearing, drawing further attention to the cultural, linguistic, racial, and class-based differences that make up the American scene; especially noteworthy for investigation of a feminine American rhetoric are Rebolledo and Rivero's *Infinite Divisions: An Anthology of Chicana Literature*, A. LaVonne Brown Ruoff and Jerry W. Ward Jr.'s *Redefining American Literary History*, and Geoffrey M. Sill, Miriam T. Chaplin, Jean Ritzke, and David Wilson's *Opening the American Mind: Race, Ethnicity, and Gender in Higher Education*. In *Redefining American Literary History* Paul Lauter calls for a new comparative model for the study of American literature and an end to the "Great River theory of American letters," the notion of a "mainstream." Such a comparativist strategy would allow us to "appreciate a broader range of conventions" and interrogate givens such as "modernism" or "realism."[16] Similarly, in *Opening the American Mind*, Gregory S. Jay argues that "it is time to stop teaching 'American' literature." Rather than a false pluralism, "our goal should be rather to construct a multicultural paradigm for the study of writing in the United States," and he urges that this project be carried out through "mapping of the located body." Racism accounts for the failures of democracy in America, he contends: false borders. "Writing in the United States" would be the title of the new course to be substituted for the old. And apropos of the American feminine rhetoric, "a multicultural pedagogy entails a process of cultural revision, so that everyone involved comes not only to understand another person's point of view, but to see her or his own culture from the outsider's perspective. This de-centering of cultural chauvinism can only be healthy in the long run, especially if it leads each of us to stop thinking of ourselves as subjects of only one culture, and prompts us to recognize the multicultural overdetermination of any individual's complex being." Thus, Jay concludes, the problematics of cultural revision would involve origins, power, civilization, tradition, assimilation, translation, bodies, literacy, and borders.[17]

In the present volume, these problematics and the shape of the feminine rhetoric(s) under study are grouped into four sections. The first group of essays presents "Voice Engendered." Here Cynthia Griffin Wolff gives us a startling insight into *Uncle Tom's Cabin*: a view of the construction of masculinity within the novel and the historical context for that construction. Deeply committed to nonviolent modes of correcting the evils of slavery, Stowe supported the "Fraternal Love" movement, a branch of abolitionism that deplored competition, conquest, and violence as the laudable and "natural" expressions of a "masculine" nature and that postulated an alternative notion of "masculinity" based upon expressions of generosity, love, and commitment to communal interests. All the major male characters in *Uncle Tom's Cabin* can be "placed" within these precepts and thus be more comprehensively understood by a modern reader. Stowe's apparent "feminization" is in reality a radical reconstruction of "masculinity" along anti-imperialistic lines. Daneen Wardrop attempts to revise the generally dismissive critical view of Helen Hunt Jackson's *Ramona* (1884) by examining the tactics Jackson devises in order to win her audience over to her radical belief that the cult of American acquisitiveness is destructive and immoral. Jackson calls attention to the "thievery" that dispossessed Native Americans of their homes, but in order to avoid alienating her Anglo (largely female) audience, she resorts to *jouissant* landscapes and mother-centered settings in hopes that the audience will pay allegiance to gender over nationality or race and recognize themselves as women who must learn to decide political questions on the basis not of convention but of their own feminine sense of justice.

Rae M. Carlton Colley examines Katherine Anne Porter's marginalia, "tiny fragments of genius, some of which saw fruition in her published criticism," which reflect her search for order amid chaos, her resulting attempt to perfect her craft, and the difficult choices she faced in a patriarchal society. Porter's notes on D. H. Lawrence exemplify these themes particularly as they reflect Porter's simultaneous disgust with Lawrence's depictions of sexuality and her admiration for him as an artist: Colley believes that "ultimately, the Lawrence marginalia shows two artists with vastly different styles addressing the common theme of a search for order" and who discover, to their horror, that sometimes order is not possible.

Wharton's ghost story "Looking Glass" (1935) is read in the context of psychoanalysis, film theory, and feminist narratology. This tale of a beautiful woman who has lost her looks turns upon the connections between visual appearance and visual perception, suggesting that, in a world in which women are to be seen but not observe, a woman will do almost anything to be looked at—and yet be unable to imagine her own desiring glance. In Susan Sweeney's view, the story's specular relations, mirror images, and narrative frames reflect the difficulty of narrating through a woman's eyes and demonstrate the extent to which feminine identity is constructed (and constricted) by the gendered gaze.

In the next section, "Race, Culture, and Diversity," Tey Diana Rebelledo, a "Chicana Guerrillera literary critic," sounds the call for a more inclusive and intellectually responsible canon, arguing her case without the luxury of virtually *any* recognition of Chicana writers, including such artists as Pat Mora and Angela de Hoyos, "fine writers . . . excluded" from the "narrowly focused feminist canon." Rebelledo discusses the problems facing Chicana writers and critics and analyzes reasons for their nearly total omission from most American literature syllabi and conference panels. Using the figure of the seventeenth-century Mexican nun Sor Juana Inés de la Cruz and a contrived text, *The Memoirs of Panchita Villa*, patterned after a Mexican novel of the 1930s, Rebelledo tells her own story within both the cultural legacy left by Sor Juana and the model furnished by the guerrillera Panchita. Rebelledo demands that we recognize the enormity of Chicanas' elision from academic discourse and then offers some surprising connections available for teaching Chicana and "mainstream" Anglo women writers.

In "What Women? What Canon?" Trudier Harris notes that even as arguments about canon formation continue to rage, it is clear that teachers, scholars, and students have already determined one for African American writers;

what modern literature course would be complete without such writers as Zora Neale Hurston, Toni Morrison, or Alice Walker, to name only a few examples? However, the tremendous amount of publishing going forward on these and other writers notwithstanding, the African American canon needs to be expanded to include lesser-known figures such as Julia Fields, Dorothy West, and Adrienne Kennedy. And, Harris insists, it is time for women scholars to become more visibly influential.

In directing attention to neglected texts, Ronna C. Johnson takes Harriet E. Wilson's *Our Nig* (1859) as illustrating the complex burdens on antebellum black, female self-representation by presenting a crucial but largely unexamined interpretive problem flagged by authorial and narrator interventions and narrative elisions: white male sexual abuse of the protagonist, Frado. In so doing, the text follows the nineteenth-century's code of "true womanhood" by effacing the reality of violation, yet indicates through its double silence and coded rhetorical figures what cannot be confessed in speech.

Lisa Marcus defends Pauline Hopkins's presentation of women and race, especially as criticized by Gwendolyn Brooks, in her analysis of Hopkins's *Contending Forces* (1900), arguing that Hopkins's project is nothing less than a radical revision of America's genealogical imagination. Hopkins subverts American concepts of racial purity by "showing the whiteness of black origins," especially as, in the story of the Montfort family's fall, she substitutes a white woman for the commonly circulated image of a black slave being beaten, "cogently exposing the engendering of race and the racializing of gender: the woman is racialized by her very placement in this scene of violence and she is engendered in her sexualized exposure to under the lash."

Shu-mei Shih explores what she calls the Korean American sensibility of the "1.5 generation" through a reading of Theresa Hak Kyung Cha's *Dictee* (1992). The term "1.5 generation," widely used in the Korean American community to describe those who were born in Korea and who immigrated to the United States at an early age, refers to a bicultural and bilingual group whose relationships with their two countries is different from those of first- or second-generation Asian Americans. Theresa Cha's imagination, Shih demonstrates, begins with "nation" but goes beyond it to a gendered and racialized reinscription of nationalism: an "ImagiNation" that at once denotes material history and evocative narratization, drawing on sources as divergent as colonialism and neocolonialism, Greek myth, Catholicism, Chinese cosmology, Korean shamanism, and French literature.

Turning to "Form and Shape: Technique," the third section of *Speaking the Other Self*, we find Elsa Nettels approaching narrrativity and gender together in her analysis of first-person narrators in *My Ántonia* and *My Mortal*

Enemy, noting how male narrators, as in the former work, differ from females as in the latter: they are more authoritative, they address a group of listeners, and they dwell more upon their own affairs. However, Nettels's incisive comparison demonstrates that the qualities exemplified by female narrators best enabled Cather to achieve the ideal of fiction defined in her 1922 essay, "The Novel Demeuble."

Jerry Dickey argues that the "narrative" devices of Sophie Treadwell's plays—works almost totally neglected even today, save her well-known 1928 work *Machinal*—are noteworthy factors in Treadwell's attempt to create a meaningful form through which women could be celebrated as subjects for the theater. In *Machinal* and the unpublished *For Saxophone*, Dickey notes, Treadwell is one of the first American women playwrights to attempt a radical restructuring of dramatic narrative for the purpose of appealing to a female sensibility in her audience; she employs a variety of expressionistic devices, such as extended interior monologues, music and song, distortion, and confessional scenes, all to dramatize a female protagonist's otherness.

In a more contemporary vein, "storytelling" is central to Grace Paley's short fiction, according to Victoria Aarons, as a link between the fragmented voices of her postmodern method and her liberal feminism within post–World War II American Jewish life. Such narrative duality is both thematic and structural, offering first an ironic chorus of comment and then the gesture of self-invention. In Jacqueline Vaught Brogan's "From Warrior to Womanist," we see the evolution of June Jordan's poetry toward a global vision combining personal, political, and poetic modes in an act of sustained resistance to the violence of her world. Her effort represents an ongoing act of faith, as well, in the redemptive power of words to highlight and subvert literal patriarchal dominance. Brogan offers readings of a number of Jordan's poems, particularly her "War and Memory," in which, amid images of World War II, the Spanish Civil War, the War on Poverty, and so on, the narrator muses: "and I remember / wondering if my family was a war / going on / and if / there would soon be blood / someplace in the house / and where / the blood of my family would come from."

Finally, in the section "Revising Tradition," we conclude by looking backward and forward, crossing borders of influence, tradition, and possibility. While narrativity as the storytelling tradition of self-expression—carnivalized, historicized, engendered, and classed—is the unifying thread in this next group of essays, their applications are even more far-reaching. Sharon M. Harris describes Tabitha Gilman Tenney's early novel *Female Quixotism* (1801) as exposing a failed sense of democracy in the new republic: using the carnivalesque to disrupt the dominant culture's discourse of harmony and unity, Tenney critiques the new order's segregation of women, foreshadowing feminist and postmodern critiques of the Enlightenment notion of reason. Tenney's book also exposes the difficulty for a writer of her time in handling the issue of race by replicating, despite the radicalism on behalf of women, the marginalization of black women. Rebecca Harding Davis devised new narrative strategies in her "The Yares of Black Mountain" (1875) in order to promote healing between North and South, suggesting that healing will arise from a new understanding of Southern women as pro-union, rebellious, matriarchal, communitarian, and "natural." Jean Pfaelzer's study of this novel explores Davis's repudiation of the narrative closures of the picturesque and the sublime as she reconfigures, instead, southern place as a gendered and historicized telos of a rebellious and articulate female community.

A pair of Wharton essays look at the functions of influence and tradition in quite different ways. Abby Werlock's witty comparison of the sexualities and varieties of humor portrayed by Wharton in *Summer* (1917) and by Walt Whitman in his poetry urges us to recognize not only Whitman's tremendous influence on Wharton but also her use of his poetic ideas to continue distancing herself from idealistic representations of romantic love. Wharton draws particularly on Whitman's "Children of Adam," "Song of Myself," "When Lilacs Last in the Dooryard Bloom'd," and "America" in her portrait of Charity Royall's rebellious sexuality. And Donna M. Campbell gives us Wharton's "rewriting" the "'rose and lavender pages'" of her sentimentalist predecessors, Freeman and Jewett, by reading *Ethan Frome* for its disruption of techniques and symbolic structures that would label Wharton as a local colorist. Viewed in this context, the much-maligned use of the male narrator becomes not only comprehensible but essential, for through her revisioning of the local-color world, especially its valuation of self-denial, Wharton seeks (naturalistically) to reclaim for her own mainstream fiction the marginal territories of the local colorists.

Laura Gutierrez Spencer explores the role of the Carmen figure in Sandra Cisneros's *Woman Hollering Creek* within the context of her use of other operatic and fairy tale figures in *The House on Mango Street*. Spencer gives an adroit and imaginative reading of how Cisneros transforms Bizet's Spanish tragedy of Carmen to a rollicking, comic South Texas conclusion in which Carmen asserts her independent nature and gets away with it—all to the strains of the Texas Tornados' "(Hey Baby) Qué Pasó?"

Finally, Paul Lauter addresses the excessive hostility directed toward Amy Lowell, still marginalized even after the feminist revival of the last quarter century. Criticized for "contradictory" practices, particularly by critics in the late 1920s and 1950s, Lowell was intent upon dissolving conventional boundaries, whether imagist and symbolist—or those surrounding her own sexuality. Renewed interest in her poetry reflects a renewed assault upon restrictive borders.

Let us turn to the many voices of *Speaking the Other Self*. As Linda Wagner-Martin observes in her Foreword, musing on Pat Mora's notion of the "nepantla," the intersections of discourse in these essays construct for us an ongoing conversation, a borderland of new possibilities, a borderland with no borders—that is, no barriers to thought and response and change, no end of possible voices and selves.

APPENDIX: READING THE *NICHO*

As created by San Antonio artists Enedina Casarez Vasquez and Arturo Vasquez, the traditional *nicho*, along with a range of *altares*, *tabletas*, and *cruzes*, embodies not only the beliefs of the Spanish Catholic Church, but also those of the Huichol Indians of Mexico. *Nichos* display portraits of Christ, the Virgin, saints, and other special figures painted in acrylics by Enedina Vasquez or cut from calendars, surrounded by special prayers or poems, tin *milagros* ("little miracles" or *ex votos* for saints' intercessions), and other decorations. Arturo Vasquez makes the boxes of wood from old wine crates or vegetable crates because he wants the wood to have had a life before it comes to them: when it is transformed into *nichos*, it symbolizes the transformations that took place in the lives of their subjects.

The Huichol symbols celebrate the abundant earth (a round symbol surrounded by small "moons"); rain (an inverted triangle atop a sphere); the wind (a jagged line); life's journey (a footprint); oneself (a sphere); and the four directions (a square cross). Christian symbols are also represented, for example, the cross, symbol of eternal life, and the many figures of the *milagros*, including those for protection of a child, for healing the body, for learning to pray. The dramatic colors of the *nichos* are symbolic as well: they celebrate heaven (blue), hope and growth (green), light and innocence (white), God (gold), moon and motherhood (silver), passion for life (red), love and truth (purple), and penance (black).

In *Libro de las Santos de EneArt*, a pamphlet accompanying their art, Enedina Vasquez writes: "When we were growing up our families had sacred places in the home where one would find religious statues, candles, rosaries, funeral cards, and pictures of the different saints or one dominant picture of a particular saint, e.g., Virgen de Guadalupe, etc. In these sacred places, usually a shelf, dresser, table or nook, either in the hallway or living room of the house, also were placed photos of family successes, such as our war heroes, or just photos of loved ones, especially the deceased members or the children of the house." The Vasquezes did not suspect that their art would become so popular that it is now sold in galleries and exhibited in leading museums nationally and internationally, including the Smithsonian Institution.

On the following pages are four of the Vasquezes' *nichos* devoted to women; they embody the voices and minds of the special women they represent. Together they form a *libro* of women's lives.

Sor Juana Inés de la Cruz (1648–1695) (fig. 1), was a nun of the Jeronymite Convent of Santa Paula in Mexico and, through her poetry, plays, and scholarly essays, one of the earliest pioneers of feminism in the western hemisphere: "We wanted to celebrate Sor Juana not only as part of our common history but as a woman who through her work and throughout her life spoke out against injustices perpetrated against the women of her time . . . and in so doing raised a storm of controversy that survives to this day. Through the quiet Sor Juana *nicho* we speak out by surrounding her with her words." The artists included smaller pictures of St. Jorge, because he fought for the oppressed, and St. Jude, because he encouraged Sor Juana to keep fighting even though the cause seemed lost.

The Virgen de Guadalupe (fig. 2) is known as the Queen of Mexico as well as the Queen of Heaven. This *nicho* was made after the death of Enedina Vasquez's mother to honor her favorite saint. On the top the Vasquezes placed a cactus to remind their son that he would encounter beautiful things in life that would cause him pain. The calendar picture is from Enedina's mother's home; they surrounded it with a prayer to the Virgin and with the Mexican *Loteria* cards the mother used to play to remind her grandson to *play* with and enjoy his family.

The *nichos* to Mary and Elizabeth and to Frida Kahlo (figs. 3 and 4) contain original watercolors by Enedina Vasquez. The one honors the Visitation of Mary and is dedicated to the Visitation House women's shelter in San Antonio in order to celebrate women helping women. The Frida Kahlo *nicho* honors the Mexican painter's courage and ability and was done as part of the touring exhibit, *La Passion por Frida*, that originated in the Diego Rivera Museum in Mexico City.

NOTES

1. Stowe, for example, is examined in arenas as diverse as her sources in Cotton Mather (Dorothy Z. Baker, "Puritan Providences in Stowe's *The Pearl of Orr's Island: The Legacy of Cotton Mather," Studies in American Fiction* 22.1 [Spring 1994]: 61–79) and her characters' "gynocentrism" (Susan Harris, "The Female Imaginary in Harriett Beecher Stowe's *The Minister's Wooing, New England Quarterly* 66 [1996]: 179–98). Susan Nuernberg ably treats Stowe in "The Rhetoric of Race," an essay in the new collection edited by Mason I. Lowance, Ellen E. Westbrook, and R. C. De Prospo, *The Stowe Debate: Rhetorical Strategies in "Uncle Tom's Cabin"* (Amherst: University of Massachusetts Press, 1994), 255–70. Some notable new contributions in Cather studies include Judith Fetterly's "Willa Cather and the Fiction of Female Development," in *Anxious Power: Reading, Writing, and Ambivalence in Narrative by Women,* ed. Carol J. Singley and Susan Elizabeth Sweeney (Albany: State University of New York Press, 1993), 221–34, and Elaine Sargeant Apthorp's "Speaking of Silence: Willa Cather and the 'Problem' of Feminist Biography," *Women's Studies* 18.1 (1990): 1–11. New, scholarly editions of Cather's works are being produced, such as

Willa Cather: O Pioneers! ed. Susan J. Rosowski and Charles W. Mignon (Lincoln: University of Nebraska Press, 1992), as well as handbooks such as Sheryl L. Meyering's *A Reader's Guide to the Short Stories of Willa Cather* (New York: G. K. Hall, 1994). One of the more interesting Wharton projects is the editing of the Love Diary by Kenneth M. Price and Phyllis McBride; see their "'The Life Apart': Texts and Contexts of Edith Wharton's Love Diary," *American Literature* 66.4 (December 1994): 663–88.

2. Andrew J. Scheiber's "An Unknown Infrastructure: Gender, Production, and Aesthetic Exchange in Rebecca Harding Davis's *Life in the Iron Mills*," *Legacy* 11.2 (1994): 101–17.

3. Some examples of the rather scarce work being done on some of these figures include the new edition of Tabitha Tenney's *Female Quixotism*, ed. Jean Nienkamp and Andrea Collins (New York: Oxford University Press, 1992); John Ernest, "Economics of Identity: Harriet E. Wilson's *Our Nig*," *PMLA* 109.3 (May 1994): 424–38; Carla L. Peterson, "Unsettled Frontiers: Race, History, and Romance in Pauline Hopkins's *Contending Forces*," in *Famous Last Words: Changes in Gender and Narrative Closure*, ed. Alison Booth (Charlottesville: University Press of Virginia, 1993), 177–96; Jennifer Jones, "In Defense of the Woman: Sophie Treadwell's *Machinal*," *Modern Drama* 37.3 (Fall 1994): 485–96. Extremely little is available on Amy Lowell. Porter scholars are examining topics ranging from her sources to the reflection of her politics in her work; see Janis P. Stout, "Katherine Anne Porter's 'Reflections on Willa Cather': A Duplicitous Homage," *American Literature* 66.4 (December 1994): 719–35; Jane P. Hafen, "Katherine Anne Porter's 'The Old Order' and *Agamemnon*," *Studies in Short Fiction* 31.3 (Summer 1994): 491–93; Thomas Austenfeld, "Katherine Anne Porter Abroad: The Politics of Emotion," *Literatur in Wissenschaft und Unterricht* (Kiel, Germany) 27.1 (1994): 27–33; and Stout, "'Something of a Reputation as a Radical': Katherine Anne Porter's Shifting Politics," *South Central Review* 10.1 (Spring 1993): 49–66.

4. See especially *The Norton Anthology of Literature by Women: The Traditions in English*, 2d ed., ed. Sandra M. Gilbert and Susan Gubar (New York: W. W. Norton, 1996), and the new *Heath Anthology of American Literature*, ed. Paul Lauter et al. (New York: D.C. Heath, 1994). Though Sandra Cisneros has probably been the Latina writer most often included on course syllabi and mentioned in criticism, there is still a dearth of scholarly work on her. June Jordan is often interviewed and discussed in more popular formats; see Peter Erickson, "After Identity: A Conversation with June Jordan," *Transition: An International Review* 63 (1994): 132–49; and Michelle Cliff, "The Lover: June Jordan's Revolution," *Village Voice Literary Supplement* 126 (June 1994): 27–29. Some intriguing work has begun to appear on Grace Paley, including Sanford Pinsker's "Grace Paley's Book of the Ordinary," *Gettysburg Review* 7.4 (Autumn 1994): 696–702.

5. See, for example, Lev Vygotsky, *Thought and Language*, trans. newly rev. and ed. Alex Kozulin (Cambridge, Mass.: MIT Press, 1986); M. M. Bakhtin, *The Dialogic Imagination: Four Essays*, ed. Michael Holquist, trans. Caryl Emerson and Michael Holquist (Austin: University of Texas Press, 1981); and Mikhail Bakhtin, *Problems of Dostoevsky's Poetics*, ed. and trans. Caryl Emerson (Minneapolis: University of Minnesota Press, 1984).

6. Jerome Bruner, *Acts of Meaning* (Cambridge, Mass.: Harvard University Press, 1990), 70, 138, 101.

7. Bruner, *Actual Minds, Possible Worlds* (Cambridge, Mass.: Harvard University Press, 1986), 149. See esp. chapter 4, "The Transactional Self," 57–69, and the "Afterword," 151–60.

8. Toril Moi, introduction to Julia Kristeva, *The Kristeva Reader*, ed. Moi (New York: Columbia University Press, 1986), 13.

9. Kristeva, "Stabat Mater," in *The Kristeva Reader*, 178, 168.

10. Suzanne Clark, "Julia Kristeva: Rhetoric and the Woman as Stranger," in *Reclaiming Rhetorica: Women in the Rhetorical Tradition*, ed. Andrea Lunsford (Pittsburgh: University of Pittsburgh Press, 1995), 306–9, 311, 314, 316.

11. Kristeva, "Women's Time," in *The Kristeva Reader*, 207; subsequent references are given parenthetically in the text.

12. Patricia Bizzell and Bruce Herteberg, "Julia Kristeva and 'Women's Time,'" in *The Rhetorical Tradition: Readings from Classical Times to the Present*, ed. Bizzell and Herteberg (Boston: Bedford Books of St. Martin's Press, 1990), 1229–31.

13. Barbara Christian, "But What Do We Think We're Doing Anyway: The State of Black Feminist Criticism(s), or My Version of a Little Bit of History," in *Changing Our Own Words: Essays on Criticism, Theory, and Writing by Black Women*, ed. Cheryl A. Wall (New Brunswick, N.J.: Rutgers University Press, 1989), 68; and Christian, *Black Feminist Criticism* (New York: Pergamon, 1985), 160.

14. Barbara Frey Waxman, introduction to *Multicultural Literatures through Feminist/Poststructuralist Lenses*, ed. Waxman (Knoxville: University of Tennessee Press, 1993), xv, xxvii–xxviii; Henry Louis Gates Jr., "The Blackness of Blackness: A Critique of the Sign and the Signifying Monkey," in *Black Literature and Literary Theory*, ed. Gates (New York: Methuen, 1984), 294.

15. Tey Diana Rebolledo and Eliana S. Rivero, eds., *Infinite Divisions: An Anthology of Chicana Literature* (Tucson: University of Arizona Press, 1993), 273–76.

16. Paul Lauter, "The Literatures of America: A Comparative Discipline," in *Redefining American Literary History*, ed. A. LaVonne Brown Ruoff and Jerry W. Ward, Jr. (New York: The Modern Language Association, 1990), 9, 29.

17. Gregory S. Jay, "The End of 'American' Literature: Toward a Multicultural Practice," in *Opening the American Mind: Race, Ethnicity, and Gender in Higher Education*, ed. Geoffrey M. Sill, Miriam T. Chaplin, Jean Ritzke, and David Wilson (Newark: University of Delaware Press, 1993), 160–61, 171, 174.

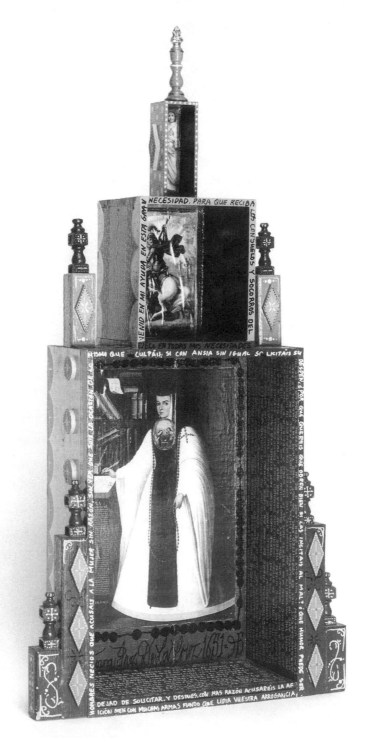

Figure 1. *Nicho Dedicado a Sor Juana Inéz de la Cruz* (1986).
Photograph by Paul Overstreet.

Figure 2. *Nicho Dedicado a La Virgen de Guadalupe* (1985).
Photograph by Paul Overstreet.

Figure 3. *Nicho Dedicated to Frida Kahlo* (1990). Photograph by Paul Overstreet.

Figure 4. *Nicho Dedicated to Mary and Elizabeth* (1994). Photograph by Paul Overstreet.

Part 1 Voice Engendered

"Masculinity" in *Uncle Tom's Cabin*

CYNTHIA GRIFFIN WOLFF

In his analysis of the three-thousand-page court record of the Beecher-Tilton adultery trial, historian Richard Wrightman Fox comments upon the difficulty of retrieving meaning from this Victorian discourse of sentiment and gender: "Both the spoken and written word meant something different to them than they do to us." [1] And if the language of 1875 is opaque to a modern reader, the language of 1852–53 is even more so, carrying as it does the freight of confusion, fear, and factionalism that followed the Fugitive Slave Act of 1850. *Uncle Tom's Cabin* was written in the immediate wake of that legislation and as a direct consequence of it. Thus, whatever our ultimate judgment of Mrs. Stowe's immensely popular antislavery novel, we must recognize the extent to which its discourse is encoded by the dense semiotics of this singular historical moment.

From the beginning, *Uncle Tom's Cabin* was controversial, and one of Stowe's consistent responses to her critics was to cite the novel's polemical aim. It was intended neither as entertainment nor as a "realistic" portrayal of slavery: "slavery, in some of its workings, is too dreadful for the purposes of art," the author observed bitterly. "A work which should represent it strictly as it is would be a work which could not be read." [2] In short, *Uncle Tom's Cabin* was composed as an explicitly political document.

Given the primacy of her propagandistic intent, Stowe had to maneuver carefully in formulating this imaginative construction of "slavery." Myra Jehlen has observed that simply by taking black men and women seriously as fictional entities—postulating that they might even become "heroic"—Stowe's literary endeavor presented "an overwhelming challenge to the existing law and order." More recently, in her major biography of the author, Joan Hedrick has concurred: "Just the mere act of carefully listening to and recording the voices of a colonized people acknowledges their presence and their self-created subjectivity." [3] Today's readers may trivialize such strategies (and may be inclined to pay more attention to the novel's undeniable traces of sentimental racism). However, at the time, these were bold, radical innovations, experiments that enraged many readers, even fellow abolitionists. [4]

For a present-day audience, then, the novel is twice difficult. First, it is informed by the Victorian language of sentiment and gender that Fox finds so surprisingly enigmatic. Second, it has unique complexities that are rooted in the antislavery politics of the period.

Writing this polemic was thus a delicate balancing act. On the one hand, Stowe could not allow her revolutionary fictional world, a novel "peopled" by black American slaves, to offend the conservative, often bigoted readers whose support of the slave system she hoped to undermine. At the same time, to avoid alienating her fellow abolitionists (people whose sentiments had already been shaped by particular allegiances or elaborate theories, people who often disagreed with one another), she was obliged to be circumspect regarding a series of issues that were being debated within the antislavery movement itself. The resultant narrative is filled with snares for an unwary or unsophisticated late twentieth-century reader.

Perhaps the single most important thing to remember is this: contrary to what we might suppose today, in the America of 1850 abolition was an unpopular, minority cause; its proponents were generally regarded as a dangerous, unsavory fringe group, radicals who were not "received" in polite social circles. "Proper" readers of all classes nurtured an appalling tolerance for the institution of slavery: the vast majority of whites believed that African Americans were by "nature" emotionally, intellectually, and morally inferior—more like farm animals than people and not worthy of sustained attention. Marketing a "sympathetic" slave novel of any length or complexity to such an audience (not to mention a novel of such Balzacian scope) was an extraordinary feat; prior to Stowe, no one had done anything like it.[5] Thus the intimacy and vast popularity of *Uncle Tom's Cabin* that we take so unthinkingly for granted today were its most astonishing achievements. The success of the novel and the seductive immediacy of its principal characters conferred unprecedented respectability on the cause of abolition.

The years 1840–1860 constituted a generalized age of reform in this country, and abolition was often associated with other causes. Some have been largely forgotten (temperance and the establishment of vegetarian communal societies); some seem surprisingly contemporary (the women's rights movement and school reform). At least one was deeply vexed, both then and now: an attempt to redefine and reform the social construction of "masculinity." In the nineteenth century, this crusade was termed the "fraternal love movement," and it was closely connected with both the theories and the practices of abolitionists.

Almost twenty years ago, Ann Douglas described a process that she termed the "feminization" of America. Douglas's work took two things for granted:

that "feminization" was an intrinsically devitalizing force and that it was associated with an essentially conservative strain of American politics in the mid-nineteenth century.[6] Both assumptions must be challenged. Current thinking (informed by feminism) compels us to wonder whether "feminization" ought ever to be casually dismissed as negative; moreover, recent scholarship makes it clear that identifying this less belligerent definition of "masculinity" with an essentially conservative process rather than with a radical attempt to expand or alter the social definitions of both genders is a significant instance of precisely the difficulty Fox has described: written and spoken words that meant "something different to them than they do to us."[7] In fact, insofar as we allude to a process of "feminization," we might equally well examine that allied process, the mid-nineteenth-century attempt to rethink the male role.

These postulations of redefined "masculinity"—formulated largely by men—were an essential element of the "fraternal love" movement; and the "fraternal love" movement itself was but one component of a much larger political campaign that had arisen in response to unpopular wars and immoral forms of oppression (of women, of Native Americans, and of blacks). Its members had begun to formulate fundamental criticisms of America's culture and of its sense of national mission, and they often had certain visible marks of "costume": "There were men who . . . bore a marked resemblance to the accepted pictures of Jesus Christ . . . [like] Charles Burleigh,—a man of tall figure, benign face . . . wearing long auburn curls and somewhat tangled tempestuous beard." Far from being a renunciation of activism, this redefinition of "masculinity" is unmistakably similar to certain rebellious elements of the antiwar movement during the Vietnam crisis of the 1960s.[8]

For both moral and practical reasons, William Lloyd Garrison had insisted that wide-sweeping reform was to be achieved solely by means of moral suasion and nonviolent resistance. The doctrine of "fraternal love" took these antiaggressive beliefs to an even more extreme level, and men like Henry Ward Beecher, Gerrit Smith, and Samuel J. May (cofounder of the American Antislavery Society and perhaps Garrison's most ardent ally) sought to integrate this more compassionate, less aggressive definition of "masculinity" into every aspect of their lives. "No ordinary bonds of friendship cemented the Garrisonian antislavery community. . . . Devotion and intimate social rituals tightly bound the outcast group, providing its members with the strength to withstand withering public scorn and personal violence. Their expressions of love imitated the biblical relationship of Jonathan and David, reflecting the Garrisonian attempt to reenact the social relations of the primitive Christian church. . . . May's religious beliefs and his social criticism stressed cooperation over competition, love and forgiveness over retribution, and a prudent submission over violent resistance."[9] "Fraternal love" entirely repudiated competition and conquest as the basis for "masculine" relationships. In their place, it encouraged expressions of lavish affection between (heterosexual) men. Male friends routinely exchanged kisses when greeting each other and passionate letters when separated: "On one occasion, Elizabeth, Theodore [Tilton's] wife, discovered [Henry Ward] Beecher on her husband's lap, both engaged in a discussion of the Sermon on the Mount. When Elizabeth entered the room, Beecher rose and greeted her with a kiss then resumed his seat with Tilton."[10] Most important insofar as abolition was concerned, the doctrine of "fraternal love" elaborated its own deeply venerated "patriotic" virtues. Because the abolitionists had always believed slavery to be an expression of oppressive, hierarchical "patriarchy," their new definition of the masculine mode mandated cooperation and harmonious communal living rather than subjugation and domination, and their attempts to put theory into practice could be found in many of the utopian communities begun during this period.

They deplored the extent to which America had always enacted its notions of masculinity through expressions of conquest and colonization; and by mid-century they were devoting their lives to eliminating the most flagrant of these: the oppression of women, the institution of slavery, and such imperialist adventures as a Mexican War (in their view, a blatant expression of rapacious, expansionist slave power). Thus in his examination of the causes and consequences of the Mexican War (1849), the abolitionist William Jay elaborated an alternative notion of "patriotism" while warning "against that admiration of *military prowess*, which, by degrading in the public estimation the virtues which conduce to the happiness and security of society, and by fostering the arts and passions which minister to human destruction, is corrupting the morals and jeopard[iz]ing the liberties of the Republic." Writing scornfully of bloody battlefield atrocities that "have been loudly trumpeted as instances of American patriotism and heroism," Jay urged a vision of masculinity and national honor that "entailed a development of that benevolence which springs from moral goodness." He exhorted Americans to turn their "efforts and costly sacrifices of time and money [to] the temporal and spiritual welfare of [their] fellow-countrymen [because] it is chiefly by such patriotism . . . that our land is clothed with moral verdure and beauty."[11]

Withal, the abolitionists' message was concise. The slave system is no less than an *internalized*, *systematized*, and *legally perpetuated* enactment of conquest and colonization; thus so long as American culture glorifies conquest, America will continue to condone some form of slavery. Moreover, to the extent that "masculinity" continues to be defined by conquest, to that extent men (as opposed to women) will be especially inclined to perpetuate the slave system. Abolition, then, requires a redefinition both of our roles as men and women and of our goals as members of an honorable republic.[12]

The man most "representative" of this radical revision of the masculine role was Jesus. "'Humanity is dual, and yet when perfected it is one'"; as that perfect "one" incarnate, Jesus had united *all* virtues, both male and female, in androgynous harmony. Moreover, far from having become weakened or ineffectual through the enactment of his nonviolent beliefs, Jesus became the ultimate (and ultimately effective) revolutionary: "He rejected vengeance but possessed the courage 'to assail wrong-doing in the highest places.' His opposition to injustice and doctrine of non-resistance could be employed to challenge the 'men of property and standing' who opposed the 'Christian' cause of abolitionism."[13]

According to *this* construction of the "Savior," the fact that he had died for our sins was a good deal less significant than the fact that he had succeeded in his mission. As the supreme radical, so the argument ran, he had put together the most effective political organization in human history, the early Christian Church, and his triumphant tactics set a standard to which these nonviolent social agitators could always appeal. Little wonder, then, that the slaves' sufferings as "portrayed in abolitionist art [are] reminiscent of scenes from sacred history" or that the final version of the masthead of *The Liberator* (first used on May 31, 1850) had the dominant figure of the risen Christ superimposed upon its images of enslaved and freed blacks.[14]

Although Garrison, May, Beecher, and the other white abolitionists often made a self-conscious attempt to enact this new notion of "masculinity" in their everyday lives, for these men the most pressing issues of "non-aggression" were generally less personal and private than political and public. Should America as a nation engage in conquest and colonization? Did the Constitution condone slavery, and if it did, should right-thinking men engage in violent means of protest? Ultimately, should the nation engage in a civil war to settle the issue of slavery? To be sure, their renunciation of violence in the service of their political aims often became a source of personal pain: as a noisy fringe group, the abolitionists were generally shunned, often harassed, sometimes subjected to violence, occasionally assassinated; and as political protestors, under all such provocations, they were obliged to respond with only passive resistance—taking blows, but never returning them. Nonetheless, as *private individuals*, they had always been free to choose between a definition of "masculinity" built upon patterns of domination and one built upon cooperation, love, and forgiveness—free to explore the possibilities for "fraternal love" (and all its implications) in safety among friends and members of their families. Even so, there were objections to Garrison's inflexibly nonviolent posture; and if some white abolitionists were uncomfortable with this commitment, the black abolitionists were even more so.

As early as 1829, *David Walker's Appeal* had called for militancy from black Americans, urging them "to prove their manhood, to rise up and take their freedom by force if necessary." Always, the relationship between militancy and "manhood" was a deeply vexed one for African Americans.[15] Unlike white men, the black men of America had never been allowed the option of aggression, conquest, and domination as a mode of asserting or defining their "masculinity"—in public or in private. Their servitude had withheld all just forms of competition and all honorable forms of authority, compelling them instead into postures of passivity and acquiescence that had been specifically designed to signify humiliation. For many, probably for most, the personal satisfaction of being able to respond with violence to the violence of a white man's tyranny was a deeply cherished hope (after Frederick Douglass's autobiography was published, some such moment may have been the most "authentic" element in the slave's narrative), and relinquishing even the *possibility* of asserting aggression as a way of proving manhood was difficult to accept.[16]

As early as 1843, the black abolitionist Henry Highland Garnet began to promote the idea of forming a political party that was defined by its antislavery agenda; in doing so, Garnet "drew upon one of the most powerful justifications for the link between physical prowess and masculinity in American gender ideals—the responsibility of men to protect their families."[17] "You act as though your daughters were born to pamper the lusts of your masters and overseers. . . . And worst of all, you timidly submit while your lords tear your wives from your embraces and defile them before your eyes. In the name of God, we ask, *are you men? Where is the blood of your fathers?*"[18] Garnet spoke for an increasing number of African Americans. Simple justice and the universal human desire for revenge both cried out for brutal retaliation against abusive slaveholders. Nonetheless, prudence dictated caution. However "justifiable" aggressive masculinity seemed, however appealing it was, "most blacks understood the dangers [that] the relatively powerless slaves faced and the probable consequences of slave rebellion," namely, massive retaliatory slaughtering of blacks by whites.[19] Thus, although he argued for militancy, Garnet "did not urge a revolution [because] 'Your numbers are too small.'"[20] He could see all too well the folly of attempting to free blacks through any means that brought about their wholesale slaughter.

What is more, it had always been the case that many black abolitionists supported only nonviolent tactics (and some version of its concomitant definition of "masculinity"). The struggle to reach freedom in the North had sobered many; they had found sanctuary in inward-looking, generally pacifist utopian communities like the Northampton Association, one of whose prominent members was Sojourner Truth, who had settled there looking for a "quiet place."[21] During the late 1840s, when Frederick Douglass began to doubt the efficacy of nonresistance, Sojourner Truth "heard him persuading an audience to believe that slavery could only be destroyed by blood. Disturbed, she waited till he sat down after his speech, and then, when a hush of deep concern had come over the audience, she called out sharply, 'Frederick, is God dead?' In a flash, the audience swung to her view."[22] Thus these issues of "masculinity" and of "fraternal love" were both complex and deeply troubling, more troubling to African Americans than to whites. The passage of the Fugitive Slave Bill in September 1850 made the question both urgent and even more problematic than it had ever been previously.[23]

At this point, the entire spectrum of violent behavior had become a matter of immediate contemplation and concern.[24] Outrage over the Compromise of 1850 was so great that virtually all abolitionists felt that a resort to violence in the protection of fugitive slaves was justifiable; still, none but the most reckless firebrands urged or supported slave rebellions, or even violent retaliation on the part of any individual slave. Common sense still understood that the insurgents themselves would be the principal casualties of such actions.[25]

Consequently, a relatively coherent nonviolent resistance movement began to emerge among blacks as even dignitaries like Frederick Douglass encountered prejudice in the North. A diversified array of strategies and techniques was developed: "Blacks made antislavery statements by refusing to compromise with racist practices. They personally challenged acts of discrimination, testifying to their courage, conviction, and commitment to equality. Sarah M. Douglass withdrew from a Quaker congregation rather than suffer the indignity of the 'negro pew.' Robert Purvise refused to pay his property tax when his children were barred from attending the public schools."[26] However, confronted with the fact that racial prejudice in the "free" North was fully as intransigent as that in the South, with the nightmare specter of slave-catchers patrolling the streets, seizing dark-skinned men and women to be shipped into slavery unless they were able to exhibit proof of their right to freedom (for the burden of proof fell always upon the victim), blacks began to wonder whether they would ever be able to make an acceptable life for themselves anywhere in America, even if slavery were abolished. Not surprisingly, they began to leave the country in droves.[27]

Once again, then, twenty years after the Recolonization Movement had been angrily rejected because of its thinly disguised racism, the possibility of blacks' emigrating from America was revived. The prominent African American minister from Rhode Island, Alexander Crummell, is a good illustration in point. During the early 1840s he had vigorously opposed the efforts of the American Colonization Society on the grounds that they represented nothing more than the vicious efforts of racist whites to rid the country of "inferior" and "troublesome" people. Like most abolitionists of that time, he had been a staunch integrationist. Little by little, however, "he became convinced of the immense potential for black development in a setting controlled by Christian, Westernized blacks. . . . Liberia, a small nation dominated by former slaves and free blacks from the United States, became the focus of Crummell's vision of the regeneration of the black race. . . . Given Crummell's strong beliefs as to the worth of 'unmixed blacks' and his hostility to the pretensions of mulattoes, his sympathies were drawn to the 'pure black' faction [in Liberia politics]."[28] By the end of the 1840s, many African Americans had turned from integrationism to separatism: separatists like Henry Bibb, the powerful editor of *Voice of the Fugitive*, had begun to look for some "place" where blacks could form an entirely differentiated and independent community; and one of the greatest proselytizers of this movement "was the influential Henry Highland Garnet. . . . 'I hesitate not to say that my mind of late has greatly changed in regard to the American Colonization scheme,' he wrote on January 21, 1848, [even before the Fugitive Slave Act]. 'I would rather see a man free in Liberia than a slave in the United States.'"[29] By the fall of 1851, Henry Bibb, J. T. Fisher, and James Theodore Holly were developing "plans for emigration and continental black unity" in anticipation of the North American Anti-Slavery Convention at Toronto.[30] Although many black abolitionists still violently opposed the "colonization" movement and would continue to do so throughout the decade, an incipient enthusiasm for black nationalism was rumbling throughout America.

Even the temperamental Martin Delaney had begun to express "back to Africa" sentiments of a sort that would come to full flower in the late 1850s. During the late 1840s, he expressed a series of confusingly conflicted attitudes toward colonization in general and Africa in particular. Originally committed to a "self-help" philosophy (the hope that America might be an "open" society in which African Americans would achieve the same kind of success as whites), Delaney began to lose faith in this vision. "Between 1849 and 1852 [he decided] that all blacks were, after all, treated as debased pariahs and subject to 'a prejudice of caste.' Having parted ways with the American Dream, it was almost inevitable that Delaney would wish to cut himself off from America itself. Emigration, then, became an alternative ideology."[31] In 1852, he wrote that "there are circumstances under which emigration is absolutely necessary."[32] His mood was despondent: "We must have a position, independent of anything pertaining to white men as nations. I weary of our miserable condition, and [am] heartily sick of whimpering, whining and sniveling at the feet of white men, begging for their refuse and offals[,] existing by mere sufferance."[33]

Thus as Wilson Jeremiah Moses has observed, "The decade preceding the Civil War was the high-water mark of classical black nationalism, not only in terms of the renewed interest in colonization, but also in terms of the philosophical writing produced."[34] This reactivated black nationalism had an interesting consequence: it seemed to offer black men ready access to *both* the social definitions of "masculinity" that had always been freely available to white men in America: perhaps a competitive, aggressive, individualistic form of the "male" identity would find its adequate arena in another land where blacks ruled themselves; or perhaps, as nationalists often argued, the black man possessed "innate Christian instincts which would suit him well for the founding of a new civilization that would stand as a shining example to the prodigal [white] Christians of Europe and America."[35]

One cannot read *Uncle Tom's Cabin* outside this context. Stowe came from a politically sophisticated family. Henry Ward Beecher (extravagantly committed to the "fraternal love" movement) was closest to her heart, and as late as 1858, two years after *Dred* appeared, Harriet Stowe herself still clung passionately to the hope that nonviolent tactics might eradicate slavery, thus avoiding the inevitable bloodletting of civil war.[36] Like many other perceptive Americans, she anticipated that such a war would be costly, and that its "solution" would be neither prompt nor enduring. Thus her most famous novel was an eleventh-hour effort to forestall that war, a supreme example of "moral suasion."

Stowe's strategies took many forms. Sometimes (especially at the beginning of the novel), she catered to her white audience's prejudiced stereotypes.[37] More often she drew heavily upon her reader's familiarity with (and tolerance of) the conventions of sentimental fiction, exalting the power of women as peace-makers and purveyors of moral wisdom.[38] But nowhere was Stowe more cunningly careful than in the construction of her principal male characters (who were the most potentially threatening to an unsympathetic audience), and here she drew self-consciously upon the notions of "masculinity" that pervaded abolitionist and reformist thinking at mid-century, especially upon those connected to the doctrine of "fraternal love"—probably because she was deeply sympathetic with them herself.

Recently, Beatrice Anderson (arguing against views of Tom that diminish his achievements because of his allegedly "submissive" behavior) recalls to us the explicit valor of his nature: "He is a strong, vital character whose motivations . . . are noble and heroic and not solely religious," she writes; moreover, Tom "'sacrifices' himself for consistently ethical (as opposed to narrowly religious) motives." She continues: "His actions are animated primarily by his anxiety for his family's welfare, by his concern for his fellow slaves both on Shelby's estate and on Legree's plantation, and always by his wise and practical weighing of consequences."[39] As part of her argument, Anderson cites the introduction of Tom: "He was large, broad-chested, powerfully made man, of a full glossy black, and a face whose truly African features were characterized by an expression of grave and steady good sense, united with much kindliness and benevolence. There was something about his whole air self-respecting and dignified, yet united with a confiding and humble simplicity." Anderson observes that this description "attests to [Tom's] good sense, power, and dignity."[40] This much is true; however, Stowe's initial construction of her hero does even more. It paints the portrait of a quintessentially "masculine" man developed along the idealized lines of "fraternal love." Moreover, a correlative expansion of the "feminine" will accompany this change: the strength of Cassie's character, her ability to work *as an equal* with Tom in their nightmarish struggle against Legree, indicates the complementary relationship between "masculinity" and "femininity"; when the first is reformulated, so (necessarily) is the second, to the ultimate betterment of both.[41]

In her hero, Stowe constructed a man whose emotional and moral life is centered not on domination or competition, but on the self-conscious, vigorous exercise of communal love, a man who unites the virtues of "kindliness and benevolence" with dignity and a "broad-chested" and "powerfully made" physique. Consistently, then, Tom's "self-sacrifice" is not a manifestation of weakness, but rather a potent and effective enactment of social responsibility: "Although it sounds paradoxical, Tom complies with a system that he judges unfair and unreasonable out of resilient strength, keen awareness of his alternatives, and intelligence, not out of blind and passive submission. . . . His actions are animated primarily by his anxiety for his family's welfare, by his concern for his fellow slaves both on Shelby's estate and on Legree's Plantation, and always by his wise and practical weighing of consequences."[42] His tactics of nonviolent opposition consistently follow the strategies of passive resistance and prudent behavior that had already been well-developed by black abolitionists who had encountered racist antagonism in the free North. Moreover, given the African Americans' particular concern that black men should be able to protect their families in the wake of the Fugitive Slave Act, Stowe takes care to make it clear that Tom's strategies are always ultimately effective in saving his loved ones. Thus her reader is presented with this paradox: nonviolent behavior may be an even more productive means of offering protection than acts of aggression (which always carry the possibility of widespread, random, violent retaliation).

Most radical of all, Stowe not only gives vivid life to the arguments of the nonviolent abolitionists who had been inveighing against America's infatuation with bloodshed, she postulates a black man as the exemplary model of this admirable behavior, a black man who is strong-hearted enough to save far more people through the heroism of personal sacrifice than might ever have been saved through vicious battle.[43] Moreover, Stowe's pointed emphasis on Tom's unadulterated "blackness" and on his explicitly "African" features prevented any of her readers from imputing his commendable behavior to some admixture of white blood (as whites were readily inclined to do). At the very least, then, this portrayal specifically refuted the mid-nineteenth-century racist claim of African Americans' intrinsic inferiority to whites in emotional and moral matters, and at the most it might be construed as confirming the sentiments that had been expressed by such black abolitionists as Crummell, that is, a belief in the black man's moral and emotional superiority (Dickens believed Stowe to be making precisely this claim).[44]

This careful political "leverage" in the creation of Tom is not unique. All of the principal males in the novel can be identified almost schematically as illustrations of the moral and emotional success or failure of different constructions of "masculinity." Thus, if the black man, Tom, is an ideal of "fraternal love" successfully enacted, the white man, Augustine St. Claire, is a grotesque distortion of that ideal, a man who has become "feminized" in the most ludicrously reductive and ineffectual understanding of the term, a fact that is especially apparent when the introductory description of St. Claire is compared with that of Tom: "[St. Claire] was remarkable for an extreme and marked sensitiveness of character, more akin to the softness of woman than the ordinary hardness of his own sex. . . . His talents were of the very first order, although his mind showed a preference always for the ideal and the aesthetic, and there was about him that repugnance to the actual business of life which is the common result of this balance of the faculties. . . . [After an unhappy marriage he was often] found lying on the sofa [pleading a] sudden sick-headache as the cause of his distress" (*UTC*, 1:200–203). Tom engages in pragmatic, nonviolent resistance and saves not only his own family, but other blacks as well; St. Claire engages in passive, intellectual daydreaming and saves no one, not even himself.

If Tom and St. Claire are equal and opposite embodiments of moral sentiment and nonviolence, George and Legree are similarly balanced enactments of "masculinity" constructed along the lines of conquest and aggressive competition. Typically, George construes his identity not communally, but in terms of domination, a category that he elaborates by consistently defining himself by comparison with other men. "My master! and who made him my master? . . . I'm a man as much as he is. I'm a better man than he is. I know more about business than he does; I am a better manager than he is; I can read better than he can; I can write a better hand,—and I've learned it in spite of him; and now what right has he to make a dray-horse of me? to take me from things I can do, and do better than he can?" (*UTC*, 1:20). By contrast, Legree is the crude, violent, phallic cartoon of such "masculinity," with "a round bullet-head, large light-gray eyes, with . . . shaggy, sandy eyebrows and stiff, wiry, sunburned hair; . . . his large, coarse mouth was distended with tobacco, the juice of which, from time to time, he ejected from him with great decision and explosive force" (*UTC*, 2:104). Thus is the legitimacy of a "patriarchal" hierarchy dismissed; thus is the authority of mere brute dominance demolished. In this fictional world, "Legree" is eponymous with naked power, and he is vile: "*I'm* your church now!" he tells his slaves. "D'ye see this fist? Heft it! . . . Well, I tell ye this ye fist has got as hard as iron *knocking down niggers*. I never see the nigger, yet, I couldn't bring down with one crack. . . . I don't keep none o' yer cussed overseers; I does my own overseeing; and I tell you things *is* seen to. You's every one on ye got to toe the mark, I tell ye; quick,—straight,—the moment I speak. That's the way to keep in with me. Ye won't find no soft spot in me, nowhere. So, now, mind yerselves; for I don't show no mercy!" (*UTC*, 2:107–9). Tom's death, then, is both a tragic loss and the definitive demonstration of social corruption: slavery's unwillingness to tolerate a resolutely good man who is also a black man.

Within the terms of this narrative, far from being a recommendation of supine passivity, Tom's strategic use of nonviolent resistance affirms several forms of "conquest": his triumph over Legree is more than the triumph of a singularly heroic black man over a savage white, more than the triumph of Christianity over sin. It is the conquest of communal, benevolent "masculinity" over a definition of gender that is built upon subjugation and aggression. "You've always stood it out agin me," Legree rages at Tom; "now, I'll *conquer ye or kill ye!*" (*UTC*, 2:204, Stowe's emphasis). When Tom dies, Stowe leaves no doubt that Legree and his vicious mode of conquest have been morally and emotionally supplanted: "'What a thing 't is to be a Christian!' [Tom whispered]. . . . He began to draw his breath with long, deep inspirations, and his broad chest rose and fell heavily. The expression of his face was that of a *conqueror*" (*UTC*, 2:212–13, my emphasis). Many of Stowe's twentieth-century readers may not sympathize with Tom's joy in Christian love. Nonetheless, all can share Stowe's hope that America will discard its imperialistic veneration of revolution, conquest, and brute force—and that it will embrace new ideals to build a more noble republic.

In this context, the consignment of George Harris and his family to a "happy ending" in Liberia is not so much problematic as it is enigmatic. His talents combine with his name to remind the reader of America's own founding father. The possibility that he might play precisely that role for his own people seems his own most ardent wish. However, are we compelled to believe that he must leave America to enact such a role? Stowe seems to claim as much:

> It is with the oppressed, enslaved African race that I cast in my lot; and, if I wished anything, I would wish myself two shades darker rather than one lighter.
>
> The desire and yearning of my soul is for an African *nationality*. I want a people that shall have a tangible, separate existence of its own; and where am I to look for it? Not in Haiti. . . . Where, then, shall I look? On the shores of Africa I see a republic. . . . There it is my wish to go, and find myself a people. (*UTC*, 2:229–30)

Black abolitionists were expressing just such expectations as these in antislavery newspapers at the time that Stowe was writing *Uncle Tom's Cabin*, their opinions initiating a mid-nineteenth-century "back to Africa" movement that would find fullest expression in Delaney and Campbell's *Search for a Place* (1860).[45] Thus one explanation for Stowe's decision is timely: she is echoing this current pro-African sentiment.

Yet the puzzling fact remains that in this fictional world, George Harris seems to have no "place"; he must be dispatched "elsewhere" (much as Dickens's unruly characters often disappeared into that nebulous never-never land, "Australia"). Another answer can be found in the reception that the character of George received after *Uncle Tom's Cabin* was published. As we have noted, the likeness of an *armed* black man had become so frightening to a white audience that such images were explicitly omitted from abolitionist propaganda after 1850. The empowerment and arming of such a man—so clearly superior, so clearly deserving of his freedom, and so justifiably enraged—was more threatening to Stowe's audience than most present-day readers can imagine. A brief anecdote will illustrate this fact. When *The Literary World* critiqued *Uncle Tom's Cabin*, its reviewer pilloried Stowe for inciting violence, and the example he gave was George Harris's "murder" of his pursuers. What *actually* happened in the novel was no more than a wounding of the pursuant slave-catchers; moreover, the fugitives take precious time to carry the wounded man to safety, where his wounds can be dressed, for, as George asserts, "It would always be a heavy thought to me if I'd caused his death, even in a just cause" (*UTC*, 1:265). Thus the "murder" and Stowe's "incitement to violence" were no more than her reader's own terrifying fantasies. Stowe's narrative implies that honorable masculinity, even constructed along the lines of conflict, will shrink from brutality and murder.

Nonetheless, even in her own day, Stowe's decision thus to banish George was sometimes criticized, condemned as a revival of the Recolonization Movement and an expression of racial prejudice. We cannot parse her conscience; however, given the narrator's explicit denunciation of this movement (see *UTC*, 2:246–48), it is plausible to infer that Stowe objected to George's enactment of "masculinity," not to his color. As Gillian Brown has astutely observed, "while the emigration of American blacks might suggest a convenient solution to white fears about the possible retribution of freed blacks, Stowe's imagination of 'this new enterprise' articulates less about fears of blacks than about fear of men" who had been trained into aggression by American culture.[46] Insofar as she was determined to force a "reevaluation of white, male systems of thought" by exalting "peer relationships" over "hierarchical" ones, all men like George would require either relocation or radical retraining.[47]

Indeed, Stowe seems to have wanted to present the full gamut of African American possibilities for "masculine" fulfillment in America; hence the somewhat awkward inclusion of a list of successful black Cincinnati businessmen just before the novel's end: "B———. Furniture-maker: . . . worth ten thousand dollars, all his own earnings. . . . C——— . . . a farmer; owns several farms in Indiana; Presbyterian; probably worth fifteen or twenty thousand dollars, all earned himself, etc., etc." (*UTC*, 2:248ff.). These stand as "proof" that men with George's ability (but perhaps without his measure of phallic rage) could make their way in this country if only the nation allowed them to do so. What is more, a knowledgeable reader in 1851–52 would have recognized this inventory as an explicit reiteration of Delaney's "self-help" theory, a notion that he developed both in his writing and in public addresses throughout the Midwest during the late 1840s.[48]

Because Stowe's intentions were consistently political and her goal revolutionary—a fundamental reorganization of American life—she aimed her work not at black readers, who needed no persuasion concerning the cause of abolition, but at whites. The most telling moment of the novel, then, may be one of its least melodramatic: the brief, all-but-silent colloquy between Senator Bird and his wife, a transaction that might take place between any public man and his spouse. Having confronted her husband with the runaways, Eliza and her child, Mrs. Bird applauds her husband's reluctant decision to aid the fugitives. "Your heart is better than your head in this case, John!" she says; and the narrator adds this wry comment: "What a situation, now, for a *patriotic* Senator, that had been all the week before spurring up the legislature of his native State to pass more stringent resolutions against escaping fugitives, their harborers and abettors! . . . Our poor Senator was not stone or steel,—as he was a man, and a downright noble-hearted one, too,—he was, as everybody must see, in a sad case for his *patriotism*" (*UTC*, 1:113, 115–16, my emphasis). Like William Jay, Harriet Beecher Stowe was concerned with civic virtues. She sought a "development of that benevolence which springs from moral goodness" and a definition of "patriotism" that was the consequence of such "benevolence, when directed to our countrymen at large."[49] She believed that this nation's abuse of its African American population would end only when reforms like these had taken place. Thus *Uncle Tom's Cabin* petitioned for a sweeping redefinition of both "masculinity" and "patriotism" in the service of that ultimate goal.[50]

NOTES

1. His comments at greater length are useful: "[The participants of the trial spoke] a language strangely different from our own (and indeed from some of their contemporaries). . . . Both the spoken and written word meant something different to them than they do to us. . . . The novels, poem, letters, memos, interviews, and official testimony produced by Beecher and the Tiltons . . . were often embedded in now-archaic discourses of power and persuasion, truth-telling and truth-shielding. . . . They were wont to engage in delicate negotiations about honor and reputation, [and] they frequently expressed emotions we have tended to suppress, such as remorse, guilt, or shame" (Richard Wrightman Fox, "The Trial of Intimacy: A New Look at the Beecher-Tilton Scandal of 1875," paper presented to the Organization of American Historians Annual Meeting, Anaheim, California, April 16, 1993, 7–9).

2. Harriett Beecher Stowe, *Uncle Tom's Cabin and The Key to Uncle Tom's Cabin*, in *The Writings of Harriett Beecher Stowe* (Boston: Houghton Mifflin, 1896), 255–56.

3. Myra Jehlen, "The Family Militant: Domesticity Versus Slavery in *Uncle Tom's Cabin*," in *Criticism* 31.4 (Fall, 1989), 385; and Joan Hedrick, *Harriet Beecher Stowe: A Life* (New York: Oxford University Press, 1994), 210. Stowe's own camouflaging remarks after the firestorm broke out (especially her claim that "God" had written the novel) have always tended to divert readers from the shrewdness with which she proceeded. As a modern commentator has observed, "The book was the greatest piece of abolitionist propaganda ever penned"; see William E. Gienapp, "Abolitionism and the Nature of Antebellum Reform," in *Courage and Conscience: Black and White Abolitionists in Boston*, ed. Donald M. Jacobs (Bloomington: Indiana University Press, pub-

lished for the Boston Athenaeum, 1993), 39. Canny abolitionists of the time (like Frederick Douglass) recognized this fact and consistently expressed their admiration for Stowe's work.

4. For example, Charles Dickens reacted negatively to the elevation of the black man's character, saying in a letter to Stowe that she had gone "too far and seeks to prove too much." Slavery had evils enough without trying to make the *African race* seem to be great! (Dickens to Stowe, July 17, 1852, in Laurie L. Harris, *Nineteenth-Century Literary Criticism* [Detroit: Gale Research Company, 1983], 3:537).

5. There had been slavery novels before *Uncle Tom's Cabin*; however, none had secured more than modest success in the crucial area of sales. For a discussion of the "unfortunate alliance between the lords of both loom and lash," see James Brewer Stewart, "Boston, Abolition, and the Atlantic World, 1820–61," in Jacobs, 101. Perhaps no account of the "disreputable" odor of abolitionism is more circumstantial or extensive than the one found through Edward L. Pierce's biography of Charles Sumner (*Memoir and Letters of Charles Sumner* [1877; New York: Arno Press, 1969]).

6. See Ann Douglas, *The Feminization of American Culture* (New York: Alfred A. Knopf, 1977), 91ff. There is no doubt that Douglas's work identified major cultural forces in the late nineteenth century, and subsequent critics (like Nina Baym and, especially, Jane Tompkins) have elaborated her notion of a "feminized" America in insightful and important ways. I do not wish to disagree explicitly with Douglas because the scope and focus of her work is different from my own, and her usage of "feminization" includes a great many things that this essay does not intend to address. My principal point of departure with several of these critics would be this: I believe that redefined "masculinity" (a *healthy and useful* "feminization" of males) might best be seen as the process by which competitive individualism is discouraged in favor of more cooperative modes of interaction.

7. Gillian Brown has recently observed that "Stowe's domestic solution to slavery . . . represents not the strength of sentimental values but a utopian rehabilitation of them, necessitated by their fundamental complicity with the market to which they are ostensibly opposed" (Gillian Brown, *Domestic Individualism: Imagining Self in Nineteenth-Century America* [Berkeley and Los Angeles: University of California Press, 1990], 18). Throughout her brilliant book, Brown assumes that "domestic" (specifically as it refers to a form of economy and a spiritual/emotional configuration) *need not necessarily be exclusively "feminine" nor need it be enacted by women.* Hence she remarks that: "*Uncle Tom's Cabin* revises Beecher's domesticity, disjoining it from patriarchal economic practices and severing it from service to any institution other than itself. Instead of ensuring industrial capitalism and supporting the government that passed the Fugitive Slave Law, the domestic might constitute an alternative system. . . . In Rachel's kitchen the boys and girls share domestic duties under their mother's guidance while their father engages in the "the anti-patriarchal operation of shaving". . . . In Stowe's model home, domesticity is matriarchal and antinomian, *a new form of government as well as a protest against patriarchy and its manifestations in slavery, capitalism, and democracy*" (18–19, my emphasis). Brown is interested in an individualistic (rather than a communitarian) view of Stowe; however, we agree in understanding Stowe's "domestic, feminine" vision as a radical form of political activism. Clearly, as in so many times

of social upheaval, mid-nineteenth-century America saw many (conflicting) reconfi-
gurations of "masculinity" and "femininity." Twentieth-century critics who disagree
may all have some piece of the "truth." Brown's work amplifies the important work of
Nina Baym and Jane Tompkins. See Baym, *Woman's Fiction: A Guide to Novels by and
about Women in America* (Ithaca: Cornell University Press, 1978), and Tompkins, *Sensational Designs: The Cultural Work of American Fiction* (New York: Oxford University
Press, 1987).

8. Thomas Wentworth Higginson, *Cheerful Yesterdays* (1898; New York: Arno Press,
1968), 118. Uneasiness about America's imperialist tendencies began almost as soon as
the country was born. Some were unhappy with the treatment of Native Americans
(see Lydia Maria Child's writings on the Indians, for example); others were well aware
of the moral disease that went with slavery; still others were concerned with women's
rights. Every "compromise" exacerbated this uneasiness; and by the 1840s, the country was already heatedly divided. Thus, it is difficult to overestimate the similarity between the period of the 1850s and the period of antiwar activism during the 1960s
(which has, in various forms, continued). This is a description of the mid-nineteenth-
century radicalism to which I refer. America's expansionist, imperialist policies were
denounced; dissidents inveighed against the stranglehold that a dominant "patriarchy"
had on various forms of power throughout the society; prejudice against minority
groups (Native Americans, women, blacks) was denounced, and efforts were made to
"liberate" them from oppression; the radicals quarreled among themselves about the
use of violence, a majority believing in the superior effectiveness of nonviolent resistance, but a voluble minority urging bloody rebellion. Emerson, a conservative,
"tersely classified" these radicals as "men with beards" (Higginson, 118). Moreover, he
voted categorically against the admission of women to the Town and Country Club (a
literary group that met for social occasions and intellectual discussion); and he voted
against the admission of Frederick Douglass and Charles Lenox Remond to the same
group because of an admitted "mild natural colorphobia, controlled only by moral
conviction" (Higginson, 173–74).

9. Donald Yacovone, *Samuel Joseph May and the Dilemmas of the Liberal Persuasion, 1797–1871* (Philadelphia: Temple University Press, 1991), 95.

10. Ibid., 100. I have included this example for several reasons. Not only does it
illustrate "fraternal love" rather dramatically; since Beecher and Tilton were both ardent abolitionists, it suggests the deeply intertwined nature of the two movements.
Finally, of course, it suggests the connection between Fox's bemused response to the
opacity of the Beecher-Tilton trial documents and the less obvious opacity of *Uncle
Tom's Cabin*.

11. William Jay, *A Review of the Causes and Consequences of the Mexican War*
(1849; New York: Arno Press, 1969), 4, 279, 288–89, my emphasis. Jay's entire chapter
on "Patriotism" is enlightening.

12. It was a fact that, in general, women were more sympathetic to the cause of
abolition than men. This is not to say that women who had been empowered by the
slave system could not be vicious in the exercise of that power (Stowe's portrait of Marie
St. Claire illustrates that sobering fact), nor that northern white women were not often
hypocritical in their "opposition" to slavery (Stowe's portrait of Miss Ophelia is an

exposure of that flaw). Nonetheless, even after these demurs have been taken into account, most abolitionists believed that women *were* more sympathetic to the antislavery movement—perhaps (as the abolitionists might argue) because their "femininity" was not captive to the exercise in unjust forms of dominance and power.

13. Yacovone, 99, 96.

14. Bernard F. Reilly Jr., "The Art of the Antislavery Movement," in Jacobs, 62; see illustration, 64. I would not want to argue that this "Christ" model was never used hypocritically (because of course it was). However, I do want to argue that it was often *not* used hypocritically. There were more "true believers" a century and a half ago than there are now, and modern readers overdiscount religious motives in this era. Nor do I deny that the *pacifism* emblematized by Christ served many purposes. Nor that one of them was to keep "dangerous" black men from being rebellious. I would merely wish to argue that this was only one of several motivations. It is true that "gradual emancipation" meant "perpetual slavery" to some self-serving whites; to others, however, it really did mean the safest and most permanent form of emancipation and enfranchisement. (One can see many of the same arguments still being rehearsed in South Africa today.) Moreover, although all black abolitionists were violently opposed to the tactics of ministers who *used* the Christian message to manipulate their congregation into lives of submission (and Stowe was more vehement than most in this regard), the majority of African Americans in mid-nineteenth-century America were *genuine* in their devotion to Christianity, and they would have been offended by a repudiation of Christianity (as opposed to a repudiation of hypocritical and immoral ministers—of whom there were many).

15. *David Walker's Appeal* (1829), quoted in James Oliver Horton and Lois E. Horton, "The Affirmation of Manhood: Black Garrisonians in Antebellum Boston," in Jacobs, 132.

16. The issue of African Americans bearing arms is a good case in point. The image of an armed black man was heavily freighted: in the South, it spelled terror—the memory of slave rebellions and the fear of rebellious retribution in the future—and even in the North it seemed portentous and threatening. Yet, paradoxically, this phobia about the danger from blacks who carried weapons existed side by side with the deeply held prejudice that African Americans would be *cowardly* in battle, that they would be more likely to run than fight, in short, that they lacked *courage*.

17. Horton and Horton, 144. His militant attitude was similar to that of the earlier African American activist, David Walker.

18. Ibid., quoting Garnet.

19. Ibid., 145. This conflict, between the moral "right" and emotional satisfaction of retaliation and its obvious folly in the face of overwhelming odds, characterizes a great deal of discussion among black abolitionists after 1830.

20. Ibid.

21. "The Northampton Association [led by, among others, Garrison's brother-in-law, George Benson] encouraged liberty of thought and speech. It had no religious creed, no antislavery creed, no non-resistance creed; but on one of his visits Garrison told the members that he took it for granted that they were 'generally antislavery, anti-war, and

temperance men'" (Carleton Mabee, *Black Freedom: The Nonviolent Abolitionist from 1830 Through the Civil War* [New York: Macmillan, 1970], 83).

22. Ibid., 83–84.

23. Mabee observes, "Understandably, black meetings protesting the [Fugitive Slave] law tended to be more violent in tone than white meetings. . . . In New York City when the chairman of a black protest meeting, occasional nonresistant William P. Powell, whom Garrison knew and admired as the manager of a black seaman's home, asked the audience if they would 'submit peaceably' to the new law, they shouted 'No, no.' The speakers who followed seemed to outdo each other in urging violence" (293).

24. All sides of the abolition movement began to anticipate inevitable bloodshed and deeply fear its consequence. One index is the rapid appearance of fictions that deal with slave rebellion: *The Heroic Slave* (1851), *Benito Cereno* (1856), *Dred* (1856), and *Blake* (1861).

25. African Americans probably appreciated this danger even more keenly than whites. Hence Frederick Douglass held himself delicately aloof from the John Brown rebellion at Harper's Ferry; he "told Brown that he was 'going into a perfect steel trap, and that once in he would not get out alive'" (quoted in William S. McFeeley, *Frederick Douglass* [New York: W. W. Norton, 1991], 196).

26. C. Peter Ripley in *The Black Abolitionist Papers*, ed. Ripley (Chapel Hill: The University of North Carolina Press, 1991), 4:352. I have cited only a brief account of this emergent non-violent movement; Ripley gives a much more circumstantial picture of it.

27. Many newspapers in the North reported this astonishing exodus (not only all abolitionist papers, but often the local press as well, an interesting fact in its own right). Not surprisingly, such a large number of escapees had difficulty finding a receptive country that would offer them the chance to make a home. While Henry Bibb gives a heartening account of "refugees" arriving safely in Canada (where they were, in the numbers that chose this northern route, not unwelcome), African Americans, accustomed to the warmth of the South, usually disliked the cold climate of even the free North and generally found the freezing cold of Canada entirely uncongenial. William Wells Brown (who lived in London) sent very pessimistic news from England concerning the hardships that awaited fugitives from American slavery. For example, to the London *Times* he wrote, "The fugitive [slave] population is now estimated at about 30,000. . . . Many of these people have, within the past six or eight months, come to this country, seeking employment and that liberty and protection which are denied them in their native land. On reaching England, they find . . . difficulties in the way of getting employment [similar to those they have encountered in] Canada, and they, therefore, become a burden to the benevolent. . . . I wish, Sir, to call the attention of those interested in the West India estates to this fact, and to suggest the propriety of adopting some measure to secure the services of as many of these fugitives as may feel inclined to go to the West Indies." And to *Frederick Douglass' Paper*: "The English are hospitable and generous, and would not see a brother-man want for bread or a night's lodging. But I would say to our fugitive brethren, if you don't want to become beggars, don't come to England. If the climate in Canada is too cold, and you must leave the

States, *go to the West Indies. But, by all means, don't come to England"* (my emphasis). Both letters were republished by William Lloyd Garrison in *The Liberator*, July 25, 1851.

28. Alfred Moss, "Alexander Crummell," in *Black Leaders of the Nineteenth Century*, ed. Leon Litwack and August Meier (Urbana: University of Illinois Press, 1988), 242.

29. Benjamin Quarles, *Black Abolitionists* (reprint, New York: Da Capo Press, 1969), 216.

30. Floyd J. Miller, *The Search for a Black Nationality* (Urbana: University of Illinois Press, 1975) 125. For additional statements about emigration to Liberia, see Granville B. Blanks, "To the Editor, *Syracuse Daily Journal*, 12 August 1852," in Ripley, 4: 131–36.

31. Miller, 119, 124.

32. Quarles, 215.

33. Delaney to Douglas, July 10, 1852, in Ripley, 4:128. Clearly what many blacks wanted was not merely safety from seizure (which they might obtain by fleeing to Canada or England), but protection from all forms of *white* oppression (which they could obtain only in a country where blacks constituted the ruling class). Delaney's initial choice (and he was clearly gropingly uncertain) was Central America; see Delaney's "The Political Destiny of the Colored Race," in Sterling Stuckey, *The Ideological Origins of Black Nationalism* (Boston: Beacon Press, 1972), 195–237. Later, he fixed his hopes and dreams upon Liberia. See Delaney and Robert Campbell, *Search for a Place*, ed. with an introduction by Hugh Bell (Ann Arbor: University of Michigan Press, 1969).

34. Wilson Jeremiah Moses, *The Golden Age of Black Nationalism, 1850–1925* (New York: Oxford University Press, 1978), 27. Moses goes on to say, "The passage of the Fugitive Slave Law in 1850 led to a resurgence of the spirit of black nationalism. Emigration schemes proliferated. . . . Africa was not the only potential site under consideration. A plan to colonize Haiti was offered by the British abolitionist James Redpath and even some of the committed integrationists like William Wells Brown and Frederick Douglass were willing to listen to his proposal." There can be no doubt that the knee-jerk racist response to America's turmoil and impending tragedy in 1850 was to "send them back where they came from" (which was understood by all abolitionists as an unacceptable reactivation of the Colonization movement). Nonetheless, it became increasingly clear that while the American Colonization Society retained its bad reputation, the prospect of *some* kind of exodus from America, some kind of "emigration," would have to be considered. A perusal of *The Liberator* is misleading: not surprisingly, that paper rather consistently reflected Garrison's own personal opinions, his powerfully pacifist sentiments and vehement opposition to any revival of the "colonization" movement. At the same time, all of the abolitionist newspapers (even *The Liberator*) carried stories about black Americans' frantic efforts to find safety somewhere *outside* the borders of the United States. Everywhere, there was genuine panic.

35. Moses, esp. 27ff.

36. Her remarks about a contemporary case are revealing. John J. Fee had been operating such superb grade schools for black children in Kentucky that white parents

sent their children to them—effectively creating integrated education. This was done entirely without violence or aggression of any sort: "The American Missionary Association decided in 1858 that Fee and his associates, working in a slave state as they were, provided a model that should be followed in every slave state. Harriet Beecher Stowe, writing in the *Independent* [November 1848] . . . pointed to the grandeur of Fee's achievement. Suppose, she wrote, the missionaries of the regular mission societies had gone into the slave states as Fee went into Kentucky, 'founding churches on principles of strict anti-slavery communion. They would have been driven out, say you? How do we know? Fee is not driven out of Kentucky.' Fee is fighting the battle in Kentucky which we should fight everywhere in slave territory. 'He is fighting it successfully— necessities, afflictions, distress, only make him stronger. Antislavery churches are rising around him, feeble indeed, in their beginning, but mighty in moral force; and every inch which Christianity seems to gain under such auspices, she really does gain'" (Mabee, 238). What Stowe seems to have feared was exactly what happened after the Emancipation Proclamation and the Civil War and Reconstruction, namely, that "free" blacks (in the South, in America as a whole) would not be much "freer" than African Americans had been while enslaved. At least *some* "gradual emancipationists" espoused that doctrine because they believed emancipation to be a necessarily slow process of reeducation; only such a process, they argued, could be lasting. Such is the thrust of Stowe's last remark, that every inch "gained" in this process was "really" gained.

37. See Richard Yarborough, "Strategies of Black Characterization in *Uncle Tom's Cabin* and the Early Afro-American Novel," in *New Essays on "Uncle Tom's Cabin,"* ed. Eric J. Sundquist (Cambridge: Cambridge University Press, 1986), 166–88. Perhaps the one "racist" belief that Stowe *did* hold (and that she shared with most mid-nineteenth-century intellectuals) was a generalized belief in "racial traits" or "racial characteristics." This belief was not, of course, limited by an exclusive application to African Americans (note how often it is applied to the Irish at this time): all groups were thought to have their distinctive characteristics. Nor was this belief always or necessarily bigoted (although it often was, of course).

38. See Cynthia Griffin Wolff, "Margaret Garner: A Cincinnati Story," in *Discovering Difference*, ed. Christoph K. Lohmann (Bloomington: Indiana University Press, 1993), esp. n. 4, where this issue is discussed at length. Nonetheless, perhaps it is worth citing one essay that has been widely influential: Elizabeth Ammons, "Heroines in *Uncle Tom's Cabin*," in *Critical Essays on Harriet Beecher Stowe*, ed. Ammons (Boston: G. K. Hall, 1980), 152–63. Ammons discerns that Stowe has "feminized" Uncle Tom "not because she is unable to make him assertively masculine, but because she does not wish to do so" (158). My own argument would suggest that half of this assertion is entirely correct: Stowe's refusal to create an aggressive hero was a matter of choice. However, I would argue, Stowe herself probably would have seen such a characterization not as "feminizing" but instead as the depiction of an *alternate and preferable form of "masculinity."* That she saw the active force of motherhood and maternity as a form of heroism is, of course, entirely true; and *Uncle Tom's Cabin* is in many ways a sanctification of these roles.

39. Beatrice Anderson, "Uncle Tom: A Hero at Last," *American Transcendental Quarterly* 5.2 (June 1991): 96, 99. Anderson also observes (and it cannot be said too often) that many of our negative stereotypes of "Uncle Tom" (and of all of Stowe's characters) come not from the novel itself, but from the countless stage "representations" of it—and from the inaccurate seepage of its constructs into popular culture.

40. Ibid., 96, quoting Harriet Beecher Stowe, *Uncle Tom's Cabin*, 2 vols., in *The Writings of Harriet Beecher Stowe* (Boston: Houghton, Mifflin, 1896), 1:28. Further references to *Uncle Tom's Cabin* refer to this edition and are cited in the text as *UTC*.

41. Stowe would have known, from a familiarity with the stories of countless slave escapes, that black men and women could and did work together more or less as co-operative equals in this heroic endeavor. One of the most notorious of escapes was that of William and Ellen Crafts (in 1849): they accomplished the astonishing feat of making their way north all the way from Louisiana by virtue of this ruse. Light-skinned Ellen Crafts cross-dressed and posed as a young "master"; William pretended to be "the young master's" body-servant. After they reached safety, they sold hundreds of engravings of Ellen Crafts in her cross-dressed disguise, thus publicizing not merely their escape but a possibility of more flexible social constructions of gender. Neither lesson was lost on Stowe, and although she never threw in her lot with the militant feminists of the period, her fictions consistently demonstrate the destructive consequences of highly polarized, bi-modal gender roles.

42. Anderson, 96–99.

43. The portrait of Tom is a specific reinforcement of the argument *against* the false "heroism" and "glory" that traditional masculine ideals of conquest invent and sustain. Anyone familiar with this strain of abolitionist sentiment can discern that Tom exemplifies the kind of plea that William Jay was making against the glorification of conquest and imperialism. For pungent examples, see Jay's chapters on "Political Evils of the War" (chapter 31) and "Glory" (chapter 34). Americans have become infected by their love of war, Jay affirms. "Dear to the warnings of history, [the American people] have apparently become infatuated with military glory, and have recently given various indications of their preference for men who have served their country in the field, over such as have merely labored to advance her prosperity and happiness, by cultivating the arts of peace" (239–40).

44. Gillian Brown astutely observes that "slave-masters like Simon Legree exemplified the extremes of capitalistic masculine self-advancement when not domesticated and regulated in a wage-labor system" (23).

45. See, for example, Granville B. Blanks (n. 30 above): "And in passing, allow me to state that after long consideration I have adopted the opinion that the western coast of Africa, and especially the Republic of Liberia, offers the most controlling inducements to our emigration" (132). See also Quarles, Miller, and Moses for many other examples. Throughout the abolitionist years, the invocation of America's own Revolutionary days was omnipresent: the spirits of patriots were often invoked, especially that of Patrick Henry, who famously demanded liberty or death. And when a black man emerged as remarkable for strength of character and leadership, he was hailed as a "George Washington" of his race. Hence Melville wrote that "Queequeg was George Washington cannibalistically developed," and the abolitionists who praised Henry

"Box" Brown for the remarkable courage of his escape called him a man who would become the "Washington of his day." Yet George Harris's character transcends that of the ordinary black abolitionist, so clearly does he seem destined for leadership and greatness. Moreover, the narrator's concluding denunciation of the racism infusing the Colonization Movement makes it clear that George's intended mission in Liberia would be one of political organization, the beginnings of black nationalism in the homeland of Africa:

Do you say, "We don't want them here; let them go to Africa?"

That the providence of God has provided a refuge in Africa, is, indeed, a great and noticeable fact; but . . . to fill up Liberia with an ignorant, inexperience, half-barbarized race, just escaped from the chains of slavery, would be only to prolong, for ages, the period of struggle and conflict which attends the inception of new enterprises. (*UTC* 2:246–47)

America, after all, had moved beyond the point where this kind of leadership was necessary; Liberia, on the other hand, was at just the point of an "inception of new enterprises," ready for its own "George Washington." Ironically, it was Delaney who most vehemently criticized Stowe's novel. According to Floyd R. Miller, "Delaney resented Mrs. Stowe's prominence as an interpreter of the Afro-American slave experience to both whites and blacks. This resentment surfaced in the spring of 1853 in several letters to *Frederick Douglass' Paper* in which Delaney criticized Mrs. Stowe for her colorizationist sentiments"; introduction to M. R. Delaney, *Blake*, ed. Miller (Boston: Beacon Press, 1970), xx. Certainly, *Blake* is a kind of "refutation" of *Uncle Tom's Cabin*. Yet that novel is itself problematic, not merely because of its fragmentary composition pattern (or because we still are lacking its conclusion), but because while deploring black "subservience," it offers no confidence in the positive outcome of black violence. Of course by the time the entire novel was printed in 1861, Delaney himself was an advocate for emigration to Liberia.

46. Brown, 31, quoting *UTC* 2:309.

47. Joan Hedrick, "'Peaceable Fruits': The Ministry of Harriet Beecher Stowe," *American Quarterly* 40.3 (September 1988): 319, 308. Some abolitionists did have colorphobia; some acknowledged it candidly. However, there is little evidence that Stowe had this prejudice, and a good deal of evidence that she did not. However, the *polemical* situation was complex: if *Uncle Tom's Cabin* was to be successful propaganda, Stowe could not afford to terrorize her readers into supposing that abolition would unleash multitudes of angry and empowered African American men who would wreak revenge upon a sinful nation. This possibility is reinforced by the unusually anti-melodramatic conclusion of the novel that foreswears the possibility of strong closure (either with Tom's death or George's emigration).

48. "In Cincinnati, for example, [Delaney] commended the many blacks working as tradesmen and thus 'amply demonstrating our capacity to take care of ourselves.' He followed this with a similar list of blacks running their own small businesses. 'This is what I desire to see,' he exalted, '—our people coming out of old employments of domestic servitude and menial occupations. This must be done is we expect ever to be elevated to an equality with the dominant class'" (Miller, 121). Given the *precision* with which Stowe follows Delaney's lead in developing this idea (he elaborated the

notion in letters to *The North Star* from various Ohio cities he was visiting, and Stowe makes her list from exactly the same region), she may well have been puzzled by his angry reaction to her novel. Or perhaps she was not, for the leadership of the abolitionist movement was involved in deep dissention by 1853–54. Delaney was not pleased with *Uncle Tom's Cabin*. For one thing, he resented this white woman's having "taken over" the intrinsically black topic of slavery and a description of the domestic relationships of African Americans. His own novel was a response to Stowe's.

49. Jay, 279.

50. A slightly different version of this essay was published in *American Quarterly*, December 1995. I would like to thank *American Quarterly* for permission to reprint it.

The *Jouissant* Politics of
Helen Hunt Jackson's *Ramona*

The Ground That Is "Mother's Lap"

DANEEN WARDROP

Today we remember Helen Hunt Jackson for three accomplishments, perhaps in this descending order of significance: she was Emily Dickinson's most astute correspondent; she was the writer Ralph Waldo Emerson called the best female poet of his time; and she wrote the novel, *Ramona*. *Ramona* appeared in 1884 as a reform novel seeking to redress the territorial grievances of the California Indians against the United States government, somewhat in the way that Herman Melville's *White-Jacket* sought in 1850 to outlaw flogging in the U.S. Navy or Harriet Beecher Stowe's *Uncle Tom's Cabin* sought in 1852 to abolish slavery. In fact, Jackson asserted, "If I could write a story that would do for the Indian a thousandth part that Uncle Tom's Cabin did for the negro, I would be thankful the rest of my life." [1] Though often overlooked today, *Ramona* was popular in the later nineteenth and early twentieth centuries and effective in causing its wide readership to become more aware of the egregious treatment of Native Americans.

A brave book, it runs the risk of alienating its largely Anglo American audience by creating a world of major characters, virtually all of whom are from a non-Anglo and non-American culture; it also risks offending its audience by using rhetoric that excoriates American values of acquisitiveness. Jackson condemns Americans as upholding "a law of thieves" and murderers. At their best they are peddlers and traders and at their worst "base," "usurping," and "seeking money, like dogs." To counteract potential alienation, Jackson flatters her audience by acknowledging their femaleness. The overwhelmingly female readership of nineteenth-century novels—and even more so, of those novels written by women—would have noticed the ways in which Jackson accorded her novel a female authority. On the conscious level they would have noticed the opening scenes teeming with women and children at the Moreno ranch. Like *Little Women*, the setting of *Ramona* depends upon an absent man (General Moreno is deceased) and a strong female community. In fact, so feminized is the opening setting that no room in the Moreno household is without a statue of the Madonna. On a more subtle and subconscious but affecting level, Jackson creates a feminized landscape that by its radical privileging of *jouissance* legitimates Ramona's identity at the same time that it emphasizes the political discourse at the heart of the novel.

Certainly, *Ramona* is not without its political inconsistencies. It should be pointed out that Jackson appropriates Indian and Chicano cultures; she does so to make a point to her Anglo audience about the culpability of the American government. Paradoxically, she appropriates these cultures in order to advocate for them. Jackson is an Anglo American author attempting to write the life of a minority protagonist, and her depictions of Ramona and Alessandro often suffer because they are anglicized and devoid of ethnicity. My thoughts here, however, remain trained on what is probably the more perspicacious side of Jackson's writings, that is, the manner in which she tries to rally her readership, largely a female, Anglo American readership, by creating a feminized landscape.

At the work's center the lovers Alessandro, an Indian sheep shearer, and Ramona, half Mexican and half Indian, escape to this feminized landscape, a wilderness hideaway that exists in the form of a large cañon. The gender implications of the cañon—rimmed with thicket, first seen in dawn's "red tints," and characterized by moss and a secret water source at the bottom—are undeniable. Ellen Moers in *Literary Women* notices the prominence of such female spaces in women's writing, especially in the latter part of the nineteenth century. Citing George Eliot's "Red Deeps," George Sand's "Black Valley," and Willa Cather's "Panther Cañon," Moers notes a pattern of female sexual landscapes that function as arenas of exultation and "earthbound ecstasy." Jackson uses her own version of the "Red Deeps" to find a feminized nature, a nature of the woman's body that can sanctify her message.[2]

Ramona and Alessandro spend three days in the cañon and emerge strengthened. The novel, too, gains power from this central topographical space of female authority. Jackson depends upon the *jouissance* that the cañon offers to *Ramona* as primary, bodily legitimation, and legitimation that her audience probably registered subconsciously. Richard Howard observes that the French word *jouissance* offers a notion of "the supreme pleasure, say, associated with sexuality at its most abrupt and ruthless pitch." The French seem to bypass the squeamishness that Americans feel about sex and can use "a vocabulary of eroticism, an amorous discourse which smells neither of the laboratory nor of the sewer, which just—attentively, scrupulously—puts the facts."[3] Hélène Cixous uses the word *jouissance* to refer specifically to orgasm-like maternal functions. Cixous's idea of *jouissance*, of rapture with the body, "a desire to live oneself within, wanting the belly, the tongue, the blood," provides a useful way of seeing Jackson's metaphoric celebration of the female body. The force of her metaphor lies in her perception of "a woman's instinctual economy" as referred to by a woman.[4] Jackson needs this metaphor to accord herself the power to speak, especially given Jackson's radical political tactic of attacking her nation's actions. Jackson gambles that her Anglo American, female readers will give primary allegiance to gender over race and nationality. She counts on women identifying with women across culture, on a kind of community of gender through the text.

I will return to Jackson's *jouissant* landscape, but first I would like to show how she establishes a mother-centered world. In order to show Ramona's mother ties, the following short summary of the novel may be helpful. Ramona, an orphan, is raised by Señora Moreno along with the Señora's son, Felipe, on the large Moreno ranch. During sheep-shearing time, the Morenos hire a band of Temecula Indians to help. Alessandro, the leader of this band and son of the Temecula chief, falls in love with Ramona, to the displeasure of the Señora. Even though Ramona is half Native American, the Señora cannot countenance Ramona's marrying an Indian. Eventually, Alessandro and Ramona flee the ranch and, as their first hiding place, use the cañon, a sort of makeshift honeymoon spot. At the same time, the American government evacuates the Temecula village for cooptation by white settlers, and when Alessandro and Ramona arrive at his village, they find upheaval. The couple becomes part of the diaspora, repeatedly displaced by American settlers. Alessandro later succumbs to mental illness caused by the displacement and eventually is murdered by an Anglo rancher whose horse Alessandro exchanged with his own during one of Alessandro's fits of disorientation. Meanwhile, Señora Moreno has died, and Felipe is freed to search the country for Ramona, whom he finds near death from the shock of Alessandro's murder. He returns to the Moreno ranch with Ramona and her baby daughter, and in time they marry and, finally, to avoid the evils of acquisitive American culture, move to Mexico.

The novel features three interlocking quests. The first, most overtly political quest is that of Alessandro for a homeland. Clearly the social import of *Ramona* lies in Jackson's precise portrayal of Alessandro's anguish as he searches for a place where he can retain his dignity. His search occupies the middle part of the novel. Felipe's quest determines the last part, as he searches southern California to find Ramona. His quest draws on the romantic convention of the lover seeking the beloved heroine. The third quest, Ramona's, informs the entire book in an understated but pervasive way. Never explicitly motivated to find her mother, Ramona nonetheless is perpetually vigilant, and we as readers are perpetually alerted to the existence of mother figures. While

Ramona never finds her biological mother, who is Native American, she finds a series of mothers, all of whom prove crucial to her development.

The nineteenth-century reader, steeped in the "cult of mother," wouldn't have missed Ramona's quest, and Helen Hunt Jackson plays upon her audience's sympathies by developing this dynamic of the maternal.[5] By forming all three quests as interdependent, Jackson fortifies them at the same time. Moreover, she uses the romantic convention of hero-seeks-heroine and the hallowed dynamic of the maternal to bolster her more radical position. In other words, Jackson takes the risk of alienating her audience by supporting Indian rights that challenge established Anglo American suppositions about race and property entitlements. She wins her audience over to her radical position by playing on their sense of feminine justice—a justice that depends upon loyalty to gender over loyalty to country.

The beginning chapter establishes a female world. A southwestern estate is presided over by the oldest member, Juanita, so ancient that her history is hazy; she endlessly shells beans so that she sits surrounded by husks. Full of "women, children, and babies," the Moreno ranch supports a women's culture. Here men are irascible and self-defeating (Juan Can, the overseer), absent (General Moreno is deceased), or ineffectual (Felipe). The Moreno ranch is a matriarchal society where, regardless of class, women know how to use social skills to attain power. Señora Moreno, especially, enacts her will in a circuitous way, never betraying her conscious desire but instead flattering and manipulating. The Señora "manouvered with her son and her head shepherd alike" to sway decisions in her favor (27). Jackson posits as a kind of genius such power that stems from the marginalization of women: "To attain one's ends in this way is the consummate triumph of art. Never to appear as a factor in the situation; to be able to wield other men, as instruments, with the same direct and implicit response to will that one gets from a hand or foot,—this is to triumph, indeed: to be as nearly controller and conqueror of Fates as fate permits. . . . But it is to be questioned whether even in these notable instances there has ever been such marvellous completeness of success as is sometimes seen in the case of a woman in whom the power is an instinct and not an attainment; a passion rather than a purpose. . . . Señora Moreno's was the stroke of genius" (12–13). A passage such as this almost reads as a desideratum for women wanting to consolidate their power, and it is reminiscent of passages in *Uncle Tom's Cabin* in which Harriet Beecher Stowe delights in showing women characters who can "wield" men "as instruments" simply by the force of their gentle influence and moral fiber. The working-class women in *Ramona* are subtly powerful, too; for instance, Marda, Ramona's nurse, rules by "sleight of hand."

Jackson uses the strategy of inventing a woman's world in order to invest women with the power to make judgments and manipulate their surroundings. She tightens this strategy even further when she appeals specifically to motherhood. Such an appeal to the ultimate authority for the majority of female readership was the best way for a woman to attempt change of the social order in the nineteenth century. Into this world of feminine power, Jackson brings Ramona, the character with the least material power but the one who enacts the most change. Jackson induces enormous sympathy for Ramona by offering a variation of the wicked stepmother story. Not only is Ramona an orphan but she is treated with wrenching indifference by the cold Señora. Presumably Jackson must make extra efforts to create sympathy for her unusual heroine, a child resulting from miscegenation. She might accordingly have been a difficult heroine for her audience to identify with.[6] As a motherless child, however, the character of Ramona would have directed the audience immediately to their primary allegiance of motherhood.

In the very first scenes in which the reader meets her, Ramona asks about her mother. It is exactly Ramona's perpetual search for acknowledgment of the mothers in her changing environment that affords her the most power. On an obvious level, she has three mothers: the nameless Native American woman who bore her; her adoptive mother and namesake, the Señora Ramona Ortegna (the infatuation of Scottish shipowner Angus Phail, Ramona's father); and her guardian Señora Moreno, the sister of Señora Ortegna. Ramona, however, involves herself with at least six other mothers as the novel progresses. Marda, who nursed Ramona and takes her side against her own biological daughter, Margarita, is a loyal maternal figure for Ramona. When Ramona returns to the Moreno ranch at the conclusion, she knows Marda "will love [her] baby" (416). Ramona's most essential initiation into the Indian village of San Pasquale occurs when the women bring the oldest woman of the tribe to meet her. After intensive scrutiny of Ramona, the woman announces her approval: "It is well; I am your mother." Ramona assents by saying, "she shall be like my mother, whom I never saw" (287–88). Yet another Native American woman stands in for Ramona's mother later, when she and Alessandro live on San Jacinto Mountain. In this woman Ramona can see "always the picture of what her own mother might perchance be, wandering, suffering, she knew not what or where; and her yearning, filial instinct found sad pleasure in caring for this lonely, childless, aged one" (364–65).

Finally, the Tennessee settler, Aunt Ri, one of the small number of sympathetic Anglo American characters, provides the most well-rounded mother figure. Salty and forthright, Aunt Ri's voice is an important one in the book's final pages, and surely Jackson meant for her to be the character with whom her typical reader might most readily identify. She speaks with common sense and compassion. At first prejudiced against both Indians and Mexicans, she easily relents because of her native charity and good will and comes to be Jackson's most articulate mouthpiece (ironically, for her accent makes her nearly incomprehensible) for championing Native American rights. When Aunt Ri finally declares herself an "Ummeriken" (341), the word carries not a little irony; certainly the spelling is meant to indicate Aunt Ri's drawl but it also seems a semideliberate slap at the dignity of "Americans." Aunt Ri is a mother figure not only to Ramona but to whole neighborhoods—to whomever she meets, it seems. She defends Ramona against dangers, worries about her loneliness, and nurses her back to health with an infusion of "old man," an herb also called "wild wormwood" that the Cahuilla Indians had already administered without effect but which, with Aunt Ri's doctoring, enacts the cure for Ramona. When Ramona finally leaves Aunt Ri, the farewell is "the hardest of all [farewells]. Ramona clung to her as to a mother" (409–10).

The most significant mothers to Ramona, however, are the mothers of spirit and of earth. It is no mistake that Aunt Ri's name derives from Maria, the mother of Jesus. The Virgin Mary provides Ramona with an essential spirit mother, and that spiritual mothering remains constant throughout the novel. We see Ramona lying on the floor at the feet of the Madonna, Ramona asking the Virgin to show her and Alessandro in which direction to turn, Ramona in San Pasquale wishing she had a statue of the saint—perhaps the only time Ramona admits to wanting anything for herself. Alessandro at one point considers that one cannot have the same feelings about a saint as about a person one knows. Ramona responds with passion. "'No, not quite,' said Ramona; 'not quite, about a saint; but one can for the blessed Virgin, Alessandro! I am sure of that. Her statue, in my room at the Señora's, has been always my mother'" (282). Ramona's connection with the Madonna gives her indomitable spiritual authority in the novel. In fact, Jackson borrows and revises the icons of Catholicism to shape her feminist agenda. Ramona's status of spiritual daughter to the Virgin allows her to become a sort of spiritual advisor to her community of women. Ramona finally acquires a statuette in their San Pasquale home, and Alessandro constructs a niche for it.[7] The village women come to Ramona's to see the statue and pray, "so that it finally came to be a sort of shrine for the whole village" (293). Ramona adopts the traits of her various mothers, the unrequited love of the Madonna, the patience of the old San Pasquale woman, the logic of Señora Moreno (28, 38), and the humor of Aunt Ri.

Finally, Ramona's most important mother is the land. Helen Hunt Jackson represents the earth as mother most particularly in the cañon to which Ramona and Alessandro escape. The episode of the cañon, the wilderness hideaway for the couple, occupies the exact center of the novel. Lest the point be missed that the cañon is a "mother earth" for Ramona, Jackson christens the earth with a sign from the mother Mary. At their first dawn there Ramona starts a prayer and is answered by a sunray illuminating the Christ on her rosary: "To both Ramona and Alessandro it came like an omen, —like a message straight from the Virgin. Could she choose a better messenger,—she, the compassionate one, the loving woman in heaven; mother of the Christ to whom they prayed, through her,—mother, for whose sake He would regard their least cry" (243). Though the scene cloys with sentimentality, Jackson's intent to hallow the mother essence in earth as well as spirit is clear. The scene, however, proves unnecessary because Jackson has already established in many secular ways the mother role of the cañon.

Furthermore, the earth, the ground that is "mother's lap" functions in another more important way for Ramona.[8] The earth is both mother and occasion for recognizing a kind of *jouissance* that comes with acknowledgment of the female body. The concept of *jouissance* implies that there is a kind of authority in the body's sensuality that is inarguable and beyond words. As Roland Barthes suggests, "pleasure can be expressed in words, bliss [*jouissance*] cannot."[9] Jacques Lacan designates *jouissance* as that which is in excess of the phallic term. Feminists utilize Lacan's notion of *jouissance* to explain ways in which women can express through the body that which cannot be articulated in words. For instance, Jacqueline Rose notes that through *jouissance* women can experience "a refusal of division which gives the woman access to a different strata of language, where words and things are not differentiated, and the real of the maternal body threatens or holds off woman's access to prohibition and the law."[10] This kind of privileging of the maternal body in order to hold off the law describes the strategy of Jackson's use of the cañon to interpose an experience for the reader more immediate than any juridical knowledge. The woman reader, in the presence of Jackson's cañon, might unconsciously subordinate her fealty to U.S. law to the rapture of female *jouissance*.

In depicting the cañon to which Alessandro and Ramona flee when they first leave the Moreno ranch Jackson achieves some of her most radical and subliminal effects. The sentimental play on the theme of the maternal—and in *Ramona* motherhood is both sentimental and strengthening—would have been noticed and championed by Jackson's readers. The imbuing of the earth with feminine sexual traits as a way to heighten the sense of female power probably would not have been noticed consciously. Jackson would have made sure to subtilize her female earth because if the metaphoric emphasis on the female body had been noticed, it almost certainly would not have been accepted.

Though Ramona is at first frightened of the cañon, once she and Alessandro have set up camp in the center of it, she feels more at home than she has previously felt: she sees it as a "friendly home," and calls it "the first home I ever had." [11] Ramona must become sensitized to the location, just as the reader must if Jackson's more overt political agenda is to gain audience. The cañon offers the process of discovery of *jouissance*; along with Ramona, the reader comes to value the female sensuality inherent in its description. Cixous defines sexual difference as that "which becomes most clearly perceived on the level of *jouissance*, inasmuch as a woman's instinctual economy cannot be identified by a man or referred to the masculine economy." The effect that *Ramona* will produce is staked largely upon the degree to which its readers will recognize that "instinctual economy" distinct from dominant male economies. In other words, the cañon provides opportunity for the discernment of a radical *jouissance*. [12]

The cañon is circled by a thicket that admits of "no apparent opening," is rimmed with ferns, and is first seen in the red dawn. Jackson makes her description explicit: The cañon "at its head was little more than a rift in the rocks, and the stream which had its rise in it was only a trickling spring at the beginning" (232). The stream issues from an unknown underground source. The entry is by way of a very narrow path. The listing above is probably enough, though it is tempting to linger over these significations of the female body after centuries of pondering the phallus. As early as 1963 Ellen Moers lamented that for the female landscape there was no "term equivalent to 'phallic symbol,' to employ in civil discourse without raising a snigger of embarrassment." Moers recognized that "certain landscapes have been good for women," including "open lands, harsh and upswelling, high-lying and undulating, vegetated with crimped heather or wind-swept grasses, cut with ravines and declivities and twisting lanes." [13] *Ramona* discovers such a female landscape and provides its readers with the opportunity to develop their instinctual economies.

Jackson takes on the challenge of representing to a female Anglo American audience the plight of Native Americans, and her problem is compounded by the fact that she has virtually no sympathetic female Anglo American characters (with the exception of Aunt Ri). Jackson's strategy is subversive in its appeal to an eroticized, explicity female nature, a cañon that is woman's body and text. She appeals to the female corpus, the still space at the center of the book.

She also prepares the reader to sympathize with the Indians' right to hold their lands by arguing, again implicitly, that the American settlers see the land as a space not of instinctual economy but of a marketplace economy. Indeed, the economics of *Ramona* deserve further study. Much of Alessandro's and other characters' scorn for Americans is based on their apprehension of the American character as grasping and acquisitive. An exasperated Alessandro tells Ramona, "'Never one Indian killed another, yet, for money. It is for vengeance, always. For money! Bah! Majella, they are dogs!' . . . The name [American] was a synonym for fraud and cruelty" (279). An interesting expression of the economics of the novel occurs in the way Jackson chooses to represent the horse. When Ramona and Alessandro escape, they take with them Ramona's horse, Baba, which had been a gift to her from Felipe. The horse acts as a sort of a test case for the economies of exchange Jackson presents. Baba, of course, has emotional value for Ramona because he was a gift, but he also has monetary value and is the main reason the lovers fear they will be pursued. They both know Ramona's claim to own the horse will hold no weight, because no capital backs it up (and the world of the novel makes clear that even a "paper" doesn't protect ownership if the commodity is held by a Native American). The alternative economy presented by Alessandro and Ramona turns on its head the notion of "Indian giving." The dire predicament of the lovers who might be apprehended with a commodity that is perceived as stolen foreshadows the tragic ending, in which Alessandro is murdered for what was mistakenly perceived to be horse thievery.

The market economy colonizes the earth as it has colonized many a woman's body, which Cixous calls the "'dark continent' trick [that] has been pulled on her: she has been kept at a distance from herself, she has been made to see (= not-see) woman on the basis of what man wants to see of her, which is to say, almost nothing."[14] Jackson's depiction of a landscape of what Moers calls "earthbound ecstasy" facilitates her desire to enlist female readers in the cause of the instinctual economy that trades in sensual values.[15] By realizing the sense of earth as erotic female space, women may resist the "dark continent trick" being pulled on the California Indians. If Stowe's implicit argument against slavery is that it kills motherhood, then Jackson's argument against colonization may be that it kills the mother's body.

Cixous sees the realization of women's writing that is authorized by women's bodies as offering the hope of establishing an alternative economy: "your body must make itself heard. Then the huge resources of the unconscious will burst out. Finally the inexhaustible feminine Imaginary is going to be deployed. Without gold or black dollars, our naphtha will spread values over the world, un-quoted values that will change the rules of the old game."[16]

Jackson had tried in her previous work, *A Century of Dishonor*, to change the rules of the game for Native Americans, who were brutally dispossessed of their lands again and again by American "thieves." In *Ramona*, at least in the center of the novel, Jackson relinquishes phallocentric rationality and instead relies upon the "inexhaustible female Imaginary" to make her case. She creates the cañon in order to be able to tap "the huge resources of the unconscious" that her female readership might find in the *jouissance* of the cañon.

Yet Jackson could not sustain the erotic female rapture of the cañon through the course of the novel and, frightened perhaps by the power of her *jouissance*, she resorted to more logocentric arguments for the remainder. She was certainly aware that she needed to divert the attention of her readers with political sugarcoating in order to deliver her tough message. To one correspondant she wrote that she hoped the reader "would have swallowed a big dose of information on the Indian question without knowing it." [17] She referred specifically to the romantic plot as a diversionary tactic. She may not have realized the more subversive diversionary tactic she devised: she excoriated the American erasure of Indian culture by appealing to the authority of the female body as inscribed in the cañon. But again, she did not sustain that kind of authority for long.

The final chapters of *Ramona* return to more conventional means of swaying a female audience. Jackson appeals to a kind of women's justice, but not one based on the body. It is based on reason and compassion and, to a lesser extent, Biblical authority. The plot seems to lead to the necessity of a court scene to resolve Alessandro's murder but instead takes an interesting shift and uses the voice of Aunt Ri as a kind of transcendent tribunal. She assures us that Jim Farrar, Alessandro's murderer, will get his just deserts, if not in legal sentencing then in the way of emotional deserts. Jackson presents Aunt Ri's sense of justice as feminine and incontrovertible. The author devalues the very legal system of her culture; the outcome of any trial sanctioned by American phallocentrism becomes a moot point.

As well it might, given the American legal system's dealings with Native American rights. As official agent to the California Indians, Jackson experienced firsthand the inefficiency and brutality of the Board of Indian Commissioners and the Department of the Interior. As a result of such experience, Jackson's preference for the impassioned jurisprudence of Aunt Ri over that of the United States might easily be understood. Jackson also revisits the conventions of the sentimental female novel by using Aunt Ri to voice the particulars of female sensibility.

She returns, too, to her dependence upon the theme of motherhood. Ramona, who very early in the novel expresses her belief that "a son is more than a daughter" (38), changes and grows through her experience of motherhood. When she and Alessandro are expecting a child, she wants to bear sons, but bears only daughters. Later, Ramona and Felipe have sons and daughters, but the novel ends with the surviving daughter of Ramona and Alessandro, Ramona's namesake, the favored child. Ramona's quest for her mother ends, finally, with the realization of herself as mother, mother to her own daughter. In finding herself in this way she dispels her earlier belief that a son is more than a daughter. Ramona as a daughter of many mothers, and as mother to an extraordinary daughter, has exonerated a world of women that Jackson would have been delighted to have her female readership notice.

NOTES

1. Helen Hunt Jackson, *Ramona* (1884; Boston: Little, Brown, 1944), 77. (Further references to *Ramona* are given parenthetically in the text.) Jackson conceived the project after the failure of *A Century of Dishonor*, her nonfiction prose work about the same topic. Jackson sent a copy of the earlier book to every member of Congress.

2. Ellen Moers, *Literary Women* (New York: Oxford University Press, 1977).

3. Richard Howard, "A Note on the Text," in Roland Barthes, *The Pleasure of the Text*, trans. Richard Miller (New York: Farrar, Straus and Giroux, 1975), v.

4. Hélène Cixous and Catherine Clément, *The Newly Born Woman*, trans. Betsy Wing (Minneapolis: University of Minnesota Press, 1986), 90, 82.

5. Critics such as Ann Douglas, in *The Feminization of American Culture* (New York: Alfred A. Knopf, 1977), explore the concept of the "cult of the mother."

6. For all the strengths of Jackson's characters, Alessandro and Ramona are still anglicized by her. For example, Alessandro speaks as if he were a Shakespearean character, perhaps because Jackson wanted to give him tragic stature. He also demonstrates an irritating reliance upon the third person (as opposed to the natural, second person) when he speaks to Ramona. Both characters use language in a stilted and formal way.

7. Ramona's relationship with the Madonna is complicated, though, when she takes the baby Jesus from her and hides the little figure until the Madonna will make Ramona's own baby well (350–51).

8. The phrase "mother's lap" is Alessandro's (240).

9. Barthes, 21.

10. Jacques Lacan, *Feminine Sexuality*, ed. by Juliet Mitchell and Jacqueline Rose, trans. Rose (New York: W. W. Norton, 1982), 137, 55.

11. Alessandro also sees it as a home. Certainly, the cañon is overdetermined by Jackson. She wants to accord it domestic sentimentality at the same time that she expects it to carry Biblical and Transcendentalist freight. The cañon must be a kind of Garden of Eden in order for the Victorian reader to avoid perceiving any blemish on the protagonist's virtue; in other words, Ramona and Alessandro are not yet married, and the reader must be able to accept their cohabitation in the cañon. Hence, Jackson casts them as Adam and Eve. Jackson, a protege of Ralph Waldo Emerson, also expects her readers to embrace Alessandro as a romantic lead by dressing him up as a kind of Transcendentalist hero. As characterized by Jackson, Alessandro is not so much a tribal

Native American as a kind of foster son of "Self-Reliance," especially as he recognizes his own sense of God in the cañon.

12. Cixous and Clément, 82. Ramona and Alessandro have two major hideouts, first in the cañon and then on the mountain, San Jacinto. It may be too much to see gender implications in both, but the stark contrast of the idyllic declivity and the tragic pinnacle forms a major organizing device in the novel.

13. Moers, 256, 262.

14. Cixous and Clément, 68.

15. Moers, 259.

16. Cixous and Clément, 97.

17. Valerie Scherer Mathes, *Helen Hunt Jackson and Her Indian Reform Legacy* (Austin: University of Texas Press, 1990), 77. She wanted them to feel only the heartache. In some ways Jackson succeeded too well in her sugarcoating objective, complaining later, "I am sick of hearing that the flight of Alessandro & Ramona is an 'exquisite ideal,' and not even an allusion to the ejectment of the Temecula band from their homes" (ibid., 83). For some readers, unfortunately, the aftertaste was all saccharine and no bitter.

Class and Sexuality in a Mexican Landscape

Katherine Anne Porter's Marginalia
on D. H. Lawrence

RAE M. CARLTON COLLEY

Katherine Anne Porter called the stories in her *Flowering Judas* collection "fragments of a much larger plan which I am still engaged in carrying out, and they are what I was then able to achieve in the way of order and form and statement in a period of grotesque dislocations in a whole society when the world was heaving in the sickness of a millennial change."[1] The same could be said of her marginalia. Just as the stories are only a small part of a never-ending grand scheme, so, too, are the marginalia: tiny fragments of genius, some of which saw fruition in her published criticism. Similarly, the themes of the marginal notes and the stories are much the same—finding order in a world of chaos, the continual perfecting of the artist's craft, and the difficult choices women face in a patriarchal society. Porter's marginalia in her books by and about D. H. Lawrence exemplify these themes. Porter shared with Lawrence a common interest in Mexico and its people, but his frank portrayal of sexuality disturbed her and colored her view of his work. However, although she did not approve of the blatant sexuality in Lawrence's work, no other artist so inspired her critical pen.

The marginalia appear in three forms: the traditional scrawl in the margins of book pages, small scraps of paper containing brief notes, and lists of pages to remember, written on the flyleaf or title page. By far, the bulk of her notes were made in the margins. Here, one may view the process of Porter's creative activity as she worked on her reviews of *The Plumed Serpent* (entitled "Quetzalcoatl") and of *Lady Chatterley's Lover* ("A Wreath for the Gamekeeper"). There are notes for other planned reviews and essays which never saw completion. Ironically, Porter's Lawrence collection is relatively small in comparison to her James, Woolf, Mansfield, and Joyce collections, for example, yet reaction to it spawned the greatest number of marginal notations.[2] Porter's general distaste for Lawrence's work explains the small size of the collection, but the books that she did own so raised her ire that the marginal notes are most extensive and provide a detailed record of Porter's method and craft. Although she strove to give the impression that her stories were produced effortlessly and at one sitting, the marginalia attest otherwise. A great deal of thought and care went into each word that Porter wrote and a great deal of reading as well.

Thematically, the marginalia vary from author to author. However, three categories of notes appear consistently: factual questions, favorite authors, and the search for order. Factual questions record Porter's doubts about such things as a date or an implied influence or motive. She was not above exercising a little genteel pedantry when she came across an error, and she habitually marked every one she found. For instance, next to a description of Lawrence's Lou Witt, who was sitting "in her well-bought American clothes," Porter wrote: "Living all over Europe and buying American clothes? Lawrence doesn't know his Americans!"[3] The second category, favorite authors, comprises Porter's delighted reactions when she discovered a mention of an author whom she especially admired. The third category, of course, is Porter's primary theme, which she looked for in all her books. A book was deemed a success or failure depending on how well its author created a sense of order. In an interview, Porter named Woolf's *To the Lighthouse*, Forster's *A Passage to India*, and Richard Hughes's *A High Wind in Jamaica* as the three "almost perfect" novels and explained that "every one of them begins with an apparently insoluble problem, and every one of them works out of confusion into order. The material is all used so that you are going toward a goal. And that goal is the clearing up of disorder and confusion and wrong, to a logical and human end."[4] In Porter's critical eye, Lawrence failed to achieve such stylistic perfection because of his inability to separate social class from sexuality.

Although she cultivated a public persona as an elegant Southern belle, Porter actually supported the emancipation of women and believed firmly that women were men's equals in all things. Her Lawrence marginalia confirm this belief. She saw in Lawrence a misogyny that deeply disturbed her and a class-consciousness that damaged his work. Lawrence's characters seemed to consist of lower-class men and the upper-class women to whom they are attracted and whom they try to dominate. This attempt at domination represents a literal manifestation of the patriarchal society Porter so despised. On the surface, Porter and Lawrence seem to be almost polar opposites, so it is no wonder that he held a peculiar fascination for the artistically proper Porter. Lawrence's work, his motives, his vision of truth all seemed muddled to Porter and without substance. Her reviews of both *The Plumed Serpent* and *Lady Chatterley's Lover* (the latter really more a diatribe against censorship than a review) reveal her confusion over Lawrence's use of his undeniable gift for ends that Porter deemed unworthy or, at least, unseemly.

In spite of their surface differences, however, particularly on the subject of sexuality, both writers shared a similar concern with Mexican primitivism that permeates their fiction. Porter disagreed with Lawrence's portrait of the Mexican Indians in *The Plumed Serpent*, calling his novel "a fresh myth of the Indian, a deeply emotional conception, but a myth none the less, and a debased one." However, she admired, almost in spite of herself, Lawrence's eye for detail, his feeling for place, and she noted that "a nationwide political and religious movement provides the framework for a picture that does not omit a leaf, a hanging fruit, an animal, a cloud, a mood, of the visible Mexico" (*Collected Essays*, 423). Yet if the "visible" Mexico was accurately and vividly portrayed, the "invisible," mystic Mexico certainly was not. Porter and Lawrence immersed themselves in the political and economic upheaval in revolutionary Mexico, with divergent results. Porter scoffed at Lawrence's fear that while in Mexico he might be murdered. She bragged, "I lived in Mexico then, in Villages and anywhere I wished to go, and never once was threatened. 1920–1925 more or less."[5] Porter overestimates both the duration of her visit and Mexico's safety. In an essay for *Century* magazine, Porter described the growing tide of violence in Mexico: "Uneasiness grows here daily. We are having sudden deportations of foreign agitators, street riots and parades of workers carrying red flags. . . . Battles occur almost daily between Catholics and Socialists in many parts of the Republic."[6] In fact, Porter herself fell under suspicion for her activities, and fearing arrest or deportation, she returned to the United States in 1921.

Porter's several visits to Mexico were inevitably colored by her first glimpse of the country in the 1920s. As a child, her father had whetted her appetite for things Mexican with his enchanting stories, so when the opportunity to travel there on assignments for *Magazine of Mexico* presented itself, Porter eagerly accepted. She arrived in Mexico City just before the inauguration of Álvaro Obregón, whose ascendance to the presidency marked a new era of national optimism for the war-weary Mexican people. Porter threw herself into the causes of the workers with characteristic enthusiasm; she taught Indian children, attended labor union meetings, and took cigarettes and fruit to prisoners of war. She sympathized with the workers who viewed the machine as their salvation, and those pro-socialist convictions found their way into her fiction, especially "Flowering Judas" and the other stories in that collection. Here she and Lawrence began to part company.

Lawrence, Porter believed, did not share her sympathy with the workers and their cause. He viewed the primitive Indians and their craft not with an eye to increasing their financial and cultural support, as Porter did, but as an expatriate who considered their art a curious form of local color. Porter wrote in

"Quetzalcoatl," her review of *The Plumed Serpent*, that Lawrence "puts in besides all his own accumulated protest against the things he hates: his grudge against women as opposed to his concept of woman, his loathing of the machine. His contempt for revolution and the poor is arrogant, not aristocratic: but he is plainly proud of his attitude. It is a part of his curiously squeamish disgust of human contact" (*Collected Essays*, 423). In Porter's opinion, Lawrence's work exhibited a class-consciousness and a misogyny that were not only violations of the artist's role but also an affront to intelligent readers.

Porter's marginalia betrayed her distaste for Lawrence's personal habits, and in typical Porter fashion she allowed her personal views to cloud her critical judgment. Most of her criticism was based on her moral misgivings, and she found much in Lawrence's work to arouse her distaste. Porter took care, however, to avoid any semblance of priggishness. She wrote in "A Wreath for the Gamekeeper" that she wished only to say "that I think that from start to finish he was about as wrong as can be on the subject of sex, and that he wrote a very laboriously bad book to prove it" (*Collected Essays*, 17). She took issue with publishers who attempted to "blackmail" readers into buying the book by saying, in effect: "If you disapprove of this book, you are proved to be (1) illiterate, (2) insensitive, (3) unintelligent, (4) low-minded, (5) 'mean,' (6) a hypocrite, (7) a prude, and other unattractive things" (18). Porter argued instead that obscene language served a specific purpose, and that it should be used for that purpose, without the attempt to glorify lovemaking. She disapproved, also, of Lawrence's own sexuality and his extramarital affairs, both homosexual and heterosexual. She blamed him completely for the disintegration of his marriage to Frieda Lawrence and felt that his low opinion of women made happiness impossible for him.

In fact, Lawrence's callous treatment of Frieda formed the basis of Porter's criticism of him both as a writer and a human being. Porter theorized that Lawrence interacted with women only within the context of a power struggle, one he was destined to lose. Further, Lawrence's sharp awareness of class division made him feel inferior to his titled, elegant wife (Frieda held the title of Baroness). He yearned for the status and power of the upper class and dreamed of attaining money and property. Class-consciousness led to Lawrence's downfall and Porter made many notes of his obsessive behavior. When Richard Aldington noted in his biography of Lawrence that he "often wanted to write about upper-class women falling in love with working men, the gamekeeper character is rather forced on him," Porter underlined the reference to class. She responded in the margins with a comment on "the obsessiveness with the relation of his father and mother in that case, Middle class with lower class but still—! and Lawrence repeated it in his own life—But this time with a real upper-class woman" (112). According to Porter, Lawrence translated his doubts about his own sexuality into a conflict between classes and gender. In other words, the woman traditionally held the higher class position but was captivated by the lower-class male. In this scenario, the male achieves the ultimate domination over the female, while proving his own superiority over the aristocracy. Porter saw this same struggle being played out in Lawrence's marriage as well as that of his parents. In Porter's view, Aldington supports this patriarchal scheme when he writes of Lawrence's "spontaneous, pleasure-loving father and the prim, self-righteous puritan woman." Underlining this phrase, Porter protests angrily, "Stop loading the Dice Aldington!" (15). She goes further in her attempts to apply this class/gender theory to other couples who were Lawrence's contemporaries. She makes notes on the inside cover of Aldington's book:

Lawrence—Frieda
K. M. [Katherine Mansfield]—Murray
Gide—Madeline
page 303—
Lawrence—Believe in *me*
Frieda I know you too well—
Compare with Madeline Gide's—"You know and I know that you are vul-
    nerable—"
The Secret Drama of my Life by Gide—

Porter seems to feel that Lawrence was right about Frieda's superiority over him. Interestingly enough, Porter herself was extremely class-conscious, and she tried, unsuccessfully, to hide her poverty-ridden childhood. This feeling, combined with her feminist leanings, probably contributes to her identification with Frieda Lawrence.

Similarly, Porter quashed any effort on the part of Lawrence to align himself with the aristocracy of his wife's family. She marks a passage in which he dreams of royalty and of subjects who will "call me king and lord!" (Aldington, 304). She asks, irritatedly, "What does he *want* with such subjects?" However, when Aldington writes of Lawrence's last days, Porter begins to sympathize with the destroyed artist. She marks Aldington's passage on the "vast far-and-wide significance" of Lawrence's life, underlining the phrase: "how clear and unquestioned is the might of the day." She wonders: "and then when you think of all the yaltering females and half-males around him—But *why* did he let them in?" (338). Aside from her distress at his tragic early demise, Porter experienced few other positive emotions for Lawrence. Any evidence of his materialism particularly annoyed her, especially his order to Frieda to "Get out of that throne, I want it." Porter comments: "Well—Jesus was a carpenter's son! What do you expect?" (Aldington, 361). Porter's awareness of Lawrence's classist views prompted her to consider writing another essay on his work, and she made notes to that end in F. R. Leavis's *D. H. Lawrence: Novelist*. She wrote in the flyleaf:

> Notes for theme of low man and superior woman theme: Lady Chatterley
>   and the gamekeeper
> Rachel and the Bargeman, (The Rainbow)
> The Virgin and the Gypsy—
> (Inscribed to Frieda, "She-Who-Was-Cynthia" with a really below the belt
>   attack on her first husband, in lowest terms—The rat passage, Page 366
> Prototype: Baroness Frieda von Richthofen and The Miner's Son—
>   Note desire to destroy what he feared—Page 371
> See Lawrence about Bennett Footnote Page 380
> 17 November 1956

Apparently she saw a pattern of male domination in several of Lawrence's novels, and she considered that the protagonist couples were all modeled, to some degree, on Frieda and Lawrence himself. Although Porter particularly enjoyed applying biographical constraints upon her critical subjects, she found that Lawrence's life permeated his work to an uncommon degree. She noted in "A Wreath for the Gamekeeper" that "the artist's life is always his material and it seems pointless to look for hidden clues when they are so obviously on the surface. Lawrence the man and Lawrence the artist are more than usually inseparable: he is everywhere, and everywhere the same" (*Collected Essays*, 25). She found in his work ample evidence to support her theories and became incensed when other critics failed to recognize her position. When Leavis asserted that "Lawrence's attitude towards his characters is not in any way affected by class-feeling. Rendering the world of back-street homes, chapel, high-tea and vernacular talk, he turns on it no different kind of spirit of interest form that which informs his treatment of life anywhere, at any social level. . . . In 'The Daughters of the Vicar,' I said, the contrast between the bright cottage and the gloomy vicarage has nothing sentimental about it," Porter responded that his claim was "Just simply not so—" (100). She found plenty in Leavis's narrative to support her contentions to the opposite. She marked an especially apt passage from "You Touched Me" in which Lawrence writes, "[Hadrian] looked at her curiously. . . . The same glamour that he saw in the elderly man he now saw in the woman. And he wanted to possess himself of it, he wanted to make himself master of it. As he went about through the old pottery-yard, his secretive mind schemed and worked. To be master of that strange soft delicacy such as he had felt in her hand upon his face—this was what he set himself towards. He was secretly plotting." Next to this passage Porter writes, "This is the exact testimony of Lawrence=the ambition of the mean charity boy to possess a superior being and reduce her to his level, or beneath it!" (316). Later, Porter notes the ultimate evidence of Lawrence's materialism in Hadrian's assertion that "he knew in his subtle, calculating way, that it was not for money he wanted Matilda. *He wanted both the money and Matilda*. But he told himself the two desires were separate, not one. He could not do with Matilda without the money, but he did not want her for the money." Porter makes a grim notation, "Here it really is in all its mean crookedness" (317). These marginal notes point to a central theme that Porter found in Lawrence's work and life: man's triumph over and domination of woman. The theme that recurs most frequently in the Lawrence marginalia is that of Lawrence's mistreating Frieda for the purpose of elevating himself. Porter marked many passages that she considered as evidence of Lawrence's debased view of all women and his desire to master and appropriate Frieda's aristocracy. She believed that his distrust of all women focused on Frieda. She ridiculed Lawrence's view of aristocracy in his essay on Thomas Hardy. Lawrence wrote: "With the men as with the women of old descent: they have nothing to do with mankind in general, they are exceedingly personal. . . . Hence the inevitable isolation, detachment of the aristocrat. His one aim, during centuries, has been to keep himself detached." She scribbled in the margin: "Through Frieda he became this authority on the aristocrat."[7] Lawrence's ill-treatment of Frieda forms the basis of much of Porter's criticism.

In Aldington's biography, Porter notes with pleasure the differences between Lawrence's and Frieda's methods of arguing when she reads that Lawrence could not see his own faults. According to Aldington, Lawrence would rather make an "illogical or absurd retort rather than admit himself beaten in an argument." She observes that "in the conversation her arguments are perfectly clear and fair," unlike those of her husband (87). Porter tried, unsuccessfully, to assume a rather blasé attitude regarding the sexual relationship between Lawrence and his wife. She marks a passage in which Aldington theorizes that his relations with Frieda began to suffer because of his infidelities. Porter remarks: "Oh God what a bore the fellow was!" (219). However, to her credit, Porter recognized that some genuine devotion existed between Frieda and Lawrence. A touching episode between the couple forced Porter to recall an especially painful experience in her own life when a man she loved succumbed to influenza while nursing Porter.[8] She marks a paragraph in which

Aldington recalls Lawrence's illness. Porter identifies with the description and notes: "For me Oct. 5 1918 / February 15 1919 / Plague in Hospital Denver" (240). The "plague" of which Porter writes is the influenza that almost claimed her life and, if reports are true, did claim the life of her young man.

More often, though, Porter felt anger with Lawrence at his attempts to subordinate Frieda's will. She notes a particularly offensive passage of Aldington's that recounts Lawrence's desire to be "lord and master." She defends Frieda's inability to sympathized with Lawrence: "Yes but it is a deep rebuke to Frieda for her refusal to believe in his *spirit*, and the mystical maleness he worshipped in men and wished her to worship. She was right not to do so—maleness alone is not a worshipped thing at is best, and in Lawrence it was very suspect and incomplete" (304). As these remarks attest, Porter was deeply offended by Lawrence's dubious sexuality and his homosexual experiences. She had several homosexual friends herself, but none of them had ever tried to hide his orientation in a marriage. Porter believed that Lawrence's philandering ruined Frieda's life, and she became infuriated upon reading stories of Frieda's unhappiness. Aldington relates that "Frieda began to get jealous" at reports of Lawrence's infidelities. To this Porter angrily notes, "He blabbed in every direction to any one who would listen, a bitter snake of treachery and spite" (305). Porter believed firmly in the privacy of marital squabbles, and Lawrence's violation of that unwritten code provided one more strike against him. Porter's notes clearly indicate that Lawrence's homosexual leanings assumed primary importance in her mind. She became disgusted when Aldington describes another public altercation between Lawrence and Frieda, in which "he flung half a glass of red wine" and "began to cry." She underlined Aldington's mention of "bitter female rows" and wrote: "Any Female row seems dignified after the petty 'male' rows of DHL" (363). Farther down on the same page she wonders. "Was it about this time or later that Frieda took a lover?" In Porter's mind, Lawrence's behavior justified Frieda's infidelity. The prospect of Frieda's affair intrigued Porter, and she tried several times to pin down the exact date of the affair's beginning. When Aldington discusses the period after the writing of *The Plumed Serpent*, Porter bemoans her lack of knowledge regarding the exact date of Frieda's taking a lover: "I *wish* I knew if this was not the date of Frieda's leaving him, in effect, for someone else—the Italian she married recently (1952)" (382). Most probably, Porter's voyeuristic interest in the marriage and sex life of Lawrence and Frieda is more complex than mere morbid curiosity. From the marginalia, it appears that Porter, like Lawrence himself, considered Frieda the superior partner in the marriage. Porter believed that Lawrence inflated Frieda's behavior into that of all women, so that Frieda became for him the arbiter of morality. In other words, should Frieda prove to be inferior to Lawrence, particularly in the matter of marital fidelity, then Lawrence would appear justified in his misogyny. The likelihood of this theory increases as one reads the other marginalia. For example, in his biography of Lawrence Harry T. Moore ascribes to Lawrence's parents the roles of lower-class, inferior male and upper-class, superior female. Porter underlines Moore's phrase, "The 'superior soul' he was to marry, Lydia Beardsall," and queries: "Why the quotes? She was 'superior' in every way to the lout she married even if they were born in the same class—so why the cheap sarcasm?" (5). Apparently, class consciousness is visible not only in Lawrence, but in Porter as well.

Porter suspected that Lawrence's obsessive behavior regarding Frieda may have been connected to her children by a previous marriage. In his book, Leavis attributes the same purity of motive to Lawrence exhibited by the protagonist of *Aaron's Rod*: "I do believe that every man must fulfil his own soul, every woman must be herself, herself only, not some man's instrument, or some embodied theory." Porter argues instead that Lawrence objectified Frieda: "Yet Lawrence saw her only as his embodied theory" (36). Porter speculated further that Lawrence looked upon his step-children as competitors for Frieda's love. Porter marks Leavis's paragraph exploring Lawrence's sense of marriage. He notes that although "the tie that holds him to his wife is insisted on, he has no feelings at all, it would seem, about his children." This passage, she felt, validated her conjectures, and she noted, "Lawrence had no children of his own, and was bitterly resentful of Frieda's and her need for them" (38). Significantly, Porter herself had no children, a lack she deeply regretted; she felt as if she were a failure at a woman's most important function. She notes a similar failed relationship between Lawrence and his sisters in Leavis's quotation from *Sons and Lovers*. Somers is reminded of his "sister, and of girls he had known when he was younger—strange glimpses of all of them, each glimpse excluding the last. And at the same time in the terrible face some of the look of that bloated face of a madwoman which hung over Jane Eyre in the night in Mr. Rochester's house." Porter comments: "His own wish that they *were* like that!" (42). Porter believed that Lawrence ultimately failed all the women who cared for him, as well as himself. She marks another episode Leavis cites from *Sons and Lovers*: "They neither of them believed in me,' [Somers] said to himself. Still in the spell of the dream, he put it in the past tense, though Harriet lay sleeping in the next bed. He could not get over it." She notes that "Both of them [his mother and his wife] had believed in him more than he had in himself. That sullen repudiating madwoman was himself" (42). Porter's feminist sensibilities are further aroused at Kate's closing remarks in *The Plumed Serpent*: "It is all very well for a woman to cultivate her ego, her individuality. It is all very well for her to despise love, or to love love as a cat loves a mouse, that it plays with as long as possible before devouring it to vivify her own individuality and voluptuously fill the belly of her own ego." Porter's reply is more than a little defensive: "This is the *man's* trick with sensuality, more than the woman's" (Leavis 72). Porter continues to pick at Lawrence's failure to produce a child with Frieda and underlines Leavis's notion that the Lawrences' problems could not be solved with the addition of a child, much like those of Anna and Will in *The Rainbow*, for "to bring into the world another life that will be faced with it is not to solve it." She cautions: "Remember his bitter jealousy of Frieda's children—their own childlessness" (150). She scoffed at Lawrence's description of Will and Anna: "The deep root of his enmity lay in the fact that she jeered at his soul." Porter scrawls: "Poor little Jackass—She jeered at nothing but saw things he had missed in his self-centered pretentiousness, which allows her no freedom of mind but must take all to its dreary little self" (149). For Porter, Lawrence took on the personality of his characters. Lawrence's appropriation of Frieda's thoughts proved his preoccupation with his own self and marked the ultimate commodification of Frieda.

However, Porter's fundamental criticism against Lawrence was, as always, moralistic. She could not reconcile his bohemian life with that of his aristocratic wife; to Porter, the two made an impossible mixture. She found clear proof of Lawrence's moral failure in the much-maligned *Lady Chatterley's Lover*. When Aldington defends the book, Porter wonders again if the novel's ill-fated lovers are not representations of Lawrence and Frieda: "Could it be that Lawrence was the sick husband and the Italian peasant lover the gardener, and so on, in this poor sick tormented and silly book? *Baroness* Chatterley?" (364). And when Moore calls the novel one of Lawrence's "major efforts," Porter underlines his phrase and sardonically comments: "A major effort and a major disaster" (358). However, she became outraged at the appearance of *The Trial of Lady Chatterley*, a thin paperback designed to appeal to a popular audience. The editor, C. H. Rolph, chose excerpts from several critical essays, including Porter's "A Wreath for the Gamekeeper," to "defend" Lady Chatterley against arguments made by critics for the prosecution. The book depicts a mock courtroom battle, and Porter is represented as one of the defense attorneys. Porter's inscription on the book's flyleaf reveals her animosity: "Rhea Johnson brought me this book about the middle of October 1961—1 year 8 months after my 'A Wreath for the Gamekeeper' was published in *Encounter*. The word 'shock' is found quite often in this transcript—all sorts of people are shocked or shocking for all sorts of reasons. Well, I am shocked too, at the utterly dishonest and malignant use and abuse of my article by the defense, the complete misrepresentation of my point of view deliberately to discredit my standing as writer and my personal reputation. . . . The whole performance is hysterical, a cross between a trial from *Alice in Wonderland* and something by Franz Kafka" (ellipses Porter's). In addition, she listed several pages on which her name was mentioned or her essay quoted: "Page 45–46–47–51–54–55–56–57–58–193–194 / reference 103–104" (flyleaf). Although Porter's interpretation of the editor's motives may be a bit extreme, her central argument is correct: the essay was misused and distorted. Porter must have been doubly insulted at the inference that she would defend Lawrence's work against charges of obscenity. In fact her complaint was just the opposite; she felt that Lawrence misused the female point of view for the sake of obscenity. She wrote that readers "have seen in his writings his hatred and distrust of women—of the female principle, that is; with some of its exemplars he managed to get along passably—shown in his perpetual exasperated admonition to woman to be what he wants her to be, without any regard to what she possibly may be—to stop having any will or mind or indeed any existence of her own except what he allows her. He will dole out to her the kind of sex he thinks is good for her, and allow her just the amount of satisfaction in it he wishes her to have—not much. Even Lady Chatterley's ration seems more in the head than in the womb" (*Collected Essays*, 25). The idea that her impassioned diatribe against Lawrence's patriarchal narrative could be used in his defense must have been particularly galling to Porter.

She denigrates Lawrence's portrayal of sexuality in his fiction and his own personal habits. She disagrees with Aldington's contention that others used Lawrence's sexuality "to bring him down." Porter argues: "Still, sex stupidity was his way of repudiating another 'dead idealism,' if you like . . . my dislike of him is based *simply* upon the *fact* that he was a nasty presumptuous, pretentious 3rd rater trying to be God" (317). Predictably she disagreed with Leavis when he praised Lawrence's entire canon, saying that "It is an immense body of living creation in which a supreme vital intelligence is the creative spirit—a spirit informed by an almost infallible sense for health and sanity. Itself it educates for the kind of criticism that here and there it challenges—it provides the incitement and the criteria. And the marvelous creative intelligence continues in full activity to the end. *The Plumed Serpent* is far from signifying the close of Lawrence's production of great art." In response to such effervescence, Porter adds tersely, "except sick on the subject of sex" (73). Leavis's devotion to his subject quickly became irritating to Porter. She refuted his claim that Lawrence's art defined a marriage which necessarily involved "the recognition that love is "not an end in itself." Porter's reply reveals her annoyance: "It *cannot* be an *end* in itself, no first rate artist has ever portrayed it so except as tragedy—disaster—a false ideal—(from Tristan and Iseult to Anna Karenina and on. Leavis will even distort George Eliot to give credit to Lawrence where he does not earn it, or need it—He is tiresomely fanatical" (137). Her aggravation reaches its apex when Leavis quotes the final passage from *The Rainbow* and adds. "The Lawrence of *Women in Love* could not have written that paragraph. And it was not really written by the Lawrence of the last part of *The Rainbow*." Porter underlines these meaningless claims and comments: "No, it was merely written by Lawrence—The real one, not his little god-monster you are so busily building up. The real Lawrence was quite often a noisy rotten writer" (170). She continued throughout the book to point out those "rotten" passages as they appeared.

Porter frankly admits that her criticism is tinged with moral overtones. She underlines Leavis's pronouncement that "Lawrence himself was a genius of transcendent social gifts and irresistible personal fascination," and responds: "This is the kind of assertion that irritates one who always found Lawrence a boor and personally repulsive" (32). She is plainly disturbed by Lawrence's lighthearted tone in a letter to Lady Cynthia Asquith. He reports that "my stomach, it has a bad habit of turning a somersault when it finds itself in the wrong element, like a dolphin in the air. The old Knight and I had a sincere half-mocking argument, he for security and a bank-balance and power, *I for naked liberty. In the end he rested safe on his bank-balance, I in my nakedness; we hated each other—but with respect. But c'est lui qui moura.* He's going to die—*Moi, non.* He knows that, the impotent old wolf, so he is ready in one half to murder me. *I don't want to murder him—merely, leave him to death*" (quoted in Leavis, 33; Porter's emphases). Porter notes: "This is the most disarming trait of Lawrence, This Ironic humor. But that 'c'est lui qui moura,' is the sinister note. Nothing should live that was not Lawrence!" Later, Porter marks an entire passage from *The Rainbow* describing a religiously tinged love scene between Will and Anna and dismisses it: "This is ghastly cheap horrible stuff / Purple patches" (Leavis, 147). She doubts Lawrence's description of Will as a young father, particularly when he "caught the baby to his breast with a passionate, clapping laugh." She underlines the words when Lawrence writes again that Will "caught it to his breast, clapping with a triumphant laugh." She disparages the passage in her notes: 'What really revolting writing because there are such wonderful things in it and he does not know what they are, and spoils everything—" (151). For a man who had no interest in his own children to write a treatise on the glories of fatherhood represented the crowning hypocrisy to Porter. She felt that Lawrence's words were a betrayal of his true voice.

However, although Porter found much to criticize in Leavis's assessment of

Lawrence's work, she did appreciate some of Lawrence's gift of language. For instance, she underlined his description of the countryside in *The Rainbow*: "she heard the ewe call, and the lambs came running, shaking and twinkling with new-born bliss." To this, Porter responds: "Ah wonderful" (158). Similarly, Porter admires Lawrence's depiction of Gerald in *Women in Love* as "emptily restless, utterly hollow," "suspended motionless, in an agony of inertia, like a machine that is without power." She notes, "This is the most terribly accurate description" (202). Porter considered Lawrence's portrait of Gerald to be a reflection of its author, particularly a sensitive passage from *Women in Love*: "His mind was almost submerged, he was almost transfused, lapsed out for the first time in his life, into the things about him. For he always kept such a keen attentiveness, concentrated and unyielding in himself. Now he had let go, imperceptively he was melting into oneness with the whole. It was like pure, perfect sleep, his first great sleep of life. He had been so insistent, so guarded, all his life. But here was sleep, and peace, and perfect lapsing out." She notes with pleasure: "This is splendid / He is always at his best about himself!" (239).

If Porter saw Lawrence in Gerald, she saw herself in another Lawrence character, *St. Mawr*'s Lou Witt. She marked a descriptive passage in *St. Mawr* that could apply to both Witt and Porter: "Lou Witt had had her own way so long, that by the age of twenty-five she didn't know where she was. Having one's own way landed one completely at sea." Porter surmised, "So, knowing Lawrence's obsession, a male force is going to get her damn *good*. Pretty soon" (280). Lawrence went on to describe Witt: "She, with her odd little museau, not exactly pretty, but very attractive; and her quaint air of playing at being well-bred, in a sort of charade game; and her queer familiarity with foreign cities and foreign languages; and the lurking sense of being an outsider everywhere, like a sort of gipsy, who is at home anywhere or nowhere; all this made up her charm and her failure. She didn't quite belong. Of course she was American: Louisiana family, moved down to Texas." Porter marveled, "Here to the word Texas could be *me*! KAP." She underlined "She didn't quite belong" and added, "Anywhere! / But I didn't want to belong, that is the difference—and God how right I was! / 1st May 1957" (280).

Ultimately, the Lawrence marginalia shows two artists with vastly different styles addressing the common theme of a search for order. Throughout her fiction, the attempt to find order in the chaos of modern society stands as an insurmountable problem for both Porter and her heroines. And both Porter and Lawrence arrive at the terrifying realization that sometimes order is impossible. At the end of Lawrence's story "The Captain's Doll," the heroine, Hannele, wonders if her lover, Alexander, is mad. F. R. Leavis finds the ending validating and calls its common sense profound. Next to his remark, Porter writes, "Neither Leavis nor Lawrence seems to realize what a very *dark* end this is—Common sense? It is a woman having at last to admit the nonsense of a man, and to 'take him on' with his nonsense, and despise him a little, but conceal it—make terms and deceive him, laugh at him for a solemn ass and yet flatter him—in fact, play the role he wants her to play To protect him from reality—and what for? because She needs him in bed! 1st May 1957 12:30 Midnight" (278).

Lawrence's kind of ending frightens Porter. He represents a world much like that of Ibsen's "A Doll's House" in which man's will overpowers that of his female counterpart. Her will is subjugated to his, and indeed, she cannot obtain equality, independence, or even sexual satisfaction. For Katherine Anne Porter, whose own identification with gender and class appears so powerfully in her fiction and marginalia, the loss of her freedom was the most horrifying prospect of all.

NOTES

1. Katherine Anne Porter, *The Collected Essays and Occasional Writings of Katherine Anne Porter* (New York: Delacorte Press, 1970), 457. Further references are cited in the text.

2. Katherine Anne Porter's library contained the following works by and about D. H. Lawrence: Richard Aldington, *D. H. Lawrence: Portrait of a Genius But . . .* (New York: Duell, Sloan and Peare, 1950); Anthony Beal, ed., *D. H. Lawrence: Selected Literary Criticism* (New York: Viking Press, 1956); F. R. Leavis, *D. H. Lawrence: Novelist* (New York: Alfed A. Knopf, 1956); Harry T. Moore, *The Intelligent Heart: The Story of D. H. Lawrence* (New York: Farrar, Straus and Young, 1954); C. H. Rolph, ed., *The Trial of Lady Chatterley* (Baltimore: Penguin Books, 1961); Stephen Spender, *D. H. Lawrence: Novelist, Poet, Prophet* (New York: Harper and Row, 1973); E. W. Tedlock, ed., *Frieda Lawrence: The Memoirs and Correspondence* (New York: Alfred A. Knopf, 1964); Eliseo Vivas, *D. H. Lawrence: The Failure and the Triumph of Art* (Evanston: Northwestern University Press, 1960).

The author wishes to thank Barbara Davis, literary trustee for the estate of Katherine Anne Porter, for permission to reprint from Porter's unpublished marginalia at the McKeldin Library, University of Maryland at College Park, Special Collections.

Although I believe this list includes all of Porter's Lawrence collection in the McKeldin Library, the list is incomplete. In her last years, Porter developed the unfortunate habit of giving away books that had already been promised to the University of Maryland. As a result, many books that Porter obviously read (i.e., *The Plumed Serpent* and *Lady Chatterley's Lover*) are missing.

3. Quoted in Leavis, *D. H. Lawrence: Novelist*, 282.

4. Joan Givner, *Katherine Anne Porter: Conversations* (Jackson: University of Mississippi Press, 1987), 89.

5. Quoted in Aldington, *D. H. Lawrence: Portrait of a Genius But . . .*, 348.

6. Joan Givner, *Katherine Anne Porter: A Life*, rev. ed. (Athens: University of Georgia Press, 1991) 156–57.

7. Beal, *D. H. Lawrence: Selected Literary Criticism*, 196.

8. Givner, *Katherine Anne Porter: A Life*, 126–29.

Mirror, Mirror, on the Wall

Gazing in Edith Wharton's "Looking Glass"

SUSAN ELIZABETH SWEENEY

Now I am a lake. A woman bends over me,
Searching my reaches for what she really is. . . .
I am important to her. She comes and goes.
Each morning it is her face that replaces the darkness.
In me she has drowned a young girl, and in me an old woman
Rises toward her day after day, like a terrible fish.
  Sylvia Plath, "Mirror"

In the last years of her life, when she was producing one exquisitely haunting tale after another, Wharton wrote a ghost story entitled "The Mirror." At some point between its composition and its initial publication in 1935, in *Hearst's International-Cosmopolitan*, she changed the title to "The Looking Glass."[1] Now, mirrors and looking glasses may seem to be the same. But Wharton is an unusually subtle, even oblique writer, whose stories depend on carefully calibrated shifts and shades of meaning; her titles, in particular, "often point toward a veiled meaning or an implied comment."[2] The change in this title indicates precisely what sort of mirror she had in mind, even as it adds to the story's latent suggestiveness. Although "mirror" and "looking glass" are essentially synonymous, the *Oxford English Dictionary* defines them differently: the first is "a polished surface which reflects images of objects"; the second, "a glass to look in, in order to see one's own face or figure." "Looking glass," then, connotes private rituals of grooming and adornment. The term implies a human spectator and such human traits as vanity, affectation, introspection. And it emphasizes not a polished surface, but the act of looking into one.

"The Looking Glass" is a good title, then, for a tale about beauty, narcissism, and a woman's awareness of herself as object of a man's gaze. Wharton's ghost story is actually an ironic psychological study of two women, a socialite and a masseuse, whose relationship is determined, in part, by their roles in the economy of female attractiveness.[3] When Cora Attlee, a retired Irish masseuse, muses aloud about "a wrong" she once did to her employer, her grand-daughter asks to hear the tale (844). As Mrs. Attlee tells it, Mrs. Clingsland was a former belle who no longer saw her loveliness reflected in her mirrors, or in men's eyes—unless "she paid for it" (849).[4] Finding proof of her beauty only in the past, Mrs. Clingsland paid Mrs. Attlee, instead, to listen to stories about how whenever she entered "a ballroom, or a restaurant or a theatre, everybody stopped what they were doing to turn and look at her" (850), and about Harry, the only man she loved, who had died years before. Mrs. Attlee worried that the unhappy woman might resort to gigolos or spiritualists, and so, to protect her from such unscrupulous people, she herself offered to bring Harry's "spirit communications" from beyond the grave (855). She asked a poor young man, well-educated but dying of alcoholism, to write them for her. At first the messages soothed Mrs. Clingsland's wounded vanity, but then she demanded an actual letter from Harry—which the young man produced at the cost of his life. Satisfied at last, Mrs. Clingsland gave a hundred dollars to Mrs. Attlee, who spent most of it on masses for the young man's soul. But now, years later, as Mrs. Attlee tells her granddaughter this tale, she feels uneasy that she never confessed the deception to her priest.

Wharton's story shows how much Mrs. Clingsland's sense of identity depends upon her beauty, an ephemeral, intangible, abstract quality that exists (or can be proven to exist) only in the eye of a male beholder. The story repeatedly plays upon this connection between looking at people and assessing their looks (not only their physical appearance, but what it implies about status, character, and temperament). Mrs. Clingsland is described as "looking like a martyred saint," "looking like a ghost," "look[ing] like a girl," and "look[ing] as if she would" die (846, 850, 851, 855). Mr. Clingsland, who "never notic[ed] any difference in her looks," cannot comfort his wife (847); other people try to do so, but Mrs. Attlee doesn't "fancy [their] looks," nor does she "like the look of" men who "are always looking out for silly old women with money" (849, 850, 851); and she thinks that growing old is harder for Mrs. Clingsland than it is for other women "who'd never had much looks beyond what you can buy" (849). The pun on "looks"—as signifying both visual perception and visual appearance—recurs in accounts of Mrs. Clingsland's lost loveliness. She associates the fading of her beauty with lines around her eyes; Mrs. Attlee compares it to blurring vision at twilight and to displacement from "an illuminated ballroom" to the darkness outside (850). Indeed, Wharton's entire story turns upon this pun, for Mrs. Clingsland has lost her "looks" in both senses of the word.

"The Looking Glass" thus illustrates a central concern of recent feminist criticism: the "gaze" and its relation to sexuality, identity, power, and cultural constructions of gender. Gazing is implicitly erotic, Freud says, because the spectator imagines possessing what he sees; Lacan explains that looking, being looked at, and looking at oneself shape one's identity; and Foucault adds that observing and being observed signify power and powerlessness in Western culture. Freud's notion of the "scopic drive," Lacan's analysis of the "mirror stage," and Foucault's discussion of surveillance as a means of discipline have made the gaze a frequent topic in literary criticism.[5] Feminist critics, in particular, have found it a useful concept with which to analyze how woman's position in patriarchy is structured within social relations, representations, and discourses, as well as within the unconscious. Ever since Laura Mulvey argued that classic Hollywood films identify woman as spectacle and man as spectator, who is looking at whom has been a provocative subject in feminist film theory and, more recently, feminist narratology.[6]

"The Looking Glass" is an ideal text for such feminist analysis, especially because Wharton's story challenges current assumptions about woman's relation to the gaze. Feminist theory suggests that the last thing a woman should want is to be looked at. And yet, as Beth Newman recently remarked, "being the object of someone's look can in some circumstances be pleasurable—even sustaining and necessary."[7] Indeed, in a world where a woman's identity is determined by her "to-be-looked-at-ness," in Mulvey's term, being unobserved is profoundly disorienting; for a famous beauty like Mrs. Clingsland, not to be noticed is not to exist. Wharton's story demonstrates not only how a woman identifies with her construction by a male gaze, but also the lengths to which she will go, if necessary, to manufacture that gaze on her own. Mrs. Clingsland even imagines her objectification as a source of power, rather than a measure of her powerlessness. And Wharton duplicates these subversive strategems—the lengths to which a woman will go—in the self-reflexive narration of the tale.[8]

Looking Glasses Everywhere, and Not a Self to See

As the story's title suggests, Wharton's heroine has no identity apart from her reflection in the glass. Mrs. Clingsland's encounters with her looking glass don't signify moments of self-recognition or self-discovery, as is usually the case in women's narratives.[9] Instead, they imitate her specularization by a male gaze. Marshall Frantz's illustration in *Hearst's* underscores this point: Mrs. Clingsland looks away from the reader and into the mirrors of her dressing table, where six shadowy masculine faces look appreciatively at her brightly smiling image. This fantasy of being the object of a man's desiring glance is repeated in specular relationships throughout the story. Mrs. Clingsland remembers Harry because of "the way he looked at" her (851); the young man who composes Harry's messages finds it difficult "making love . . . to a woman you've never seen"; and Mrs. Attlee realizes that he too is dead when his eyes look at her "as if he didn't see" (856). Mrs. Clingsland herself looks at no one but Mrs. Attlee; and her glances at the masseuse, like those at the mirror, merely enact her objectification.[10] One such encounter eerily emphasizes that she has no look of her own: "She opened her great eyes and looked at me; and I seemed to see the wraith of her young beauty looking out of them" (855). It is the specter (and spectacle) of her former loveliness, not Mrs. Clingsland herself, which seems to regard Mrs. Attlee here, and even that gaze may be Mrs. Attlee's own, reflected in her mistress's eyes.

Wharton uses the simple act of looking into a mirror, then, as a haunting metaphor for her heroine's lack of identity. One such scene, which I want to consider at length, exemplifies Mrs. Clingsland's desperate attempts to convince herself of her desirability and thus her very existence.[11] Mrs. Attlee remembers that only moments after a social encounter had restored Mrs. Clingsland's "faith in her beauty," she would seek it again—in vain—in her mirrors: "I've seen her run upstairs with the foot of a girl, and then, before she'd tossed off her finery, sit down in a heap in front of one of her big looking glasses—it was looking glasses everywhere in her room—and stare and stare till the tears ran down over her powder" (847). Mrs. Clingsland seems to exist here only as a spectacle, a girlish vision of face powder and finery, a lovely reflection in the glass. And yet she cannot even find that image of herself, no matter how long she stares into her mirror.

Mrs. Clingsland's search for a certain image in the glass, and the mingled fascination and fear with which she regards it, accords with Lacan's analysis of the "mirror stage." In the mirror, Lacan says, the small child first sees a marvelously ordered and unified image of himself, but because this image remains outside of and separate from the self, it is "alienating" as well as pleasurable: the child experiences no such wholeness in his body, only in his reflection. Lacan explains that for the male child, this imaginary realm of endless reflections of himself is disrupted by the father and the larger, symbolic world of social relations and differences that he represents; as the child approximates more and more the social ideal of a complete self in a whole body, he gradually develops his own identity.[12] But the female child's experience may be quite different, as feminist theorists point out.[13] She may find that the larger world, where looking and being looked at have gendered meanings, perpetuates and even exacerbates the frightening difference between her image and herself, making it difficult to progress beyond the mirror stage. Jenijoy LaBelle explains that the female child may see in her reflection a "radical otherness" and yet also a self, "an image privileged with a truth beyond the subjective and at the same time taken to be the very essence of that subjectivity."[14] She may remain alienated from her reflected image even as she identifies with it.

Mrs. Clingsland's estranged response to her reflection suggests that she is still in the mirror stage: she identifies with others' images of her, rather than integrating them into a coherent identity. Indeed, this account of Mrs. Clingsland staring and staring into her mirrors stresses not her wholeness but her distortion, disintegration, and decomposition. The breathless eagerness with which she runs upstairs, as if to a waiting lover, emphasizes her alienated, narcissistic relation to her reflection. That she runs with the "foot of a girl," in particular, may mean that even in her youth she cannot find the image in the glass that she seeks. This paradox suggests not only that no reflection could possibly reassure her, but also that she has never had—because no human being could—the kind of perfect loveliness that she imagines. And each time the momentary illusion of her beauty fades (since beauty is so much a matter of belief), the lightfooted "girl," dressed in "finery," again becomes merely an old woman sitting "in a heap" before her mirrors—just as, after the ball is over, Cinderella's regalia turns back into rags (847).

The description of the mirrors themselves further emphasizes Mrs. Clingsland's fragmentation. Her body would be inevitably diminished in "one of her big looking glasses"; and since her bedroom has "looking glasses everywhere," her body would be reduced still more, and repeated to the point of vanishing utterly, by the dizzying *mise en abyme* effect of mirrors reflected in mirrors." Finally, the artful repetition of certain words ("looking glasses—it was looking glasses"; "and stare and stare") duplicates within the passage precisely what the passage is describing: the mirrored multiplication of both Mrs. Clingsland's reflection and her self-regarding gaze. Significantly, these repeated words draw the reader's attention to the looking glass and the act of looking into it, rather than to Mrs. Clingsland. She herself disappears, even as she searches for a self within the glass.

The passage demonstrates, then, that Mrs. Clingsland's search for a unifying image only further fractures her psyche. In order to retain her identity, she attempts to become a spectacle; and in order to do that, she pretends to be her own spectator—until, finally, this precarious, hypothetical, psychological structure collapses, and her tears, running "down over her powder," distort the carefully made-up image even as they blur her vision of it. The shattering consequences of her looking-glass quest recall the Queen's plight in the fairy tale "Little Snow-White." (Indeed, Wharton's title, "The Looking Glass," may allude directly to the Queen's magic mirror.)[15] Like Mrs. Clingsland, the Queen relates to the world only through her mirror, depending on it to tell her that she remains "the fairest of them all." Sandra Gilbert and Susan Gubar even argue that Snow White merely represents part of the Queen's fragmented identity: her reflection in the glass, the perfect and passive image of female beauty to which she must conform.[16] Thus the Queen sees no unifying image in her mirror, either, but only finds herself also further divided into the roles of spectacle (Snow White, the female object of desire) and spectator (the male voice of the mirror, which passes judgment upon her).

A woman who gazes into her looking glass, then, may lose her self in the process. As Jenijoy LaBelle says of another woman's encounter with her reflection, in Jessamyn West's *Cress Delahanty*: "The subject (that which perceives) becomes the fictive male, and the [woman's] image in the mirror becomes the female object he perceives." This reversal of gender roles and subject/object relations is further complicated by "the fact that the 'real' person here becomes in the mirror the object of an imaginary subject."[17] John Berger speculates that the gendered construction of subjectivity through the gaze forces a woman to divide herself so: "The surveyor of woman in herself is male: the surveyed, female. Thus she turns herself into an object."[18] Stephen Heath agrees that a woman can express her subjectivity in specular terms only when she "see[s] herself seeing herself."[19] But Wharton's story suggests that then there is no self there.

Through a Glass Darkly

A woman transfixed before her looking glass does not make for much of a story, however. A plot develops when the glass no longer gives back her image of herself, and she sets out to regain that image, whether by eliminating her rival, as in "Little Snow-White," or by finding a better mirror, as in "The Looking Glass." As Mrs. Attlee recounts her tale to her granddaughter, then, she emphasizes the progressive stages of Mrs. Clingsland's search for a mirror that might still depict her as young and lovely.

This search inevitably addresses the same problem raised by Wharton's revision of the story's title: how to define "looking glass." As the story progresses, the very meaning of the term changes, from one of Mrs. Clingsland's many bedroom mirrors to anything that might provide the image of herself she seeks: another's gaze, another's words, or a mere "sheet of paper scribbled over in pencil" (857). Mrs. Clingsland has always defined the term figuratively rather than literally: from the beginning, she uses other people "as looking glasses" (850). But when she no longer finds her beauty reflected in actual mirrors or in others' eyes, she seeks it instead in spoken words. A looking glass becomes not only someone who responds visibly to her appearance, but anyone who describes it aloud—rather like the magic mirror in "Little Snow-White." As Mrs. Attlee explains, "she had to be always hunting for new people to tell her she was as beautiful as ever; because she wore the others out, forever asking them: 'Don't you think I'm beginning to go off a little?'" (849). And just as the Queen asked her mirror each morning "Who is the fairest of them all?" so Mrs. Clingsland asks Mrs. Attlee, in a similar daily ritual, to tell her that she is still lovely—and "every morning," Mrs. Attlee says, "she believed me a little less" (847).

Eventually, when Mrs. Attlee's compliments and cajoleries no longer convince her, Mrs. Clingsland seeks yet another looking glass among the dead, and it is then that "The Looking Glass" becomes a ghost story. Of course, this tale of a woman enthralled with her own reflection is already a ghost story. A reflection is an optical ghost, and Mrs. Clingsland, merely "the wraith of her young beauty" (855), the shadow of her own image in the glass, is no more than the ghost of a ghost. In folklore, moreover, mirrors represent "the realm of souls, spirits, and the dead"; as Freud explains, they evoke the "uncanny," that eerie feeling that what should be inanimate is actually alive.[20] Given these associations between mirrors and the supernatural, it is perhaps inevitable that Mrs. Clingsland's search for a looking glass should end up "Over There" (854).

Mrs. Clingsland specifically seeks the ghost of the man whose utter stupefaction, the first time he looked at her, seemed to provide the perfect reflection of her beauty. But because Harry has been dead for many years, his gaze must be refracted, and reenacted, by two other figurative looking glasses: the clairvoyant or "clear seeing" Mrs. Attlee and the eloquent young man who shapes in words what Harry supposedly saw. Gazing at Mrs. Clingsland through Harry's eyes involves hearing (Mrs. Attlee "sees" long-ago scenes she has heard about from her mistress) as well as speaking (the young man expresses Harry's vision in words that Mrs. Attlee repeats in turn to Mrs. Clingsland). Indeed, Mrs. Attlee and the young man must each *imagine* looking at a sight, Mrs. Clingsland's youthful beauty, that neither actually sees. That is the same sight, of course, that Mrs. Clingsland herself imagines but cannot see in her mirrors. These acts of imagined looking are interdependent, moreover; in order for Mrs. Attlee and the young man to convince Mrs. Clingsland that she is still lovely, they must believe that she once was, which means that she must convince them as well. That is, they must convince her, and she them, that *Harry* believed her to be lovely—since female beauty only exists, in this story, in the eye of an imagined male beholder.

Earlier in the story, Mrs. Clingsland divided herself before her bedroom mirrors; now she needs other, external participants to bring her ideal spectator to life. Harry's distant gaze not only requires further disintegration of her own agency; it is also more tenuous than any other mirror she has tried. It reflects her beauty neither in discernible glances nor in direct speech, but in disembodied words: a series of secondhand messages and a forged letter that seems even more intangible because it isn't quoted in the text. Any reflection in such a mirror must be dim, distorted, even dismembered, a point that Wharton underscored in revising the story by adding "the cracked looking glass" that Mrs. Attlee holds to the mouth of the dead young man and the "cracked laugh" with which he has told her, "It's damn difficult, making love for a dead man to a woman you've never seen" (856; cf. "Mirror" 32, 33). And yet, no matter how unreliable this particular mirror may be, it yields the only reflection that satisfies Mrs. Clingsland.[21] The ideal looking glass turns out to be . . . a dead man.

But isn't that what Mrs. Clingsland has sought all along? As Mrs. Attlee explains, "what she wanted, and couldn't do without, was the gaze of men struck dumb by her beauty" (849). What *this* woman wants—"the gaze of men struck dumb," the stilled, silenced, but manifestly *visible* evidence of her own visual loveliness—resembles nothing so much as a mirror. In fact, Mrs. Attlee clarifies her mistress's desire, a few paragraphs later, in precisely those terms: "What she wanted was a looking glass to stare into; and when her own people took enough notice of her to serve as looking glasses . . . she didn't much fancy what she saw there" (850). Mrs. Clingsland doesn't want men merely "to serve as looking glasses," then. She wants them to be blank, mute, regardless objects which reflect nothing of herself except what she wishes to see.

That is why she relishes Harry's first message from the grave: "'He was so blinded by [her] beauty that he couldn't speak.' . . . Blinded by her beauty; struck dumb by love of her! Oh, but that's what she'd been thirsting and hungering for" (853). She wants all men who look at her (even "the actors on the stage" when she enters a theatre, who are themselves the focus of others' eyes) to be blinded, silenced, transfixed, their very "breath [taken] away" by the sight (850, 854). Such immobilized figures, which exist only to confirm her own existence, suggest the reflections of the self—"statues," "phantoms," "automata"—in the mirror stage; they also exemplify the fate of *all* the male characters in "The Looking Glass."[22] What is most striking, however, is the violence implied by this figurative process of blinding, paralyzing, and muting. Indeed, Mrs. Attlee describes the death of the young man, who has tried so hard to imagine Harry's vision of Mrs. Clingsland, in those very terms: "He laid there in his bed as if he didn't see me, though his eyes were open. . . . He neither moved nor spoke" (856).

Mrs. Clingsland never meets the anonymous young man, and she learns of his existence from Mrs. Attlee only after he is dead. Nevertheless, it is his attempt to look at her—through Harry's eyes—that apparently causes his death. A man has died, then, from gazing at Mrs. Clingsland, and *that* is what she has wanted from the beginning. "Stopped" or "stopped short" by her beauty (850, 851)—a state that, in this story, signals death (856)—men will never stop looking at her. In their eyes, she will remain beautiful forever. This fantasy, in which Mrs. Clingsland "stops" men merely by appearing before them, is startling not only because it reveals such fear and rage, but also because it uses the gendered construction of "looks," in both senses of the word, to express those very emotions. Indeed, Mrs. Clingsland seems to fancy herself a Medusa, a woman whose dreadful eyes turn every man who sees her into stone.[23]

Wharton, who was fond of classical mythology and frequently alluded to it in her fiction, apparently identified Medusa with the erotic power of the gaze. In "The Eyes," for example, she invokes the Gorgon's reflected image in order to describe an exchange of sexually charged glances.[24] The myth of Medusa, moreover, is yet another tale in which a mirror signifies a woman's specularization. Perseus evades Medusa's transfixing gaze and transfixes her instead—by decapitating her—because he looks not at *her* but at her reflection in his bronze shield. Freud speculates, in his essay "Medusa's Head," that this myth expresses "a terror of castration . . . linked to the sight of something"; Tobin Siebers observes that Medusa's head always "represent[s] what cannot be represented or what should not be represented"; and Stephen Heath argues, more precisely, that it embodies male fears of being castrated by a female gaze.[25] But the female gaze, that persistent specter of feminist film theory and feminist narratology, doesn't exist for Mrs. Clingsland. Instead, she is merely projecting her own objectification by a male gaze, her experience of what Wharton elsewhere called "the benumbing effect . . . of a man's eyes," onto the male spectator himself.[26] In her fantasy, he is blinded, paralyzed, and silenced not because she looks at him, but because she is so beautiful to *look at*.

"The Looking Glass" may seem, then, to turn the tale of woman's objectification into a subversive narrative of female power. In a gendered world of specular relations, Wharton suggests, a beautiful woman may do almost anything to continue being seen: Mrs. Clingsland even covets a dead man's approving stare. And yet she can't conceive of her own desiring female gaze. Even in her angry fantasy about the death of men who look at her, she remains the object, not the subject, of the glance. And if imagining a look of her own is so difficult for Mrs. Clingsland, then imagining a female *narrative* gaze—as

Wharton tries to do for Mrs. Attlee, the other woman in this story—must be nearly impossible.

Framing the Looking Glass

Narration often involves the gaze. Writers frequently use specular language and imagery to tell a story, just as theorists use visual terms—"point of view," "perspective," "focus," "frame"—to describe the process of narration. At the beginning of "The Looking Glass," for example, Wharton indicates the thoughts of Mrs. Attlee and her granddaughter by describing how they *look* and how they *look at* each other: "Moyra Attlee interrupted her listless stare down the empty Sunday street . . . and turned an astonished glance on her grandmother"; "Mrs. Attlee's eyes grew sharp behind her spectacles, and she fixed them half distrustfully on the girl's face" (845, 846). In using such "listless stare[s]," "astonished glance[s]," and "fixed" glares to narrate her fiction, Wharton resembles many writers. But this particular story reveals more profound connections between narration and the gaze. The range of specular relations, mirror images, psychological structures, and narrative frames in "The Looking Glass" reflects the story's own narration, and, in particular, the difficulty of narrating it through a woman's eyes.

Wharton's story is so self-reflexive, in part, because modernist narration itself resembles a series of reflections as much as a play of glances. Narratives have often been compared to mirrors, in order to stress their faithful representation of reality, from classical accounts of literature as a mirror held up to nature, to the frequent use of "mirror" in Renaissance book titles, to Stendhal's famous definition of the novel as a mirror carried along a road. But modernist narratives resemble not mirrors, but looking glasses: they emphasize not a mimetic surface, but the act of gazing into one. James and other modernists paid more attention than earlier writers to the psychology of narration, and they even described it as a process of *reflection*.[27] Wharton also thought of narrative focalization as a looking-glass technique. In her book on *The Writing of Fiction*, she defines it in Jamesian terms as the "reflecting consciousness," the "reflector," "the mind chosen by the author to mirror his given case," and she argues that "to choose this reflecting mind deliberately" is the storyteller's first concern.[28] Because Wharton identified narrative focalization with reflection, it is significant that she uses mirror imagery to narrate her characters' thoughts in "The Looking Glass." She uses the verb *to reflect*, for example, to signify moments of backward glancing or inward looking: "Mrs. Attlee once more reflected" on the past; "Moyra reflected that [her grandmother] was probably asleep" (847, 847–48). Moreover, Wharton chose such imagery deliberately: in revising the story, she added the phrases "she reflected" and "her thoughts . . . came to the surface" and changed "reflect" in one instance to "consider," presumably because she had already used the word twice on that page (844, 847; cf. "Mirror" 2, 9). Wharton's concept of narrative focalization as a process of reflection, and her use of mirror imagery to narrate this particular tale, suggests that the many mirrors in "The Looking Glass" may elucidate her own narrative technique in the story.

The looking glasses in this story already signify Mrs. Clingsland's identity as a visual object, of course, but they also represent the narrative process that reveals her objectification to the reader, through the eyes not only of a female "reflector," but of the very woman who serves as her figurative looking glass within the tale. Mrs. Attlee is at first, like her mistress, merely the object of a narrative gaze, "sitting back in her comfortable armchair by the fire, her working days over, and her muscular masseuse's hands lying swollen and powerless on her knee" (844), but she herself soon becomes the narrator: when she begins her embedded tale in section 3, the quotation marks and reportorial tags surrounding her speech disappear and the frame narrator never returns. And whereas Mrs. Clingsland remains a spectacle in one looking glass after another, Mrs. Attlee actually wears "spectacles," or glasses for looking—as if to make her "sharp eyes," "fixed" upon her listener, even more acute—while she tells the tale of the other woman's lost reflection (846). Mrs. Attlee's spectacles have the same significance as eyeglasses worn by women in Hollywood films, which Mary Ann Doane calls "one of the most intense visual clichés of the cinema"; that is, they indicate not "a deficiency in seeing but an active looking, or even simply the fact of seeing as opposed to being seen."[29] Even when Mrs. Clingsland loses herself in a masquerade of mirrored glances, then, Mrs. Attlee is still able to observe and thus narrate her plight: "*I've seen her* . . . stare and stare till the tears ran down" (847, emphasis mine). And within her story about the wrong she once did to Mrs. Clingsland, Mrs. Attlee embeds still other stories of what she has seen: visions of Harry and of what *he* saw when he looked at Mrs. Clingsland years before. Mrs. Attlee thus serves as Mrs. Clingsland's figurative looking glass, what Wharton calls a "reflecting consciousness," in two distinct senses: in her narration of the other woman's story, and in her actions as an embedded narrator within that story.[30]

"The Looking Glass" is not the first tale of a woman's identity as spectacle to be narrated by a literal or figurative mirror. "Little Snow-White" features the Queen's looking glass, which knows and speaks the truth (whether Snow White is dead, for example) and thus exemplifies the story's own omniscient, authoritative, third-person narration. Sylvia Plath's poem "Mirror" is narrated in the cool, indifferent voice of the mirror itself.[31] In both "Little Snow-White" and "Mirror," however, the looking glass is identified with the judgment of an imaginary male spectator. Wharton's story uses the mirror, instead, to articulate a *female* gaze in a world where women are to be seen but not to observe. Wharton thus turns traditional ideas of narration and vision to her own purposes. She transforms the mirror, which already signifies both narrative looking and feminine "to-be-looked-at-ness," into a specifically female narrative gaze.

In order to represent this female narrative gaze in "The Looking Glass," Wharton brings together several related motifs: female "reflectors"; mirror reflections; clairvoyance; and the pictorial technique of chiaroscuro. Mrs. Attlee's narration is associated, for example, with the acute vision symbolized by the spectacles she wears. The stories that she tells her granddaughter evoke "pictures," "glimpses," and "scenes of half-understood opulence and leisure, like a guide leading a stranger through the gallery of a palace in the twilight, and now and then lifting a lamp to a shimmering Rembrandt or a jeweled Rubens." They bring to life "dazzling" images and "shimmering" paintings, framed and polished surfaces, in other words, which prefigure other looking glasses in the story. Mrs. Attlee's oral storytelling thus communicates visual, rather than aural, information. It seems to elide the distinction between modes of perception or to convey mental pictures to her listener in a way that transcends ordinary seeing. More important, her narration illuminates dim, twilit, "half-understood" scenes that would be imperceptible otherwise (845). As she prepares to tell Moyra the story of how she wronged Mrs. Clingsland, for example, her "sharp eyes [seem] to draw back behind a mist of age" that Moyra cannot penetrate (846). Mrs. Attlee begins that story, moreover, by remarking: "Well, my dear, I'd always had a way of seeing things" (848).

Wharton identifies Mrs. Attlee's narration not only with looking glasses, then, but with a kind of looking-glass vision: second sight, "a way of seeing" that transcends mere seeing, or "clairvoyance," the ability to *clearly see* in a mysterious, shadowy, uncanny realm (848). In thus describing Mrs. Attlee's narrative gifts, Wharton may have had in mind a famous biblical passage that compares degrees of spiritual understanding to gazing into a mirror: "For now we see through a glass, darkly; but then face to face: now I know in part; but then shall I know even as also I am known" (1 Cor. 13:12). Religious parables and prophecies are a common subtext in Wharton's fiction; this particular verse establishes the same connections between mirrors, occult power, and clarity or obscurity of vision that are found in "The Looking Glass." It also associates looking with the expression of subjectivity and the possession of forbidden knowledge—"then I shall know even as also I am known"—just as

Wharton's story does. And the larger context of this verse, Paul's warning that prophecies are only partly true, raises questions of narrative reliability and narrative framing that are also addressed in "The Looking Glass."[32] The biblical subtext emphasizes that Wharton associates Mrs. Attlee's storytelling—and her own story's narrative technique—with mirrors and second sight.

Wharton thus identifies the female narrative gaze with less direct, less tangible, less reliable modes of seeing. By identifying a woman's narration with looking-glass vision, in particular, Wharton characterizes it as eerie, uncanny, even unnatural. Such stratagems may have been necessary for her even to imagine a woman's look, something that cultural constructions and psychological structures alike make almost inconceivable. Such stratagems may also reveal, themselves, the deep unconscious taboo against a woman's possession of the gaze. As Stephen Heath warns, "If the woman looks, the spectacle provokes, castration is in the air, the Medusa's head is not far off; thus, she must not look."[33]

Indeed, every instance of Mrs. Attlee's looking in "The Looking Glass," whether she is "seeing things" or narrating what she has seen to other women, emphasizes the forbidden nature of her glance, as well as what it perceives. Just as Mrs. Clingsland fantasizes about the death of men who look at her, so the "things" that Mrs. Attlee sees are dead, immobilized, inanimate male bodies. She claims that she can see dead Harry "as clear as if he was in the room with us" (852), and she later inspects the dead body, as well as the belongings, of the poor young man who gazed at Mrs. Clingsland through Harry's eyes. Mrs. Attlee confirms the young man's death with a "cracked looking glass," takes "a quick look" at his room, "look[s] among his few books and papers," and then "turn[s] back for a last look at him" (856). Although this scene may suggest the uncanny power of Mrs. Attlee's glance, it also emphasizes the danger, for a woman, of appropriating the male gaze. A man must be dead, apparently, before a woman may safely regard him: her looking occurs only belatedly, after the fact, as *second* sight. Even then, her looking may remain inconceivable. In illustrating this very scene for *Hearst's*, for example, Marshall Frantz completely eliminated Mrs. Attlee's glances at the male body: not only are her eyes cast down as she reads Harry's letter, but the young man appears in the background, his body almost indistinguishable from the bedclothes and his face turned away from Mrs. Attlee, and from Wharton's female reader. And even if a woman's looking is conceivable, it may be only as something that will cost her dearly. In classic Hollywood films, "any female brazen enough to assume the agency of the gaze" is inevitably punished.[34] In "The Looking Glass," Mrs. Attlee's visions are expressly prohibited by patriarchal authorities such as her church and her priest, and she herself believes that by "seeing things" she risks eternal punishment at the hands of an angry male God (848).

Given these unconscious taboos and explicit proscriptions against the female gaze, it is not surprising that Mrs. Attlee narrates her visions only to other women, whether telling her female clients about "things they wanted [her] to see" or showing her granddaughter "dazzling glimpses" of the past (846, 845). But these furtive stories of a woman's looking are also prohibited. Moyra's mother "could tell" her about her grandmother's clairvoyance, Mrs. Attlee explains, "only she wouldn't, because after a bit the priest got wind of it, and then it had to stop . . . so she won't even talk of it any more" (848, Wharton's ellipsis). Even telling tales about what another woman has seen is dangerous. Accordingly, the narration of this story, which concerns one woman's fatal good looks and another's uncanny looking, is structured by Wharton's awareness of such strictures against the female gaze.

"The Looking Glass" is framed, at both "diegetic" and "extradiegetic" levels, as a series of confessions made by one woman to another. (Such confessions are looking-glass narratives, in a sense; each woman sees her own plight more clearly as she recounts it to a quiet, receptive listener.) At the diegetic level, Mrs. Clingsland confesses her fear that she has lost her beauty, prompted by Mrs. Attlee's comforting words: "you can tell Cora Attlee what's the trouble. . . . Come, now, you tell me, and it'll help you" (846). At the extradiegetic level, Mrs. Attlee confesses her deception of Mrs. Clingsland, in turn, to her granddaughter; she is afraid to tell her priest, even though "its being unconfessed lurked disquietingly in the back of her mind" (846). Each narrative level, then, features a psychological and generational mirroring between a bemused old lady and a younger woman who watches her, waits on her, and listens to her stories.[35] That relationship serves, moreover, as a self-reflexive model for Wharton's interaction with her own readers. Elderly Mrs. Attlee, recounting her ghost stories and tales of a glamorous bygone age, is in part a whimsical portrait of Wharton herself. And "listless," "inattentive" Moyra—who is "rous[ed] to sudden curiosity" by one of her grandmother's remarks, who asks to hear the story behind it, and whose listening presence is acknowledged as that story is told—is Wharton's figure for her reader. The story is framed, then, in a series of receding "reflectors," like the mirrors within mirrors in Mrs. Clingsland's bedroom. Shoshana Felman describes a similar effect in James's "The Turn of the Screw": "the story's frame is nothing other than a *frame of mirrors*, in which the narrative is both reflected and deflected through a series of symmetrical, mutual glances of couples looking at themselves looking at themselves." In James's ghost story, this "transferential narrative chain" features a series of seductive relationships based upon sexual difference.[36] In

Wharton's ghost story, however, it forms a series of narcissistic relationships based upon shared gender identity. Each narrative level in "The Looking Glass" emphasizes, in particular, that the tale of a woman's looking is for female eyes only.

"The Looking Glass" thus acknowledges, in several ways, the transgression implied by a woman's possession of the gaze. The tale of a woman's look is forbidden by male characters, framed as a series of guilty confessions between women, and disguised as a ghost story by Wharton herself. Although Wharton does articulate a female narrative gaze in "The Looking Glass," then, she remains at best ambivalent about its validity. She narrates the story primarily through Mrs. Attlee's eyes and develops the plot by means of Mrs. Attlee's uncanny visions; yet she consistently undermines her narrator's reliability. She casts doubt on the authenticity of Mrs. Attlee's embedded stories, as well as the instances of "clear seeing" they describe. Wharton also contrasts female orality with male literacy in "The Looking Glass," just as she does in other short fiction. Even as she describes her narrator as a storyteller of uncanny power and insight, then, she disparages her ability as a writer; as Mrs. Attlee herself admits, "Writing wasn't ever my strong point" (853). Indeed, Wharton implies that Mrs. Attlee has neither invented, nor narrated, nor composed the "spirit communications" that she gives to her mistress. Mrs. Attlee's messages merely echo what Mrs. Clingsland has already told *her*; when Mrs. Clingsland asks for Harry's description of her dress "that first evening at dinner," for example, Mrs. Attlee readily supplies it because, she says, "she'd described that dress to me so often" (854). And the messages are not only constructed from Mrs. Clingsland's own memories; they are also narrated in a dead man's voice and composed by a dying man's hand. Mrs. Attlee's already tenuous narrative authority seems even more dubious when she tells Moyra how she obtained Harry's letter, the only written text in the story: after she found it half-hidden under the young man's bed, she literally "cop[ied] out" its text, scarcely comprehending the words as she wrote them down (857). In "The Looking Glass," as in her other stories, Wharton portrays female authorship as furtive, forged, or fabricated.[37]

Mrs. Attlee, apparently, needs a male narrator and a male author to describe her visions, just as Mrs. Clingsland needs a man's admiring glance to confirm her beauty. Neither woman requires an actual man, however, only the merest vestige of masculine authority. (As is often the case for Wharton's female characters, their lives are still shaped by men even when the men are no longer there.) Even a dead man will do, will enable each woman somehow to express her own subjectivity through the gaze, whether as spectacle or as spectator. At the levels of both form and content, then, Wharton shows in this story the extent to which feminine identity is constructed, and constricted, by the gendered gaze.

Other Reflections in the Glass

Wharton also reflects her own image in "The Looking Glass." Throughout her life, Edith Wharton was anxious about the female gaze, especially as it is manifested in reading and writing. Her childhood cast the primal scene, that first narrative of forbidden looking, in literary terms: for Wharton to read romances in her father's library despite her mother's warnings, Paula Berggren suggests, would have been "figuratively [to] gaze upon her father's nakedness."[38] Indeed, Wharton's novels and stories often compare the act of reading, especially a woman reading a text that belongs to a man, to voyeurism.[39] "The Looking Glass" associates reading with voyeurism, for example, when Mrs. Attlee describes her mistress perusing Harry's long-awaited letter: "I waited a long time, looking away from her; you couldn't stare at a lady who was reading a message from her sweetheart, could you?" This climactic scene expresses Wharton's anxiety about forbidden looking, and about reading and writing masculine letters, in the hesitant, indirect, "stealthy" gaze of her female narrator (857).

The story's doubts about the accuracy of Mrs. Attlee's vision and the authenticity of her authorship thus suggest Wharton's own "anxious power," her ambivalence toward the appropriation of masculine discourse.[40] More precisely, Mrs. Attlee's narration in "The Looking Glass" evokes Wharton's anxiety about "seeing things": that is, reading and writing texts in a mode, literate discourse, that she felt was prohibited to women in general, and in a genre, the ghost story, that as a child she had been specifically forbidden to read. It is especially significant that Mrs. Attlee, like Wharton herself, is a teller of ghost stories. Wharton apparently associated ghost fiction with the awful power of the glance: in addition to "The Looking Glass," she devoted another tale, "The Eyes," to a habitual "spectator" who becomes himself the object of ghostly eyes, discovers that "being thus gazed at was far from pleasant," and finally sees the eyes staring out at him from his own mirrored reflection.[41] More important, Wharton identified writing ghost stories with the same uncanny looking-glass vision that she associates, in "The Looking Glass," with the female narrative gaze. In her preface to *Ghosts*, she calls the writer of supernatural tales a "ghost-seer," someone who makes "them visible to us," and she describes the composition of such tales in terms of vision, clairvoyance, and chiaroscuro: "nobody knows better than a ghost how hard it is to put him or her into words shadowy yet transparent enough."[42] In fact, Wharton's ghost stories, which describe "seeing" the invisible, offer an implicit critique of literary realism and its associations with detection, positivism, and masculine authority.

Wharton's ambivalence toward her identity as a female writer also explains her contradictory attitudes toward women's looks and women's looking in "The Looking Glass." Wharton often imagined herself as split between two roles, the female ornament and the male author, that seemed incompatible or even contradictory.[43] "The Looking Glass," which most critics agree is at least partly autobiographical, dramatizes that split. Like Mrs. Clingsland, like many other women who try to see themselves, Wharton found it necessary to divide herself in two, or rather, into two characters: Mrs. Clingsland, the spectacle, and Mrs. Attlee, the spectator. One woman is the protagonist, who clings to her striking looks and imagines the death of every man who sees her; the other is the narrator, who claims an uncanny "way of seeing" with which to gaze at those men in turn. Readers of "The Looking Glass" have disagreed over whether Wharton extends her sympathy to Mrs. Clingsland or to Mrs. Attlee.[44] This dispute can be resolved, however, by identifying the two women with these two different aspects of Wharton herself. Indeed, "The Looking Glass" suggests a new way to read the mirror images, female doppelgängers, and ambivalent bonds between women that recur throughout Wharton's fiction.

"The Looking Glass" reflects the image of its readers, too. Reading a narrative, we engage in "insight," in imaginative looking, in identifying with another's imaginary gaze as well as with the others that that gaze perceives. We thus find ourselves reflected in the text. Reading "The Looking Glass," in particular, makes us more aware of that process. In this sense, too, Wharton's story functions not as mirror but as looking glass: it draws our attention not to the tale's polished surface, but to our own act of gazing into it. "The Looking Glass" does this most explicitly when, at the end of the story, Mrs. Attlee finally looks at Mrs. Clingsland after her mistress has finished reading Harry's letter. Reading the letter seems to have utterly transformed Mrs. Clingsland: "there she lay on her pillows . . . the letter clasped tight in her hands, and her face smoothed out the way it was years before, when I first knew her. Yes—those few words had done more for her than all my labor" (858). By withholding the letter's "few words," the story emphasizes instead their uncanny effect on Mrs. Clingsland. Her "smoothed out" face not only suggests the letter's unfolded page but even takes its place as the text that we must interpret. Has Mrs. Clingsland been successfully duped by her masseuse? Has she actually received a message from Harry (since this is a ghost story, after all)? Or is her *belief* that the letter is from him the only thing that matters?

By leaving such questions unanswered, Wharton makes the story's ending a matter of belief for her readers, too. Indeed, by not returning to the story's frame (the third-person narrator's description of Mrs. Attlee's storytelling), Wharton leaves us within it, unsure of our position in relation to the story being told. Frantz's title illustration in *Hearst's* exemplifies this self-reflexive *mise en abyme* for female readers, in particular: the words "The Looking Glass" are superimposed upon a hand mirror that contains the image of Mrs. Clingsland's haggard, unhappy face, so that Wharton's female reader seems to regard her own reflection within it. Indeed, I find, as a woman reading this story, that I identify with both Mrs. Attlee and Mrs. Clingsland, with both narrator and heroine, with both spectator and spectacle, in a complex, contradictory pyschological response that seems to echo Mrs. Clingsland's own fragmentation before her mirrors. In "The Looking Glass," Wharton brilliantly analyzes such self-division in terms of the gendered construction of looking and being looked at. But she also challenges her readers to imagine being, and looking, beyond the looking glass.[45]

NOTES

1. The handwritten manuscript of "The Mirror" is at the Beinecke Rare Book Room and Manuscript Library at Yale University. This story was among the handful of tales that Wharton sold to Hearst in the 1930s, despite her disdain for "the present standard of American picture magazines" and for Hearst's publications in particular; see *The Letters of Edith Wharton*, ed. R. W. B. Lewis and Nancy Lewis (New York: Charles Scribner's Sons, 1988), 574. "The Looking Glass" appeared in *Hearst's International-Cosmopolitan* 99 (December 1935): 32–35, 157–59, accompanied by melodramatic illustrations and cautionary précis: "What every woman knows: that the truth can be hidden from her friends, but not from her mirror. . . . A powerful short story by a distinguished American novelist" (33). (Barbara A. White, in *Edith Wharton: A Study of the Short Fiction* [New York: Twayne, 1991], 174, cites this version under the incorrect title "The Mirrors" and without full pagination.) For its appearance in *Hearst's*, Wharton made her story simpler and less ambiguous: she retained most of the dialogue but condensed the narration (thus placing less emphasis on Mrs. Attlee's introspection and her spiritual dilemma); she divided the text into shorter paragraphs; she eliminated all ellipses; and she added exclamation points. Wharton reprinted "The Looking-Glass" a year later, however—with its original text restored and expanded—in *The World Over* (New York: Appleton-Century, 1936), 243–77. R. W. B. Lewis later included this version in his edition of Wharton's *Ghosts* (New York: Charles Scribner's Sons, 1973)—in place of "A Bottle of Perrier"—and in *The Collected Stories of Edith Wharton* (New York: Charles Scribner's Sons, 1989), 2: 844–58. Unless otherwise noted, all quotations from "The Looking Glass" are from *The Collected Stories*, and references will be given parenthetically in the text. References to the manuscript (hereafter identified as "Mirror") and to the first published version (hereafter identified as *Hearst's*) will also be cited parenthetically in the text.

2. Jean Frantz Blackall, "Edith Wharton's Art of Ellipsis," *Journal of Narrative Technique* 17.2 (1987): 157.

3. Sherrie A. Inness, "An Economy of Beauty: The Beauty System in 'The Looking Glass' and 'Permanent Wave,'" *Edith Wharton Review* 10.1 (1993): 8–9.

4. Mrs. Attlee's name emphasizes her persuasiveness, diplomacy, and working-class background: Clement Richard Attlee, a British politician, was elected leader of Britain's Labour Party in 1935, several months before "The Looking Glass" appeared in print. Mrs. Clingsland's name suggests, by contrast, her conservative and aristocratic clinging to the past. (Its similarity to "Mrs. Clayburn" supports the thesis that "The Looking Glass" and "All Souls'," Wharton's last story, are "paired" [Allan Gardner Smith, "Edith Wharton and the Ghost Story," in *Modern Critical Views: Edith Wharton*, ed. Harold Bloom (New York: Chelsea House, 1986), 91]. Both "Mrs. Clingsland" and "Mrs. Clayburn" begin with the same consonantal cluster, combine two monosyllabic words, and denote an earthly destination.) The name of Mrs. Attlee's priest, Father Divott, connotes both earthliness and spirituality: according to the *Oxford English Dictionary*, a "divot" is a bit of sod as well as an archaic Scottish word for "devout."

5. Sigmund Freud, *Three Essays on the Theory of Sexuality, Standard Edition of the Complete Psychological Works of Sigmund Freud*, ed. James Strachey (London: Hogarth, 1959), 17:149–59; Jacques Lacan, "The Mirror Stage as Formative of the Function of the I as Revealed in Psychoanalytic Experience," *Ecrits: A Selection*, trans. Alan Sheridan (New York: Norton, 1977), 1–7; Michel Foucault, *Discipline and Punish: The Birth of the Prison*, trans. Alan Sheridan (New York: Vintage, 1979).

6. Laura Mulvey, "Visual Pleasure and Narrative Cinema," *Screen* 15.3 (1975): 6–18. On the gaze in feminist film theory, see Teresa de Lauretis, *Technologies of Gender: Essays on Theory, Film, and Fiction* (Bloomington: Indiana University Press, 1987); Mary Ann Doane, "Film and the Masquerade: Theorizing the Female Spectator," *Screen* 23.3–4 (1982): 74–87; Stephen Heath, "Difference," *Screen* 19.3 (1978): 51–112; and E. Ann Kaplan, "Is the Gaze Male?" in *Powers of Desire: The Politics of Sexuality*, ed. Ann Snitow, Christine Stansell, and Sharon Thompson (New York: Monthly Review Press, 1983), 309–27. On the gaze in feminist narratology, see Beth Newman, "Getting Fixed: Feminine Identity and Scopic Crisis in *The Turn of the Screw*," *Novel* 26.1 (1992): 43–63; Newman, "'The Situation of the Looker-On': Gender, Narration, and Gaze in *Wuthering Heights*," *PMLA* 105.5 (1990): 1029–41; Carol J. Singley and Susan Elizabeth Sweeney, "Forbidden Reading and Ghostly Writing in Edith Wharton's 'Pomegranate Seed,'" in *Anxious Power: Reading, Writing, and Ambivalence in Narrative by Women*, ed. Singley and Sweeney (Albany: State University of New York Press, 1993), 197–217; and Robyn Warhol, "The Look, the Body, and the Heroine: A Feminist-Narratological Reading of *Persuasion*," *Novel* 26.1 (1992): 5–19.

7. Newman, "Getting Fixed," 43.

8. On Wharton's fascination with the gaze and its significance in her ghost fiction, especially in relation to narrative poetics, see Singley and Sweeney, "Forbidden Reading," 205–8. On her "extensive dramatization of women who are their images in the glass" (63) in several novels—*The House of Mirth, The Reef, The Custom of the Coun-*

try, The Mother's Recompense, and *Summer*—see Jenijoy LaBelle, *Herself Beheld: The Literature of the Looking Glass* (Ithaca: Cornell University Press, 1988), 59–63, 78–79, 87–90.

9. See LaBelle, 2.

10. Wharton is aware that the gaze is structured by class as well as gender. Just as men stare at Mrs. Clingsland, so she stares at Mrs. Attlee—"her great eyes burning into me like gimlets," "her eyes blazing" (852–53, 857)—while waiting for Harry's messages. Mrs. Attlee, however, takes only "a stealthy look" at her mistress as she reads Harry's letter (857).

11. In identifying her self with her beauty, Mrs. Clingsland resembles Aphrodite. As LaBelle notes in *Herself Beheld,* Aphrodite's servant "walks before her carrying a mirror, so that she may constantly look at herself . . . not because she is vain, but because she needs to see that she is still beautiful. She only exists for herself (and for the world) as a beautiful being" (31). Mrs. Clingsland also evokes other legendary female figures—the Queen in "Little Snow-White," the Medusa in classical mythology—as I will explain later in the essay.

12. Lacan, 2, 5–6.

13. See Luce Irigaray, *The Speculum of the Other Woman,* trans. Gillian C. Gill (Ithaca: Cornell University Press, 1985); Julia Kristeva, *Desire in Language,* ed. Leon S. Roudiez, trans. Thomas Gora, Alice Jardine, and Roudiez (New York: Columbia University Press, 1980); and Juliet Mitchell, *Psychoanalysis and Feminism* (New York: Penguin, 1975).

14. LaBelle, 9.

15. See Jacob and Wilhelm Grimm, "Little Snow-White," *Grimm's Fairy Tales,* trans. Margaret Hunt, rev. James Stern (New York: Pantheon, 1944), 249–58. "The Looking Glass" thus exemplifies the middle stage of what Theodore Ziolkowski calls "disenchantment": the historical process in which magical images from folklore are rationalized, then psychologized, and finally parodied in literature. On "catoptromantic" mirrors, which are a source of knowledge, see Ziolkowski, *Disenchanted Images: A Literary Iconology* (Princeton: Princeton University Press, 1977), 149, 162–68; on fairy-tale themes in Wharton's novels, see Elizabeth Ammons, *Edith Wharton's Argument with America* (Athens: University of Georgia Press, 1980).

16. Sandra M. Gilbert and Susan Gubar, *The Madwoman in the Attic: The Woman Writer and the Nineteenth-Century Literary Imagination* (New Haven: Yale University Press, 1979), 39, 41.

17. LaBelle, 53.

18. John Berger, *Ways of Seeing* (New York: Penguin, 1972), 47.

19. Heath, 92.

20. Ziolkowski, 160; Freud, "'The Uncanny,'" *Standard Edition,* 17:219–56. Mrs. Clingsland's lost reflection may also represent her soul: Mrs. Attlee, who calls her employer a "poor soul" twice on one page (855), muses that "it was true I'd risked my soul . . . but then maybe I'd saved hers" (858).

21. Wharton leaves open the possibility that the letter actually came from Harry. In its redemptive effect on Mrs. Clingsland, and its textual absence from the story, it resembles the "word which made all clear" at the end of *The House of Mirth* (New York:

Charles Scribner's Sons, 1905), which passes between Lily and Selden but is withheld from the reader (532). On the secret love letter as emblem of forbidden sexuality and textuality in Wharton's fiction, see my essay "Edith Wharton's Case of Roman Fever," in *Wretched Exotic: Essays on Edith Wharton in Europe*, ed. Katherine Joslin and Alan Price (New York: Peter Lang, 1993), 325–26.

22. Lacan, 2–3. At the diegetic level, Mr. Clingsland, Harry, the young man, and the priest are all dispensable, dead, dying, or desexualized; at the extradiegetic level, Mrs. Attlee's husband and son are both deceased (she is a widow who lives with her widowed daughter-in-law).

23. Mrs. Clingsland's fantasy also recalls the "evil eye" of folklore. Lawrence Di Stasi, in *Mal Occhio: The Underside of Vision* (San Francisco: North Point Press, 1981), traces this phenomenon not to Lacan's mirror stage but to Melanie Klein's account of the weaning process (54–56). Di Stasi identifies the evil eye's contradictory powers of punishment and protection with the ambivalent maternal goddess (93) and with the paired figures of mother and son, "the devouring feminine eye or the penetrating masculine eye" (135).

24. The interplay of glances at the end of Wharton's "The Eyes" (*Collected Stories*, 2:114–30), a ghost story about male homosexuality, directly parallels those in the myth. Frenham, Culwin's minion, hides his face so as not to meet Culwin's gaze; Culwin, like Medusa, sees himself "in the mirror behind Frenham's head" and confronts his own image "with a glare of slowly gathering hate"; the narrator, like Perseus, glimpses Culwin's reflection in the glass and observes his face without being himself observed (130).

25. Freud, "Medusa's Head," *Standard Edition*, 18: 273; Tobin Siebers, *The Mirror of Medusa* (Berkeley and Los Angeles: University of California Press, 1983), 8; Heath, 91–92.

26. Wharton, "The Eyes," 120.

27. In his preface to *The Princess Casamassima*, for example, James remarks on the necessity of "placing advantageously, placing right in the middle of the light, the most polished of possible mirrors of the subject," and he cites Strether (in *The Ambassadors*) as "a mirror verily of miraculous silver" (*Theory of Fiction: Henry James*, ed. James E. Miller Jr. [Omaha: University of Nebraska Press, 1972], 240).

28. Wharton, *The Writing of Fiction* (New York: Charles Scribner's Sons, 1925), 87, 88, 46.

29. Doane, 81.

30. Wharton, *Writing of Fiction*, 87.

31. Sylvia Plath, "Mirror," *The Collected Poems*, ed. Ted Hughes (New York: Harper and Row, 1981), 173–74.

32. Paul's assertion that a "gift of prophecy" is "nothing" without charity (2 Cor. 13: 2) also reminds the reader that Mrs. Attlee deceives her mistress partly out of pity and that Mrs. Clingsland herself had "a loving nature, if only anybody'd shown her how to love" (849). On religious subtexts in Wharton's fiction, see Carol J. Singley, *Edith Wharton: Matters of Mind and Spirit* (New York: Cambridge University Press, 1995).

33. Heath, 92.

34. Jackie Byars, "Gazes/Voices/Power: Expanding Psychoanalysis for Feminist

Film and Television Theory," in *Female Spectators: Looking at Film and Television*, ed. E. Deirdre Pribram (London: Verso, 1988), 113.

35. On narrative levels, see Gérard Genette, *Narrative Discourse: An Essay in Method*, trans. Jane E. Lewin (Ithaca: Cornell University Press, 1980), 228.

36. Shoshana Felman, "Henry James: Madness and the Risks of Practice (Turning the Screw of Interpretation)," *Writing and Madness* (Ithaca: Cornell University Press, 1985), 177.

37. On orality, literacy, and ambivalence toward female authorship, see my "Edith Wharton's Case," 323–27.

38. Paula Bergrren, "Seeing the Gorgon: Edith Wharton and the Problem of Knowledge," paper read at the Modern Language Association Convention, panel on Edith Wharton and Women, San Francisco, December 30, 1987.

39. See Singley and Sweeney, 205–9.

40. Ibid., 197.

41. Wharton, "The Eyes," 115, 120.

42. Wharton, preface to *Ghosts, Collected Stories*, 2: 875, 877.

43. Amy Kaplan, "Edith Wharton's Profession of Authorship," *ELH* 53.2 (1986): 433–57.

44. Margaret B. McDowell, in "Edith Wharton's Ghost Tales Reconsidered," *Edith Wharton: New Critical Essays*, ed. Alfred Bendixen and Annette Zilversmit (New York: Garland, 1992), 291–314, compares "The Looking Glass" to other late tales, arguing that Wharton's "autobiographical identification is even more transparent" here: she makes Mrs. Attlee a comic character, "but extends her full sympathy to Mrs. Clingsland" (296). White, in *Edith Wharton: A Study*, agrees with McDowell that the story is autobiographical; however, she claims that Wharton also extends sympathy to Mrs. Attlee and that the servant's revenge reveals "the aristocratic writer's guilt and fear" (97). The relation between mistress and servant is clearly at issue; accordingly, Inness, in "An Economy of Beauty," points out "the differences between the beautiful, elite women who accept their status as glorified objects" and women like Mrs. Attlee, "who, by manipulating the conventions of the beauty system, gain agency that they would otherwise lack" (8).

45. I am grateful to Audrey Jaffe, James Phelan, Carol J. Singley, and Sarah Stanbury for their comments on this essay. I presented an earlier version at the American Literature Association Symposium on American Women Writers in San Antonio, Texas, October 1993; it was first published in *Narrative* 3.2 (1995): 139–60.

 **Part 2**   Race, Culture, and Diversity

The Chronicles of Panchita Villa

A Chicana Guerrillera Literary Critic

TEY DIANA REBOLLEDO

Mother, father
there's no passing
the cup
I'm going to be a troublemaker
when I grow up.
Demetria Martínez

The topic of this essay is Chicana literature, Chicana criticism, and the canon. It is a subject about which I have written many times but which evolves depending on the historical moment, what has happened to Chicana literature and Chicana critics during the time immediately preceding, and how angry I am about the situation at any given time. In its various manifestations these thoughts have been called "Chicana Studies: The Missing Text," "Is There a Place for Chicana Studies in Women Studies?" "Lost in America," and, when I am really angry, "Et tu Bruta?" an aggressively relentless play on the feminist betrayal of women of color, but doubly nasty because in Spanish Bruta is not only the feminine of Brutus but also means "stupid" or "dumb." I am sorry to have to give yet another transformation of these ideas here, but I will try not to be offensively aggressive. The problem is that in all the years I have been speaking about this, I have not seen things change much. Chicana critics have to continue to be guerrillera fighters.

To begin, I want to clarify what canon I am discussing here, as there canons of which Chicana literature might be a part, although the reality is that it is not part of many. Certainly we are not even mentioned in the larger context of Anglo/European literature, nor are we considered within Latin American literature. Neither are we included within the canon of general American literature. In the canon of Chicano and other minority literature, the women are clearly and importantly recognized and included, particularly in recent years. Here I want to discuss the inclusion of Chicanas in the more narrowly focused feminist canon: a place where a few Chicana writers such as Sandra

Cisneros, Ana Castillo, and Gloria Anzaldúa are sometimes included, and the rest of such fine writers as Pat Mora and Angela de Hoyos excluded. And in the main, it is a canon where Chicana literary critics are excluded. In the mainstream of feminist journals such as *Signs*, very few, if any, Chicana critics have been published, and in other journals such as *Critical Inquiry* or *PMLA* we cannot even imagine being included. When I wrote "Lost in America" I commented that we are lost because Chicana writers and critics are not included in mainstream anthologies, journals, or books. And until recently we were not really integrated in Chicano anthologies, which focused mainly on male writers. We are lost in Women's Studies because, except in exceptional cases, scholars in Women's Studies programs often feel that studying the latest French feminist theory or postmodern theory is more important than spending time in the study of minority women.

The problems facing Chicana writers are many. Until recently Chicana writers were cut off from the national market because of region and the newness of their literature. It has only been within the last ten years that we have begun to see their work consistently published even by Chicano publishers such as Arte Público and the Bilingual Press. Before then, many Chicana writers self-published in chapbooks issued in small numbers and distributed among family and friends. There was no regional or national distribution of these texts. In the last several years some university presses have begun to publish Chicana writers and critics: The University of Arizona Press, The University of New Mexico Press, The University of Texas Press, and a few others. And lately some authors, beginning to make use of literary agents, have been able to break through into New York publishing houses, riding on the current interest in all things hot and Latino. This has happened with fiction, with poetry, and, especially interesting and worthwhile, with children's books. Yet except for these few big splashes, Chicana literature remains unknown. However, academics can no longer complain about a lack of literary texts and critical works written by Chicanas. In my research for *Infinite Division: An Anthology of Chicana Literature* I came across thousands of texts written by Chicanas, and creative work continues to pour out.[1] And while Chicana literature is young, the high quality of the work shows that is also mature. But I want to discuss the problems that beset those of us in academia who are struggling to find a place for Chicana literature at least within academic circles, if not with the general public.

One issue is the role of the Chicana critic. We all have faced the problem of working in what are thought of as "marginal areas": women and minority women. We are asked what kind of a market can there be for that? Is it academically legitimate? Are the writers good enough? Do they have a sufficient body of work? Do you as a critic have enough theory? Does standard theory apply to minority writers? This is the sort of questioning that comes from your department, your college, your colleagues. At the same time we face interrogation about political correctness and multiculturalism from the right, for example, from the National Association of Scholars ("the nasties," I call them), who are trying to maintain power in the face of change. This makes us the target for an inquisition that can include public and private harassment (I know: a Chicana colleague and I have been the subject of such harassment) as well as other attempts at silencing.

Rather than discuss these issues in the abstract, I would like to talk on a more personal level. In 1985 I was invited to give a Last Lecture at the University of New Mexico. The Last Lecture Series was conceived as being the last, and perhaps most important, lecture that you would give during your lifetime. Clearly such a responsibility weighs heavily on your mind, even though you might not intend it to do so, and I approached my task with severity and enthusiasm. I titled my lecture, "Meditations on Two Texts of Some Importance: *The Letter of Sor Juana Inés de la Cruz*, and the *Memoirs of Panchita Villa*." Sor Juana's *Carta Atenagórica*, the seventeenth-century Mexican nun's feminist reply to patriarchal colonial Mexican society, is an important document in our Mexicana/Chicana intellectual history, one which defended women's right to knowledge and to education. In her *Carta* she not only saw knowledge as being female and herself as the descendent of a long line of learned women, she had the temerity to claim that women were the originators of laws, propagators of Greek wisdom, and teachers of great philosophers and kings. She also asserted that a woman invented the Latin language, the basis of all writing and knowledge in the church. At one point, ordered by authorities to put away her books, she continued to make scientific observations: "And what could I tell, my lady, of the secrets of nature that I discovered while cooking? I observe that an egg binds and fries in butter and oil but breaks up in sugar syrup; that the yolk and white of the same egg are so opposed that each one separately will mix with sugar, but not both together . . . but my lady, what can we women know except kitchen philosophy? Lupercio Leonardo aptly said, 'it is possible to philosophize while preparing dinner.' And I often say, observing these trifles: 'If Aristotle had been a cook, he would have written much more.'"[2] Sor Juana has left an intellectual and culturally legacy that has been eagerly taken up by Chicana writers and critics. *The Memoirs of Panchita Villa*, the other text I referred to in my Last Lecture, is also an ironically contrived text, patterned after a Mexican novel of the 1930s. Martín Luis Guzmán wrote *The Memoirs of Pancho Villa* to record the life and times of the Mexican revolutionary hero. Panchita Villa, our contemporary heroine, was constructed as a literary revolutionary, fighting against the academic establishment as a Chicana, and as a woman. The author is Concepción Galindo, better known in her family as Concha (also the name of her grandmother). Concha was born in a small town in northern New Mexico. She came from a family of writers, and her mother wrote a novel about growing up during the Mexican Revolution, unpublished, to be sure, in the tradition of so many women writers. Nevertheless, the novel influenced all three daughters, who would go to the trunk where it was generally stored to read about the time their mother, fleeing roving revolutionaries, was put on a train where wounded and dying soldiers had been moved, her white dress totally covered, to her horror, in blood. And about the time their grandmother, the first Concepción, saved their grandfather from being shot. In time this contemporary Concha grew up and became a university professor. So in *The Memoirs of Panchita Villa*, she details the struggle that Chicana academics, intellectuals, and writers had to wage in order to gain acceptance in the larger canonical worlds. In 1985 it was a chronicle mainly against the narrowmindedness of male-centered academic life and intellectual inquiry. In the novel, the heroine, Panchita, questions various people she meets. For example, she asked how are minority women, students, faculty, and staff treated at universities? Welcomed or silenced? To the males of her culture she asked whether there was also a place for Chicanas in their revolution? Why was not the study of women and women's knowledge, especially that of minority women, considered valid? Now it is true that in the intervening years some of this has changed, but unfortunately two of her questions are still timely. In one Panchita asks other women, in particular feminists, "Why do you wish only to mirror and reproduce yourself in terms of your scholarly interests?" And she asks why Chicanas are not represented in the curriculum of Women's Studies and American Literature. Why, why, why, why, why? Because of its densely thick narration, its outlaw structure, we can clearly define the *Memoirs* as a novel of questioning. And, as I was finishing my discussion of the *Memoirs* I said, "Well, enough is enough. It is true that some revolutions and some revolutionaries are more exciting than others. The type of everyday guerrilla warfare that Panchita engages in is on par with the observations of Sor Juana as she mixes egg yolks with sugar. But then perhaps if Aristotle had been a woman he could have been a better revolutionary."

Then volume 2 of the *Memoirs* appeared (it seems the author has at least six volumes in mind). Two central issues are addressed: how to include and integrate Chicana literary texts into the curriculum and into the canon, and how to include and integrate Chicana critics into the canon. Since Panchita Villa has undertaken a thorough discussion of those issues that you can read for yourself, here I will only add my own personal observations about Chicana literature and the feminist canon.

Most Women's Studies programs are led by feminists who range in perspectives from traditional to liberal to radical. At times they remember that they need to include minority women in their courses and on their faculties. Certainly in recent years, with curriculum integration projects and with loud commentary from minority women, many programs have made significant progress in inclusion. Many have not, and I truly believe, even with women who regard themselves as "liberals," there is still insensitivity, tokenism, and the necessity for us constantly to be educating. This attitude reminds me of a poem written in the early seventies by Marcela Christine Lucero Trujillo called "No More Cookies, Please" in which she states how tired she is of attending coffees with liberal feminists, constantly having to be nice and to explain herself, educating them.[3] For Chicana writers and critics, it seems to me, not much has changed. If any group of minority women have been able to cross boundaries, I believe it is black women. More often than not they are included in the curriculum, and their works are read. Chicanas are not half so well represented; Asian-American and Native American women are almost invisible. We are still having trouble breaking into the mainstream, although a select few are doing quite well. We continue to be asked the questions, is the work any good? Are the writers any good? Are you any good? Or are you good enough? (And since we ourselves ask these questions of ourselves often enough, it doesn't take much to discourage us.)

I want to outline several areas that, for me, continue to be problematic.

Integrating our research into mainstream books, journals, and so on. For a long time I have firmly believed in working on projects that would integrate our work into the larger canon. To this end I have published chapters in such works as *The Desert Is No Lady* and *For Alma Mater*, while continuing to publish extensively in Chicana/Chicano publications.[4] Several years ago I received a letter, however, which has made me question the value of such integration. I would like to give you excerpts from it (names withheld), which will aptly illustrate what I am talking about. It may strike a familiar chord in some of you.

"Dear Professor Rebolledo:

"My coeditor and I have just signed an advance contract with a university press for a collection of essays on the fiction and/or autobiographies of twentieth-century British and American women writers. For some time now we have been searching for someone to write and essay on mothering in the fiction of a Chicana or Latina Woman writer." (At this point and throughout I am going to do a Chicana deconstructionist analysis of this letter. To begin,

I must mention that I did not know these women at all. I read that the volume is already put together since they have an advance contract. The editor at the press told them that they needed to find a Chicana or Latina—it doesn't matter which—so that their volume will not appear to be racist. They have already preselected the topic, mothering, but they don't know any Chicana or Latina critics, or really anyone who knows any, since they have been searching for some time. In addition they don't know any universities where such knowledge might be found.) "Your name was given to me by the Women's Studies Director at the University of ——. She also suggested a possible novel—*The Ultraviolet Sky*—but we are certainly open to suggestion about this."[5] (Here they have chosen the novel for me, but if I complain loud enough they would be willing to change. After all, they have not read the novel, so it doesn't make all that much difference.)

"We are limiting each essay to 8250 words (23 pages, excluding bibliography), and our deadline is October 15, 1989. In fact it would be preferable if we could have an initial draft in September so that we can make editorial comments. Given the short notice, we do realize that this may be difficult to achieve." (Ah yes, deadlines. The letter to me was dated July 14, with the "14" crossed out and "18" written in; I received it on July 28. This gave me exactly a month and a half to write a paper on a subject chosen for me. Because what I write might not be any good, they ask for it a little early so they can edit it, for it might be really radical—or, the more likely possibility is that, since I am a Chicana and speak other languages, it will be badly written in English, so changes will have to be made. It also assumes that I have nothing to do but to write this paper. I was only involved in trying to finish books, write a paper for MALCS, finish a promised chapter for a book on Chicano colonial literature, get my classes organized, and coordinate the National Association for Chicano Studies Conference for 1990.)

The final paragraph. "Please let me know as soon as possible. You may phone me at home or at State University. But I am rarely in my office during the summer. You may, of course, also write to me at the above address. I do hope to hear that you will contribute an essay to this book." (Deconstruction: Even though I have nothing to do with this project, she not only patronizes me but she places the burden of responsibility on me. I may phone her, and, moreover, I should track her down. Barring not finding her, I can write to her, soon—immediately—with my excitement about having been invited to participate in this project.)

Now perhaps some of you will think I am overreacting to this letter. When you have received enough of them you will see how serious this is. Question: What to do? I took the easy way out: I didn't answer. Advice from colleagues ranged from writing them an angry letter telling them *"que se chinguen,"* to a letter educating them by refusing to participate but explaining why I am offended, to doing a Chicana deconstruction of it. This letter is serious because the project has never been from the start an integrated project with input from minority writers about how best to combine these various papers and perspectives; it is tokenism at its worst because it is so genuinely insensitive and it makes so many assumptions about our work.[6]

It is very important to generate public programs on issues that minority women feel strongly about. But minority women have to be at the center of the planning for such programs. When they are, you can have great results. Erlinda Gonzales-Berry and I planned a program on Redesigning the Traditional Literary Canon, invited female and male speakers, collaborated between departments, and it was a great success. But there have been other programs where this precisely has not been the case, and they have resulted in memorable disasters. One case in point is the Dark Madonna Conference held at UCLA several years ago and sponsored by the UCLA Center for the Study of Women and cosponsored by many minority groups, such as the African Studies Center, Chicano Studies, and the Hispanic Women's Council. It seemed a well-planned conference, but, on the night of the opening plenary session, with over five hundred women in the audience, it quickly became apparent that all was not well. Of six speakers on the podium there were no minority women. (We had all been relegated to sessions the next day). The evening dragged endlessly on with discussions about women and uses of convention and garden clubs. When time was allowed for questions a woman stood up and I recognized her, Roberta Fernández. She said, and I paraphrase, "As you look at the audience you can see that we are of all races, and the program was advertised as the Dark Madonna with an obviously black virgin and child on its cover. Why are there no minority women on the plenary session?" As you can imagine, this left the persons on the stage in total confusion with all sorts of embarrassing statements to be said, such as, well, there *are* minority women on the program tomorrow, we *tried* to include minority women (and they had invited quite a few of us), we didn't think, and, it's not *my* fault, for I am not the organizer. My point here is that this happens again and again. When there are no minority women on the planning committees, we are forgotten. I would like to interject here that the organizers of the ALA Symposium on American Women Writers did not fall into the above traps. They have energetically and conscientiously searched out, invited, and integrated minority women into the conference. I feel that they have done a thoughtful job inviting Chicana and Asian American writers and critics. More effort needs to be made to include Native American women.

I think that perhaps the greatest impact that we have been able to make vis-á-vis Women's Studies has been in curriculum integration. I am not so sure about integration in the American Literature and English curriculum. At least at the University of New Mexico, all the Women's Studies courses taught must have a strong racial and ethnic component in them. Truly integrating Chicanas on projects, however, has been a different story, even on projects of curriculum integration. I have often worked with a Regional Women's Studies Program on different projects, and for some years now I have been telling them that they need to have Chicanas on their advisory board and to consult with Chicanas on their projects instead of presenting them as a fait accompli. The program often makes attempts to be inclusionary on their projects, inviting minority women to participate in small numbers. Several years ago they received a grant from the Ford Foundation to participate in a curriculum integration project of a different sort: to integrate the work of minority women into the Women's Studies curriculum. I was asked if our program wanted to participate. I asked what minority women were on the planning committee: well, none. I asked who the project director was (well, an Anglo), and I asked who the coordinators were (well, an Anglo and a Chicano). I said no, no thank you, that we didn't want to participate because we had no input. In their January 1989 newsletter I read that of thirteen campus coordinators for the project only one was a Chicana, although two Chicanos were also included.

When one takes into consideration how these different projects are being put together and presented, it becomes clear that, for the most part, we Chicanas are not only not represented, but that others are speaking for us, others who may be sympathetic but who cannot presume to speak from our perspective. Once again others are shaping our worldview and presenting it as ours. Is this better than not being represented at all? I will leave this for you to cogitate.

What can Chicanas do about this besides complain? For one thing, at this time many Chicanas feel we need to concentrate on our own research, our own classes, our own agendas. We need to finish our dissertations, our articles, our books. We need to be clear on our perspectives and to look at other Chicanas as a source of support. When we are invited to be speakers, present papers, collaborate on books, we must ask who the organizers are, who the planners are. Have they have had input from minority women; are they asking for ours? Are we invited at the beginning of the project so that we may take a role in shaping it? If the answers to our questions are not satisfactory, we might perhaps refuse to participate, particularly if we are being used as tokens and are matronized. If we are feeling generous we might explain why we are refusing. We must express our concerns. If this is heard from enough of us, perhaps the message will sink in, and I won't be the only one who is difficult to work with.

If you feel I have exaggerated the exclusion of Chicana writers and critics from the canon, let me finish by recounting an incident that happened just last month. I received a call from an editor from a distinguished press in New York, asking me if I could review an anthology proposal for a book on American women writers from 1600 to the present. After I had agreed and received the proposal, I saw that there was not one Chicana or Latina writer included. However, there were 255 items by Emily Dickinson (make no mistake, I think Dickinson is a fabulous writer) and 30 sonnets by Edna St. Vincent Millay. While African American women writers were generously included, Native American writers were scattered throughout, and only two Asian American writers, Tan and Kingston, were present. And once again "The Yellow Wallpaper" was reproduced in its entirety (as it is endlessly). In my answer I said, "I have to tell you to begin, that I am totally shocked that in 1993 not one Chicana or Latina writer would be represented in an anthology of this magnitude. If the author would like to call this the *Anthology of Anglo American Women Writers* then it might be acceptable, or perhaps it could be called *Emily Dickinson and Some Other Writers*, but to call it American Women Writers is truly a travesty. . . . I think it would be an embarrassment for your press to publish this text as it stands. Moreover, to simply tack on Chicana/ Latina writers without meaningful integration would be an absurdity." To add insult to injury, after last week I received a form letter from the press thanking me for my review and asking if they could use any of my remarks for publicity.

Please do not misunderstand me: I am for working together to integrate works by women of color into the canon. But I am tired of being marginalized, matronized, and colonized. I want the texts to be fully integrated from the beginning in a meaningful way, texts that talk to each other in both the minority and the traditional canon: texts that are selected from a perspective of women of color and not the other way around. What can you personally do about all this? Be thoughtful, include the work of women of color in your classes, place their work side by side with a more traditional work. You might be surprised by the dialogue generated as the texts speak to each other. At the Symposium on American Women Writers one of the keynote speakers noted that she thought we could not create a canon that included minority writers, because it would not be historically accurate. However, if one were to recognize that part of the Chicana tradition could (and should) include Mexican writers such as Sor Juana Inés de la Cruz, (after all, the Southwest was part of Mexico until 1848) and stories from the oral traditions of Hispana/Mexicana and Native American writers, we could construct a much more creative (and historically significant) canon. Other suggestions would be to buy (not xerox) our books—encourage your students to buy our books. Selling books encourages publishers to publish more. Invite us to lecture, include us from the beginning in your programming for conferences, enjoy our humor, our ironies, educate yourself, be revolutionary.

As I end I would like to confess what you have already guessed, that the *Memoirs of Panchita Villa* result from another female tradition, the apocryphal text, that they are attributed to Concha Galindo, who in reality is me, that they are a not-yet-existent text, a discourse in progress. To finish, I would like to acknowledge all my revolutionary co-troublemakers who function on the Theory of Bad Conduct, who resist tradition and easy answers, who want to revolutionize the world to make it more just for all its people, who desire a system of knowledge and learning that is truly egalitarian, and who support teachers, texts, and critics who represent the Other. I acknowledge those troublemakers who are not afraid to question established systems and who are on the edge of the wave of new learning. And especially I want to acknowledge Sor Juana, who questioned and who clearly understood that language and knowledge are tools in the stairway to the pyramid of the mind.

I would like to end this discussion, which is just a beginning, with a poem by a Nuevo Mexicana writer, Gloria Gonzales:

> There is nothing
> so lonesome
> or sad
> that
> papas fritas
> won't cure.[7]

NOTES

1. Tey Diana Rebolledo and Eliana S. Rivero, eds., *Infinite Divisions: An Anthology of Chicana Literature* (Tucson: University of Arizona Press, 1993).

2. Margaret Sayers Peden, ed. and trans., *A Woman of Genius: The Intellectual Autobiography of Sor Juana Inés de la Cruz*, 2d ed. (Salisbury, Conn.: Lime Rock Press, 1987), 63; I have modified the translation.

3. In Dexter Fisher, ed., *The Third Woman: Minority Women Writers of the United States* (Boston: Houghton Mifflin, 1980), 402–3.

4. Vera Norwood and Janice Monk, eds., *The Desert Is No Lady* (New Haven: Yale University Press, 1987); Paula A. Treichler, Cheris Kramarae, and Beth Stafford, *For Alma Mater: Theory and Practice in Feminist Scholarship* (Urbana: University of Illinois Press, 1985).

5. Alma Luz Villenueva, *The Ultraviolet Sky* (Tempe, Ariz.: Bilingual Press, 1988).

6. At the Symposium on Women Writers where I read this paper, several Chicana colleagues came up to tell me they had received identical letters. This means the editors blanketed everyone. What would have happened if we had all accepted?

7. Gloria G. Gonzales, "There Is Nothing," in *Las Mujeres Hablan: An Anthology of Nuevo Mexicana Writers* (Albuquerque: El Norte Publications/Academia, 1988), 184.

What Women? What Canon?
African American Women and the Canon

TRUDIER HARRIS

While I am not certain that continued discussions about the canon are irrelevant, it is clear that a canon of African American women's literature has been formed with or without those discussions. It has been formed by scholars, teachers, editors, graduate students, and publishers. Anyone who teaches, it seems to me, teaches from the perspective of what she or he has determined to be the canon for that particular subject matter (unless she or he just superimposes weird and idiosyncratic personal tastes). This is no less true for those of us who teach the works of African American women writers. Few of us would consider such courses complete without the inclusion of writers like Harriet Jacobs, Zora Neale Hurston, Gwendolyn Brooks, Lorraine Hansberry, Toni Morrison, Alice Walker, Sherley Anne Williams, Rita Dove, and Toni Cade Bambara.

In fact, focus on black women writers has been so intense that some black male academics are feeling compelled to teach courses these days on "Black Male Writers," and there is a recently founded *Journal of Black Male Studies*. I'm not exactly sure that I understand the rationale, but the pattern is clearly emerging, as is a general focus on what is called a "black masculinist tradition" in African American literature (as if it were anything *but* that before 1970 or so). These reactionaries are clearly responding to what they perceive to be the unimpeachable establishment of black women writers as part of the literary canons in many universities. And this is not simply in courses devoted exclusively to African American women writers. These authors have gained a place in contemporary novel courses, traditional American novel or general literature courses, Women's Studies courses, sociology courses, history courses, African American studies courses, liberal studies courses, and a host of other interdisciplinary adventures in learning.

A corollary to this trend of inclusion is that everybody—her cousin and her stepcousin—wants to use texts by black women writers in their theses and dissertations these days. It seems as if black women writers are the new testing ground upon which graduate students are earning their diversity brownie points (and that is the case with a few established scholars as well). One African American woman friend of mine refuses to supervise any more masters theses where Toni Morrison is one of the authors treated. Another friend maintains that she is so sick of teaching Zora Neale Hurston's *Their Eyes Were Watching God* (1937) that she is just going to take it out of her syllabus for a couple of years. It's not that these women have any less love for these authors or works, it's just that they are somewhat jaded trying to keep pace with this constant demand upon their responsive intellectual energies.

In the past few years, Toni Morrison's *Beloved* (1987) and *Song of Solomon* (1977), Alice Walker's *The Color Purple* (1982), and Gloria Naylor's *Mama Day* (1988) have all been selected as the text that *all* freshmen are required to read in large, predominantly non-black universities where there are no or few black faculty members. That has been the pattern for a school the size of Clemson University. But smaller schools, such as Emory & Henry College in Virginia, have followed a similar pattern; *Beloved* is a standard selection in their Great Books program. In the fall semester of 1993, I learned that Morrison's *Beloved* is not only required for the *agregation*, the national examination the French government uses to recruit college teachers—which means that it is taught in all French universities—but that two French professors have completed a collection of essays on the book in order to enhance the learning process for their students.[1]

In the spring semester of 1988, when I taught a doctoral seminar on Toni Morrison's works, I had to answer questions such as "Has she written enough to have a course by herself?" "What else has she published besides *Beloved?*" My, how the times do change. In the short six-year period since then, when only *two* full-length critical studies were available on Morrison, we have gone to a plethora of books, including Barbara Rigney's *The Voices of Toni Morrison* and my own *Fiction and Folklore: The Novels of Toni Morrison*; collections of essays, such as Nellie Y. McKay's *Critical Essays on Toni Morrison*; inclusions in various critical studies, such as Henry Louis Gates's *Black Literature and Literary Theory* and Houston A. Baker Jr. and Patricia Redmond's *Afro-American Literary Study in the 1990s*; and a general sanctioning of the legitimacy of teaching a course on Morrison.[2] As of September 29, 1993 (three days before I presented this paper at the San Antonio conference), the MLA CD-ROM Disk listed 269 items on Morrison (works published since 1981 and primarily in the past five years).

And when the big guys get into the act, you know the writer has been canonized. Around 1988, I received an invitation to contribute a chapter to a book that a very well-known European American scholar was editing on Toni Morrison for Chelsea House. I asked some questions about the project, and I never heard from him again. His collection of essays on Morrison appeared in 1990. His collection on Zora Neale Hurston appeared in 1986, and he published another collection specifically on *Their Eyes Were Watching God* in 1987. That pattern continues. In 1993, Henry Louis Gates Jr. edited *Toni Morrison: Critical Perspectives Past and Present* and *Alice Walker: Critical Perspectives Past and Present*, both distributed by Penguin.[3]

Therefore, while we are still discussing what a canon should comprise, very well-established scholars and the publishing industry are in the process of sanctioning the one we already have in place. I don't know of any publisher who sets out on money-*losing* ventures; consequently, the numerous projects already published, or currently underway that include African American women exclusively, or include them in conjunction with black male writers, are a testament to the durability of what someone has determined *is* a canon. And we might start this citation with the critical role Oxford University Press has played in this attention-getting that leads to canon formation. Their publication in 1988 and 1991 of the thirty-plus-ten volumes of the Schomburg Library of nineteenth-century black women writers, under the general editorship of Henry Louis Gates, was certainly an historic moment for reevaluation of the previous place African American women writers had held on the American literary stage.

The Oxford Companion to Women's Writing in the United States, edited by Cathy Davidson and Linda Wagner-Martin, has a healthy selection of essays on black women writers. The corresponding *Oxford Companion to African American Literature* is even more detailed in its inclusion of those writers.[4] Gale Research Company published a total of six volumes in its *Dictionary of Literary Biography* series on African American writers, when it originally had planned to publish only two; the in-house editors severely miscalculated the numbers and quality of African American writers. Some of those volumes have gone into second and third printings, and they sell for an average of one hundred dollars each.[5] In 1991, there was discussion about yet another such volume, for at the time of the original publication a writer like Gloria Naylor, who is so well known today, had not met standards for inclusion in the series. (Amazing, isn't it?)

The New Cavalcade, a huge two-volume project on which Joyce Ann Joyce expended a lot of energy, appeared in the past couple of years.[6] The D. C. Heath Anthology has a generous selection of African American writers and works. Norton and Houghton-Mifflin have anthologies of African American literature currently in production, and a huge African American encyclopedic project is underway at Columbia University. The twenty-volume *American National Biography* has included black women writers from Lucy Terry

(1746) to J. California Cooper (1993). In 1992, Jessie Carney Smith's *Notable Black American Women* appeared, with black women writers forming a significant portion of that compilation. Noted historian Darlene Clark Hine completed a similar project, *Black Women in America: An Historical Encyclopedia*, in 1993, which she published as two volumes and which also includes numerous entries on black women writers.[7] Thadious M. Davis's biography of Nella Larsen appeared in February of 1994, and biographies are underway on Frances Ellen Watkins Harper, Lorraine Hansberry, Gwendolyn Bennett, and Paule Marshall.[8] The University of South Carolina has requested a volume not just on black women writers, but on *Southern* black women writers. If we've reached the point where we can discriminate regionally, we must surely have arrived in American letters.

And I am sure you are aware of HarperCollins having undertaken, at the encouragement of Henry Louis Gates, the publication of the entire corpus of Zora Neale Hurston's works, those previously published as well as those not published before. Beacon Press has a reprint series on black women writers edited by Deborah McDowell, which has reissued works such as Ann Petry's *The Street* and such classics as Alice Childress's *Like One of the Family . . . Conversations from a Domestic's Life*, and other presses are interested in similar ventures.[9] Critical volumes on such writers are proliferating at a rate that no normal teacher or scholar can keep up with, unless she quits her job and reads full-time.

Equally important are the contributions that black writers themselves have made in the shaping and perpetuation of the canon. The most notable example is the role Alice Walker played in recentering Zora Neale Hurston in African American women's literature. Certainly Robert Hemenway published the award-winning biography of Hurston, but it was Walker's devotion to Hurston and her search for Hurston's grave in Florida that added a dramatic dimension and urgency to the necessity of reclaiming writers such as Hurston.

It seems to me, therefore, that the question is not so much about *forming* a canon anymore as it is about reshaping it, correcting errors and omissions, lobbying for the inclusion of more neglected writers, and training students who are competent to engage the works critically as well as in the classroom. And we have to insist upon criteria for inclusion. No matter her popularity, Terry McMillan is simply not Alice Walker or Toni Morrison. On the other hand, writers like Georgia Douglas Johnson, Adrienne Kennedy, Julia Fields, Dorothy West, and Lucille Clifton have clearly been neglected or have received far less attention than they deserve. Johnson, Fields, and Clifton would broaden our conceptualization of black women's poetic traditions and would serve, along with the inclusion of other often-overlooked poets, to expand focus from the slave narrative and fiction strands that now seem to dominate. Johnson's romanticism, Fields's roots in the South, and Clifton's recreation of mythic African ties provide diverse ways in which to think of black women's literary production, and these poets offer scholars who have entered the canon of black women's literature through other genres another way of fleshing out the skeleton of black women's literary history.

Similar arguments could be made for playwright Kennedy and other dramatists. Writing against the grain of the dominant strand of black nationalism in the sixties, Kennedy makes clear as well the diversity of black women's voices. Her expressionistic, symbol-laden dramas beg for more instructional and scholarly attention, as do the plays of P. J. Gibson, Kathleen Collins, Elaine Jackson, and other contemporary playwrights. Critical collections of essays such as Carol P. Marsh-Lockett's forthcoming *As the Curtain Rises: Black Female Visions on the American Stage* will serve yeoman work in clarifying the necessity for inclusion of many of these playwrights.

We scholars, teachers, students, and editors, especially women, can encourage more expansive inclusion by offering suggestions to those book representatives who plague our offices, writing directly to publishers, and completing the wonderful studies that will further encourage publishers to keep certain works in print. We as scholars and readers do have a *public* role to play in what gets canonized, but so far it seems as if women have been more content to teach and write dissertations on African American women writers, with an occasional scholarly study, while men have played more aggressive and visible roles in catapulting the women to national and international prominence.

Ultimately, canonization for African American women writers is not unlike that for any other group of writers. By what we write and teach, what we recommend for publication, we convey to our students and disciples what is acceptable. The irony of all this canon-formation talk is that no one ever reinvents the process. We simply follow an historical pattern of displacement, believing—and acting upon the premise—that, at any given moment, our preferences are infinitely more sane, intelligible, inclusive, and valuable than those of the idiots who refuse to see the worth of our writers/goddesses.

NOTES

1. Genevieve Fabre and Claudine Raynaud, *Essays sur "Beloved" de Toni Morrison* (Paris: Cetanla, 1993).

2. Barbara Hill Rigney, *The Voices of Toni Morrison* (Columbus: Ohio State University Press, 1991); Trudier Harris, *Fiction and Folklore: The Novels of Toni Morrison* (Knoxville: University of Tennessee Press, 1991); Nellie Y. McKay, ed., *Critical Essays*

on *Toni Morrison* (Boston: G. K. Hall, 1988); Henry Louis Gates Jr., *Black Literature and Literary Theory* (New York: Methuen, 1984); Houston A. Baker Jr. and Patricia Redmond, *Afro-American Literary Study in the 1990s* (Chicago: University of Chicago Press, 1989).

3. Henry Louis Gates Jr. and K. A. Appich, eds., *Toni Morrison: Critical Perspectives Past and Present* (New York: Amistad, 1993); *Alice Walker: Critical Perspectives Past and Present* (New York: Amistad, 1993).

4. Cathy Davidson and Linda Wagner-Martin, eds., *The Oxford Companion to Women's Writing in the United States* (New York: Oxford University Press, 1995); William L. Andrews, Frances Smith Foster, and Trudier Harris, eds., *The Oxford Companion to African American Literature* (New York: Oxford University Press, 1997).

5. Thadious M. Davis and Trudier Harris, eds., *Afro-American Fiction Writers After 1955* (Detroit: Gale Research Company, 1984) and *Afro-American Writers After 1955: Dramatists and Prose Writers* (Detroit: Gale Research Company, 1985); Trudier Harris and Thadious M. Davis, eds., *Afro-American Poets Since 1955* (Detroit: Gale Research Company, 1985); Trudier Harris, ed., *Afro-American Writers before the Harlem Renaissance* (Detroit: Gale Research Company, 1986); *Afro-American Writers from the Harlem Renaissance to 1940* (Detroit: Gale Research Company, 1987); *Afro-American Writers, 1940–1955* (Detroit: Gale Research Company, 1988).

6. Arthur P. Davis, J. Saunders Redding, and Joyce A. Joyce, eds., *The New Cavalcade* (Washington, D.C.: Howard University Press, 1992).

7. Jessie Carney Smith, *Notable Black American Women* (Detroit: Gale Research Company, 1992); Darlene Clark Hine, *Black Women in America: An Historical Encyclopedia*, 2 vols. (Brooklyn, N.Y.: Carlson, 1993).

8. Thadious M. Davis, *Nella Larsen, Novelist of the Harlem Renaissance: A Woman's Life* (Baton Rouge: Louisiana State University Press, 1994).

9. Ann Petry, *The Street* (1946; Boston: Beacon Press, 1985); Alice Childress, *Like One of the Family . . . Conversations from a Domestic's Life* (1956; Boston: Beacon Press, 1986).

Said But Not Spoken

Elision and the Representation of Rape, Race, and Gender in Harriet E. Wilson's *Our Nig*

RONNA C. JOHNSON

Many critics and historians have established the idea that rape and its threat, as well as struggles to meet dictates of the code of "true womanhood," placed intertwined burdens on the narrative self-representation of antebellum black women. In Harriet E. Wilson's *Our Nig: or, Sketches from the Life of a Free Black*, white male sexual abuse is a powerful if unspoken threat to the protagonist, Frado, though a threat suggested only indirectly, by means of the author's and the narrator's interventions and narrative elisions. Wilson's representation of Frado's vulnerability to sexual abuse fits into her promise of a narrative that discloses southern slavery's "appurtenances North" but one that does not "divulge every transaction" constituting the life of the "Free Black" subject.[1] Nevertheless, to date commentators have sought primarily to situate *Our Nig* within the historical and literary discourse of related period texts, such as those by Harriet Beecher Stowe, Frederick Douglass, Harriet Jacobs, and Elizabeth Keckley, focusing on Wilson's use of the received structures of the sentimental novel and the slave narrative.[2] Though many commentators have noted what Henry Louis Gates Jr. has termed the text's "silences and lacunae," these have not been examined in connection with a sustained and powerful, albeit oblique, representation of sexual abuse.[3] Yet these lacunae and other narrative discontinuities allusively divulge a history of abuse of the indentured Frado that is elided in the tale.

Our Nig's representation of Frado's indenture follows codes for true womanhood by inscribing elisions in the narrative. This discursive activity produces and preserves a surface of narrative modesty that attests to authorial "concern for discursive respectability."[4] But by coding sexual abuse of the protagonist in narrative irregularities that point to its elisions, the text subverts its avowed reticence to suggest the full implications for gender and sexuality of a northern indenture that replicates southern slavery. That is, *Our Nig* says figuratively through narrative structure what cannot be confessed in speech: the sexual transgression against the black female. Constituting what

Claudia Tate correctly characterizes as the text's "deliberately constructed double-voiced representations," narrative irregularities replicate structurally the double silences of sexual exploitation and its socially and formally coerced denial.[5] Further, *Our Nig*'s assertions of omissions match lacunae in representations of the Bellmont men, and their trespasses, once recognized, provide conjunctions that unify the otherwise disjunctive narrative of the tale.

We are invited to trace a coded subtext by *Our Nig* itself. The text both announces its narrative inhibition and hints at the causes. Statements made in the preface by Wilson and in the conclusion by the omniscient narrator alert us to confessional constraints on the text that prompt its inscription of an enigma. Assertions in the preface that "every transaction" of Wilson's and Frado's often conflated stories is not "divulged," that Wilson has "purposely omitted what would provoke most shame" in white abolitionists, and the warning in the text's closing that "some part of [Frado's] history is unknown save by the Omniscient God" all imply narrative inhibitions and elisions that challenge assumptions about the tale as told. These admonitions resonate with sexual implications that cannot be stated directly; indeed, from *Clarissa* to *The Color Purple*, confidences entrusted by women in narrative to "the Omniscient God" have signified sexual violation. In this, *Our Nig*'s claims to narrative silence ominously remind us that for black women, the southern slavery to which Frado's northern indenture is compared meant rape. And the egregiousness of this common trauma was doubled by patriarchal ideologies of racism and of slavery as an institution, both of which made it virtually impossible to declare the occurrence of rape without inculpating the (black female) victim and exculpating the (white male) perpetrator.[6]

Thus *Our Nig* reserves a subtextual discursive space in which is inscribed what antebellum dominative discourse forbids, assertions of white male exploitation of black female sexuality. Or, the narrative expresses subtextually experiences that, in Wilson's words in the preface, she "do[es] not pretend to divulge"; this labored phrase itself typifies the text's "double-voiced representations" because it suggests that textual reticence "pretends" to keep secret something that is nevertheless said. The allusive subtext of *Our Nig* signifies through disruptive signifiers, destabilizing tropes, and effaced analogies that constitute a second, encoded narrative voice, which may be called that of the signatory "Our Nig," who mediates between author Wilson and protagonist Frado. The subtext signifies structurally in correspondences between avowed lacunae in the narrative and discrepancies and discontinuities in storytelling that the surface tale reveals but denies are there. Exemplifying this double-voiced textuality, the preface offers oblique, coded explanations for narrative inhibition that contextualize the story's elisions. In Wilson's usage in the preface, slavery itself is a veiled reference to or code for rape, for the word "slavery" occurs in conjunction with a shame that she wants to avoid by censoring disclosure. Wilson claims that she would not "palliate slavery at the South, by disclosures of its appurtenances North" and that she has "purposely omitted what would most provoke shame in our good anti-slavery friends." Her insistence on omissions effects a complicated double move that practices what Elizabeth Fox-Genovese calls "discursive respectability" but simultaneously inscribes the incidence of something shameful, and discursively binds it to slavery.

Moreover, establishing the coded relationship with the narrative that characterizes the subtext, this avowal of an unnamed shame associated with slavery flags, and is correlated with, a marked omission in the text's account of Frado's indenture. The narrative explicitly recounts Frado's endurance of virtually every form of psychic and physical violence associated with slavery, except the shame often imposed on the black female subject, rape. The relentless account of abuses Frado suffers calls into question Wilson's claim of omissions and, because it is so graphic, the account uneasily points to sexuality. This reading foregrounds gender, which is first displaced by Wilson in the preface onto political discourses via abolition, and then underplayed in the narrative's account of Frado's indenture. Foregrounding gender clarifies that Wilson's concern for discursive modesty expressly limits narrative self-representation with regard to sexual experience. Just so, sexual exploitation is the one "shame" specific to black women's experience of slavery that is conspicuously missing from the narrative's list of abuses. This absence works with other irregularities to evoke allusively the full implications of slavery for the black female body in Frado's northern indenture. Tropes, eccentric signifiers, and narrative discontinuities palpably signify the repressed material of the subtext and permit us to identify and name as a presence an absence that is said to be omitted.

This dimension of Wilson's narrative and the subtext's detectable referent of sexual abuse are elucidated by a textual reading cast from feminist, historicist, and Freudian perspectives. Because women are objects, not subjects, of dominative discourses of sexuality, Wilson's inability to state directly aspects of Frado's experience reflects power hierarchies that forbid black women from representing their sexuality. To contend with these environmental constraints on women's self-representation, Hortense Spillers has argued that it is incumbent on feminist critics to "supply the missing words" of female sexual experience by "actively imagin[ing] women in their living . . . confrontations with experience (at least, the way they report it)."[7] The subtext of *Our Nig* must be "actively imagine[d]" in order to bring into view what Wilson warns has been "purposely omitted" but what, as Freud notes of repressed material, returns to be detected. Attention to the manner of *Our Nig* resorts to inscribing crucial aspects of Frado's life aslant, in enigmatic allusions; as Barbara Christian aptly characterizes its contingent expressions, "scenes of attempted or covert seduction . . . might be implied in scenes in *Our Nig*'s transgressive subtext, which resists black female disempowerment in gender- and race-coded antebellum discourses by saying without speaking its confession to 'the Omniscient God.'"[8]

Our Nig's coded, subversive expressions take the form of textual elisions and narrative inconsistencies, such as those inhering in representations of the Bellmont men, as well as charged rhetorical figures, such as the eye rhyme Frado/Fido (the name of a dog) and the repeating signifier of a silver half-dollar. Anomalous fictive material in the text's opening chapters, which recount the life of Frado's mother Mag Smith, provides for a displaced representation of aspects of Frado's experience that are effaced in the tale. And in the tale's closing, an encoded biblical metaphor connects sexual impropriety with slavery and with Frado's indenture. These elements constitute the obscured subtext wherein the revelations alluded to by the text find discursive expression, where otherwise unspoken instances of Frado's experience are inscribed in tropic figures, textual reticences, and narrative discrepancies and allusions. A speaker of the unspoken is named on the title page, where it is said that *Our Nig* is "By 'Our Nig.'" The Signatory "Our Nig" is neither the historical personage Harriet E. Wilson nor the fictive protagonist Frado, but a disembodied figure that mediates between these two textual positions. A signifier for the subtext and a discursive product of the mystified aspects of the narrative, "Our Nig" is resonantly manifest in the encoded biblical metaphor with which the tale ends.

The symbolically supercharged sentence that concludes the tale mirrors and elaborates Wilson's assertions that parts of Frado's story remain untold. The text concludes with Chapter 12, subtitled "The Winding Up of the Matter," which recounts Frado's marriage to Samuel, a black man posing as a runaway slave, his abandonment of Frado after the birth of their son, and Samuel's untimely death from yellow fever. The final paragraph of the chapter acts as a coda to the tale's account of Frado's life; it summarizes the fate of members of the Bellmont family. This survey of the Bellmonts and the tale itself ends with this sentence: "Frado has passed from [the Bellmonts'] memories, as Joseph from the butler's, but she will never cease to track them till beyond mortal vision" (131). This magisterial pronouncement intoned by "Our Nig" suggests a motive of revenge in the preceding narrative, which, as a text that may survive its time, is a vehicle for tracking its objects beyond the living sight of its enunciator. The revenge of "Our Nig" is effected in the subtext of *Our Nig*, which is likewise a vehicle for surpassing narrative limits into an ineradicable, continuous present; the subtext is ineradicable because, like "Our Nig," it is not directly inscribed and thus is not vulnerable to expurgation. Although the subject Frado is the forgotten object of the Bellmont family memory, their perfidy is unforgotten, preserved subtextually in the biblical allusion that posits a metaphoric equivalence between Frado and the Bellmonts and Joseph and the butler.

The metaphor alludes to Genesis 39–42, which recounts the tale of Joseph, a Hebrew slave, and the Egyptian butler, both confined to Pharoah's prison. Joseph correctly interprets a dream the butler has about fertility and charges the butler to intercede with Pharoah on his behalf. The butler forgets Joseph until Pharoah has an enigmatic dream; then he recalls the clever interpreter still in prison. Joseph is summoned and correctly interprets Pharoah's dream of seven years of feast and seven years of famine. He is pardoned and rewarded with a high position in Pharoah's service, a happy ending to the ungrateful butler's lapse of memory. On its surface the analogy likens the Bellmonts to the butler as self-absorbed forgetters of their debt to a "slave," Frado. But the story of how Joseph came to be in Pharoah's prison, as well as his talent for renarrating or interpreting dreams, are significant buried elements of the biblical allusion, and they point to a similarly obscured sexual discourse in *Our Nig*.

The story of how Joseph came to be in prison might be said to be a slave narrative, while the last line of *Our Nig* suggests that it is an allegory of or analogous to Joseph's slave narrative. Before his imprisonment, Joseph is overseer of his master's house. He is recognized because he is "handsome and goodlooking" (Gen. 39:7), in the same way that Frado is initially valued by Jack for being "real handsome and bright, and not very black either" (25). Joseph becomes an object of sexual interest to his master's opposite, Potiphar's wife, who "cast her eyes upon" him and behind Potiphar's back repeatedly begs Joseph to "lie with her," an invitation Joseph steadfastly refuses (Gen. 39: 8–13). The analogy to Frado locates her as an object of sexual interest to her mistress's opposites, the Bellmont men, and indeed the story of their activities behind Mrs. Bellmont's back forms the subject of the tale's subtext. The gender bias of the dominative mode is evident in the sexual politics played out in the continued parallels between the biblical tale and the antebellum one. Frado's seduction is elided in the text because black women's discursive disempowerment assures that it would be read as implicating her. And this is precisely the same reason that Joseph's seduction by Potiphar's wife *can* be disclosed: it implicates the female. In both cases men are exonerated of desirousness or desirability; both are ascribed to women.

In the biblical story, Potiphar's wife, the spurned sexual aggressor enraged by her defeat, steals Joseph's garment to prove her false accusation that Joseph "came in to lie with" her (Gen. 39:8). Occupying the social position that ensures her version will prevail, Potiphar's wife reverses the facts with her lie and causes Potiphar to send Joseph to prison for refusing her; she mobilizes patriarchal power to effect her revenge. Still, like the antebellum tale that survives the Bellmonts and proves (their) northern white racism, the biblical tale that survives Potiphar's wife testifies to her perfidy. In the biblical tale, the victim of sexual aggression (the "slave" Joseph) is discursively rendered the predator by false testimony. Just so, on the plantation white male sexual violence was falsely ascribed to black female carnality, for prevailing essentialist ideologies of race assigned lasciviousness to the black female and masked white male culpability and sexual agency. In *Our Nig*, the Bellmont men are likewise invisible to their exercise of patriarchal "law." Joseph is never cleared of the charges of Potiphar's wife, even though they are shown to be fabricated; the stain of sexual transgression is never bleached from his person. But when Joseph interprets Pharoah's dream, when he retells a narrative to foreground its hidden meaning, he is freed and promoted to power. Similarly, the signatory "Our Nig" is never cleared of Frado's humiliating experience, but nevertheless achieves power and subjectivity by conveying hidden aspects of Frado's indenture in a metaphoric subtext of the narrative.

Thus the metaphor likening Frado and the Bellmonts to Joseph and the butler provides an allusive entry to the subtext or effaced sexual discourse of *Our Nig*. The subtext preserves yet subverts discursive modesty; it asserts black female subjectivity by alluding to white male sexual abuse without implicating Frado. Its double-voiced, indirect inscriptions are the means by which, in Gates's terms, the black-as-object may transform herself into the black-as-subject (1983, lv), eluding inculpation (here, the charges of sexual impropriety from which Joseph is never exonerated) by effacing the sexual discourse of the biblical slave narrative to which Frado's life is likened.[9] "Enough," the omniscient narrator insists at the tale's close, "has been unrolled to demand your sympathy" (130); enough, that is, has been provided to effect Frado's discursive status as a subject who renders her oppressors the objects of her discourse. The biblical metaphor represents Frado's shift from object to subject by drawing a connection between one common occasion for narrative, the restoration of (the Bellmonts') "forgotten" memories, and a part of Frado's experience that remains undivulged, (the Bellmonts') sexual predation. The text's unnameable "shame" is thus figured slantwise, as it were, and figured as the Bellmonts' transgression, in the metaphor's repressed allusion to Potiphar's wife. Matching this allusive manner of inscription and reiterating its claims, the text's opening chapters provide an account of Frado's mother that offers further correspondences to its avowed omissions and likewise points to a repressed discourse of sexual experience.

The question of Wilson's autobiographical relation to *Our Nig* has been of strong interest to scholars wishing to authenticate the text. The outline of Frado's experience has been matched to known facts of Wilson's life, permitting a general identification of author and protagonist. The exception to these equivalences is *Our Nig*'s account of Mag Smith, which occupies the first two chapters. Claudia Tate concludes that "all the events in the first two chapters must be presumed fictional inasmuch as their factual construction is beyond the competence of a young child's memory and understanding." Similarly, Henry Louis Gates maintains that "these early chapters describe events far removed from the author's experiences . . . [which] she cannot claim to recollect clearly and some which she cannot recollect at all, such as the courtship and marriage of her mother." Gates suggests that disparities in the text's opening chapters, where first-person chapter titles head third-person narration, evince Wilson's "anxiety about identifying with events in the text which she cannot claim to recollect," whereas later in the text, when Wilson treats events within her living memory, (auto)biographical and fictional points neatly overlap. It is salient that the events with which *Our Nig* begins, events Gates terms a source of authorial anxiety because they eclipse Wilson's experience, represent transgressions of female sexuality and respectability. Specifically, as Tate notes, these events are "elaborately constructed mitigations of what Mag's white culture regards as numerous transgressions of feminine virtue." They represent unfortunate sexual experiences that have befallen a *white* woman. The racial distinction is a determinative element of the subtextual allusions encoded in the parallels between Mag's story and Frado's.[10]

The first two chapters of *Our Nig* recount events of Mag Smith's life that Wilson could not have witnessed in her own mother's life. The authorial anxiety they reveal coincides with their content of female sexual experience, material that antebellum black female authors were unable to treat directly in their narrative self-representations. Differences in narrative candor with regard to Mag's and Frado's sexual experiences and conjugal histories measure inequities in discursive and experiential possibilities and privileges that derive from racial caste disparities. Mag is white, her daughter Frado, though half-white, is designated black. The limits in the antebellum era (as today) of what might be said of (and by) white women and of (and by) black women about their sexual experiences diverge significantly at the point at which the female is blamed for male desire. The lapses of white women like Mag Smith, as *Our Nig* shows, may be charitably adduced to misfortune and poverty; for black women who like Frado are conscripted into virtual slavery because of the social meaning given to their color, no charitable explanations obtain. In racialized antebellum codes for the feminine, black women are either virtuous or fallen. Any account of Frado's sexuality that might compromise her virtuous status must be repressed or told by indirection. Let us then consider the fictive story of Mag Smith's life as a displaced representation of parts of Frado's story, as the first-person chapter titles imply. And as the third-person narration of these chapters intimate, this story of Mag Smith cannot be ascribed to Frado/Wilson, a strategy that preserves their good repute. Read as an allusive inscription of parts of Frado's story that are prohibited from the narrative of *Our Nig* because of its era's "social requirement for female sexual reticence," the story of Mag Smith correlates to Wilson's claims of omissions.[11]

Key parallels between Frado's narrated life and Mag's place them in a discursive, rather than solely familial, relation, and the narrative's directness in recounting Mag's life allows us to perceive what is veiled in its account of Frado's. Both Mag and Frado are "early deprived of parental guardianship, far removed from relatives" (5); Mag is said to have "merged into womanhood, unprotected, uncherished, uncared for" (5), a phrase repeated when Frado enters maturity (115). Both women marry black men in hopes of improving their economic lot: Mag can either "beg my living, or get it from" Jim (13), while Frado's marriage to Samuel promises her "the relief of looking to another for comfortable support" (127). Both mother and daughter are rendered destitute by the unexpected deaths of their black husbands; both are left to maintain children, and each in desperation sends a child out to foster care. Mag's relinquishment of Frado begins the story that constitutes the tale proper, while Frado's relinquishment of her son is one of the events with which this same tale closes. This reversed parallel calls attention to the opening and the closing of the narrative.

Further differences in structural correspondences between Mag's and Frado's stories point to lacunae in the narrative. In another reversed parallel, Mag's destitution and desperate marriage to a black man form the near beginning of the account of her life, while Frado's parallel destitution and marriage to a black man end the account of hers. Mag's story begins before her marriage, with her seduction and subsequent abandonment by an unseen, unnamed, implicitly white man who deceives her. This event, which precedes marriage to a black man, has no explicit parallel in the account of Frado's life before *her* marriage to a black man. The story told about Mag's seduction before her marriage suggests an effaced correspondence in the story of Frado's indenture: the elision of sexual experience preceding her marriage. Frado's metaphoric equivalence to the sexually wronged Joseph of Genesis in the text's last line and the repression of Joseph's sexual history in the metaphor point to a repressed story that is conveyed subtextually in structural juxtapositions and parallels between Frado's life and Mag's.

Turning from structural to figural inscriptions of Frado's sexual exploitation, we turn to *Our Nig*'s indictment of northern white racism. This discourse encompasses the text's apparent origin in maternal economic necessity and its allusions to slavery and connects them to an effaced discourse of sexuality. Because Frado is the child Mag must leave with another family to ensure her own economic survival, Frado becomes the abused "nig" whose experiences provide the narrative. Because she is later a mother who must herself put her son in foster care to ensure his survival, Frado is provided the occasion of telling her story. Because Wilson must provide maintenance for son and self, she produces *Our Nig* as a commercial "experiment," as she says in the preface. Only the signatory "Our Nig" lacks an economic motive for narrative; the biblical metaphor suggests a wish to revenge the Bellmonts' ingratitude, or their racism. As a discursive figure mediating the textual positions of Wilson and Frado, "Our Nig" also mediates economic motives and those of revenge, connecting and subordinating maternal economic necessity to northern white racism. Alluding to slavery's exploitation of the black female body by showing that racist assumptions underlie Frado's northern indenture, disruptive tropes and signifiers suggest that the narrative's economic motive is a screen. These narrative figures expose the sexual aspect of the antebellum economic exploitation of the black female body by conveying subtextually Frado's carnal commodity value for the Bellmonts.

Our Nig undertakes to represent and thus to expose the way race overdetermines northern indenture as a replication of slavery for the black female subject. Evelyn Brooks Higginbotham notes that "race came to life primarily as the signifier of the master/slave relation and thus emerged superimposed upon class and property relations."[12] Just so, Frado is conscripted to virtual slavery in the white Bellmont household because "the nigger in the child" (26), as Mrs. Bellmont puts it, signifies that her "time and person belonged solely to" the family (41). Her "shade" (39) means Frado may be "train[ed] up . . . from a child" (26) to do Mrs. Bellmont's work; for Mrs. Bellmont as for the plantation owner, a "dozen" children so complected would be "better than one" (26). Thus the Bellmonts' "Two-story White House, North" is conflated with the white-pillared southern plantation, where pigmentation differentiates master from slave. Yet even this apparent, if provocative, equation of northern indenture with southern slavery is complicated by figural inscriptions or transgressions denied *both* north and south. Frado's indenture is amplified in *Our Nig*'s subtext as a racialized condition that implicates her body beyond compulsory labor and corporal punishment. Disruptive tropes and signifiers effect the text's embedded social critique by suggesting that Frado's body is available to satisfy not only Mrs. Bellmont's avarice and sadistic impulses, but also (white male) carnal desires suppressed in the text.[13] For example, the disconcerting eye rhyme Frado/Fido constitutes a trope for Frado's commodification and conveys otherwise unspoken aspects of her status. Forged in the slippage between the names Frado and Fido, the rhyme problematizes signification by playing the terms against each other and thus destabilizing apparently innocuous narrative contexts. This figural play insists that the text's allegory of slavery represents the black female body in ways not directly expressible.

First, the narrative posits Frado's equivalence to a dog in the eyes of the Bellmont men when the son Jack remarks, "'Father is a sensible man . . . He would not wrong a dog. Where *is* Frado?'" (35–36, emphasis Wilson's). Jack's association to Frado from the dog his father would not wrong conflates the two and fixes the child in an animal register of discourse. Jack's remark occurs when his sister Mary has accused Frado of lying about an event in which Mary is to blame for her misfortune. The full context of his remark links the child's discursive equivalence to an animal with racialized privileges of speech and with representations of violence that have sexual connotations.

"It is very strange you will believe what others say against your sister," retorted his mother, with flashing eye. "I think it is time your father subdued you."

"Father is a sensible man," argued Jack. "He would not wrong a dog. Where *is* Frado?" he continued. (35–36)

Pointing to the fictive and intentional nature of this discourse, pointing to the hand of "Our Nig," Frado is not present for this exchange; she is in another part of the house, "her mouth wedged apart, her face swollen, and full of pain" (36). That is, she is being tortured and silenced for providing testimony that contravenes (Mary's) privileged white control of representation. Moreover, the threat Frado's speech poses to white hegemony is also ascribed to Jack, who ought to be "subdued" for his imputed preference for Frado over his white kin. This preference circularly implies an incestuous connection (he should prefer his sister to Frado, according to Mrs. Bellmont), a taint that is underscored by the suggestion of bestiality in Jack's elliptical association of Frado to a dog. Earlier, Mary herself wishes "to use physical force 'to subdue [Frado],' to 'keep her down'" (33); the repetition of "subdue" with regard to Jack's behavior discursively links him to Frado: both commit offenses to his sister and his mother. Jack's preferences should be "subdued" by an intervening father, but the Bellmont father "would not wrong a dog." This curious, eccentric figure of speech calls further attention to a transgressive subtext, for what can it mean to say that a person is so "sensible" that "he would not wrong a dog." The referent of the metaphor is Jack; he is the dog in question. But it is Frado who occasions the metaphor, Frado to whom Jack's thoughts turn, so the metaphor becomes a discursive turn by which a carnal link is established between Jack and Frado in the animal register of discourse. Furthermore, because his father is too "sensible" to "subdue" Jack, the alliance or link between Jack and Frado contravenes only Mrs. Bellmont's privilege. For it is Frado, the racial other, and her "jollity" (a racialized code word) whom Mrs. Bellmont would differentiate through the exercise of her power to subdue or "quench by whipping or scolding" (38); it is this racially differentiated Frado whom Jack prefers, defends, and conflates with a dog. As Jack's remark implies, it is Frado whom the Bellmonts treat like a dog.

Then a real dog, Fido, enters the narrative in another curious inscription: Jack "resolved to do what he could to protect [Frado] from Mary and his mother. He bought her a dog, which became a favorite with both" (37). The juxtaposition of Jack's resolve to protect Frado with his procurement of a dog both he and Frado enjoy forms an unsettling non sequitur that suggests something is elided between resolution and procurement. It enigmatically aligns the dog's purchase with Frado's physical vulnerability, which is earlier specifically linked to her testimony, the very act of discursive subjectivity that challenges and contravenes white control of representation. Further, the cryptic phrase "do what he could" flags a variance between Jack's real power as a white male to protect Frado and his procurement of a pet for her, a token more suggestive of an exchange than an act in her defense. The subtle irregularity of this passage recounting Jack's purchase of the dog typifies the narrative's encoded subtextual discourse of "transactions" not "divulged," in Wilson's words.

In the same indirect and asymmetrical way, the eye rhyme Frado/Fido is charged with commodity and carnal associations. These associations are part of the discourse of slavery and serve to define Frado's indenture as an enslavement. The rhyme posits what Jack's remark conflating Frado with a dog implies, that a dog is Frado's discursive equivalent. The slippage between the names Frado/Fido inscribes Frado's status as the Bellmont's pet, a status borne out by the amusement of the Bellmont males and their hired men at her capering and prank-playing. Not only an extension of the child, the dog is a projection of a self split off from Frado in the narrative; he embodies her commodity value. Fido is bought by Jack, sold by Mrs. Bellmont, and "obtained" again by Mr. Bellmont (61–62). Like the people traded on plantations, Fido possesses exchange value: in him, Frado's debased chattel status is inscribed;

through him, her indenture is equated with slavery. Moreover, Jack's purchase of the dog suggests the protection bribed sexual exploitation may have afforded female slaves, as does his subsequent gratification because the "gift" of Fido to Frado "answer[ed] his intentions" (42). Like the silver half-dollar he later gives the child, Fido may answer his intention to reward or bribe Frado for services that the dog's animal representation of her enslaved self suggests are carnal. Commenting on Fido's "dog-agility" in learning tricks—itself a phrase containing the potential for sexual double entendre about positions and dexterousness in intercourse—Jack "pronounced him very knowing" (42). This anthropomorphic phrase alerts us to a discontinuity between subject and rhetoric that suggests a premature knowing or expertise in the child for whom Fido represents a split-off self. This knowing is discontinuous with what the narrative represents overtly, but it correlates with the text's warnings of omissions. In one of many phrases that establish the eye rhyme, it is said that "Fido was the entire confidant of Frado" (41); he is the repository and embodiment of secrets suppressed in this narrative said to contain omissions.

Thus the eye rhyme Frado/Fido indicates the narrative's encoded subtext, and Fido marks discursive space signifying the unspeakable in Frado's life among the Bellmonts. Wilson observes in the preface that her life would be "declare[d] unfavorable in comparison with treatment of legal bondmen." So too Frado's treatment by the Bellmonts is unfavorable in comparison to Fido's. Thus, parting with Fido at the end of her indenture, Frado leaves behind her status as pet, her degrading obligation to entertain in order to survive, her life that is worse than the life of her dog. Fido signifies the child Frado was and simultaneously evokes the one she was never permitted to be. *Our Nig* represents de facto slavery in the North in its depiction of Frado's treatment as property acquired and nurtured for the purpose of whites' economic gain and comfort. Although the economic motives and exploitive racist views that render Frado's northern indenture the image of southern slavery are overtly depicted, undertones of sexuality complicate the process of signification. Racial differentiation, profit, and violence are discursively interrelated in unsettling, transgressive figures, as in the following exchange between the senior Bellmonts:

"Why, according to you and James, we should very soon have her in the parlor, as smart as our own girls. It's of no use talking to you or James. If you should go on as you would like, it would not be six months before she would be leaving me; and that won't do. Just think of how much profit she was to us last summer. We had no work hired out; she did the work of two girls—"

"And got the whippings for two with it!" remarked Mr. Bellmont.

"I'll beat the money out of her, if I can't get her worth any other way,"
retorted Mrs. B. sharply. (89–90)

The Bellmont men would like to "go on" with Frado in a way that ostensibly
threatens categories of racial differentiation and Mrs. Bellmont's power, her
"right" to "beat the money out of" Frado, a phrase linking profit to violence.
But the men's imputed wish to have Frado in the parlor marks discursive space
for another kind of transgression, one that does not destabilize hierarchies of
racial difference. Barbara Omolade observes of slavery's binary racial ethos
that "the category 'white' would also mean that the people designated 'black'
could be held in perpetual slavery." [14] The converse also holds true, that the
category "black" means that those designated "white" would embody and enjoy hegemonic power and freedom. These are race-coded privileges Mrs. Bellmont retains by preserving distinctions between Frado and her daughters that
define Frado as an economic asset and proof of white power, to which the
stripes that scar her body attest. But, and this is to the point, these distinctions
may be securely preserved even if the men's wish to have Frado in the parlor
is realized. For their desire to "go on" with Frado evokes another register of
profit made at her expense, that of sexual exploitation, a kind of profit authorized by empowered categories of racial differentiation and which nevertheless infuriates Mrs. Bellmont. [15] The allusion to an unrepresented desire of the
Bellmont men points to the text's declared silences and the subtext that voices
them, to aspects of the female slave narrative that are repressed in *Our Nig*.

The narrative of *Our Nig* plainly describes the protagonist's endurance of
starvation, torture, beating, overwork, exposure to natural elements, sadistic
psychological conditioning, and spiritual deprivation. Which is to say that the
unexpurgated narrative plainly describes acts committed by Mrs. Bellmont,
an admitted "right she-devil" (17). Because they are recounted, these acts
cannot correspond to the text's avowed reticences. Let me say here that I appreciate and in no way intend to diminish or mitigate the text's depiction of
white middle-class female brutality in the abuse meted out to Frado by Mrs.
Bellmont and Mary. *Our Nig's* representation of white female agency and responsibility for racial exploitation constitutes a fundamental indictment. Set-
tling for this indictment at face value, however, risks a reading that underesti-
mates its complex sophistication of expression. Such a reading also in effect
repeats the silencing of women which sexual violence at least in part aims to
achieve, and it preserves the immunity of white male sexual privilege, the
privilege to trespass without penalty. Thus it is important to note that while
Mrs. Bellmont is emphatically visible in her cruel displays of "vixen nature"
(41), the men who are Frado's reputed allies are curiously invisible in their

practice of sympathy, which is not to say that they do not intervene, only that their intervention is unrepresented in the narrative. Discrepancies and discontinuities in representations of the Bellmont men create a narrative vacuum that is inscribed as elision. These elisions reserve discursive space for the only abuse that is not explicitly represented in the narrative: sexual exploitation.

The Bellmont men are said to be, in the person of the father, the "law" whose "word once spoken admitted of no appeal" (31), yet they present themselves as Mrs. Bellmont's subordinates. The father claims he cannot stop his wife's abuse of Frado because "women rule the earth, and all in it," and his intervention would consign him to "live in hell meantime" (44). This claim blatantly contradicts what the tale repeatedly dramatizes, that his word *is* "law"; that he is an intercessor in domestic affairs "who could not be denied" (83). Mr. Bellmont is the patriarch of "determined eye" and "decisive manner" whose direct order "'not [to] strike, or scald, or skin'" Frado (47) in fact does stop his wife's abuse, with no apparent cost to himself. His claim to the contrary suggests a cover-up, especially considering its distortion of white women's worldly power, which, even in the nineteenth-century middle-class home, was far inferior to that of white males, as indeed Mr. Bellmont's infrequent but always successful interventions demonstrate. His claim of inferiority to Mrs. Bellmont is further contradicted by its textualization as direct discourse, which reifies his subjectivity and power of self-representation. Moreover, although the men represent themselves as powerless before a sadistic Mrs. Bellmont, she is said to be "always foiled" (87) when she complains to them of Frado. And the men who alone possess the absolute power to intervene do so mostly in one way: they repeatedly take Frado to her room, or to theirs, to comfort her. For example, after one terrible scene, Jack, who "pitie[s]" Frado, "comforted her as well as he knew how, sat by her till she fell asleep, and then left for the sitting room" (36). That is, the men express their alleged discomfort with Mrs. Bellmont's violence by closeting themselves with Frado in a bedroom away from her, a response that vitiates their supposed beneficence. Evincing patriarchal privilege, what goes on in those closeted bedrooms is unseen, undramatized, elided; it is an exercise of patriarchal "law" that correlates to the text's claim of omissions.

The "deleted sexuality" Claudia Tate feels "looming in these episodes" may also provide a deleted explanation for Mrs. Bellmont's violence.[16] Harriet Jacobs, Frederick Douglass, and numerous historians document that, rather than identify with black female victims of rape, white mistresses often brutally punished black women for the sexual transgressions of their white men.[17] Thus Mrs. Bellmont's violence may also register rage at trespasses her men commit; it may express more without explicitly disclosing anything other than her well-known "vixen nature" (41). The men's prerogative of "law" above all ensures their sexual freedom, which they possess exclusively and whose exercise is not explicitly represented but may be felt to reverberate in Mrs. Bellmont's violence. Her violence is so excessive that it suggests a displacement that masks a shame even she is not empowered to speak. This interpretation is advanced by the narrative's manipulation of a silver half-dollar, a signifier for sexual transgression that inculpates the son Jack by its repetition in a later scene involving Mrs. Bellmont. The textualization of the coin provides an example of what Tate calls the text's tendency to "unsettling narrative repetitions"; it is one of those fraught "textual disruptions," because in both instances that Frado receives a silver half-dollar (from Jack and from Mrs. Bellmont), Fido is dramatically or discursively invoked, infusing the half-dollar signifier with carnal associations established in the dog.[18]

The coin first appears in a scene of Frado's resistance to Mrs. Bellmont's tyrannical regime. In this scene, Frado is commanded by Mrs. Bellmont to eat from her used dinner plate instead of a clean one.[19] Frado resists this humiliation with a gesture of contempt for Mrs. Bellmont: she bids Fido to lick the plate clean, "then, wiping her knife and fork on the cloth, she proceeded to eat her dinner" (71); predictably, Mrs. Bellmont explodes. Her comeuppance especially amuses her son Jack. "Boiling over with laughter" (72), he recounts the scene to James in Frado's presence and, "pulling a bright, silver half-dollar from his pocket, he threw it at Nig, saying 'There, take that; 'twas worth paying for'" (72). The half-dollar is an ambiguous signifier of payment to Frado for Jack's satisfaction because of the male-coded sexual innuendo in the phrase "boiling over." Jack ostensibly rewards Frado for her comic performance, which recalls literary and historical accounts of slaves rewarded for providing their masters' entertainment.[20] But Frado's humiliation of Jack's mother inscribes a darker association to chattel slavery, for slaves were surely not rewarded for mocking their masters. In this, the coin evokes payment often made to female salves, as bell hooks notes, to encourage their entry into prostitution or to reward their submission to white male sexual demand.[21] Demonstrating his approval of Frado's humiliation of his mother, Jack is linked to Frado in a transgressive behavior that is represented with sexual overtones and which is offered in his ambiguous, sexualized way as an explanation of his mother's rage and violence.

Historians note both that a female slave's acquiescence to white male sexual advances might offer a modicum of protection for herself or her family and that sexual exploitation was "used as a punishment or demanded in exchange for leniency."[22] *Our Nig* depicts the Bellmont men as sources of such protection for Frado. James provides Frado "shelter" from "maltreatment" (67) and "shield[s] her from many beatings" (76). Jack "resolves to do what he could to protect her from . . . his mother" (37); "with Jack near [Frado] did not fear her" (71). What Frado pays for this shelter may be inferred from an exchange that precedes Mrs. Bellmont's humiliation at the dinner table:

> "Where are your curls, Fra?" asked Jack, after the usual saluation.
> "Your mother cut them off."
> "Thought you were getting handsome, did she? Same old story, is it; knocks and bumps? Better times coming; never fear, Nig."
> How different this appelative sounded from him; he said it in such a tone, with such a rogueish look!
> She laughed, and replied that he had better take her West for a house-keeper. (70)

Jack's persistent attention to Frado's "glossy ringlets" (68) recalls his first comment about her, which sets an ominous tone for her indenture: "'Keep her,' said Jack. 'She's real handsome and bright, and not very black, either'" (25). She is black enough to define white but not so black as to repel whites. In Jack's eyes, Frado is an attractive object, "that pretty little Nig" (47) he writes of to his brother James. All this intrusive attention to Frado's body resounds in Jack's question, "Where are your curls, Fra?" (70) and challenges its apparently innocuous jocoseness. The narrative's acquiescence to the hated "appelative" "Nig" implies the conditions of his protection: a coerced, sexualized familiarity or intimacy or possession. Frado's rejoinder that he should take her away for his housekeeper is understood as a wish to escape Mrs. Bellmont, although in this context it sounds coy. However, it is reported in indirect discourse, which discursively demonstrates Frado's submission to Jack's terms of interest, but in a disembodied way that precludes her subjectivity. The phrase implies Frado's acquiescence in her abused object status, but in fact it also shows Frado's objectification, which is manifest in the text but not spoken (and therefore not agreed upon) by her; she is stripped of subjectivity in the phrases that imply her cooperation. And that is the point: Jack's interest in Frado, signified by his trivializing attention to her shorn hair and beaten body ("knocks and bumps") is the sign of her objectification, not its antidote. Thus *Our Nig* shows that Bellmont male protection against maternal violence is sexualized and is itself a source of Frado's objectification.[23] This is one reason the narrative comes into being: so that the signatory "Our Nig," who mediates between Wilson and Frado and reigns in the subtext that neither author nor protagonist can own may condemn and subvert the hated "appelative" "Nig."

The sexualized associations of the silver half-dollar are intensified with its repetition. Frado's indenture finally ends in her eighteenth year, and we are told that "Mrs. Bellmont dismissed her with the assurance that she would soon wish herself back again, and a present of a silver half-dollar" (117). The outrageous idea that Frado will regret her liberty calls attention to and taints this silver half-dollar, which, echoing the earlier scene of Mrs. Bellmont's humiliation, evokes Jack and links him to his mother's abuse.[24] The appearance of Mrs. Bellmont's unprecedented gift of a silver half-dollar in a context devoid of her customary violence encourages the inference that a customary violence is also elided in Jack's earlier such payment to Frado for his satisfaction. The repeated signifier linking son to mother connects the unseen to the seen, staining the son's reputed beneficence with the mother's violence. The repetition of the silver half-dollar disrupts the surface tales's gender asymmetry of good sons/bad mother, white male benignity/white female malevolence, and shows that sons and mother, white males and white females occupy the same discourse, the same subtext of omissions: a northern exploitation of Frado equivalent to that of the plantation and the sexual significance of that equivalence for the black female.

The silver half-dollar that subverts claims of white male beneficence by linking it to white female violence suggests that Mrs. Bellmont may provide a safe narrative site for expressing what cannot be said about the Bellmont men without connecting discourses that exonerate white male aggression with discourses that figure the "black woman as chronically promiscuous," in Angela Davis's words.[25] The transgressive subtext of *Our Nig* suggests that the Bellmont men do not view Frado in any significantly different way than does Mrs. Bellmont, but to name their violence would unroll a mobius strip of racist, patriarchal antebellum inversions that revise accounts of material reality to protect white men and to indict black women—indict Frado. Thus *Our Nig's* subtext of omissions, its manipulation of signifiers, as well as its textual elisions and discrepancies in story-telling suggest that the Bellmont men also partake of the "opportunity" Frado signifies to Mrs. Bellmont "to indulge her vixen nature" (41); they too partake of what is described as Mrs. Bellmont's "manifest enjoyment" in abusing Frado (66), her "excite[ment] by so much indulgence of a dangerous passion" (82). Indeed, such representations of Mrs. Bellmont's sadistic pleasure may signify sites of displacement for an indulgence the men practice unseen and that cannot be named except in the encoded subtextual discourse of the signatory "Our Nig."[26]

By coding white male sexual violence against the black female protagonist in the narrative's structures and figures rather than directly in the narration itself, *Our Nig* figures at once both the silence to which the female victim of sexual exploitation is enjoined and the invisibility enjoyed by the white male perpetrators. As a text coded for sexual transgression in its announced reticence, in its erasure of sexual violence and its effacement of perpetrators, *Our Nig* provides an account of its era's race and gender conventions. It is axiomatic that, above all, dictates of true womanhood oblige Wilson's indirection with regard to sexuality, the one part of Frado's story that is "unknown save by the Omniscient God" and prohibited from expression. Or from direct expression. *Our Nig* endeavors to say without speaking them the unnameable aspects of Frado's experience. It this, it conforms to true womanhood's prescriptions for female chastity and modesty, but it also indicates the fall of "slavery's shadows" on the indentured body of a "Free Black" woman, and by allusively inscribing her sexual exploitation, attests that the rule of the plantation and its masters also holds sway "In a Two-story White House, North."

NOTES

1. These quotations are taken from Harriet E. Wilson, *Our Nig: or, Sketches from the Life of a Free Black* (1859; New York: Vintage, 1984). Subsequent references will be given parenthetically in the text.

2. Hazel V. Carby, *Reconstructing Womanhood: The Emergence of the Afro-American Woman Novelist* (New York: Oxford University Press, 1987); Henry Louis Gates Jr., introduction to *Our Nig*; and Claudia Tate, *Domestic Allegories of Political Desire: The Black Heroine's Text at the Turn of the Century* (New York: Oxford University Press, 1992). The focus common to all three writers is succinctly summarized by Tate when she calls *Our Nig* a "complex variation on the intersection of the conventions of sentimental fiction and the slave narrative" (39). See also Gates, "Parallel Discursive Universes: Fictions of Self in Harriet E. Wilson's *Our Nig*," in *Figures in Black: Words, Signs, and the "Racial" Self* (New York: Oxford University Press, 1987), 125–63.

3. Gates, "Introduction," xxxv. Carby pronounces *Our Nig* "an allegory of a slave narrative, a 'slave' narrative set in the 'free' North" (43), focusing her argument on the violence of the white mistress, but she does not pursue possible sexual transgressions of the white masters, which would complete the slave narrative allegory as it particularly pertains to black women. Tate identifies a "reticent sexual discourse in the novel" (35) but confines her discussion to the protagonist's relationship late in the tale with her husband Samuel. Gates finds in Frado's "complex relationship" to the Bellmont son James "a curious blend of religion and displaced sexual desire," but he approaches the "dormant passion" as if it is Frado's repressed wish ("Introduction," xlix). Thus these critics and others imply and even recognize a repressed but pervasive sexual element in the narrative of *Our Nig*, yet they each follow the text's own protocol and account for the mysterious element in ways that preserve its indirection or obfuscating displacement.

4. Elizabeth Fox-Genovese, "My Statue, My Self: Autobiographical Writings of Afro-American Women," in *Reading Black, Reading Feminist*, ed. Henry Louis Gates Jr. (New York: Meridian, 1990), 198.

5. Tate goes on to identify "deliberately constructed double-voiced representations"

in *Our Nig* (39), a formulation that also describes the narrative's practice of inscription by elision through a transgressive subtext that conveys material left out of the surface narrative of *Our Nig*.

6. Wilson's contemporaries Harriet Jacobs and Elizabeth Keckley address their sexual exploitation in slavery but, endeavoring to maintain decorum, they resort to telling it slant. Rennie Simson, in "The Afro-American Female: The Historical Context of the Construction of Sexual Identity," in *Powers of Desire: The Politics of Sexuality*, ed. Ann Snitow, Christine Stansell, and Sharon Thompson (New York: Monthly Review Press, 1983), 229–35, calls attention to Elizabeth Keckley's elided and indirect locations for the narration of sexual coercion in *Behind the Scenes*, pointing to Keckley's statement, "I do not care to dwell upon this subject [of being the object of sexual lust of the second of two white men who pursue and ravish her] for it is one that is fraught with pain. suffice it to say, that he persecuted me for four years, and I—I became a mother" (Simson, 231; Elizabeth Keckley, *Behind the Scenes: Or, Thirty Years a Slave and Four Years in the White House* [1868; New York: Basic Books, 1985], 33). Keckley's text was published in 1868, within the same period as that of *Our Nig* (1859) and Harriet Jacobs's *Incidents in the Life of a Slave Girl* (1861; Cambridge: Harvard University Press, 1987). In Keckley's account, as in Wilson's, modesty and indirection prevail (she will not "dwell" on "this subject" "fraught with pain"); omission is indicated by the phrase "suffice it to say"; and elision is graphically inscribed by the dash between the two *I*s required for her to confess sexual exploitation, gestured to in the appositely demure figure of achieved motherhood. As in Jacobs's and Wilson's accounts, the verb "persecuted," a charged word used somewhat eccentrically becomes in this context a trope for sexual violation or penetration, while the phrase "for four years" indicates duration and suggests the repeated trauma that is too "fraught."

7. Spillers cautions against the disabling effects of face-value assessments of black female self-expression with regard to sexuality and insists that "in order to supply the missing words in the discourse of sexuality, we would try to encounter agent, agency, act, scene, and purpose in ways that the dominative mode forbids. . . . To dissipate its energies requires that the feminist critic/historian actively imagine women in their living and pluralistic confrontations with experience (at least, the way they report it), and perhaps the best guarantee of such commitment is the critic's heightened self-consciousness with regard to the conceptual tools with which we operate" ("Interstices: A Small Drama of Words," in *Sexuality*, ed. Hortense Spillers [Boston: Routledge, 1984], 94).

8. See Barbara Christian, Introduction to Mrs. A. E. Johnson, *The Hazeley Family* (1894; New York: Oxford, 1990).

9. See Gates, "Introduction," iv.

10. Tate, 35; Gates, "Introduction," xxxv–xxxvii.

11. Tate, 38.

12. Evelyn Brooks Higginbotham, "African-American Women's History and the Metalanguage of Race," *Signs* 17. 2 (Winter 1992): 256.

13. See Tate, 44.

14. Barbara Omolade asserts that in U.S. race relations, the (black) "body could not

be separated from its color" ("Hearts of Darkness," in Snitow, 353–55). So, too, in *Our Nig*, the conspicuously designated black body of Frado signifies that the Bellmont men do not view her any differently than does Mrs. Bellmont, though their sex implicates them in a further level of exploitation they would have been able to regard—and to take—as their racial due within the reigning racial discourses of the day: sexual transgression of black female subjectivity. Or as Angela Davis puts it, the white male "license to rape emanated from and facilitated the ruthless economic domination that was the gruesome hallmark of slavery" (*Women, Race and Class* [New York: Random House, 1981], 175). As slavery is the "gruesome hallmark" of Frado's indenture, so too is an undisclosed but subtextually inscribed sexual exploitation.

15. Harriet Jacobs and Frederick Douglass both depict the fury of white women at white male sexual transgression. Both authors show that this transgression does not destabilize categories of racial difference but in fact preserves them and foregrounds gender as a central determinative of white (male) race privilege, the chief entitlement enacted in the sexual exploitation of black female slaves, or, in *Our Nig*, of Frado. See Jacobs and Frederick Douglass, *Narrative of the Life of Frederick Douglass, An American Slave* (1845; Garden City, N.Y.: Doubleday, Anchor Books, 1973).

16. Tate, 243.

17. My reading of the Bellmont men's transgression against Frado as a further and deleted explanation of Mrs. Bellmont's violence is supported not only by the work of Barbara Omolade, but also by bell hooks. See hooks, *Ain't I A Woman: Black Women and Feminism* (Boston: South End Press, 1981), 15–49. See also Jacqueline Jones, *Labor of Love, Labor of Sorrow: Black Women, Work and the Family, from Slavery to the Present* (New York: Basic Books, 1985), and Eugene D. Genovese, *Roll, Jordan, Roll: The World the Slaves Made* (New York: Random House, 1974), among others, which substantiate the claim that that sexual exploitation of black female slaves by white masters was further exacerbated by the white mistresses' violence against the women for the males' transgressions. Omolade asserts that "most white women sadistically and viciously punished the black woman . . . for the [sexual] transgressions of their white men" (356–57); she also notes that white women competed for white male favor in "the social relationship of supervisor of black women's domestic labor" (351, 357), and, thus, "ultimately, white men were politically empowered to dominate all women and all black men and women: this was their sexual freedom" (352).

18. Tate, 44.

19. James exercises his male word of "law" when he "calmly, but imperatively" insists that Frado dine with the family and "eat such food as we eat" (68) instead of her usual way, "standing, by the kitchen table" eating scraps, forbidden to "be over ten minutes about it" (29). That is, his word of "law" sets the scene that will result in the transgression of Mrs. Bellmont's word of law; white women's power is inferior and subsidiary to white men's. Indeed, without James's agency, Frado would not be in a position to administer Mrs. Bellmont's comeuppance.

20. This aspect of the scene recalls one from *Uncle Tom's Cabin* that captures the patronizing expectation of slavers to be amused by their slaves. Eliza's young son Harry is bidden to dance, sing, and perform imitations for the entertainment of Mr. Shelby

and the trader Haley and is rewarded for his cleverness with raisins, a piece of orange, and Haley's disastrous desire to take the boy in acquittal of Shelby's debt. Topsy is similarly bidden to entertain Augustine St. Claire and his sister Ophelia on the day when St. Claire "gives" Topsy to Ophelia.

21. hooks, 24, 27.

22. Jacquelyn Dowd Hall, "'The Mind That Burns in Each Body': Women, Rape, and Racial Violence," in Snitow, 332. See also Jones, 37; Melton A. McLaurin, *Celia, A Slave* (Athens: University of Georgia Press, 1991).

23. The omniscient narrator—"Our Nig"—observes that the image of a "frail child, driven from shelter by the cruelty of his mother, was an object of interest to James" (50): read through the subtext that subverts the cover story of Bellmont male benefi-cence, this sentence suggests that James's "interest" is what makes Frado an "object."

24. Indeed, in the sentence before, rather incongruously, we are told that Frado must leave Fido behind. This information evokes the Frado/Fido eye rhyme, the identifi-cation of pet and child, the dog's provision as gift to bribe or placate or reward the child, and the dog's narrative value as signifier for a split off part of the protagonist. Fido is not only Frado's "entire confidant" (41), the embodiment and repository of what may not be told directly in the narrative, he is Frado's accomplice in the humilia-tion of Mrs. Bellmont, which provides the occasion of her first gift of a silver half-dollar.

25. Davis, 182.

26. It cannot be named because it "would most provoke shame in our good anti-slavery friends," as Wilson says in the preface. That is, it cannot be named because it would cause shame for Wilson as well as for Frado. It cannot be named without incul-pating its victim, for discourses, institutions, and laws in Harriet Wilson's time as well as in our own conspire to protect white male patriarchal privilege with invisibility, in this case by associating black women with carnality (Hall, 333) and, as the historian Richard Hofstadter explains, by blaming white male interest in black women (and the access to them permitted by their privilege) on myths of the women's lasciviousness (see Omolade, 365).

"Of One Blood"

Reimagining American Genealogy in Pauline Hopkins's *Contending Forces*

LISA MARCUS

Since the beginning of the nation, white Americans have suffered from a deep inner uncertainty as to who they really are. One of the ways that has been used to simplify the answer has been to seize upon the presence of black Americans and use them as a marker, a symbol of limits, a metaphor for the "outsider." Many whites could look at the social position of blacks and feel that color formed an easy and reliable gauge for determining to what extent one was or was not an American. . . . But this is tricky magic. Despite his racial difference and social status, something indisputably American about Negroes not only raised doubts about the white man's value system but aroused the troubling suspicion that whatever else the true American is, he is also somehow black.

Ralph Ellison

A genealogy will never neglect as inaccessible the vicissitudes of history. On the contrary, it will cultivate the details and accidents that accompany every beginning; it will be scrupulously attentive to their petty malice; it will await their emergence, once unmasked, as the face of the other.

Michel Foucault

Little Bursts of Righteous Heat

"Words do wonderful things," Gwendolyn Brooks asserts in her afterword to Pauline Hopkins's *Contending Forces*: "They pound, purr. They can urge, they can wheedle, whip, whine. They can sing, sass, singe. They can churn, check, channelize. They can be a 'Hup two three four.' They can forge a fiery army of a hundred languid men."[1] However, Pauline Hopkins's words do not pound, wheedle, whip and whine according to Brooks, who suggests that Hopkins "has not chosen from her resources words and word jointures that could make changes in the world" (404). Instead, Brooks asserts, "often doth the brainwashed slave revere the modes and idolatries of the master. And Pauline Hopkins consistently proves herself a continuing slave, despite little bursts of righteous heat, throughout *Contending Forces*" (404–5). Brooks, writing in 1978, was certainly echoing her literary and political moment. African American writers were actively defining themselves against accommodation, and, as Brooks herself writes, *Contending Forces* "is not *Native Son, Invisible Man, Jubilee, Roots*. Pauline Hopkins is not Richard Wright, Ralph Ellison, Margaret Walker, Alex Haley. Unlike Margaret Walker, in the fire of *For My People*, Pauline Hopkins is not herein urging that 'martial songs be written'; she is often indignant, but not indignant enough to desire Margaret's 'bloody peace'" (403).[2] Ironically, Brooks's litany of "not"s appears in an edition of *Contending Forces* that attempts to reclaim it as part of a "Lost American Fiction" series; the attempt to resurrect Hopkins's novel is nearly undermined by Brooks's frustration with what she calls Hopkins's "assimilationist urges" (409).[3]

Yet, Hopkins was by no means an accommodationist; in fact, she was considered radical enough by forces loyal to Booker T. Washington to be removed from her editorship of the *Colored American Magazine* in 1904, because "her attitude was not conciliatory enough" to white readers, as Abby Arthur Johnson and Ronald Maberry Johnson suggest in their study of the politics of African American magazines.[4] Indeed, Johnson and Johnson argue (in a chapter significantly entitled "Away from Accommodation") that Hopkins, as an editor, refused to compromise her political agenda. The *Colored American Magazine*, for which Hopkins wrote from its inception in 1900 and which she edited between 1902 and 1904, was far from assimilationist. A story called "Black Is, as Black Does" by Angelina Grimké, published in the magazine's founding year, is a fictional dream in which God saves a beaten and mutilated black soul while banishing the white, bloodsoaked murderer to hell.[5] Illustrative of Hopkins's militant editorial stance is a confrontation that took place within the pages of the *Colored American Magazine*. A white reader had written to cancel her subscription, protesting the interracial love affairs that dared to flourish in the pages of the magazine's fiction. Hopkins's own short story "Talma Gordon" had been published in the magazine's fifth issue and, as I discuss below, its interracial love story offered a strong argument in favor of the amalgamation of the races, an argument that turn-of-the-century whites could hardly stomach.[6] In response to the lost subscription, Hopkins published a vituperative reply bidding good-riddance to the subscriber and defending her own fictional and editorial choices: "my stories are definitely planned to show the obstacles persistently placed in our paths by a dominant race to subjugate us spiritually . . . I sing of the *wrongs* of a race that ignorance of their pitiful condition may be changed to intelligence and awaken compassion in the hearts of the just." She concluded, "I am glad to receive this criticism for it shows more clearly than ever that white people don't understand *what pleases Negroes*" (emphases in original).[7]

Gwendolyn Brooks's sincere lament is that Pauline Hopkins was not angrier, not revolutionary in spirit or agitative enough in her writing. I propose that Hopkins's fiction does embody a radical project, in its genealogical revision of America's national family tree. Suggesting, in an historical moment of deep national fear of integration and miscegenation, that America's racial identity has been forged in a violent history of power and domination, Hopkins iconoclastically challenged her readership to reinvent their understanding of American citizenship. All of her major fiction genealogically reimagines America's national psyche and physiognomy. *Contending Forces* (1900) proposes that modern America descends both metaphorically and genetically from the rape of African American women during slavery. Likewise, *Winona: A Tale of Negro Life in the South and Southwest* (1902) amalgamates white, black, and Native American blood to reinvent the racially hybrid American subject. Practically all the white characters in *Hagar's Daughter: A Story of Southern Caste Prejudice* (1901–2) discover the (tragic) mutability of identity when many of them turn out to be of African American origin. Finally, *Of One Blood, or, The Hidden Self* (1902–3) reaches across physiologic, psychic and spiritual space to suggest a grand Ethiopian origin of civilization and an African America.[8]

Pauline Hopkins believed in the transformative possibilities of fiction, what Brooks calls the "wheedle, whip and whine" that "forge[s] a fiery army of a hundred languid men." Accordingly, she wrote in her preface to *Contending Forces*: "Fiction is of great value to any people as a preserver of manners and customs—religious, political and social. It is a record of growth and development from generation to generation. *No one will do this for us; we must ourselves develop the men and women who will faithfully portray the inmost thoughts and feelings of the Negro with all the fire and romance which lie dormant in our history*, and, as yet, unrecognized by writers of the Anglo-Saxon race" (14, emphasis in original). Hopkins's apocalyptic vision of fire and romance is historically generated and radically nationalist in that her project includes a revision of American subjectivity—hardly a diminutive burst of heat.[9]

Race and Gender on the Threshold of a New Land

America, a country that has always been obsessed with miscegenation and racial difference, is constitutionally consanguineous. Contemporary African American chronicler Shirlee Taylor Haizlip has recently traced her own roots to "The First Lady of Whiteness," Martha Washington, and reintroduced her family to an entire branch of relations who had conceived of themselves as caucasian. In fact, she suggests that many Americans whose families have been in this country since the Civil War are likely to contain mixed blood.[10] Hopkins's fiction anticipates Haizlip's testimonial in the epigraph to her book, "I am in all America / All America is in me," that America's citizens are bound by filiation. "Races are like families," Hopkins's narrator says in *Contending Forces* (198), and the novel goes on to argue that America is a racially conglomerate family. Indeed, *Contending Forces*'s genealogical romance stages a kind of Foucauldian critique of American history. As Foucault argues, genealogy exposes the accident of any origin and the historical contingency of supposedly absolute human categories. The historical search for homogeneity will instead reveal difference, the "face of the other."[11] Hopkins opens *Contending Forces* with just such an accidental birth, subverting American concepts of racial purity by showing the whiteness of black origins, how blackness in the United States has been, literally and forcefully, fathered by whiteness.

From the opening pages of *Contending Forces*, Hopkins stresses that her African American heroine's identity and destiny are intertwined with her white progenitor. The novel opens with a "retrospective of the past," reaching back to the early nineteenth century to tell the story of the dissolution of the Montfort family. Charles Montfort is introduced as a Bermuda slaveowner who "perverted right to be what was conducive to his own interests, and felt that by owning slaves he did no man a wrong" (22). Montfort moves to the more slavery-friendly shores of America when it is rumored that Great Britain plans to abolish the slave trade. By initiating her genealogical romance with this heavily ironized "owner of seven hundred slaves," Hopkins locates her story's foundations in a colonialist, paternalistic, and auspiciously white family. Even this slaveowner's whiteness is thrown into doubt, however, by the narrator's foreshadowing suggestion that the Montfort's eventual decline is connected to the possibility of "a strain of African blood polluting the fair stream of Montfort's vitality, or even his wife's" (23). The book's frontispiece depicts a similarly ambiguous image of racial confusion: a troubling illustration of the near-fatal whipping of Montfort's possibly "polluted" wife (see fig. 1). This picture of an ostensibly white woman being beaten links the Anglo and African characters and their destinies in this novel. By substituting a "white" woman for the commonly circulated abolitionist image of a black slave being beaten, Hopkins cogently exposes the engendering of race and the racializing of gender: the woman is racialized by her very placement in this scene of violence, and she is engendered in her sexualized exposure under the lash.[12] By publishing her novel with this frontispiece, Hopkins inverts standard

Figure 1. Frontispiece to the 1900 edition of Pauline Hopkins's *Contending Forces*.

racial equations, insisting on the continuous threat of white male violence and sparing the black female from its brutal outcome.[13]

The racializing of gender that culminates in the scene depicted on the frontispiece begins the moment Grace Montfort is spied from the shores of the United States. Two lowly white "idlers" oversee the arrival of the Bermuda planter and his slaves, and their speculations on the arriving merchandise include Grace Montfort: "never seed sich a booty in my life" (41), exclaims Hank. Bill replies, as he "scratched his head meditatively: 'Strikes me, Hank, thet thet ar female's got a black streak in her somewhar'" (41). Hank ultimately agrees that "thar's too much cream color in the face and too little blud seen under the skin for a genooine white 'ooman" (41). And so begins the racialization that brings down the Montfort clan. This scene takes place on the threshold of a new world; for Charles Montfort it seems to promise prosperity, but for Grace Montfort, crossing the border of this new world exposes both her gender and her race to violent speculation.

The racialization of Grace Montfort is particularly interesting because Hopkins goes to great lengths to emphasize her white appearance: "Grace Montfort was a dream of beauty even among beautiful women. Tall and slender; her form was willowy, although perfectly molded. Her complexion was creamy in its whiteness, of the tint of the camellia; her hair, a rich golden brown, fell in rippling masses below the waistline; brown eyes, large and soft as those seen in the fawn; heavy black eyebrows marking a high white forehead, and features as clearly cut as a cameo, completed a most lovely type of Southern beauty" (40). Hopkins's African American heroine, Sappho Clark, is described in strikingly similar terms. She is "tall and fair, with hair of a golden cast, aquiline nose, rosebud mouth . . . a combination of 'queen rose and lily in one'" (107). Brooks criticizes Hopkins for making Sappho Clark so conspicuously white, but I would like to explore how this racial confusion works in the opposite direction: what are we to make of the fact that Hopkins makes Grace Montfort subject to a community that constructs her as black? Perhaps Hopkins is not simply denigrating black beauty, as Brooks suspects, but establishing a metonymic connection between her white and black female characters in order to radically revise American genealogy.

In her fiction Hopkins consistently rewrites the conventional racial narrative, dramatizing the nation's sinful story upon the bodies of ostensibly white women. By substituting Grace Montfort into the black woman's victimized posture, Hopkins forces a reconsideration of the interplay between race, gender, and sexuality. Shifting the focus away from the stripped down and sexualized black woman, Hopkins exposes the white woman's body as a potentially vulnerable crossroad of historical significance. Though the white woman is racialized in the metonymic substitution that she undergoes, the aggressor remains constant. The threatening violence comes not from the mythical black male rapist; the constant threat is actually from the white man.[14] Hopkins's novel, written while black men were being lynched all over the South because of white hysteria about racial purity, provides a revisionary narrative revealing that white women had more to fear from the men of their *own* race.

As I have suggested, the story of Grace Montfort originates the history of the "contending forces" that define the novel: Grace is racialized by the white community, ostensibly because they find her skin too "creamy" but mainly in order to instigate the deflation of her husband's wealth and power. Indeed, the suspicion of Grace's black blood enables the community's "civil defense fund" to justify her husband's murder and Grace's brutal whipping and perhaps rape. The "committee on public safety" meets shortly after the Montforts have settled into their new home. The committee decides that their "Klan" cannot tolerate the possibility that Montfort will soon free his slaves, and they determine to issue a stern warning to Charles about his conduct. When Hank Davis, who we remember from his idle speculation on the dock, arrives to caution Charles about the "rules of the commoonity," Charles administers a "sound flogging" to this offensive man. As the narrator comments, Hank "receive[d] personal violence of a character that was most galling to the spirit of any free-born Southern man—an ordinary cowhiding, such as he would mete out to his slave" (59), and this flogging provokes the vengeance that will lead to Montfort's death. Simultaneous with this battle between the racializing idlers and Charles Montfort, there is another battle silently brewing in the breast of the villain Anson Pollock, whose intense desire for Grace Montfort is fueled by the "blackness of her whiteness."[15] Indeed, her "creaminess" turns him on and feeds his appetite to possess her. When Hank appears with his battle scars, Pollock is ready to destroy Charles so that he can have Grace as a spoil of war.

The action that follows is the fundamental—literally, the generative—event of this text. Once Charles has been murdered, Grace is dragged to the whipping post, and Hank Davis ruminates: "This woman's husband had flogged him—he would have a sweet revenge. Those lily-like limbs, the tender flesh that had never known aught but the touch of love, should *feel the lash as he had*" (68, emphasis in original). It is clear here that Grace's "lily" whiteness particularly exaggerates Hank's pleasure in his project. Hank "tear[s] [Grace's] garments from her shrinking shoulders" and his "savage instinct" takes over. He and Bill Sampson whip her alternately with a "snaky leather thong" cutting patterns out of her white flesh.[16] Hank's work in this scene builds upon his earlier speculation: whereas earlier he read race onto the body of the arriving Bermuda woman, he now writes race upon that body as if it were a blank page: "Hank gazed at the cut with critical satisfaction, as he compared its depth with the skin and blood that encased the long, tapering lash" (69). This scene illustrates Mae Henderson's lucid argument that together the inscription of the whip and the ascription of the white male gaze "produce the meaning of black female subjectivity in the discursive domain of slavery" (26). Interestingly, though, Pauline Hopkins has metonymically substituted a white woman into this equation, suggesting by this substitution that not only are white women vulnerable (because of their dependence) to the savagery of white men, but that whiteness itself can be rendered mute in the racializing of gender that takes place when fueled by sexual and vengeful desire. Whereas, for Henderson, "the black woman becomes a tabula rasa upon which the racial/ sexual identity of the other can be positively inscribed," in Hopkins's tale the white woman's body is presented as a tabula rasa that is then racialized in the experiencing of gender.

It is important to notice that the white men cut patterns out of Grace's flesh and stand back to critically admire their work. Carving into the white woman's body this critical design, the white "savages" demonstrate their ability to inscribe racial history. Grace's body becomes a text upon which white men can inscribe their ownership of women, both black and white. Grace does not preserve this inscription for long: she drowns herself, seemingly ending her textual body's inscription and ascription. But, notably, the text of Grace's body does not disappear; it circulates silently as the prehistory to the subsequent narrative, never letting the reader forget that her body instigated the genealogy that issues forth through the novel. Once Grace Montfort is officially marked as black by the community, her descendants emerge as a black family into which Sappho Clark eventually marries.

Black and White Metonymies

Grace Montfort's unravelling white womanhood provides the narrative threads out of which Hopkins weaves her African American heroine. The extinguished white family is supplanted by Hopkins's subsequent narrative and regenerated through the novel's African American community. In particular, Sappho Clark is incarnated as the novel's replacement for the deceased Grace Montfort; Sappho conveniently appears as the novel's heroine as soon as her progenitor expires. Hopkins's metonymic linking of these two characters is an example of what Hortense Spillers has described as the complicatedly entangled narratives of white and black women: "African American women's community and Anglo American women's community, under certain shared cultural conditions, were the twin actants on a common psychic landscape, were subject to the same fabric of dread and humiliation. Neither could claim her body and its various productions—for quite different reasons. . . . In fact, from one point of view, we cannot unravel one female's narrative from the other's, cannot decipher one without tripping over the other." [17]

Like Spillers, Hopkins insists that the narratives of Grace Montfort and Sappho Clark, though intertwined, are not identical or interchangeable. Sappho Clark suffers a much more brutal pattern of violence than the one that drives Grace Montfort to suicide. Sappho is revealed to be "Mabelle Beaubean," in a harrowing tale that not only reveals her less-than-idyllic origins, but also illustrates a political debate against accommodation and passivity in the wake of Southern lynching. Luke Sawyer tells the audience at the American Colored League the story of the young Mabelle, who, at fifteen, was savagely raped and forced into prostitution by her father's "white" half-brother. Saved by Sawyer, she buries herself in a convent, gives birth to a child, and escapes to reinvent herself. Sawyer tells this story unaware that Mabelle, now Sappho Clark, is in his audience. Unfortunately for Sappho, no history remains repressed in *Contending Forces*, and Sappho's is brought to bear on her by the insidious John P. Langley, whose middle initial "P" turns out to link him to the evil Anson Pollack of Grace Montfort's inaugural story. After her history is exposed, Sappho flees once again to the convent, running from the man she loves, fearful that he will reject her "tainted" body. Things turn out all right in the end for Sappho, because Hopkins chooses to resurrect her as a model of African American womanhood.

I want to stress how Hopkins hinges her narrative on the distinction and discontinuity between Grace and Sappho as much as on their metonymity. Though her body "manifests the stigmata of past events," Sappho emerges as the heroine of the novel because she survives the violence that Grace cannot.[18] This is not an essentialist rendering of weak white womanhood in opposition to "persevering" African American women. Hopkins is supplanting a nineteenth-century ideological construction of femininity with a more modern apparatus for thinking about womanhood. Thus, Hopkins's racial manipulations do not, as Gwendolyn Brooks suspected, simply lighten Sappho's skin; instead, Hopkins deflects onto a white character the sexualized violence habitually inscribed on black bodies, so that she can reimagine African American womanhood. Shifting the terms of the discussion, Hopkins suggests that the brutality of rape suffered under the auspices of Southern paternalism does not exclude African American women from leading productive (and virtuous) lives. The desire for an uncolonized black female body is a "pretend history," suggests Hazel Carby, who argues that turn-of-the-century black feminists, including Hopkins, "understood that the struggle [for a new model of African American womanhood] was to be characterized by redemption, retrieval, and reclamation—not, ultimately, by an unrestrained utopian vision."[19] Grace Montfort, then, figures as a kind of sentimental homage to "True Womanhood": her whiteness, her weakness, and her ultimate failure are supplanted by a new version of womanhood for a new century.[20]

Hopkins charts the terms of this new vision of African American womanhood in a chapter entitled "The Sewing Circle." The sewing circle encompasses what Claudia Tate calls a "gynocentric space" in *Contending Forces*.[21] Here, the women of the African American community gather to raise money to pay the mortgage on their church. Stitching together the fabric that will solidify the community's congregation, the women demonstrate that their piecework is a politics. A blackboard detailing "events of interest to the negro race" is a conspicuous nucleus of the room, revealing it to be not only a site of domesticity, but a place of discourse and political agitation. The topic for the day is "the place which the virtuous woman occupies in upbuilding the race." The matriarch who holds forth at the meeting, Mrs. Willis, a woman whose activism Sappho finds simultaneously repugnant and attractive, eagerly argues for a redefinition of virtue. She tells the young women that "it will rest with you and your children to refute the charges brought against us as to our moral irresponsibility, and the low moral standard maintained by us in comparison to other races." Sappho becomes the living embodiment of Mrs. Willis's argument: she is not the tragic sentimental heroine who is "ruined," as Grace Montfort is; Sappho is virtuous, moral, and responsible despite her rape.

Hopkins's attempt to challenge the intersecting discourses of feminine virtue and racial purity reflects the larger Reconstruction project represented by the work of Anna Julia Cooper and W. E. B. Du Bois. In 1892, Cooper wrote that "the colored woman of to-day occupies, one may say, a unique position in this country. In a period of itself transitional and unsettled, her status seems one of the least ascertainable and definitive of all the forces which make for our civilization. She is confronted by both a woman question and a race problem."[22] As Cooper herself suggests, African American women are "heirs of a past which was not our father's molding" (28), their inheritance a seemingly degraded and impoverished womanhood. Though euphemistic, Cooper refers to what Du Bois would later call the "red stain of bastardy" brought about by the widespread rape of female slaves by white men.[23] As Du Bois poignantly argued, "the rape which your gentlemen have done against helpless black women in defiance of your own laws is written on the foreheads of two millions of mulattoes, and written in ineffaceable blood" (137). This "hereditary weight," this "stamp" of race, has marked out its inheritors who bear the history of their legal defilement. Prefiguring Foucault's genealogical project of "expos[ing] a body totally imprinted by history," both Du Bois and Cooper reject the opposition of purity and bastardy.[24] Du Bois argues against "counting bastards and prostitutes" (50), and for exposing the history of racial and sexual violence "written in ineffaceable blood" and imprinted on the bodies of African Americans.

Rather than yearning for a "pretend history" of undefiled womanhood, the practical women of *Contending Forces*'s sewing circle simply redefine the terms of discussion. They cannot reinvent their history, so they name their aggressor and seek to "reconstruct womanhood," to borrow Hazel Carby's apt phrase. Mrs. Willis suggests that "our definitions of virtue are too narrow. We confine them to that conduct which is ruled by our animal passions alone. It goes deeper than that—general excellence in every duty of life is what we may call virtue. . . . We are virtuous or non-virtuous only when we have a *choice* under temptation" (149). Mrs. Willis goes on to argue that "the fate of the mulatto will be the fate of the entire race" (151). Hopkins goes further: because Grace Montfort is constructed as a mulatto by the racializing community, and because Sappho's son is born of America's national sin, Hopkins's genealogy suggests that the fate of the mulatto will be the fate of America.

Pauline Hopkins's fiction participated in the Reconstruction project of revising the stereotype of black female wantonness. This project has often been associated with an aspiration toward white bourgeois gentility, and thus some readers, such as Gwendolyn Brooks, have viewed the racial hybridity in Hopkins's fiction as an attempt to "whitewash" her black heroines. Yet, as I have attempted to show, writers such as Hopkins, Du Bois, and Cooper were not surrendering to a fantasy of whiteness, but rather questioning the intersecting discourses of racial purity and female virtue. Seen in this context, Hopkins's metonymic linkings of white and black characters appear not as an acquiescence to the allure of white womanhood, but as an attempt to create a fictional space for a new representation of African American female subjectivity. As Hortense Spillers argues, the "captive body" has been read as "the source of an irresistible, destructive sensuality."[25] At the turn of the century, this myth of sensuality that attached itself to African American women still prevailed; thus, there was a need for fictional and critical representation that would not simply reduce African American women to subjugated bodies. Hopkins's metonymic connection between Grace Montfort and Sappho Clark addresses this need. The sexualized violence that inaugurates the genealogy of *Contending Forces* deflects onto a white character the iconic violence that the literature of slavery habitually inscribed upon black bodies, thereby shifting attention away from the sexualized black female body. Thus Hopkins permits her heroine to transcend the fictional plot that conventionally consumed the black woman. Claudia Tate argues that "the ideology of Western beauty had conditioned readers—black and white alike—to expect fair heroines and to bestow sympathy on the basis of the purity of character, aligned to the purity of their caucasoid comeliness," and surely this is apparent in nineteenth century American narrative. The "caucasoid comeliness" of post–Reconstruction fiction seems, however, not only to reflect, as Tate concludes, a capitulation to conventions of "True Womanhood" in order to "counter the racist stereotype of black female wanton sexuality." [26] That "white" and "black" characters can stand in for each other, functioning as virtual metonymies in Hopkins's novel, is suggestive of a more daring project, a project that questioned the very definitions of racial difference and American womanhood. [27]

Family Ties

There is another genealogy in *Contending Forces* that springs from Grace Montfort, and it is to this story of family ties that I would like now to turn. Not only does Grace Montfort produce an African American lineage; she is also progenitor of a "white" British family who become heirs to her story and her suspect blackness at the end of Hopkins's novel. Let us return briefly to the scene of the Montforts' demise. Charles Montfort's murder and Grace's suicide do not extinguish the Montfort clan. They leave behind two sons, Jesse and Charles Jr. Jesse's grandson is the virtuous Will Smith whom Sappho Clark later marries; this is the outcome of the African American genealogy that I have discussed above. While both Montfort boys are made into slaves by the evil Anson Pollock, Charles Jr. is "sold" to a British mineralogist (who promptly frees him) and becomes ancestor to a "white" British parliamentarian whom we meet later in the novel as "Mr. Withington."

It is crucial to note that these two genealogies, one of blackness, the other of whiteness, work together to produce the meaning of family, history, and national belonging in Hopkins's text. On the one hand, Grace Montfort's ambiguous racial status, evident in her too "creamy" complexion, instigates the Africanizing of her offspring when they are "remanded" into slavery; on the other, it simultaneously reconfirms her aristocratic white heritage when Charles Jr. circumvents his bondage to become white once more. Thus, when Charles Montfort Withington, British parliamentarian, discovers his cousinage to "Ma" Smith (Jesse's daughter) at the end of *Contending Forces*, Hopkins has concocted a fairy tale of international racial amalgamation that links these diasporic characters in a genealogy of familial and civic kinship.

While I have focused much of my discussion of *Contending Forces* on Grace Montfort and Sappho Clark, the novel centers a good deal of its story in the Smith family boardinghouse. It is here that Sappho Clark comes to begin a new life after shedding her "hidden self" (Mabelle Beaubean), and here that she meets and becomes engaged to the meritorious Will Smith, a thinly disguised Du Bois protégé. It is here also that *Contending Forces* "cements the bond of brotherhood among all classes and all complexions" (13), by revealing Mr. Withington's kinship with the Smiths. Will Smith meets his "uncle" at a Canterbury Club dinner where the British guest has come to discover "fine specimens of the genus homo" (290). Withington reveals that his mission in the United States is to ascertain why "the two races do not mix, and to all appearances never will" (296). He worries that "there seems to be no common ground between them; they cannot live together harmoniously" (296). Of course, Withington soon learns that "appearances" are misleading in the context of the American racial situation. Not only does Withington eventually discover the harmony of racial admixture within his very own body, but he sees in the body of Will Smith the contradictory sign of both the violence of slavery and the promise of amalgamation. The parliamentarian is impressed by Will's assertion that "the peace, dignity and honor of this nation rises or falls with the Negro" (300). Will proves that the threat of the mythical black male rapist, a fabrication notorious even in Withington's Britain for supposedly preventing the races from living together harmoniously, is patently false. Will Smith, arguing with a white Southerner at the club dinner, uses his own body as evidence that white men are the true culprits of rape: "Take the representatives of my race who are with you tonight. How did we get our complexions, soft curls and regular features? Our ancestors were black, flat-featured, and had many other racial marks. Your race does not intermarry with Negroes, does it? That being the case, the answer is self-evident" (299–300). Withington, impressed by Will and the other "manly specimens" at the dinner, vows upon his departure to promote "sentiment" for African Americans in Great Britain.

Some months later, when he is again in the United States, Withington visits the Smith boardinghouse to call on Will. He tells "Ma" Smith that Will "possesses rare intellectual gifts" and says, "I must confess to a feeling of curiosity to learn how such characters are nourished among a people like yours" (372). It is soon revealed that these people are also his people. The "art of necromancy" that had produced "such a distinguished woman" in Ma Smith "from among the brutalized aftermath of slavery" has also worked its *black* magic upon this British aristocrat of "distinguished address." Will, it seems, is not at home, so Ma Smith entertains Withington with "a story of faithful fathers bearing insult and injury to keep the meanly paid employment; of mothers 'spending weary days and nights over the washtub and ironing board in order to get money to educate their children'" (372). This, Hopkins tells us, is a story "common enough among Negroes," but it is a "revelation" to Withington, who empathizes with the "monstrous injustice" that African America has suffered. As Ma Smith introduces the story of her life to Withington, she tells him that "there are strangely tangled threads in the lives of many colored families" (373). Withington soon discerns that Ma Smith's "romantic history" is also his own, that they share the same story. He embraces this "kinswoman" and upon Will's entry, he embraces his black "kinsman." Hopkins cheerfully (and optimistically) concludes this narrative: "So noble was the nature of this man that he never once thought of the possible ridicule that might come to him through his new kinspeople. He thought only of the tie of blood" (377). Withington's lighthearted incorporation of his kin (his "blood") is a crucial moment in Hopkins's genealogical project; the orphaned Montfort sons are reunited in this posthumous and cross-racial embrace. The "nobility" in Ma's "romantic history" of struggle and triumph inspires Withington to recognize his "tie of blood" with African America. Hopkins has thus defined a diasporic genealogy of shared blood and shared history.

Hopkins's desire to construct such a utopian family plot can be understood in light of Hortense Spillers's suggestion that the offspring of the enslaved community in the United States are subjects "on the boundary," anticipating filial attachment beyond the violent alliances enforced by slavery. Hopkins wants to chart an affiliative narrative that claims America's orphans as international "brotherly" subjects. Spillers notes that "in the context of the United States, we could not say that the enslaved offspring was 'orphaned,' but the child does become, under the press of a patronymic, patrifocal, patrilineal, and patriarchal order, the man/woman on the boundary, whose human and familial status, by the very nature of the case, had yet to be defined." [28]

For the enslaved, as Spillers reminds us, kinship is rendered meaningless because it is vulnerable to arbitrary encroachment. This threat explains Hopkins's desire to construct a genealogy that survives the dispersements, discontinuities, and displacements of slavery. In contrast to the patrilineal family structure designed to guard sexual, racial, and national legitimacy, Hopkins imagines a diasporic family that is affirmed horizontally rather than through vertical, patrilineal descent. [29] Hopkins's genealogy expands kinship to a more inclusive, amalgamated family, thereby legitimating an African American national subjectivity. Arbitrary encroachment is, however, the fate of Grace Montfort's two sons. Charles Jr., adopted away from his home and from his kin, is given his wife's family name in a move that legitimates him in Great Britain and obscures his own polluted patronym. Jesse too had taken his wife's family name of "Whitfield" (Ma Smith's maiden name). Hopkins thus appears to grant legitimacy to a genealogy generated and authenticated by women. Yet these obscuring female names must be unveiled to reveal the (Montfort) family narrative that adheres remarkably through *Contending Forces*. Thus, although the diasporic family is engendered by women, Hopkins appears anxious to replace her matrilineal ties with a return to the more traditional legitimacy afforded by the Montfort name. Still, it is *Grace* Montfort, not Charles, who engenders this genealogy.

Kin, Spillers suggests, "has no decisive legal or social efficacy" for the enslaved; family is a "revered privilege of a free and freed community." This, I think, is why Hopkins is so obsessed with reestablishing family ties and confirming African American social and legal citizenship. She goes quite far in her work to show that in fact kinship can (and will) ultimately command legal and social authority. Once the Smiths discover their British cousins, they not only recover a lost bloodline, they rescue the lost Montfort fortune that has been successfully sued from the American government. Of course, the supreme irony here is that the wealth the Smith family inherits has been accumulated by the sweat of slave labor. The social legitimacy granted by kinship is, of course, not always uncontaminated.

Laura Doyle has argued that "behind Mr. Withington's brotherly gesture of kinship lies a past of violated kinship; behind the fairy tale reunion lies a suppressed nightmare separation," and surely, as we have seen in Grace Montfort's story, this is true.[30] Yet, the violent story that precipitates the harmonious family reunion at the end of *Contending Forces* is America's own story, and Hopkins is keen to stress this. While brotherly love is cemented across class and complexion by the resolution of her "homely tale," the Montforts and their immediate heirs are not party to the happy reunion of the races. They are sacrificed for the sake of future racial amalgamation and national, even international, harmony. *Contending Forces* thus does not simply erase the violence of this national story. Hopkins's family romance does, however, optimistically hope that the shared history of white and black Americans has secured African Americans a place in America's national family. "Not only does Hopkins claim," Doyle argues, "that most negroes have some white blood, but she also hints through this history that many whites, such as Mr. Withington, have negro blood." This is important: by stressing that blackness is (forcefully) fathered by whiteness in the United States, Hopkins describes a context in which whiteness, too, is always potentially, and suspiciously, black. And yet ultimately, the necromancy of blood and color is arbitrary, and filiation is random and surprising. In the American scene, Hopkins would later suggest (not uncomplicatedly), we are all "of one blood."[31] This is a radical assertion: where bloodlines confirm family as a privilege, Hopkins wants to insist upon the family ties of the nation to confer the privileges of social and legal authority that kinship grants. "Races are like families," Hopkins writes in *Contending Forces* (198). Not only are races like families, but the nation is a family, no matter how tangled its threads.

Old Wives' Tales and New National Subjectivity

I would like to end this piece with two old wives' tales and a fantasy of new national subjectivity. First for the new national subject: Ralph Ellison, in his well-known essay "What America Would Be Like without Blacks," asserted that "something indisputably American about Negroes . . . aroused the troubling suspicion that whatever else the true American is, he is also somehow black."[32] This "troubling suspicion," the racial repressed of America's national psyche, Ellison's "troubling suspicion" was brilliantly and exuberantly illustrated in a photograph of "The Young Colored American," printed in the autumn 1900 issues of *The Colored American* and sold as a Christmas keepsake to raise money for the future of the magazine (see fig. 2).[33] The representation of a baby sitting upon the unfurling American flag is a dramatic portrait of centennial optimism. As the century turned, the editorial staff at the magazine, including Pauline Hopkins, marketed this hopeful image of a new American for a new century. The baby, flag rippling beneath his nearly naked body, is indisputably representative of a newly born black national subject, but also, and importantly, of a newly begotten *American* national subject. The magazine was clearly asserting the manifest Americanness of their young figurehead, and the readership bought it; indeed, it was so popular that new photographs had to be issued.

If, as Pauline Hopkins has shown us, the post-Reconstruction African American subject is the offspring of violent trespass, then for all the white hysteria about racial admixture that marked the Reconstruction period, no separation of the races could erase the "red stain of bastardy" that whites had inflicted upon African America. In effect orphaned by country and kin, as Hortense Spillers has pointed out, African Americans at the turn into the twentieth century were reconstructing familial ties previously violated by slavery's thefts. Yet, the "young colored American" of the photograph is by no means an orphan, he is America's child, claimed by all who bought his

Figure 2. "The Young Colored American," *The Colored American Magazine*,
October and November 1900.

chimerical image. Adopted into the homes of the black middle class, together the young colored American *and* the flag hail the new century with a bright and shining optimism.

Pauline Hopkins's genealogical fiction attempted to grant legitimacy to America's orphaned citizens by proving the consanguinity of all America. Indeed, her work both responds to Du Bois's assertion that African Americans "have woven ourselves with the very warp and woof of this nation" (275) and prefigures Ellison's bold statement that "whatever else the true American is, he is also somehow black." But Ellison also reminds us that even if "the true American is also somehow black," this frequently provokes unease and a "troubling suspicion" among whites. The "troubling suspicion" was fueled, in part, by America's obsession with a fantasy of whiteness particularly evident in the literature of the 1890s, and in the "one drop" of black blood rule affirmed in the famous 1896 *Plessy v. Ferguson* Supreme Court decision.[34] It was also fueled by a fear of the blackness at the heart of America's "white" civilization (a fear and a fantasy that one might well argue is still with us today). Ellison's "troubling suspicion," that there is a blackness in the constitution of America, strained African Americans' attempts to depict new American subjectivities for the new century. These tensions are explored in two short, turn-of-the-century narrative pieces that meditate on America's consanguinity. Both stories are "old wives' tales" in that their plots hinge on the surprise revelation of marital attachment to secret wives who are produced virtually from narrative itself, with each "old" wife appearing as a result of a romantically woven and very public "tale." For one writer this means a marriage to history itself (particularly the history of slavery) while for the other, the "old wives' tale" offers a lesson in imagining the future of interracial community.

Published in Boston in 1899, the same city and the same year in which Hopkins copyrighted *Contending Forces*, Charles Chesnutt's story "The Wife of His Youth" similarly explores racial heritage and filiation.[35] Chesnutt's narrative opens with the protagonist, Mr. Ryder, meditating on the haunting paleness of Tennyson's "fair women," while he plans a toast to honor the light-skinned beauty who anticipates his proposition of marriage that evening. His dream of pale women is interrupted by the return of the racial repressed. The dark-skinned "wife of his youth" halts his fantasy of whiteness and returns him to a racial morality, which eventuates in his public claim of affiliation with the dark (and feminine) other who is his past. "The Wife of His Youth" centers on the renunciation of a fantasy of whiteness; for Chesnutt, history is embodied in the ancient black woman, and the protagonist must accept this history, the history of slavery and the stigma of race. Chesnutt's pale woman, the object of Mr. Ryder's affections, is a "Blue Vein": she is light-skinned enough to see the "blue veins" of her blood vessels beneath her pale wrists. She is also of free birth and has accumulated wealth and social status, thus gaining access to the "Blue Vein Society," Chesnutt's infamous group of "talented tenth" African Americans, around whom the story is situated. The light-skinned woman, to Chesnutt, represents a rejection of history and a genteel ambition to reproduce whiteness, and she is necessarily supplanted by the return of her precursor. However, even in his eventual rejection of the pale woman, Chesnutt traps his protagonist "Mr. Ryder" within a paradigm of stereotyped, bifurcated racial and sexual representations. Mr. Ryder must renounce the sexually desirable, youthful, cultured, light-skinned woman, for the aged, rural, dialect-speaking black woman, who appears to be more a mother than a wife.

This renunciation of the "future" seemingly embodied in the pale woman occurs in a very public display, in which the wife of Ryder's youth is conjured up in a romantic and moral fable that he delivers instead of his planned toast of betrothal. This fable tells of the ex-slave Liza Jane's dedication to rectify the familial encroachments of slavery by locating her long escaped husband Sam Taylor. She has been unwittingly successful, it seems, having encountered "Sam Taylor" in the person of Mr. Ryder that afternoon. Liza Jane has approached Ryder with a "daguerreotype" of "Sam Taylor," and Ryder recognizes the distinct features in the photograph as his own. Sending Liza Jane away without identifying himself, Ryder does manage to scribble down her address on the flyleaf of his volume of Tennyson. The black woman, and the history she embodies, is thus written over the romantic "dream of fair women," canceling out the romance incarnated in Tennyson's fantasy. Similarly, when Ryder later gazes at himself in the mirror of his dressing case, his romantic new self is effaced by his own degraded history of double abandonment: the revelation of this mirror scene is clearly that the self is bound to history. When, later that evening, Ryder entertains the guests with a moral fable about racial obligation, it turns out to be his own story in disguise. He asks the guests whether "Sam Taylor" should acknowledge his "Liza Jane" and his nearly betrothed speaks for the crowd by counseling that indeed he should. In the extraordinary denouement, not only is "Liza Jane" conjured up quite literally from the tale, but "Sam Taylor" is conjured up as well, as the narrative of assimilationist "progress" surrenders to the history of slavery.

In contrast, as we have seen in *Contending Forces*, Pauline Hopkins's embrace of history and racial filiation is designed to *destabilize* racial categories, thereby opening fictional space for a vision of African American womanhood that transcends the dichotomous and fossilized racial categories confining Chesnutt's women. In fact, Hopkins's story "Talma Gordon" may well have been written in response to Chesnutt's morally charged fable. "Talma Gordon" was published in the October 1900 issue of *The Colored American Magazine*, a year after Chesnutt's volume *The Wife of His Youth* appeared.[36] "Talma Gordon" takes place during a meeting of the Canterbury Club of Boston, a site where we remember first meeting Mr. Withington in *Contending Forces*. At this meeting, "some rare opinions were to be aired by men of profound thought on a question of vital importance to the life of the Republic," the question being "Expansion: Its Effect upon the Future Development of the Anglo-Saxon throughout the World" (271). Dr. Thornton, the host, has a wife, not so old and not quite in the attic, but certainly hidden away, who he produces later as evidence for his argument that a "superior being" will be born of the intermarriage resulting from imperialism, both within and outside of America's borders. Thornton's fascinating argument includes this oration: "Given a man, propinquity, opportunity fascinating femininity, and there you are. Black, white, green yellow—nothing will prevent intermarriage. Position, wealth, family, friends—all sink into insignificance before the God-implanted instinct that made Adam, awakening from a deep sleep and finding the woman beside him, accept Eve as bone of his bone; he cared not nor questioned whence she came. So it is with the sons of Adam ever since, through the law of heredity which makes us all one common family. And so it will be with us in our re-formation of this old Republic" (273). In this world of white Adams lying down (or at least waking up) with green, yellow, or black Eves, expansion becomes a metaphor for intercourse, and the United States' imperial project is likened to the Anglo-Saxon's copulation with the globe's green, yellow, and black populations. Thornton's imagery cites erotic attraction as instinctual evidence of the "law of heredity that makes us all one common family"; racially other Eves are the bone of white Adams' bones. Moreover, intermarriage is not a pollution or degeneracy, but an invigoration: the "old Republic" of America will undergo a "re-formation" in this imperialist marriage.

Thornton's argument about expansion reflects Hopkins's own complicated position on United States imperialism.[37] As Hazel Carby points out, by the end of the 1890s "the United States had acquired the basis of its empire," having annexed the Philippines, Puerto Rico, Guam, Hawaii, and half of Samoa.[38] This empire, Carby reminds us, was composed primarily of people of African, Indian, Polynesian, Japanese, and Chinese descent, the so-called "darker races." Thus Thornton's argument that "if we are not ready to receive and assimilate the new material which will be brought to mingle with our pure Anglo-Saxon stream, we should call a halt to our expansion policy" (273), reminds both the club audience and us readers that the United States had its own internal problems regarding expansion and amalgamation: both the African American population that white America did not want to assimilate and the Native Americans who were being virtually destroyed through U.S. "expansion." Hopkins's linking of domestic and international imperialism seems to work in two directions. On the one hand, given America's racist history, international expansion is at best a problematic endeavor. On the other hand, Hopkins's argument, as voiced by Dr. Thornton, attempts to use international expansion to envision an amalgamated Republic beyond America's racial divisions.

Thornton's story, his "old wives' tale," catalogues America's own internal imperialism; he tells the listeners that the story "came under his observation as a practitioner" (273). We soon learn that he is not only a practitioner of medicine, but a practitioner of amalgamation. The tale that Thornton tells to "make his meaning clearer" is, like Ryder's story in "The Wife of His Youth," delivered to a very public and "blue-blooded" audience with similar results: the secret wife of Thornton's middle-age is produced quite literally to "illustrate" his tale. Thornton's long, convoluted tale of the Gordon family presents a family whose whiteness and social status is based on both foreign piracy and domestic exclusion.

As Hopkins tells us, "the Gordons were old New England Puritans who had come over in the 'Mayflower'" (274). Captain Gordon, having amassed and lost a fortune in the East India trade as an imperialist and a pirate, "restored [his] old Puritan stock to its rightful position" in a fortuitous first marriage to a wealthy Boston heiress. When this first wife gives birth to a third child with suspiciously dark skin, Captain Gordon violently confronts her, causing a crisis that kills both mother and child. Gordon has kept this ancestry secret from his two surviving daughters, though he plans to quietly disinherit them. His second marriage produces a white (and therefore right) heir to the Gordon fortune, which, we remember, he has acquired from his "black" first wife. Gordon, the new wife, and the young "white" heir are murdered one night, and, although Gordon's daughter Talma is tried for the crime, there is not enough evidence to convict her. She and her sister Jeanette flee public opprobrium and take up residence in Europe, where Talma becomes engaged to a successful young painter and Jeanette dies. Jeanette leaves Talma a revealing letter that unmasks the Gordon girls' heritage, the "blackness of their whiteness," or what Talma's fiancé calls "the pollution of Negro blood" as he packs his bags. With her engagement fallen through, Talma retires (perhaps also to die of blackness) to Thornton's sanitarium, which has been established on the old Gordon estate. It turns out that Jeanette (and not Talma) had indeed plotted to murder the Gordons, having learned of her father's plan to disinherit. Though another villain beat her to the task, she did manage to destroy the will and thus restore the girls' financial inheritance. The murderer, it turns out, is a man named Simon Cameron, conveniently dying at Thornton's sanitarium. Thus Dr. Thornton holds all the keys to the Gordon mystery. The murder was Cameron's revenge against Gordon's piracy in East India; it is revealed that Gordon himself slaughtered Cameron's father for gold. Gordon, it seems, is punished not only for his imperial enterprises abroad, but for his domestic imperialism as well: having murdered Cameron's father, it becomes apparent that he all but murdered his first wife and first son too. This is the end of Thornton's narration to the Canterbury club; the Gordon mystery is solved. Expansion abroad is thus likened to piracy, whereas expansion at home is a theft of another kind: Captain Gordon had "stolen" his "black" first wife's money, but refused to incorporate her or her daughters as kin. Thornton, in contrast to Gordon, turns out to be a benevolent practitioner of "expansion," having incorporated Talma and her story as his own. When the Canterbury Club guests ask curiously, "what became of Talma Gordon?" Thornton rises and says, "I shall have much pleasure in introducing you to my wife—née Talma Gordon" (290). The "romantic" and "beautiful" wife who the club members have all heard about is thus revealed to be Thornton's black Eve, an embodiment of his expansionist argument.

Both Chesnutt and Hopkins employ the motif of secret wives, yet to very different effects. For Chesnutt, the "wife of his youth" exposes the African American's marriage to history, particularly to the history of slavery: this is a marriage of indebtedness, obligation, and though it is morally courageous, it is not presented as a particularly appealing option in Chesnutt's story. Thornton's public embrace of his "black" wife, on the other hand, provides a vision of an amalgamated American future that emerges from, but is not wedded to, this history. Histories, and particularly oppressive histories, certainly shape the present and the future for Hopkins, yet the tragedies of history are overcome and incorporated into the living present. It may be disturbing to some that both the "black" woman and her story are incorporated within the white doctor's narrative, and it may be disturbing that only the near-white African American woman can function as a liminal figure, whose undecidable racial status marks her as a subject on the border. It seems to me, though, that these undecidable figures are merely metaphors for new Americans and more of an argument against writers like Charles Carroll, who suggested in his venomous account *The Negro a Beast* (1900) that amalgamation would "corrupt the flesh of the nation."[39] Instead Hopkins was interested in a figure who would incorporate, literally within the flesh, both the violence of history *and* the future's promise. The history of slavery is thus never stagnant, never a "quicksand" that pulls its progeny down; instead it shapes the future of all America's black *and* white citizens.[40] We do well to remember here that Hopkins's story is about "white" people, and it is narrated to the ostensibly Anglo-Saxon Canterbury Club. Talma Gordon is of excellent stock; a descendant from the *Mayflower*, she is by all accounts truly an American, yet to paraphrase Ellison this "true" American is "also somehow black."

The near-white heroines of *Contending Forces* and "Talma Gordon" are not so much evidence of a bourgeois surrender to "purity, piety and submissiveness" then, but a blurring of racial boundaries. These "figures on the border" are illustrations of America's interwoven subjectivities, historically bound together, as Du Bois put it, "with the very warp and woof of the nation." Hopkins's apparently bourgeois figurations are, it seems to me, suggestive of her double embrace of both the violent history of slavery *and* a future that promises racial accord. Her fiction attempts to transform the discord embodied in America's already amalgamated citizenry into a symbol of national consanguinity. This distinctly "American Grammar," as Hortense Spillers might put it, is best described in the last pages of Hopkins's last novel: "The slogan of the hour is 'Keep the Negro down!' but who is clear enough in vision to decide who hath black blood and who hath it not? Can any one tell? No, not one; for in His own mysterious way He has united the white race and the black race in this new continent. By the transgression of the law He proves His own infallibility: 'Of One Blood have I made all nations of men to dwell upon the whole face of the earth,' is as true today as when given to the inspired writers to be recorded. No man can draw the dividing line between the two races, for they are both of one blood!"[41] Hopkins's visionary reckoning that "No man can draw the dividing line between the two races" is directed to resist efforts to "Keep the Negro down." Adopting a tone of providential rhetoric, Hopkins's declaration that we are "of one blood" asserts a radical genealogy that both challenges the political exclusions of American subjectivity and imagines a new Eden and new Adam and Eve.[42]

NOTES

1. Gwendolyn Brooks, afterword to Pauline Hopkins's *Contending Forces* (1899; Carbondale: Southern Illinois University Press, 1978), 403–4. Subsequent references both to Brooks's afterword and to *Contending Forces* will be given parenthetically in the text.

2. On accommodation, see, for example, Alice Walker's *Meridian*, published in 1976, and Toni Morrison's *Song of Solomon*, which came out in 1977. The eighties

saw a shift in interest back toward earlier African American writers as many authors returned thematically to rewrite the plots of slave narratives and racial romances. See Shirley Anne Williams's *Dessa Rose* (1986), Octavia Butler's *Kindred* (1979), and Toni Morrison's *Beloved* (1987).

3. I am not arguing here that Brooks is a flawed reader of Pauline Hopkins, or even that her reading of Hopkins is questionable. Brooks is right that Hopkins's voice would not indicate a revolutionary spirit in the 1960s or 1970s, especially following Wright and company. I argue with Brooks, however, because in her historical moment, Hopkins did intend her genealogical fiction to "wheedle, whip and whine" and to "forge a fiery army of a hundred languid men." Critics of Hopkins's work tend to ignore or downplay Brooks's comments because she is one of the twentieth century's most brilliant poets and because her own work is so insightful about race oppression in America. Hazel Carby, however, also takes issue with Brooks's characterization of Hopkins's "assimilationist urges" (*Reconstructing Womanhood: The Emergence of the Afro-American Woman Novelist* [New York: Oxford University Press, 1987], 140).

4. Abby Arthur Johnson and Ronald Maberry Johnson, *Propaganda and Aesthetics: The Literary Politics of Afro-American Magazines in the Twentieth Century* (Amherst: University of Massachusetts Press, 1979), 9. Subsequent references will be given parenthetically in the text.

5. Angelina Grimké, "Black Is, As Black Does," *Colored American Magazine* 1 (August 1900): 163; quoted in Johnson and Johnson, 7.

6. For example, Charles Carroll in his *The Negro a Beast* argued (not unsurprisingly, given his title) that amalgamation "destroys the standing of the nation or continent in the eyes of God, lays its civilization in ruins, and transforms its population into barbarians, idolaters and savages" (319) and William Calhoun characterized miscegenation as "one of the greatest evils consequent upon the two races" that would result in the disappearance of the Negro and the mongrelization of the Caucasian. They were not alone in their sentiments: amalgamation was characterized alternately as "race decadence" and "perilous contamination" by others. See Charles Carroll, *The Negro a Beast, or In the Image of God* (1900; Miami: Mnemosyne Publishing Co., 1969); William P. Calhoun, *The Caucasian and the Negro in the United States* (1902; New York: Arno Press, 1977); and William Benjamin Smith, *The Color Line: A Brief in Behalf of the Unborn* (New York: McClure, Phillips, 1905).

7. "Editorial and Publishers' Announcements," *Colored American Magazine* 6 (March 1903): 398–99; quoted in Johnson and Johnson, 8.

8. The publication dates for *Winona, Hagar's Daughters*, and *Of One Blood* reflect the span of their serialization in the *Colored American Magazine*. These novels did not appear in book form until they were published as part of the Oxford University Press Schomburg Library series in 1988. See *The Magazine Novels of Pauline Hopkins* (New York: Oxford University Press, 1988).

9. Hopkins's nationalism is akin to the "literary black nationalism" discussed in Wilson Moses, *The Golden Age of Black Nationalism, 1850–1925* (New York: Oxford University Press, 1978). Though his references to Hopkins's work are condescending, the nationalism that his project describes is certainly appropriate for thinking about her oeuvre.

10. Shirlee Taylor Haizlip, *The Sweeter the Juice* (New York: Simon and Schuster, 1994); subsequent references will be given parenthetically in the text.

11. Michel Foucault, "Nietzsche, Genealogy, History," in *Language, Counter-Memory, Practice: Selected Essays and Interviews*, ed. Donald F. Bouchard, trans. Bouchard and Sherry Simon (Ithaca: Cornell University Press, 1977), 144.

12. I take these terms from Mae Henderson, who extends Teresa De Lauretis's formulations. See Mae Henderson, "Speaking in Tongues: Dialogics, Dialectics, and the Black Woman Writer's Literary Tradition" in *Changing Our Own Words*, ed. Cheryl Wall (New Brunswick: Rutgers University Press, 1989), 19. Subsequent references will be given parenthetically in the text.

13. Hopkins would have had a good deal of control in choosing the illustrations for her book because it was published by the newly formed Colored Cooperative Publishing Company in 1900. An all African-American collective, the publishers felt that *Contending Forces* was a "powerful race book" and were hardly censorious of her work. Additionally, the collective started the *Colored American Magazine* the same year that they published *Contending Forces*, and they brought Hopkins onto the staff of the magazine. The frontispiece to *Contending Forces* was also published in the *Colored American Magazine* when they serialized the opening chapters in the November 1900 issue.

14. See Angela Davis's brilliant study, "Rape, Racism and the Myth of the Black Rapist," in *Women, Race, and Class* (New York: Random House, 1981).

15. I am reversing the terms that Lauren Berlant employs in her discussion of *Passing* in "National Brands/National Body: Imitation of Life," in *Comparative American Identities*, ed. Hortense Spillers (New York: Routledge, 1991), 111.

16. Hazel Carby (132) reads this scene as a symbolic rape.

17. See Hortense Spillers, "Mama's Baby, Papa's Maybe: An American Grammar Book" *Diacritics* 17.2 (Summer 1987): 77.

18. Foucault, 148.

19. Carby, 315.

20. For a more detailed discussion of the ramifications of "True Womanhood," see Barbara Welter's discussion in "The Cult of True Womanhood" (*American Quarterly* 18 [1966]: 151–74). Hopkins's white contemporary Kate Chopin was also exploring the oppressive ramifications of "true womanhood" in *The Awakening*, which was published in 1899, just prior to *Contending Forces*. Chopin's white heroine drowns herself like Grace Montfort, though unlike Grace, Edna escapes to a watery death because there is no place yet in the world for a white woman who would live outside the constraints of conventionality.

21. Claudia Tate, "Allegories of Black Female Desire; or, Rereading Nineteenth-Century Sentimental Narratives of Black Female Authority," in Wall, 122.

22. See Anna Julia Cooper, *A Voice From the South* (1892; New York: Oxford University Press, 1988), 134. Subsequent references will be given parenthetically in the text.

23. See W. E. B. Du Bois, *The Souls of Black Folk* (1903; New York: Signet, 1969), 50. Subsequent references will be given parenthetically in the text.

24. See Foucault, 148.

25. Spillers, "Mama's Baby," 67.

26. Claudia Tate, *Domestic Allegories of Political Desire* (New York: Oxford University Press, 1992), 63.

27. I agree with Ann duCille that "the near-white heroines who dominated the pages of nineteenth-century novels—no matter how distasteful their pale skin, piety, and purity may be to modern readers—served important political and literary functions. They stand as signs of the racist contradictions at the heart of American society" (*The Coupling Convention: Sex, Text, and Tradition in Black Women's Fiction* [New York: Oxford University Press, 1993], 47).

28. Spillers, "Mama's Baby," 74.

29. My thinking here is informed by Spillers's argument that "'family,' as we practice and understand it 'in the West'—the vertical transfer of a bloodline, of a patronymic, of titles and entitlement, of real estate and the prerogatives of 'cold cash,' from fathers to sons and in the supposedly free exchange of affectional ties between a male and female of his choice—becomes the mythically revered privilege of a free and freed community" ("Mama's Baby," 75).

30. Laura Doyle, "The Folk, the Nobles, and the Novel: The Racial Subtext of Sentimentality," *Narrative* 3.2 (May 1995): 179.

31. Here I refer to Hopkins's last serialized novel, *Of One Blood, or, The Hidden Self*, where she suggests that black and white Americans share "one blood" and also, more importantly for her story, that black Americans share "one blood" with a grand Ethiopian civilization.

32. Ralph Ellison, "What America Would Be Like without Blacks," *Going to the Territory* (New York: Random House, 1986), 110–11.

33. The photograph appeared in both the October and November 1900 issues of *The Colored American Magazine* and was offered to the public for the price of one dollar.

34. For an interesting discussion of the impact of *Plessy v. Ferguson* on the literature of the 1890s, see Eric Sundquist, *To Wake the Nations: Race in the Making of American Literature* (Cambridge: Harvard University Press, 1993), especially 225–70.

35. Charles Chesnutt, *The Wife of His Youth and Other Stories of the Color Line* (1899; Ann Arbor: University of Michigan Press, 1968). My discussion of Chesnutt's story as an "old wives' tale" is informed by Werner Sollers's compelling reading of Chesnutt in *Beyond Ethnicity: Consent and Descent in American Culture* (New York: Oxford University Press, 1986), 156–66.

36. Pauline E. Hopkins, "Talma Gordon," *The Colored American Magazine* 1.5 (October 1900), 271–90; subsequent references given parenthetically in the text.

37. For a provocative discussion of Hopkins's position vis-à-vis America's imperial project, see Kevin Gaines, "Black Americans' Racial Uplift Ideology as 'Civilizing Mission': Pauline E. Hopkins on Race and Imperialism," in *Cultures of United States Imperialism*, ed. Amy Kaplan and Donald Pease (Durham: Duke University Press, 1993), 433–55.

38. Carby, 133.

39. See n. 6.

40. I am alluding to the title and theme of Nella Larsen's 1928 novel, *Quicksand*. See *Quicksand and Passing* (New Brunswick: Rutgers University Press, 1987).

41. *Of One Blood*, in *The Magazine Novels of Pauline Hopkins*, 607.

42. I wish to thank the following people for their generous and thoughtful responses to earlier versions of this essay: Cora Kaplan, Cheryl Wall, Marianne DeKoven, Mary Dougherty, Jaime Hovey, Eve Oishi, Lynne Dickson, and Jim Albrecht. I also thank Anthony Toussaint and Diana Lachatanere at the Schomburg Library for their assistance locating and reproducing the frontispiece to *Contending Forces*.

Nationalism and Korean American Women's Writing

Theresa Hak Kyung Cha's *Dictee*

SHU-MEI SHIH

Not quite the Same, not quite the Other, she stands in that undetermined
threshold place where she constantly drifts in and out. Undercutting the
inside/outside opposition, her intervention is necessarily that of both a
deceptive insider and a deceptive outsider.
  Trinh T. Minh-ha, When the Moon Waxes Red

As subject for history, woman always occurs simultaneously in several
places. Woman un-thinks the unifying, regulating history that ho-
mogenizes and channels forces, herding contradictions into a single
battlefield. In woman, personal history blends together with the history of
all women, as well as national and world history.
  Hélène Cixous, "The Laugh of the Medusa"

Given our postcolonial histories, it seems to me that it is only in the teeth
of violence that we can speak the unstable truth of our bodies, our
human lives.
  Meena Alexander, "Piecemeal Shelter: Writing, Ethnicity, Violence"

The project of "claiming America," the dominant agenda of identity
politics in Asian American discourse since its inception, has recently
been dealt serious challenges from new immigrants and a younger generation
of scholars. The infusion of transnational consciousness that resulted from an
increasingly globalized culture industry and flexibility of locational/national
boundaries threatens to make the kind of Asian American cultural nationalism
as promulgated by Frank Chin inconsequential. This is not really because of
Chin's militaristic tropes of empowerment with their strong masculinist bias,
but rather because of the changing demographics of Asian Americans (overwhelmingly more immigrants than native-born) who perceive their multiply
situated identities to be incompatible with a nation-bound definition of "Asian
American."[1] The consequences of these challenges to the "claiming Amer-

ica" agenda are yet to be thoroughly mapped or understood, but the debate on the question has been not unlike that about the incompatibility between politics and postmodernism: a domestic identity politics is politically more viable and effective in attaining for the minority the rights of national citizenship and representation, while a transnational conception loses its political edge, if it does not become politically paralyzed.[2]

But we do well to remember an earlier moment in Asian American discourse and writing when similar challenges were repressed. Theresa Hak Kyung Cha's 1982 work *Dictee*, a text that did not speak to any activist agenda, was ignored for almost a whole decade, only reemerging in recent years as one of the most important works of Korean American literature.[3] The history of the text's reception, first considered non–Asian American, finally becoming some kind of authentic representation of the hybrid, interstitial Asian American subjectivity, underlies the shift in discursive paradigms intimately connected to the rise of a stream of postcolonial theory that may be termed postmodernist. While the text does speak to a kind of deterritorialized, denationalized consciousness, what I find compelling instead is the *pains* and *traumas* of such consciousness that Theresa Cha all too eloquently writes about. Reading through Cha's torturous negotiations with various tropes and locational politics of nationalism, one may be able to rethink the reified oppositional relationship between claiming America and transcending America and instead see how these opposed agenda might be speaking to each other in dialogic, though paradoxical, ways.

The 1.5 Generation Imaginary and Nationalism

In this paper, I propose to read *Dictee* as the work of a "1.5 generation" (*il-jum-o-se*) Korean American woman writer. While no component of this designation—"1.5 generation," "Korean," "American," "woman," and "writer"—neither singly nor in various combinations, can fully account for Cha as a writer or for her text, as a working category "1.5 generation" not only offers a useful point of entry to the text, but also a specific way to approach notions of the "interstitial," the "in-between," "hybridity," and "heterogeneity" valorized in recent discussions of Asian American literature. The category "1.5 generation," though widely used within the Korean American community, has been largely subsumed under the rigid denominations of first, second, and third generations in Asian American discourse. Born in Asia but emigrating at an early age, the 1.5 generation comes to America and grows up often as fully acculturated as second generation, but there is usually a less adamant rejection of the Asian country from where the family emigrated. Though not always

bilingual, they are often bicultural, and they maintain a profoundly ambiguous relationship to both the country in which they grow up and the country
of their birth. They are simultaneously the immigrant whom American-born
Asian Americans may despise and attempt to alienate, and the acculturated
American who shares the language and experience of the American-born.[4]
Hence they are in a sense neither "Asian," "American," nor "Asian American,"
while at the same time being all of these. The simultaneity of their being
neither/nor and both/all is in a sense what distinguishes the 1.5 generation
from both immigrant Asians and American-born Asian Americans.

Notions such as "in-between" and "interstitial" are insufficient spatial metaphors here since they cannot account for such simultaneity. Although they
are conceived in opposition to the inside/outside binarism, they are actually
catechrestic because without set boundaries for inside and outside there can
be no in-between. In other words, spatial categories will always already spell
out the boundedness of space unless they are endowed with a temporal dimension. We see in Cha's work, for instance, how borders both form and
coalesce, contest and yield; hence there is no set "in-between" or "interstitial"
location. As borders shift in time and space, so does the location of the subject.
It is impossible to frame a specific "in-between" space. Just as space is fragmented, so is time: occupying multiple places and shifting locations means
being in different temporalities at the same time.

"Hybridity" and "heterogeneity," on the other hand, can be used only with
caution. The celebratory use of the terms undermines differences in kind and
thereby essentially empties them of their significance, turning them into utopian designations with universalistic overtones. Just as the shifting locality of
Theresa Cha may differ in specifics from that of a second generation Korean
American, or another member of the 1.5 generation for that matter, each hybridity and heterogeneity is also constituted differently. A basic distinction between metropolitan and postcolonial hybridities, made by R. Radhakrishnan,
is useful in illustrating how "all hybridities are not equal." Radhakrishnan
claims that postcolonial hybridity is an expression of "extreme pain and agonizing dislocations," "an excruciating act of self-production by and through
multiple traces," not a celebratory, comfortable "jouissance" of metropolitan
hybridity, which hides "the subject of the dominant West." If the picture of
the "self" that emerges in Cha's work appears to be composite, fragmentary,
unstable, and nonunified, it still bespeaks her desire to articulate, however
difficult or impossible the task, a sense of one's self, or what Radharkrishnan
calls an "inventory of one's self," where *agonizing* heterogeneity and hybridity
continue to explode the notions of a unified self, a stable identity, and political

representation based on such closed, reified boundaries.[5] The hybridity witnessed in the work of Theresa Cha powerfully registers such a painful process of self-production, but the forces with which she negotiates are distinct from other postcolonial hybridities, not all of which are equal or the same.

The basic, most immediately recognizable components of Cha's agonizing hybridity may be very broadly described: colonial and postcolonial Korean national culture and history, memory of Korea, growing up in America as a racialized and gendered subject, Western artistic and poetic traditions. In *Dictee*, Korean national history becomes foregrounded as perhaps the most painful source of Cha's memory. An obsession with the Korean nation and Korean nationalism, however, underlies the work not only of Theresa Hak Kyung Cha, but of a majority of Korean American writers. This explains in part the inevitability of nationalism or, more precisely, diasporic nationalism, as subject matter in Cha's work and the need to reinscribe that subject matter from individual and individuated perspectives. A history still palpably warm with bloodshed—Japanese colonial rule (1910–45), the division into North and South Korea (1945), the Korean War (1950–53), the American neocolonial military presence after the war, the autocratic rules of Rhee Syngman and Park Chung-hee until 1979, and numerous political coups and demonstrations from the 1960s to the present day, including the bloody Kwangju incident (1980)—ineluctably forces itself on Korean American literary imagination, perhaps because of both its closeness in time and intensity of its impact on all Korean immigrants. Masculinist inscriptions of nation and nationalism in such texts as Peter Hyun's *Man Sei: The Making of a Korean American* (1986) and Richard Kim's *The Martyred* (1964) and *Lost Names* (1970) seek to establish an equation between the male subject and the national subject by making national history serve as the catalyst for the formation of male subjectivity, identity, and agency. In the by-now canonical *Clay Walls* (1987) by Kim Ronyoung, a feminine probing into the various ways the discourse of nationalism has been put to use reveals a regime of gender bias within those uses, while Mary Paik Lee's *Quiet Odyssey* (1990) and Margaret Pai's *The Dreams of Two Yi-min* (1989) background nationalist activities in Korea, Hawaii, and the continental United States as pivotal to Korean American experience.[6] Theresa Hak Kyung Cha, along with the poet Myung Mi Kim, presents by far the most lyrical renderings of the obsession with the nation and nationalism, albeit in a lyricism seeped in violence, darkness, and tragedy.[7] Recent scholarship on the constructed nature of nationalism in the West and in East Asia, on the colonial prehistory of Third World nationalism as derivative discourse, on the limits and violence of nationalist ideology, reflects a growing awareness of the fluctuating boundaries of nationhood, one that 1.5 generation Korean American women writers like Cha and Kim "experience" culturally, linguistically, corporeally, and viscerally.[8]

The discourse within which I would further locate Cha's reinscription of nationalism is that of ethnic feminism simultaneously within and beyond Korean and Korean American contexts. Two issues are relevant here: a feminist critique of the homosocial basis of nations and nationalism, and a racialized/ethnicized critique of the connection between the nation state and racism.[9] Deniz Kandiyoti argues that nationalist movements often invite the participation of women through interpellating them as "national" actors but also concurrently reaffirm the boundaries of gender difference.[10] Valentine M. Moghadam also notes that although the trope of women is often the basis upon which the nation is imagined, there is within each nation a definite gender economy.[11] Partha Chatterjee goes so far as to conclude that nationalism in colonial states such as India actually sharpens the division between genders because women are made to embody cultural authenticity and tradition.[12] A reading of male Korean American narratives of nationalism, such as the texts mentioned above, unambiguously reveals such an agenda. Floya Anthias and Nira Yuval-Davis, on the other hand, argue that boundaries of all "imagined communities" such as nation, ethnicity, and culture are inevitably racialized. Race and racism, they contend, serve as "a structuring principle for national processes, by defining both the boundaries of the nation and the constituents of national identity." Commenting on the fact that people of different ethnicities and races have different access to the state and its resources, they further claim the existence of an internal colonialism in various nation-states.[13] In this regard, the history of legalized racism against Asians and Asian Americans in the United States indeed leaves no room for comfort. As bell hooks also unambiguously remarks in regard to black women: "To white women, full participation in the growth of the U.S. as a nation often included acceptance and support of white racial imperialism, while black women, even those who were most politically conservative, were often obliged to denounce the nation because of its racist policies."[14] What compounds the difficult situation for Korean Americans is that their status as recent immigrants is taken as justification to further delegitimize them as full citizens of the state. Before a 1.5 generation Korean American writer understands the complexity of her relationship to the American nation, then, she is already multiply disenfranchised by her immigrant status, ethnicity, and race. In a similar manner, her relationship to the Korean nation is anything but unambiguous: strictly circumscribed by a patriarchal nationhood, no longer a Korean citizen, and often unable to speak the language, she is ostracized or, at best, left out.[15] In sum, the 1.5 generation imaginary cannot extricate itself from either the discourse of transcending America (because of its postcolonial hybridity) or that of claiming America (because of its unequal access to the nation-state).

Gender, Nation, and Blood Writing

A text profuse with images of dismemberment, *Dictee* is composed of fragments: words, phrases, incomplete sentences, paragraphs, poems, pictures, diagrams, calligraphy, and photos. Korean and diasporic Korean history and shamanistic myth, Greek mythology, Roman Catholic religious discourse, French literature, and Chinese cosmology also play their intertextual roles. Immensely difficult to decipher, the text often seems to drown in its own fragmentation, refusing to make any straightforward, easily consumable signification. It draws attention to the way words and phrases sound as they are juxtaposed and truncated, to emphasize the experiential quality of language, so that searching beyond the play of signifiers often seems to yield little result. This is because Cha does not merely tell us something, but also writes about telling, about speaking, but the text's rejection of straightforward signification is also the result of Cha's desire to unlearn and to unwrite the "colonial consolations" of the English and French languages through typographic and orthographic innovations, as well as semantic and syntactic disruptions to conventional representation.[16] She records the painful processes by which utterances, speech, and writing are made, through both a complex negotiation with linguistic colonialism and imperialism, patriarchal injunctions, as well as the physical, physiological impediments to speech, always connecting the historical and the mythical with the personal and the corporeal. In the process, Cha narrates herself as a voice or voices through the orchestration of numerous female voices (historical and mythical) and the re-membering and coordination of disparate speech organs (physical, physiological).

This narrativization of the self within a multiplicity of voices is generally grounded in a narration of the Korean nation and its modern history. The book opens with a rubbing of Korean words carved on the wall of a coal mine in Japan, allegedly inscribed by conscripted Korean laborers and sadly expressing the most elementary of longing: "I miss my mother. I am hungry. I want to go back to my hometown."[17] The first of the nine Greek muses Cha invokes, whose names become the discernible section headings in the text, is Clio, the muse of history, who tells the history of the Korean independence movement under harsh Japanese rule. Cha begins her narration of this national history with an enlarged photo of the female revolutionary Yu Guan Soon, with her dates of birth and death printed in large letters on the adjoining page. What strikes the reader immediately is the extreme brevity of her life—seventeen years—explicitly revealing the cruelty of those who executed her. The female body demolished (for participating in independence activities during the March 1, 1919, demonstration and afterward, Yu Guan Soon was imprisoned and later dismembered by the Japanese) then becomes a metaphor for the decimated nation: "She is given seven years prison sentence to which her reply is that the nation itself is imprisoned" (37).

The female body thus deployed in the name of the nation becomes the register of the materiality of history its bloodshed, that, to borrow Lisa Lowe's words, "exceeds textualization."[18] This materiality is what escapes linguistic representation: "Japan has become the sign. The alphabet. The vocabulary. . . . The meaning is the instrument, memory that pricks the skin, stabs the flesh, the volume of blood, the physical substance blood as measure, that rests as record, as document. . . . To the other nations who are not witnesses, who are not subject to the same oppressions, they cannot know. Unfathomable the words, the terminology: enemy, atrocities, conquest, betrayal, invasion, destruction. . . . Not physical enough. Not to the very flesh and bone, to the core, to the mark" (32). History is here opposed to historiography, the former infused with blood, flesh, and bone, the latter mere words. Yu Guan Soon's photograph, along with the photograph of Korean martyrs crucified in a graveyard awaiting execution by Japanese soldiers (39), visually addresses the impossibility of historiography (words) to capture history's concrete, material, physical, and above all bloody reality, one filled with "decapitated forms."

The text is in this way punctuated throughout by fragments of Korean historical reference. This is the case even when the text seems to leave the realm of Korean national history for more philosophical musings on the nature of language and writing. At these points, the physical narrations of the nation present themselves as even more stark and intrusive. In the "Melpomene Tragedy" section, Cha, again with visual eloquence, shows us a map of Korea severed in two by a thick Demilitarized Zone across the middle. Divided against her will by neocolonial powers, particularly the United States, Korea was deprived of the right to self-determination even though the Japanese colonial era was already over by the end of World War II.[19] "We are severed in Two by an abstract enemy an invisible enemy under the title of liberators who have conveniently named the severance, Civil War. Cold War. Stalemate" (81). Words of violent separation such as "severance" and "incision" permeate this section, echoing the severance of the national body with the demolition of the female body of Yu Guan Soon and the "decapitated forms" of Korean revolutionaries.

Again when the text seemingly moves beyond and away from Korea as a frame of reference after the "Melpomene Tragedy" section, a picture of a sea of Korean faces suddenly appears without explanation: people dressed in early-twentieth-century-style clothing, traditional *hanbok*, their faces anguished and indignant (122). The photo depicts a crowd of onlookers, men, women and children, standing on one side of a street in front of a temple, supporting the independence marchers of March 1, 1919. It speaks visually, and it speaks through those mouths agape, most probably shouting support for a nationalist theme not verbally articulated by Cha.

This national history is also intertwined with personal history, specifically that of Cha's mother, who was born and raised in Manchuria during the colonial era by parents who had earlier fled from the Japanese. When Manchuria too fell to the Japanese in 1931 after the Mukden incident, they came under Japanese colonial rule, therefore again deprived of their language and culture, except that this time the Chinese-born mother was not even allowed to speak Chinese, let alone Korean. In the section entitled "Calliope Epic Poetry," speaking Korean is described as risking death, because Japanese colonizers forbade its use, metaphorically tying the tongue (the physical organ) and literally usurping the tongue (Korean language). Theresa Cha therefore deliberates on mother tongue, mother's tongue, mother's language, "mother" as the first utterance, and so on, as she explores the connection between nation, language, and gender. Addressing her mother, Cha writes, "you speak the tongue the mandatory language like others. It is not your own. Even if it is not you know you must. You are Bi-lingual. You are tri-lingual. The tongue that is forbidden is your own mother tongue. You speak in the dark. In the secret. The one that is yours. Your own. . . . To utter each word is a privilege you risk by death. Not only for you but for all. All of you who are one, who by law tongue tied and forbidden of tongue" (45–46). Political coercion by the Japanese in Manchuria disallows Cha's mother from speaking her own mother tongue, hence tongue-tied "by law."

National and personal history are further conjoined in Cha's depiction of Korean history after the partition of the Korean peninsula, and here we begin to see Theresa Cha's explicitly gendered inscription on nation and nationalism. A few historical facts are necessary to understand her critique. The Korean nationalist movement, born out of the independence movements of the early twentieth century against Japanese occupation, has a long history both in Korea and in such sites of diaspora as Manchuria, Hawaii, and Los Angeles. This Korean nationalism, sponsored by the Korean government after independence, nevertheless proved to be very problematic. Directly under neocolonial control of the United States, a series of repressive regimes coopted the rhetoric of nationalism in the service of a totalitarian state. While the anticolonial, "original" nationalism under Japanese occupation was meant to be liberationist, the state-sponsored, "derived" nationalism after independence proved to be its opposite, hence the rise of grassroots nationalism in opposition to the state and an unending series of student demonstrations.[20]

In 1980, Theresa Cha returned to Korea and was shocked by a sense of history repeating itself. Distant historical memories of the 1919 independence march and more recent ones of student demonstrations in the early 1960s against the autocratic rule of Rhee Syngman were revived as she witnessed more bloodshed of students demonstrating against the totalitarian rule of Park Chung-hee. A description of a 1962 demonstration in which young men were killed uncannily describes the current one: "Orders, permissions to use force against the students, have been dispatched. To be caught and beaten with sticks, and for others, shot, remassed, and carted off. They fall they bleed they die" (83). To the bloodstains of the revolutionaries under the colonial rule are added the blood of students opposing the government. All these stains cannot be erased: "I heard that the rain does not erase the blood fallen on the ground. I heard from the adults, the blood stains still. Year after year it rained. The stone pavement stained where you fell still remains dark" (85). History repeats itself, only this time those who are shooting the students are Koreans, like an "Insect that eats its own mate" (88). The section overflows with the sorrow of a mother whose son is killed, as inconsolable as the bloodstain is ineradicable. The name of the oppressor has changed, but the pain has remained for the people, especially women. The heart-wrenching cries of the mother who begs her son not to go to the demonstration not only brings into crisis the mandate of the nationalist state to protect and represent its people but also that of a political demonstration against that state. What indeed is national political struggle for a mother? "Running to the front door, Mother, you are holding my older brother pleading with him not to go out to the demonstration. You are threatening him, you are begging to him. . . . You are pulling at him you stand before the door. He argues with you he pushes you away. You use all your force, all that you have" (83). The politicized young students arrayed against the state are thus obliquely paralleled by the instrumentalized police and soldiers deployed to use violence against them. Cha creates this parallel by noting how students wear uniforms as do the soldiers, both "uniformed" (57) without individual identity or voice, representing a "school" or a "post" (83, 85). Implicitly, Cha articulates a connection between nationalisms (whether for or against the nationalist state) and the uniform instrumentalization of the human will and the human body.

A gendered critique of Korean nationalisms is further coupled with a racialized examination of American nationalism. In a satiric voice, Theresa Cha notes what it means to become a naturalized American citizen: "I have the documents. Documents, proof, evidence, photograph, signature. One day you raise the right hand and you are American. They give you an American Pass port. The United States of America. Somewhere someone has taken my identity and replaced it with their photograph. The other one. Their signature their seals. *Their own image*. And you learn the executive branch the legislative branch and the third. Justice. Judicial branch. It makes the difference. The rest is past" (56, emphasis mine). Cha questions what it means to be "naturalized," which in effect "denaturalizes" one by imposing a national identity, which demands ideological, cultural, and other forms of submission. Does becoming "American" mean memorizing the three branches of government? Cha asks ironically. What then is to become "American" for an ethnic, racialized female? R. Radhakrishnan observes that naturalization into American citizenship for a diasporic person is a process of minoritization, one's previous national identity is turned merely into the qualifier "ethnic."[21] This spells out, from a different angle, the immense sense of loss and ambivalence that Cha articulates above.

This sense of loss and ambivalence, however, is extended also to the country of her origin. Immediately following this passage is Cha's discovery that in Korea a returned Korean is faced with equal disregard: "[Koreans] treat you with indifference" (56). Her own difference—"I speak another tongue now, a second tongue a foreign tongue" (80)—also disallows her from returning to the prediasporic state. Nationalism and nationality, to her, cannot but be reifying categories, categories as exclusionary, instrumentalized, and repressive as the uniformity of soldiers and policemen.

Cha's narration of these different nationalisms, then, provides a shifting sense of allegiance and puts the notion of geopolitical nationalism under erasure just as she has powerfully erected it, a simultaneous double movement of recalling and effacing. In a similar manner, evocations of the nation and nationalism as sites of symbolic meanings are also entwined with the materiality of history. In one instance, national history serves as a metaphor, the blood of revolutionaries and demonstrators becoming the most eloquent "writing" of history. As opposed to the kind of historiography that is mere words, Cha conceives of writing, any writing, as a form of bleeding: the image of blood, punctured from the skin, flowing and gushing from the veins, splattered on paper, becoming stain, like writing, or rather, becoming writing itself. "Something of the ink that resembles the stain from the interior emptied onto emptied into emptied upon this boundary this surface. More. Others. When possible ever possible to puncture to scratch to imprint. Expel. Ne te cache pas. Révèle toi. Sang. Encre. Of its body's extention of its containment" (65). The thickest ink, the "near-black liquid ink" (64), is the blood (sang/encre); writing is to puncture, to scratch, to imprint, to expel the blood.

Stone to pigment. Stone. Wall.
Page.
To stone, water, teinture, blood. (166)

This conception of writing as blood is a reciprocal metaphor: blood as the physical "writing" (imprint/stain) of history's violence, and writing as the process in which one discharges "blood" (ink). The ominous suggestion of death pervades both cases. The connection is further endowed with nationalist meanings: namely, the ritual of "blood writing" (hyulso) conducted by Korean revolutionaries (including Ahn Joong Kun, whose name appears on page 28) and student demonstrators to pledge their commitment to the cause of national liberation and democracy.[22] Instead of a metaphor, here writing in blood or blood writing becomes a literal act of sacrificial self-mutilation, again exemplifying the coexistence of the corporeal and the symbolic in Cha's signifying system.[23]

Writing and blood are here inextricably linked via the discourse of the nation, so that the nation returns once more as the text for which bloods/words are shed/written. Yet the national does not serve as the ultimate signified, but rather functions as a metaphor that Cha borrows for the investigation of a theme obsessively treated in the text: the physicality and corporeality of writing and speech. Time and again, the Korean nation and its history are evoked as a possible location of a nationalized, historicized female identity, while simultaneously the text deterritorializes nationalism and exposes the limits of its ideology from a gendered and racialized point of view.

Cha's gendered rethinking of nationalism is linked, moreover, to her critique of patriarchy as a form of colonialism. When the linguistic colonialisms of Japanese, French, and English (in order of lessening severity) are targeted as the agents that deprive one of one's true tongue, Cha conjoins such a critique with the patriarchal injunction against women's speech. For instance, she relates the silencing of Korean women by patriarchy; women tongue-tied by virtue of their gender. Describing her mother's relationship with her father, she says, "He is the husband, and she is the wife. He is the man. She is the wife. It is a given. He does as he is the man. She does as she is the woman, and the wife. Stands the distance between the husband and wife the distance of heaven and hell. . . . You only hear him taunting and humiliating her. She kneels beside him, putting on his clothes for him. . . . She yields space and in her speech, the same. Hardly speaks. Hardly at all. The slowness of her speech when she does. Her tears her speech" (102–4). The mother is multiply "tongued-tied": by law under Japanese colonialism, and now in her marriage by virtue of her gender. Theresa Cha, in fact, obsessively dwells on the theme of the silencing of women's tongues. Thus the prevalence of the figure of a Greek *diseuse* (a female teller, a sayer) whose voice, in Cha's puns, has been disused. She has no voice of her own and as a medium only transmits other voices. When she speaks, she is always already speaking a foreign tongue. The tongue is a foreign object in her mouth. Like a shaman, whose voice is used by others, Cha as a writer also speaks many languages—Korean, French, English, Latin, Chinese, and sometimes Italian—speaking in other voices, other languages. Hence the hesitations, the halting, stops and starts, and fragmentary utterances, both spontaneous and deliberate. Spontaneously fragmented, because Cha speaks with great difficulty; deliberately fragmented, because she is also subverting linear representation. Her tongue is hence "cracked" and "broken" in the sense that it speaks with impediment and also in the sense that it is divided into many tongues. Cha thereby emphasizes the corporeality and physicality of words and language as visualized in the cracked tongue of a female speaker. The multiply colonized tongue becomes the physical and visual corollary to the imprisonment of women under patriarchal and other colonialisms.

The text dramatizes the difficult process by which women come to speech not only on a political level (history of colonialisms), but also on the physiological and mythical levels, and here again the national becomes merely one of the many frames of reference. In the twenty-one pages prior to the first discernible section ("Clio History"), there begins the ritual of evocation by the Greek *diseuse* mentioned earlier. A voiceless woman who nonetheless has an urgency to speak, she mimics the physical movements of speech; she takes dictation and translation exercises in French to acquire a language. But when she fails to utter anything, she resorts to allowing others to speak through her: "She allows others. In place of her. Admits others to make full" (3); "*She would take on their punctuation. She waits to service this. . . . The relay. Voice. Assign. Hand it. Deliver it. Deliver.* She Relays the others. Recitation. Evocation" (4, italics in the original).

Allowing others to speak through her, particularly in the case of her dictation/reception of the French and English languages, again implicates the tongue as the site of a more subtle form of colonization, distinguished from the overt, institutionalized linguistic colonialism of the Japanese. French imperialism, as conveyed through translation and dictation exercises Cha relates, interpellates those who learn the language through cultural, religious, and ideological inculcation. In these exercises Cha records (Cha attended Catholic school and learned French as a child, later getting a B.A. in Comparative

Literature with French emphasis), we see the presence of a subtle imperialist trajectory: patriotic invocation of the French national anthem (16), a regiment of order and hierarchy (18) and total supplication of the female (St. Thérèsa de Lisieux included) to the "Man-God" (13) in the French Catholic church, and a crude Francocentrism in such statements as "Paris is not only the capital of France, it is the capital of the world" (15). Theresa Cha's response to such inculcation is subversion through acts of ironic submission: while taking dictation, she spells out the punctuation marks instead of using symbols (1); during acts of contrition in the Catholic church, she makes up sins not only "[f]or the guarantee of absolution" (16) but also because to conduct a confession is "[t]o make words. To make a speech in such tongues" (17). By similar processes, allowing yet ironically twisting the voices of dictation, the *diseuse* finally borrows a voice, acquiring utterance through relaying: "Begins imperceptibly, near-perceptible. (Just once. Just one time and it will take.) She takes. She takes the pause. Slowly. From the thick. The thickness. From weighted motion upwards. Slowed. To deliberation even when it passed upward through her mouth again. The delivery. She takes it. Slow. The invoking. All the time now. All the time there is. Always. And all times. The pause. Uttering. Hers now. Hers bare. The utter" (5). The process by which she acquires speech is fundamental to the structure of the book and its major underlying "desire," the desire of self-narration. The invocation of the nine Greek muses for nine sections of the text continues the *diseuse's*/Cha's search for speech, and the completion of the invocation is the acquiring of speech (and writing) and the narration of the self, which is the book. To speak and to write is to make possible a physical existence, as exemplified in the physical presence of the book as object.

The number nine holds a constellation of meanings relating speech and writing to life and regeneration. Cha names the nine discernible sections of the text after the nine Greek muses, each muse's specialty offering thematic and symbolic cues to the text that follows.[24] The Catholic religious ritual of novena (a nine-day ritual of prayer and devotion) that Cha recounts is an occasion for making words (writing this book), as it is also the process of birth, "the novena of the Immaculate Conception" (19). The nine-day period in which Demeter awaits the return of her daughter Persephone from Hades (133) brings the promise of the regeneration of the earth and the restoration of spring when the nine days are over, made possible by the reunion of mother and daughter. The Korean myth of princess Pali (*Pali kongju*) relayed by Cha tells of the princess's search for remedies for her ill mother and her acquisition of nine pockets of medicines from the well-keeper (167–70), again highlighting a theme of regeneration through mother-daughter bonding.[25] A sense of completion is then conveyed by the number ten in the cosmological structure of "Chung Wai: Tenth, a circle within a circle, a series of concentric circles" (173), by the evocation of the "tenth muse" Sappho in the beginning of the book, and by the tenth pocket of medicine that the well-keeper gives to princess Pali herself.[26] The twenty-one pages leading to the nine sections, and the dozen unnumbered pages with pictures and words preceding the twenty-one pages, can also be considered as the tenth section. The text is circular, beginning numerous times and never really ending, the pages between the front cover photo (an Egyptian ruin) and the back cover photo (female revolutionary Yu Guan Soon with her friends) forming a nonlinear continuum, self-contained in its gathering of fragments, and yet autonomous as a book-object. A completion in itself, the book in its physical presence articulates a sense of salvation and transcendence of the darkness, dismemberment, and tragedy depicted inside.

As evidenced from the numerical structuring, the text draws from multiple codes of reference, which are carefully made to echo or correspond to one another. The myth of princess Pali needs some explication in relationship to the figure of the *diseuse* and the Greek myth of Demeter and Persephone (who are also called *diseuses* by Cha). This myth is most often evoked in Korean shamanistic rituals for the dead. Princess Pali, the little girl in Cha's tale, is considered by Koreans as the original shaman from whom the tradition has descended. During a *kut* (shamanist performance) for the deceased, the female shaman calls the spirit of Pali by chanting the ballad of the princess and asking her to guide the deceased through the underworld. This is because in a different version of the myth, princess Pali descends to the underworld to find a magic herb with which she restores her mother's health.[27] The *diseuse* in this context corresponds to the possessed shaman (*naerim mudang*) through whom the voices speak, and they both become metaphors for the writer coming into her voice through a kind of exorcism of voices.[28] The mother and daughter bond in the myth of Demeter and Persephone finds its correspondence in princess Pali's own filial devotion to her mother, both having to do with a journey, whether voluntary or not, to the underworld.

The text in fact weaves a complex tapestry of multiple self-narration through the convergence, interweaving, correspondence, as well as disjunctions among various female characters: Persephone, princess Pali, a Korean shaman, a Greek diseuse, Yu Guan Soon, Joan of Arc, St. Thérèsa de Lisieux, Theresa Cha's mother Hyung Soon Huo, to name the immediately recognizable ones, besides the nine muses and Sappho. The multiple relationships of these characters to Cha and among themselves are important indications of the characteristics of the self being narrated. For instance, the connections among Yu Guan Soon, Joan of Arc, and St. Thérèsa de Lisieux are established directly in the text via their shared martyrdom. Before Yu Guan Soon dies, she utters the names of Joan of Arc (28); St. Thérèsa de Lisieux desires to be a religious martyr just like Joan (117); Theresa Cha's own first name echoes that of the saint; and finally, Cha prints in her text stills from Carl Dreyer's silent film "La Passion de Jeanne d'Arc" (1928). These women coalesce into the universal figure of the heroine: "The identity of such a path is exchangeable with any other heroine in history their names, dates, actions which require not definition in their devotion to generosity and self-sacrifice" (30). Theresa Cha too can be said to be a heroine via artistic martyrdom, dying for the sake of art, because one writes with one's blood and it can run dry: *"The ink spills thickest before it runs dry before it stops writing at all"* (133, italics in the original).

This universalism of the heroine, however, is once again disrupted by Cha through her gendered perspective, which questions the submission of women to another master narrative, religion. St. Thérèsa's self-imposed submission to the "Man-God," for instance, is unambiguously paralleled with Cha's mother's involuntary submission to her husband. Cha cleverly does this by juxtaposing these two narratives of submission on alternating pages in the ironically titled section "Erato Love Poetry." Religion, like patriarchy, demands a total capitulation of the female, to the point of masochistic self-negation. Theresa Cha therefore quotes the most gruesome details of the imagined martyrdom of St. Thérèsa from her autobiography, where she wants to be "scourged," "crucified," "flayed," "plunged into boiling oil," and her neck presented to the sword (117), while paralleling them with her mother's forced devotion to her husband, her silence, tears, and objectification (she is his "possession"). Through Cha's gendered critique, nationalism, religion, and patriarchy are presented as totalities that manage female subjects, so that even female heroism can only be expressed through submission and self-negation.

Moreover, the connection between nationalism and Western missionary education questions these totalities from a racialized perspective. Yu Guan Soon attended the Yihwa Girl's School (*Yihwa hakdang*) in Seoul run by American missionaries. There she received her formative education, and there also her nationalist aspirations were nurtured. How can this nationalism, a "derivative discourse," liberate the nation from the grips of colonial and neocolonial powers, when the discourse itself was borrowed from those very same powers?[29] This question is especially urgent for modern Korea because of the extent to which the Christian church and its religion served as the seedbeds of Korean independence activities during the colonial era. Furthermore, Theresa Cha herself attended Catholic schools, and the text, as discussed earlier, shows her ironic submission to religious catechisms as well as to the French language taught there. The question, "Whose nationalism is it?" is made even more poignant by the question, "Whose religion is the Catholicism or Christianity that helped foster nationalism in Korea?"

The mother-daughter narrative of Demeter and Persephone, of princess Pali, of Theresa Cha and her own mother, of St. Thérèsa and her religious "Mothers" for whom she wrote her autobiography *Story of a Soul*, again form several parallels.[30] Writing or narrating is here a process by which one speaks to, for, about, and from the mother, thereby engendering the birth of a self whose locus is the polyphonic gathering of voices and bodies of mothers and daughters in history and myth. The self is here located in the axis of a mother-daughter continuum, which ultimately transcends temporal/spatial and natural/supernatural distinctions.

The interrelationships among the figures within this polyphony, as indicated by this initial reading, are extremely complex. This suggests the impossibility of narrating a coherent, unified self, but equally expresses a strong desire for excavating an inventory of the self, even though that self may never be properly territorialized. Cha thoughtfully excavates universalistic implications, parallels, and correspondences in the formation of female subjectivities across time and across cultures, but she also forcefully exposes the violence committed against women by such totalities as nationalism, patriarchy, and religion that are often excused in the name of universalism.

Ultimately, it is still toward articulation and writing that Cha strives as a means of locating a self. Though such a multiply situated identity may be forever beyond reach, Cha finds writing as the place where self-identity and the forces that shape it, including the moments of life and death, are represented. But perhaps even more, writing holds the hope of transcending these mortal confines: "She says to herself if she were able to write she could continue to live. Says to herself if she would write without ceasing. To herself if by writing she could abolish real time. She would live. If she could display it before her and become its voyeur" (141, italics in the original). Written words can be immortal, like ruins on the landscape. Fossilized so that they remain as eternal markings on otherwise blank spaces:

Words cast each by each to weather
avowed indisputably, to time.
If it should impress, make fossil trace of word,
residue of word, stand as a ruin stands,
simply, as mark
having relinquished itself to time to distance (177)

The Egyptian ruins on the cover of the book are the metonymic counterpart to words. The Korean engravings on the wall of the Japanese coal mine literally epitomize words as ruins, and by emphasizing their corporeality, Theresa Cha gives words a physical dimension. Published after Theresa Cha's own tragic death, *Dictee* is the ruin of words that she left behind so that she may "continue to live."

NOTES

1. For the cultural nationalism of Frank Chin, see his "Come All Ye Asian American Writers of the Real and the Fake," in *The Big Aiiieeeee*, ed. Frank Chin et al. (New York: Meridian, 1991), 1–92.

2. See the special issue of *Amerasia Journal* 21.1–2 (1995), entitled "Thinking Theory in Asian American Studies," for the recent debate.

3. Theresa Hak Kyung Cha, *Dictee* (New York: Tanem Press, 1982); page references are to this edition and are cited in the text. (A reprint edition is available from Third Woman Press, Berkeley, Ca.). Four critical essays on *Dictee* were grouped together in *Writing Self, Writing Nation*, ed. Elaine Kim and Norma Alarcon (Berkeley, Ca.: Third Woman Press, 1994). Elaine Kim's opening essay solidly exemplifies the road activism has traveled from prioritizing the "American" in "Asian American" to extolling the "in-between," the "interstitial," and the "third space" beyond binarisms.

4. For a discussion of the persistent desire to alienate immigrant Asians in Asian American literature, see Shirley Lim, "Assaying the Gold: Or Contesting the Ground of Asian American Literature," *New Literary History* 24.1 (Winter 1993): 147–69.

5. R. Radhakrishnan, "Postcoloniality and the Boundaries of Identity," *Callaloo* 16.4 (Fall 1993): 753.

6. Peter Hyun, *Man Sei: The Making of a Korean American* (Honolulu: University of Hawaii Press, 1986); Richard Kim, *The Martyred* (New York: George Braziller, 1964) and *Lost Names* (New York: Praeger, 1970); Kim Ronyoung, *Clay Walls* (Seattle: University of Washington Press, 1987); Mary Paik Lee, *Quiet Odyssey*, ed. Sucheng Chan (Seattle: University of Washington Press, 1990); Margaret Pai, *The Dreams of Two Yi-min* (Honolulu: University of Hawaii Press, 1989).

7. See Kim's 1991 collection of poetry, *Under Flag* (Berkeley, Ca.: Kelsey St. Press, 1991).

8. For references see the following books: Benedict Anderson, *Imagined Communities* (London: Verso, 1992); E. J. Hobsbawn, *Nations and Nationalism since 1780* (Cambridge: Cambridge University Press, 1992); Harumi Befu, ed., *Cultural Nationalism in East Asia: Representation and Identity* (Berkeley: Institute of East Asian Studies, University of California, 1993); Partha Chatterjee, *Nationalist Thought and the Colonial World* (Minneapolis: University of Minnesota Press, 1993); Julia Kristeva, *Nations without Nationalism*, trans. Leon S. Roudiez (New York: Columbia University Press, 1993); Edward W. Said, *Culture and Imperialism* (New York: Alfred A. Knopf, 1993).

9. See Andrew Parker et al., eds., *Nationalisms and Sexualities* (New York: Routledge, 1992), for powerful critiques of the "fraternity of men" (Benedict Anderson's phrase, quoted by the editors) underlying the imagination and formation of nationalisms.

10. Deniz Kandiyoti, "Identity and Its Discontents," in *Colonial Discourse and Post-Colonial Theory*, ed. Patrick Williams and Laura Chrisman (New York: Columbia University Press, 1994), 380.

11. Valentine M. Moghadam, "Introduction: Women and Identity Politics in Theoretical and Comparative Perspective," in *Identity Politics and Women*, ed. Moghadam (Boulder: Westview Press, 1994), 1–22.

12. Partha Chatterjee, *The Nation and Its Fragments* (Princeton: Princeton University Press, 1993), 115–19.

13. Floya Anthias and Nira Yuval-Davis, *Racialized Boundaries* (New York: Routledge, 1992), 32–40.

14. *Ain't I a Woman* (Boston: South End Press, 1981), 175.

15. Even today, young Korean American women who attempt to integrate into Korean society are often ostracized in a hostile manner in a culture that privileges homogeneity. Their dress and behavioral codes are mocked as too licentious and Westernized, their inability to speak fluent Korean as selling-out. Often they are maliciously associated with the "Western Princesses" (*yanggongju*)—Korean prostitutes who serve American GIs—because of their appearance and behavior.

16. Meena Alexander's term; see her "Piecemeal Shelter: Writing, Ethnicity, Violence," *Public Culture* 5 (1993): 622.

17. Hyun Yi Kang notes that the words may actually have been inscribed in a tunnel in Nagano Prefecture. In either case, they powerfully convey Japanese exploitation of Korean labor and the Korean laborers' longing for their homeland. See Kang, "The 'Liberatory Voice' of Theresa Hak Kyung Cha's *Dictee*," in Kim and Alarcon, 99.

18. Lisa Lowe, "Feminisms of Color: Heterodoxy and the Writing of History," paper presented at "The Feminist Future" conference, UCLA Conference Center, Lake Arrowhead, Ca., November 1993, p. 2.

19. The division of the Korean peninsula into North and South at the 38th Parallel was ordered in General Order 1 drafted by the Operations Division of the American War Department in the Pentagon; see David Rees, *A Short History of Modern Korea* (New York: Hippocrene Books, 1989), 78–79.

20. The terms liberationist "original nationalism" and postindependence oppressive "derived nationalism" come from C. J. H. Hayes, as quoted in Floya Anthias and Nira Yuval-Davis, *Racialized Boundaries*, 29. Opposing the government-sponsored nationalism, a grass-roots nationalist movement called "Minjung" rose to reclaim for Koreans a peasant-culture-based "pure" national culture untainted by Western capitalism, to achieve national unification, and to drive out neocolonial forces. For an overview of the *Minjung* movement, see Nancy Abelmann, "*Minjung* Theory and Practice," in Befu, 139–65. Also see Chungmoo Choi, "The Discourse of Decolonization and Popular Memory: South Korea," *Positions* 1.1 (Spring 1993): 77–102.

21. R. Radhakrishnan, "Ethnicity in an Age of Diaspora," *Transition* 54 (1991): 104–15.

22. Ahn Joong Kun (1879–1910) was an important figure in the early twentieth-century anti-Japanese activities. Most famous for cutting his finger for "blood writing" as mentioned above, he attempted to assassinate a Japanese general in Harbin, Manchuria, in 1909 and was captured and executed by the Japanese in 1910. See Yu Keng-huan, *Ahn Joong Kun* (Seoul: T'aekuk ch'ulp'ansa, 1970). An interesting connection between Ahn Joong Kun, Yu Guan Soon, and Theresa Cha is their Catholic background; Christian and Catholic churches functioned as havens of independence activities throughout the colonial era in Korea.

23. I would like to thank Kyung-hee Choi of Indiana University for inspiring me to look into this connection between blood writing and Cha's conception of writing as flowing of blood.

24. This structure is reminiscent of Marguerite Yourcenar's *Feux* (1936), whose nine sections are named after figures from Greek mythology, literature, and the Bible, each given a symbolic attribute as the nine muses in Cha's text. Yourcenar being one of Cha's favorite authors, the intertextual links to Yourcenar's text can be illuminating. For instance, both texts share a profound lyricism (being made up of what Yourcenar called "lyrical prose pieces"), highly experimental form, and themes of time, love, and death.

25. In the most commonly known version of the myth, princess Pali waits on the well-keeper of the Western sky for nine years to obtain medicinal well-water for her ill mother. So again the number nine is significant.

26. On page 154, Cha gives the Chinese characters for "*Chung Wai*," which I suspect is a misrecognition of "*Chung wei*." The former means being thickly surrounded by an enemy or obstacles, while the latter means a series of concentric circles. In Chinese, the latter also denotes completion and reunion, as in the phrase *pojing chongyuan*, "the broken mirror becomes whole again," an apt metaphor for the sense of completion achieved through the gathering of fragments in the text.

27. Laurel Kendall, *Shamans, Housewives, and Other Restless Spirits* (Honolulu: University of Hawaii Press, 1985), 154.

28. A *naerim mudang* is one who becomes possessed by a spirit or the deceased and speaks in that person's voice. A shaman, in other words, can role-play various parts and voices. See Yi Du-Hyun, "Role Playing through Trance Possession in Korean Shamanism," in *Shamanism: The Spirit World of Korea* ed. Richard Guisso and Chai-shin Yu (Berkeley: Asian Humanities Press, 1988), 162–180.

29. For a discussion of nationalism as a derivative discourse in the Third World, see Chatterjee.

30. Saint Theresa wrote *The Story of A Soul* at the request of Mother Agnes of Jesus, Mother Marie de Gonzague, and Sister Marie of the Sacred Heart. See *The Story of a Soul*, translated by Michael Day (Westminister, Pa.: The Newman Press, 1953). Note the coincidental connection here with Theresa Cha; who attended the Convent of the Sacred Heart as a child. See Moira Roth, "Theresa Hak Kyung Cha, 1951–1982: A Narrative Chronology," in Kim and Alarcon, 151.

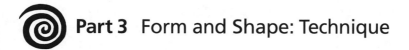

Part 3   Form and Shape: Technique

Gender and First-Person Narration in Willa Cather's Fiction

ELSA NETTELS

First-person narrators appear throughout Willa Cather's fiction, from her earliest stories to her last completed novel. What initially impresses the reader is the preponderance of works narrated by male characters: *My Ántonia*, "Tom Outland's Story" in *The Professor's House*, and nine of the short stories.[1] A female character narrates *My Mortal Enemy*, four stories, the original introduction to *My Ántonia*, and the epilogue of *Sapphira and the Slave Girl*. Of the male narrators, all but Tom Outland appear in the first part of Cather's career, before 1922. The most memorable female narrators—Nellie Birdseye in *My Mortal Enemy* and Cather herself, who concludes *Sapphira and the Slave Girl*—belong to the later period.

These facts suggest several related questions: Why did Cather so often use a male narrator in the first part of her career but not in her later years? What differences are to be observed between her male and female narrators, especially as these differences are revealed through comparison of the two major works narrated in the first person: *My Ántonia* and *My Mortal Enemy*? In what ways does the female narrator in *My Mortal Enemy* enable Cather to realize her ideal of fiction defined in her best-known essay, "The Novel Démeublé," published in 1922?

Cather's use of a male narrator was questioned early in her career by her most important literary friend and mentor, Sarah Orne Jewett, who had herself been warned against the practice by William Dean Howells. After reading Jewett's story, "Hallowell's Pretty Sister," Howells, then editor of the *Atlantic Monthly*, wrote to the author in friendly admonition: "It appears to me impossible that you should do successfully what you've undertaken in it; assume a young man's character in the supposed narrator . . . when it comes to casting the whole autobiographical being in a character of the alien sex, the line is drawn distinctly."[2] Thirty-two years later, Jewett, in an often-quoted letter to Cather, praised the portrayal of wife and husband in Cather's story "On the Gull's Road" but continued, "The lover is as well done as he could be when a woman writes in the man's character—it must always, I believe, be something of a masquerade."[3]

Cather's letters to Jewett in the Houghton Library at Harvard University contain no reference to Jewett's criticism of "On the Gull's Road," but we know that for Cather the idea of "masquerade" was congenial. Her fascination with performance and impersonation is evident in her first novel, *Alexander's Bridge*, originally published in *McClure's Magazine* as "Alexander's Masquerade," which represents the dual identity of the actress Hilda Burgoyne on and off stage and the double life of the protagonist, an engineer, bound to his wife in Boston, attached to his mistress in London.

Cather herself in adolescence assumed the masquerade of boys' clothes; in later years, as Bernice Slote observed, "she could be a consummate actress in language and print."[4] According to Mildred Bennett, Cather aided in the writing of Ellen Terry's autobiography.[5] As the managing editor of *McClure's*, Cather easily assumed the perspective of the writers whose work she edited, and she created the personality of the magazine in her professional correspondence. Her last service for McClure was to capture his voice and his idiom in the autobiography she wrote for him.

Cather cited this experience in justifying to Will Owen Jones, editor of the *Nebraska State Journal*, her choice of Jim Burden as the narrator of *My Ántonia*. In a long letter to her old associate and friend (May 20, 1919), she attributed her confidence in writing the novel as Jim Burden's story to her success in recreating the character of McClure in his autobiography, which his wife and his partner John S. Phillips had praised as a completely successful representation. Initially feeling herself confined within McClure's personality, she had come to find the assumption of another's identity so stimulating that she had wished to repeat the performance by assuming the identity of a different kind of man.[6] In terms reminiscent of Jewett's observation to her that "one must know the world *so well* before one can know the parish," she explained in her letter to Jones why, in the introduction to *My Ántonia*, she had stressed the narrator's wide knowledge of the world beyond the Nebraska of his childhood.[7] In the importance she placed on this knowledge she followed Edith Wharton, who so often found in the male narrator of high professional and social standing what she believed a story required, reflection by a mind "so situated and so constituted as to take the widest possible view of it."[8] The majority of Cather's male narrators are professional men, journalists ("Behind the Singer Tower" and "The Willing Muse"), an artist ("The Namesake"), a diplomat ("On the Gull's Road"), a geologist ("The Affair at Grove Station"), and Jim Burden, a lawyer for a railroad.

Likewise, recent critics have attributed Cather's use of male narrators to her desire to transcend limitations traditionally imposed on women. Hermione Lee observes that men have a natural claim on literary genres such as the epic and the pastoral that inform *My Ántonia*.[9] Sharon O'Brien distinguishes between male narrators whose gender, she believes, is "not contradicted by the text" and those who are "masks of lesbian feelings," allowing Cather to "explore a woman's passion for another woman" without appearing to represent "unnatural" love.[10] Sandra Gilbert and Susan Gubar, who associate Cather's assumption of male dress with her creation of male narrators, also describe these narrators as masks, which enable the author not merely to disguise feelings but to assume the authority and "linguistic potency" identified with male authorship.[11] Similarly, Anne Robinson Taylor sees the transposition of gender as a "literary masquerade" that liberates the author from prescribed gender roles and allows her or him to achieve wholeness through identification with the other sex.[12]

The creation of male narrators may have been liberating for Cather, but she was not moved to liberate her female narrators from the attitudes and responses that conventional society expected of women. It is true that Cather, unlike Edith Wharton, did not make her female narrators inferior to the male narrators in class or linguistic culture. Jim Burden, Nellie Birdseye, and Marjorie ("Uncle Valentine") are equally privileged as exponents of Cather's literary art. The male narrators, however, are more given to pronouncements and judgments than are the female narrators. The tone of the men's narratives is authoritative and decisive. Characteristically, the male narrator feels himself intellectually or socially superior to those he is observing. His self-assurance may be reflected in pity ("A Wagner Matinee") or in the epigrammatic wit and wordplay with which the narrator of "A Willing Muse" pronounces on his unworldly friend: "There must be either very much or very little in a man when he refuses to make the most of his vogue and sell out on a rising market."[13]

Except for the narrator of "The Diamond Mine," a sophisticated woman of wealth and worldly knowledge, the female narrators seldom pronounce judgment, often profess uncertainty and disclaim knowledge. No male narrator begins as does the female narrator of "Jack-a-Boy": "I am quite unable to say just why we were all so fond of him, or how he came to mean so much in our lives" (*CSF*, 311). Of her Aunt Charlotte, the narrator of "Uncle Valentine" confesses: "I find that I did not know her very well then," that "I began really to know her" only after her death.[14] She never states what becomes apparent to the reader, that Charlotte's love of the young composer was the great passion of her life.

Indicative of their assurance and sense of their authority and importance, male narrators, more than the female narrators, make themselves and their feelings the subject of their narratives. The narrator of "On the Gull's Road" is more preoccupied with his response to the mortally stricken woman he meets on shipboard than he is with her suffering. His sentiments seem rather factitious beside those of the female narrator of "The Joy of Nelly Deane," whose love of her schoolmate suffuses the story and expresses itself as a tribute to the girl whose beauty and vitality charmed a whole town. Even Carrie, the narrator of "The Diamond Mine," who unsparingly judges the exploitative relatives and lovers of the singer Cressida Garnett, even she never upstages the protagonist, but within the story and in narrating it she puts herself wholly at the service of her friend.

In keeping with their roles as observers subordinate to others, the female narrators rarely quote themselves when they engage in conversations, unlike the male narrators, who give themselves prominent speaking parts. The female narrator of "Uncle Valentine," a story four times longer than "On the Gull's Road," contributes fewer words to the dialogue than the male narrator of the shorter tale. Two of the male narrators ("The Namesake" and "Behind the Singer Tower"), but none of the female narrators, address a group of friends, thus turning their narratives into public performances that test the speaker's power to justify his monopoly of the conversation.

The differences evident in the short stories are fully illustrated by the male and female narrators of Cather's longest first-person narratives: Jim Burden in *My Ántonia* and Nellie Birdseye in *My Mortal Enemy*. Each novel places at its center a woman who more fully than anyone else captures the imagination of the narrator without determining the course of the narrator's life. Jim is effectively separated from Ántonia when he enters high school and she becomes a hired girl. For twenty years, during which she marries and bears ten children, he does not see her at all. Nellie Birdseye observes Myra Henshawe at three different stages in their lives, separated by months or years: their first meeting when Nellie is fifteen; her visit to New York several months later; and ten years later, her chance encounter with the Henshawes, now poverty-stricken, living out Myra's last days in a jerry-built apartment-hotel in a city on the West Coast.

The difference in the relation of narrators to their subjects is apparent at once. Although four years younger than Ántonia, Jim always has the advantage of his grandparents' established place in Black Hawk and the privileges of education accorded to males of his social standing. At their first meeting, he becomes Ántonia's instructor when he begins to teach her English words. Throughout the novel, he is constantly judging her by *his* standards, criticizing her behavior, even shunning her when she fails to conform to his conventional ideal of gentility.

When Nellie, aged fifteen, first meets Myra Henshawe, a commanding woman in her forties, Nellie is immediately aware of herself as an object of scrutiny, perceiving that the visitor "saw my reflection in a mirror" before they speak.[15] Jim sees Ántonia's eyes as warm reflecting surfaces, "full of light, like the sun shining on brown pools in the wood."[16] Nellie feels appropriated by Myra Henshawe's "deep-set, flashing grey eyes [that] seemed to be taking me in altogether—estimating me" (*MME*, 12). From the beginning, Myra dominates the relationship. At their first meeting Nellie feels herself the one to be judged: "I had begun to think she was going to like me" (*MME*, 13). Unlike Jim Burden, who repeatedly engages in conversation with other characters, Nellie is a silent observer who does not speak at all in the first two episodes. In the last part, she makes an occasional remark but she remains essentially the audience of Myra Henshawe's one-woman performance.

The difference between the assertive male narrator secure in his judgments and the reticent female narrator is, of course, a measure of the differences between Ántonia and Myra Henshawe and the different methods by which Cather reveals them. The picture of Ántonia builds gradually, scene by scene, as Jim and Ántonia mature together. The novel represents a process of memory in which Jim's insights and reflections are always in the foreground. Nellie Birdseye's narrative records a series of revelations from which the portrait of Myra Henshawe slowly emerges. First knowing of Myra through the romantic stories of her elopement told by Nellie's mother and aunt, the narrator perceives more fully at each encounter the mundane or sordid realities behind the romantic legend. As Susan Rosowski has observed, at the beginning of each of the three sections, Nellie has illusions about the Henshawes that the ensuing scenes dispel.[17] But she does not speculate, then or later, on the meaning of the words and actions that disturb her, although because she is narrating from an adult's perspective she might be expected to comment on the significance of what she observed.

Nellie's name, Birdseye, has prompted some critics to see her as an unreliable narrator whose vision remains limited by naivete and romantic yearning she never outgrows. For Marilyn Callander, Nellie remains "frozen in a kind of Snow White/Sleeping Beauty self-absorption," longing to continue "in a state of adolescent sleep."[18] Janis Stout credits Nellie with some insight in the last part of the novella but she finds Nellie, even at the end, a "fallible center" whose vision is "clouded" by her need to see the Henshawes as romantic figures.[19] But as several critics have noted, Nellie, looking back on her younger self, indicates by her ironic comment her awareness of her innocent naivete. According to Hermione Lee, "a dry voice of experience undermines whatever idealization there may have been."[20]

At the same time, the narrator seeks to capture the experience of her younger self, to convey the sense of wonder and excitement that gripped the observer who naturally sees more than she can understand or analyze. A fifteen-year-old girl seeing a couple for the first time in their New York apartment could not be expected to know exactly what lies behind situations: a gift of topaz sleeve-buttons, a quarrel over a key ring. Nellie observes Myra Henshawe advise an actor in his love affair, minister to a dying poet, send the most expensive Christmas holly tree to Helena Modjeska, and entertain artists and singers on New Year's Eve; she can sense the pulse of emotion in these acts but cannot then, and does not later, generalize them as expressions of a woman, without genius herself, who craves association with it and can satisfy her longing to create beauty and exercise power only through a generosity often indistinguishable from manipulation.

Compared to Jim Burden, always ready to sum up characters and interpret actions, Nellie seems a shadowy figure: "colorless, devoid of personality, lacking in self-definition," according to one critic; "the least obtrusive of [Cather's] narrators and window-characters," according to another.[21] That she and other female narrators are less authoritative, more self-effacing, than male narrators, may make them seem "weaker," but reticence and self-effacement may be an artistic strength. A narrator who does not force interpretations on the reader allows for a more subtle representation of character, in which words, gestures, and actions become signs to be read by the discerning reader and the narrator together. Such a narrator may seem more sensitive to shades of behavior and complexities of character than the analyst always prompt with his conclusions.

The absence of analysis and interpretation, then, need not evidence limited perception but may be the means by which Cather achieved effects defined in her essay, "The Novel Démeublé": "The inexplicable presence of the thing not named, of the overtone divined by the ear but not heard by it, the verbal mood, the emotional aura of the fact or the thing or the deed."[22] A perfect illustration of the "inexplicable presence" occurs in *My Mortal Enemy*, when Nellie reflects on the power of her memory of the Casta Diva aria sung at the New Year's Eve party to recall the "hidden richness" of Myra Henshawe's nature: "a compelling, passionate, overmastering something for which I had no name" (*MME*, 61, 60). How appropriate that "the overtone divined by the ear," "the verbal mood," should be evoked by the memory of music, by words the narrator sings to herself. How much would be lost were the narrator to fix a name to the "overmastering something."

Nellie as the adult narrator remains true to the limited understanding of her adolescent self in refusing to interpret scenes, but even a single word can convey an attitude, govern a reader's response and capture the essence of a character. One of countless examples occurs as Nellie recalls the Henshawes at the climax of the novella's most memorable scene, as they listen to a young Polish woman sing the Casta Diva aria. "I remember Oswald, standing like a statue behind Madame Modjeska's chair, and Myra, crouching low beside the singer, her head in both hands" (*MME*, 60). How much of Myra's fierce primal energy, potentially explosive, is contained in the word *crouching* (repeated a few lines later), with its manifold suggestions of a humble worshipper, a cringing servant, and an animal tensed to spring. How different the effect had Myra *knelt* beside the singer.

The novel démeublé does not require a female narrator, but the reticence, the refusal to judge and define, essential to evoking "the presence of the thing not named"—these are traditionally considered feminine rather than masculine traits. The contrasting methods of *My Ántonia* and *My Mortal Enemy* are also consistent with Cather's identification of men but not women with self-conscious literary composition. (In revising the introduction to *My Ántonia* Cather removed the passage in which the female narrator proposes that both she and Jim Burden "set down on paper" their memories of Ántonia, but even in the original version she confesses to making only "a few straggling notes," admits that "my own story was never written," and presents the novel as "Jim's manuscript, substantially as he brought it to me" [*MA*, xii, xiv].)

Jim Burden is not a professional writer, but his narrative, which he claims "hasn't any form" (*MA*, xiv), is a written text expressive of his awareness of himself as a character within a story and also the composer of that story. A "self-reflexive narrator," as Blanche Gelfant terms him, he draws on a novelist's vocabulary in composing the past as narrative.[23] His departure for Harvard concludes one division of his story: "My Lincoln chapter closed abruptly" (*MA*, 397). In retrospect, he most values Ántonia for her power to transform his memories into pictures "like the old woodcuts of one's first primer" (*MA*, 397). He might be describing himself when he says of Frances Harling's interest in the country people: "She carried them all in her mind as if they were characters in a book or a play" (*MA*, 171). He presents Mrs. Steavens's moving account of Ántonia's suffering after her desertion by Larry Donovan as an archetypal tale within a frame, a story to be heard. The ambiguity of the title, "The Pioneer Woman's Story," which could refer to Ántonia's experience or to the Widow Steavens's narration of it, increases the distance between the self-conscious writer-narrator and the other characters. Whether Cather intended it or not, the Widow Steavens's narrative, an unself-conscious, unstudied expression of grief and love, makes Jim's professions of feeling for Ántonia seem fabricated, a literary construct that affords what Ann Romines terms "the private satisfactions of ordering and control, as accomplished by an artist."[24]

My Mortal Enemy is not cast as a written text or a narrative told to an audience. Like all the other female narrators, Nellie Birdseye is an autonomous narrator who does not see herself as the chief actor or the composer of the story she tells. Her shifting feelings about Myra Henshawe are of the essence, but she presents them as important not in themselves but as they reveal the variable, capricious nature of the woman who dominates the novel. Jim Burden in the original introduction to *My Ántonia* tells the female narrator that if he is to write about Ántonia, "I should have to do it in a direct way, and say a great deal about myself" (*MA*, xiii)—which indeed he does. In contrast, Nellie Birdseye says practically nothing about herself and her own affairs.

Because Jim Burden produces a manuscript, he may seem to exercise more authorial power than Nellie Birdseye. But Nellie, no less than Jim, shapes meaning in selecting and arranging the contents of the narrative. In Deborah Carlin's words, "Nellie, like a critic, reconstructs the text of Myra's life into a narrative in order to make some sense of it."[25] In fact, the existence of Myra's life story seems more dependent on the narration of Nellie Birdseye than the existence of Ántonia's story seems dependent on Jim Burden's manuscript. Jim memorializes Ántonia but he does not call her into being. Myra Henshawe, one feels, would not exist if Nellie were not there to transform the figure of a romantic legend into the real woman.

Jim Burden seems to appropriate Ántonia, but her inexhaustible vitality precludes a narrator's possession of her. In ignorance of Ántonia's life struggle, Jim may transform her into an icon, as several critics have contended (Jim thus reversing the process of de-mythicizing that Nellie represents), but Ántonia cannot be confined by another's mental processes. Many readers, I believe, would agree with Susan Rosowski that Ántonia "breaks through [Jim Burden's] narrative, and thus through his attempts to possess her by writing about her."[26] Nellie Birdseye at their first meeting feels that Myra's eyes are "taking me in altogether," but as narrator, Nellie always holds Myra in her gaze. By effacing herself, by subordinating herself to Myra, Nellie makes herself the reality-giving presence; she becomes the source of Myra Henshawe's reality. The female narrator who refuses to formulate her subject and offers only tentative readings of her ambiguous words actually assumes a kind of novelistic power that none of the male narrators commands.

This is not to imply that within *My Mortal Enemy* Nellie is manipulative or domineering. No character could be less so. Her refusal to name the "something" in Myra's nature that she so strongly feels reflects her respect for the integrity of the other person, as does the absence of any attempt on Nellie's part to answer the questions her narrative raises. What was Oswald's relation to the giver of the topaz sleeve-buttons? What door was opened by the key over which the Henshawes quarreled? Were Myra Henshawe's jealous suspicions groundless? Was Nellie right to feel in Oswald Henshawe's attitude "indestructible constancy" (*MME*, 120)? We may assume that Nellie herself does not know the answers. But because she does not speculate, because she does not impose her concerns between herself and Myra Henshawe, she binds that character to her more tightly than if, like Jim Burden, she had converted the story of another person into the story of herself.

It is, of course, possible for a male narrator to be self-effacing, but Cather did not see her important male characters in this way. Whether they are narrators or "window characters" like Niel Herbert or protagonists of third person narratives, they are ego-centered, preoccupied with their own affairs and impressions. Some of Cather's female characters, it is true, such as Thea Kronborg, Myra Henshawe, and Sapphira Colbert are no less self-absorbed, but they are not narrators whose ostensible purpose is to portray another person. The effect of the self-concerned narrator such as Jim Burden suggests Virginia Woolf's image of the shadow across the page cast by the self-confident male voice: "a straight dark bar, a shadow shaped something like the letter 'I' "—an intrusive presence that obstructs one's view of the world around it.[27]

For one final illustration of the value Cather came to place on the female narrator, we may consider the contrast she presents in her essay on Katherine Mansfield, written in 1923. Cather begins by recording a "glimpse" of her subject "through the eyes of a fellow passenger" on a ship from Naples, an elderly bachelor from New England who had met Katherine Mansfield when she was a child.[28] His encounter also took place on shipboard, on a boat from New Zealand to Australia. He had been charmed by the child, he told Cather, but years later he read a story by Mansfield that he found "artificial, and unpleasantly hysterical, full of affectations" and consequently he had no desire to see the writer again.[29]

In the second half of the essay, Cather presents her own view of Katherine Mansfield, whom she judges a writer of genius, possessed of the power Cather most valued, the power to convey through words what is never actually stated on the page, "the inexplicable presence of the thing not named." In Mansfield's best work she felt this presence, "this overtone, which is too fine for the printing press and comes through without it." [30]

Cather does not mention the elderly man again, but the essay suggests that it is the female reader, and by implication the female narrator, who best senses the unspoken in others' texts and commands the power to evoke it by her own words. As Cather in her essay summons to life and death the writer who in her last days "read Shakespeare continually, when she was too ill to leave her bed," so three years later she created a female narrator to portray a woman who, like Mansfield, is sustained at the end by poetry, by the "inexhaustible richness" of Shakespeare's language. What Cather draws from Mansfield's *Journal*, Nellie Birdseye draws from Myra Henshawe's life: a narrative that is "not the story of utter defeat."[31] Unlike the elderly passenger fixed on the shadow of his own feelings, Cather and her female narrator distill themselves in their subject and so preserve the integrity of the woman their unshadowed vision creates.

NOTES

1. I have not included the narrator of "Two Friends"—whose sex is not indicated—in the list of male narrators, although a boy would be more likely than a girl to frequent the places where men gather in this story.

2. Letter of 10 June 1876, *Selected Letters of W. D. Howells*, ed. George Arms and Christoph K. Lohmann (Boston: Twayne, 1979), 2:130.

3. Letter of 27 November 1908, *Letters of Sarah Orne Jewett*, ed. Annie Fields (Boston: Houghton Mifflin, 1911), 246.

4. Bernice Slote, introduction to *Uncle Valentine and Other Stories: Willa Cather's Uncollected Short Fiction, 1915–1929*, ed. Slote (Lincoln: University of Nebraska Press, 1973), xiii.

5. Mildred Bennett, in a letter to Dorothy Canfield Fisher (March 19, 1951), explained why she believed that Cather had helped write the autobiography of Ellen Terry: "The opening pages of the Terry book have a definite Cather flavor and later comes the thesis that first impressions are the deepest—a prominent Cather belief" (Special Collections, University of Vermont Library, by permission).

6. Willa Cather Collection, Manuscripts Department, Alderman Library, University of Virginia.

7. Willa Cather, preface to *Alexander's Bridge*, in *Willa Cather: Stories, Poems, and Other Writings*, ed. Sharon O'Brien (New York: Library of America, 1992), 942.

8. Edith Wharton, *The Writing of Fiction* (New York: Charles Scribner's Sons, 1925), 46.

9. Hermione Lee, *Willa Cather: Double Lives* (New York: Pantheon Books, 1989), 153.

10. Sharon O'Brien, "The 'Thing Not Named': Willa Cather as a Lesbian Writer," *Signs* 9 (1984): 597, 593.

11. Sandra M. Gilbert and Susan Gubar, *No Man's Land: The Place of the Woman Writer in the Twentieth Century*, vol. 2, *Sexchanges* (New Haven: Yale University Press, 1989), 201.

12. Anne Robinson Taylor, *Male Novelists and Their Female Voices: Literary Masquerades* (Troy, N.Y.: Whitston, 1981), 5.

13. *Willa Cather's Collected Short Fiction, 1892–1912*, introduction by Mildred R.

Bennett (Lincoln: University of Nebraska Press, 1956), 116. Hereafter abbreviated *CSF*, with page numbers given in the text.

14. *Uncle Valentine and Other Stories*, 8.

15. *My Mortal Enemy* (New York: Alfred A. Knopf, 1926), 11. Hereafter abbreviated *MME*, with page numbers given in the text.

16. *My Ántonia* (Boston: Houghton Mifflin, 1918), 26. Hereafter abbreviated MA, with page numbers given in the text.

17. Susan J. Rosowski, *The Voyage Perilous: Willa Cather's Romanticism* (Lincoln: University of Nebraska Press, 1968), 146.

18. Marilyn Berg Callander, *Willa Cather and the Fairy Tale* (Ann Arbor: UMI Research Press, 1988), 44.

19. Janis P. Stout, *Strategies of Reticence: Silence and Meaning in the Works of Jane Austen, Willa Cather, Katherine Anne Porter, and Joan Didion* (Charlottesville: University Press of Virginia, 1990), 84.

20. Lee, 212.

21. Callander, 44; Theodore S. Adams, "Willa Cather's *My Mortal Enemy*: The Concise Presentation of Scene, Character, and Theme," *Colby Library Quarterly*, Series 10, September 1973, 138.

22. Willa Cather, *Not Under Forty* (New York: Alfred A. Knopf, 1936), 50.

23. Blanche H. Gelfant, "Art and Apparent Artlessness: Self-Reflexivity in *My Ántonia*," in *Approaches to Teaching My Ántonia*, ed. Susan J. Rosowski (New York: The Modern Language Association of America, 1989), 127.

24. Ann Romines, *The Home Plot: Women, Writing and Domestic Ritual* (Amherst: University of Massachusetts Press, 1992), 143.

25. Deborah Carlin, *Cather, Canon, and the Politics of Reading* (Amherst: The University of Massachusetts Press, 1992), 29.

26. Susan J. Rosowski, "Writing against Silences: Female Adolescent Development in the Novels of Willa Cather," *Studies in the Novel* 21 (Spring, 1989): 68.

27. Virginia Woolf, *A Room of One's Own* (New York: Harcourt, Brace, and World, 1929), 103.

28. *Not Under Forty*, 123. Hermione Lee (188–92) considers the importance of this essay in her discussion of Cather's modernism.

29. Ibid., 134.

30. Ibid., 137.

31. Ibid., 145, 144.

The "Real Lives" of Sophie Treadwell

Expressionism and the Feminist Aesthetic in *Machinal* and *For Saxophone*

JERRY DICKEY

Although Sophie Treadwell authored seven plays produced on Broadway stages and composed over forty plays during her entire career, she remains best known today only for a single work, the acclaimed drama *Machinal*. By the time *Machinal* appeared at the Plymouth Theatre in 1928, Treadwell had already mastered the difficult task of pursuing dual careers in journalism and playwriting. Working as a reporter first for the *San Francisco Bulletin* and then for the *New York Herald Tribune*, Treadwell was one of the first women in America to serve as an accredited foreign war correspondent. She had also completed an extensive interview with Mexican President Obregón during the revolutionary turmoil and a follow-up exclusive interview with Pancho Villa in his hideaway in Chihuahua. In the first half of the 1920s, Treadwell fused her ability to investigate real-life personages with her talents in creating fictional dramatic portrayals, authoring *Rights*, a play about Mary Wollstonecraft, *Gringo*, featuring a Mexican bandit bearing more than a surface resemblance to Pancho Villa, and *Poe*, a docudrama created from extensive research into the private papers of Edgar Allan Poe.

Machinal allowed for Treadwell's apotheosis as an artist who fused real life with dramatic fiction. This expressionistic play was inspired by one of the most sensational murder trials of the first half of the twentieth century, the Snyder-Gray case, in which Ruth Snyder was convicted of conspiring with her lover, Judd Gray, to murder her husband, resulting in their executions by electric chair. Although Treadwell did not officially cover the trial for the *Herald Tribune*, she attended the courtroom proceedings, and many of the details of the trial scene in *Machinal* parallel those of the case.[1] Due in part to the sensational nature of the play and in equal measure to the novelty of the form Treadwell employed, *Machinal* was an enormous critical success. Although many of Treadwell's previous plays reflected her familiarity with the realistic, well-made play structure, her sudden employment of expressionistic techniques in this play should not be dismissed as opportunism, as riding the crest of the expressionistic wave that washed over New York theater throughout the 1920s.[2] Rather, *Machinal* signals a first attempt by Treadwell to create an alternative aesthetic that would activate the imaginations of those in her audience.

Machinal, though, was not Treadwell's only experiment in the radical restructuring of dramatic narrative.[3] She achieved her boldest innovation in a four-act musical play entitled *For Saxophone*, copyrighted in 1934 but never published or produced. Although the play does not have its origins in a true-life subject such as Ruth Snyder, it depicts the pursuit of a different type of "real life" as a young woman seeks self-validation despite social obstructions. *Machinal* had made wide use of sounds, verbal images, offstage voices and figures, and extended interior monologues to produce a theatrical metaphor for the mental state of its central character. *For Saxophone* similarly utilizes most of these devices, yet increases its reliance on lighting effects and especially musical underscoring for emotional effect. Treadwell's opening stage directions for the work even go so far as to suggest that the play is "really words for music."[4] Taken together, *Machinal* and *For Saxophone* compose one of the earliest concerted attempts by an American woman dramatist to create an alternative, non-realistic narrative form through which women could be celebrated as subjects in drama.

The narratives of both plays begin with a rather familiar dramatic approach that depicts the women as desired objects of male possession, both being the sought-after prizes in impending marriages. In *Machinal*, the opening scene introduces the audience to an ordinary "Young Woman" in her twenties (it is not until the play is half over that we learn her real name, Helen Jones). Here, the Young Woman's office coworkers enviously discuss her as the object of the boss's affections and speculate on how her working life will turn to one of leisure after marriage. Similarly, *For Saxophone* begins with an objectification of the focal character, Lily, a high-society maiden who has recently returned to America after a secluded education in a French convent. In the opening scene of this work, socialites at a prenuptial dance gossip on the good fortune of Lily's coming marriage to a rich young man. Through symbolic nomenclature, Treadwell immediately strips Lily of her individuality by melding her personality into that of her husband-to-be, Gilly. Lily and Gilly; it is hard to think of one without the other.

Yet after the opening objectification of the female characters, Treadwell quickly subverts audience expectations by employing a variety of expressionistic techniques that move the women into the subject position of the dramas. In an unpublished manuscript version of *Machinal*, Treadwell's opening stage directions clearly reveal the function of one of these techniques, the introspective monologues, in the development of the dramatic narrative: "Does their place in the plan of the play—connecting links, or better,—connecting channels of action—demand that the thought move through them in an approximately straight line, or can one be permitted a nearer approach to the scatteredness, unexpectedness of the relaxed meditating mind?" Treadwell hoped that her use of these various techniques would create a sensational stage effect "by accentuation, by distortion . . . and perhaps by the quickening of still secret places, in the consciousness of the audience, especially of women."[5] Treadwell provides even more specific preliminary remarks on the activating effect of these devices in *For Saxophone*:

> This script is written to be played with an almost unbroken musical accompaniment. . . .
>
> Much use is made of voices (of people not seen)—bits of conversation here and there—incomplete—suggestive. . . .
>
> The play is done in sixteen scenes, seven of which are voices with only one moment seen—the focal moment (something like a close-up in pictures). All the scenes of each act go one into the other through lights, voices, and music, so that the effect is of something seen, moving-by, and something overheard,—from all of which, a bit here and a bit there inconsequential and seemingly unrelated, the audience discovers,—writes the play. (n.p.)[6]

Treadwell's statement that these devices will have their greatest effect upon women in the audience derives in part from the fact that audiences come to the action of the plays through each female character's point of view. Audiences are not allowed to engage in the narrative through the familiar manner of empathic identification with a male character who views the female as Other. Instead audiences experience each woman's frustrations at being relegated to the role of outsider in various social relationships, as Other to her boss, her family, her husband, her lover, and ultimately herself.

In her influential study, *Feminism and Theatre*, Sue-Ellen Case addresses the issue of whether or not a dramatic form exists that particularly expresses female experience or sensibility. Borrowing from French writers and literary theorists, Case introduces the concept of "contiguity," an organizational device described variously as a "nearness," a form "constantly in the process of weaving itself . . . embracing words and yet casting them off," avoiding explicitness in favor of that which is "touched upon."[7] Case summarizes the contiguous structure as "elliptical rather than illustrative, fragmentary rather than whole, ambiguous rather than clear, and interrupted rather than complete. This . . . form seems to be without a sense of formal closure—in fact, it operates as an anti-closure."⁸ Both *Machinal* and *For Saxophone* share an affinity with such a contiguous structure, as a few brief examples from the lesser-known *For Saxophone* will reveal.

After their marriage, Lily and Gilly face consummation of their nuptial in a sleeper car of a train en route to their Miami honeymoon. Through sound, suggestive allusion, and fragmented, interrupted episodes, Treadwell represents Lily's anxiety about impending sex with a man she barely knows, a man who has been chosen for her by her father:

> *Gilly:* A clean getaway. Your husband engineered that! (She says nothing)
>   Your husband, hear that?
> *Lily:* I hear it.
> *Gilly:* Your husband! How does it sound?
> *Lily:* Don't say it yet!
> *Gilly:* Don't you like it?
> *Lily:* I have to get used to it.
> *Gilly:* You'll get used to it. (Sound of wheels) Happy?
> *Lily:* Are you?
> *Gilly:* Am I! (Sound of the wheels) (1.5.22)

In the moments that follow, Lily gently spurns Gilly's tentative amorous advances, executed to the music of a portable victrola, while similarly rebuffing his attempts to relax her with a drink from his flask of alcohol; a porter provides momentary respite by entering and taking their tickets; Gilly tries to lure Lily into the bed by pretending to be sleepy; the porter returns and asks if he should "make the bed down now," to which Lily responds with a weak, "Not now" (1.5.27–28). Treadwell further implies that Gilly's persistent physical advances may lead to overt coercion as he again tries to get Lily to drink from his flask, even attempting to hold her nose when she refuses so she will not smell the alcohol. Silence and more sounds of train wheels punctuate their brief exchange. Gilly wishes to himself he had brought a maid along, presumably to provide discreet assistance to his reluctant bride. Lily asks that the window be opened to relieve her sense of the closeness of the sleeper room, but the deafening sound of the wheels soon forces its closure. Finally, the scene ends as Gilly "pulls down the shade. The stage darkens. Their voices are heard":

> *Gilly:* Here, take some of this.
> *Lily:* Just a little—just a— (*Curtain*) (1.5.31)

Lily's inhibitions, largely fostered through gender enculturation, prohibit her from directly challenging Gilly's authoritarian pursuit of his conjugal rights.

Treadwell achieves dramatic power in this short episode through detention and circumvention, rather than unbroken delineation, of the scene's fundamental issue. Treadwell's approach is, in Hélène Cixous's terms, a "working [of] the in-between."[9]

Six years later, Gil and Lily return to the Miami hotel where they spent their honeymoon. Lily has insisted on a different room because she remembers the original one had "a spot in the ceiling, right over the bed" (2.2). A maid tells Lily that the twin beds in this new room are typical of the accommodations desired by the hotel's married social elite. "The best people don't seem to care for doubles," she tells Lily. "Sometimes a single will want a double, but doubles generally want singles" (2.7). The maid's observation intensifies Lily's desperate desire not to become one of the multitude of women who remain acquiescent in financially comfortable but spiritually stifling marriages. Perhaps, Lily may surmise, sexual fulfillment is to be found only illicitly, in relationships created outside formal social sanction.

From this point, Treadwell weaves an episodic chronicle in which Lily pursues, through a montage of disparate scenes, three overlapping courses of action, each of which ultimately proves problematic. Lily's affair with a knife-throwing Russian folk dancer leads simply to victimization, as the Russian's idea of sex contains only self-gratification. Her sense of guilt over her prolonged affair undermines her dogged efforts to remain in her marriage to Gil. Treadwell dramatizes Lily's resulting anguish through several of her so-called "focal moments," such as a scene in which spot lighting narrowly focuses on Lily, alone and restless in the bedroom of her home, while the theater reverberates with amplified voices of her cook and maid gossiping and moralizing on her behavior.

The third course of action appears at first to offer promise, as Lily follows the advice of a sympathetic author of psychological novels who urges her to defy the social expectations that lead to compulsive self-denial. Emotionally detailing her experiences to the novelist, Lily removes, for the first time, the censors that have forced her to circumvent rather than question inhibiting social constraints. She soon discovers, however, that her previous socialization has never taught her how to create a meaningful, independent life, and she tells the writer that after their initial meeting she desired but could not carry through with suicide. "It wasn't that I was afraid," she tells him. "I just felt as though I couldn't die before I had ever lived. . . . After I was with you, I felt that I had become real, and I wanted a real life" (4.4.31). Although she leaves both Gil and her lover, Lily is at a loss as to how to construct this "real life" of her own. She follows the writer back to his home in Vienna, an action that demonstrates Lily's inability even to conceive of herself as the subject of her own life. She relies once more on another to provide her with meaning and purpose. Rather than indicting her for this failure, Treadwell retains sympathy for Lily, condemning instead an indifferent society that subtly devalues her pursuit of personal and sexual freedom.

As Treadwell prepares to bring resolution to these narrative threads, she inserts a striking scene, one that seems unrelated to the previous story lines but serves to reintroduce the social pressures that silence Lily's process of individuation. Now alone and confused, Lily seeks rest and treatment at a European spa. Treadwell uses afternoon tea at this spa to surround Lily with a disheartening collage of disenfranchised women. A Viennese dance orchestra plays jazz music throughout, while Lily sits at a table with a middle-aged Englishwoman with a persistent pain in her side and another lonely woman of about fifty with a face haggard before its time. Behind them, women vie with each other to hire male waiters as dance partners, while other women dance together. At the table, the Englishwoman speaks to Lily with disgust about a scientific treatise she is reading called "Enduring Passion."

> *Woman with Book:* Who wants [passion] to last a lifetime? I don't for one, do you? . . . If a woman has a quirk against her husband, that doesn't mean she needs a lover, it means she needs . . . to lose some egoism. Women demand too much of life.
> *Lily:* Why shouldn't they?
> *Woman:* Because they don't get it. Life hasn't got it to give. . . . Nothing is really right—perfectly right—ever. Why should we expect it of marriage? . . . At least we have our good manners and our sense of humor with which to wangle it . . . (Pause) . . . and our endurance. (4.5.43–45)

The woman echoes exactly all the traditional attitudes and roles that Lily has previously believed women must enact: endure the marriage, sex is not pleasurable or important, get rid of your egoism and self-interest. Around her in the spa, Lily sees bountiful examples of women who have accepted society's equation of spinsterhood with a life of failure. Lily mistakenly assumes that because the woman's words have the solid ring of familiarity to them they must be truths.

Given this final reinforcement of cultural gender inscription, it is not surprising that the narrative of Lily's plight ends unhappily. A closing scene in a cafe before Lily's planned return to Gilly in America features a performance by her old lover, the knife-throwing Russian dancer. Treadwell brings resolution to *For Saxophone* in the same manner she did in *Machinal*, defeat through death: here, Lily is stabbed by one of the dancer's knives. Although the narratives of both plays reach a state of tragic resolution, Treadwell avoids any scene providing emotional catharsis to the audience, choosing instead to cut the narratives off exactly at the point of the women's deaths. While creating works that depict women as subjects of the drama, Treadwell cannot yet envision them completely empowered or victorious, but she refuses to allow her audiences to feel comfortable with their defeat. The characters' emotional frustrations at the hands of a society that inhibits their creation of a meaningful "real life" remain within the empathic audience after the plays have ended.[10]

Although Treadwell's complete works encompass a wide range of styles and subjects, in *Machinal* and *For Saxophone* she became one of the first American women dramatists to attempt a radical restructuring of dramatic narrative. Unlike other American expressionistic plays of the 1920s, such as Elmer Rice's *The Adding Machine*, these works by Treadwell avoid literal, uncontested readings, relying instead on a complex cluster of sounds, movement, images, and music for suggestive effect.[11] Also, unlike the majority of plays by her female contemporaries, Treadwell's works freely abandon the form of the realistic, well-made play in favor of attempting an alternative feminist aesthetic, an alteration devised for the expressed purpose of placing women in subject positions in drama while attempting to appeal to a female sensibility in her audience.

NOTES

1. For a detailed discussion of the play's relationship to the Snyder-Gray trial, see Ginger Strand, "Treadwell's Neologism: *Machinal*," *Theatre Journal* 44 (1992): 163–75; and Jennifer Jones, "In Defense of Woman: Sophie Treadwell's *Machinal*," *Modern Drama* 37 (1994): 485–96.

2. Treadwell's use of the well-made play form can be found in a number of her early dramatic manuscripts housed at the University of Arizona Library Special Collections (UALSC). This collection also contains a series of unpublished lectures by Treadwell on playwriting, in which she outlines her knowledge of the realistic play construct.

3. Earlier Treadwell experiments in nonrealistic play structure include a scenario for a musical version of her comedy *Madame Bluff* (1915–16), in which song and dance are used to advance the story, as well as *The Eye of the Beholder* (1919), in which the characterization of a young woman changes in each of the play's four scenes to reflect the attitude by which she is alternately viewed by her husband, her lover, her lover's mother, and her own mother.

4. Sophie Treadwell, *For Saxophone*, typescript, n.d., Sophie Treadwell Papers, UALSC, Box 13. Subsequent references to this manuscript will be given parentheti-

cally in the text. The manuscript is numbered with reference to act, scene (except for act 2, which has only one scene), and page.

5. Sophie Treadwell, *Machinal*, typescript, n.d., UALSC, Box 11. This stage direction does not appear in any of the published versions of the play.

6. After reading the play in manuscript, the noted scene designer Robert Edmond Jones praised the originality and dramatic potential of these devices in *For Saxophone* in a letter to Treadwell: "You have a great idea here, the germ of a new theatre idiom . . . here is a bold step into a new dimension, full of power. . . . There are passages in *Saxophone* that are so original and brilliant I simply have no words for them" (quoted in Nancy Edith Wynn, "Sophie Treadwell: The Career of a Twentieth-Century American Feminist Playwright" [Ph.D. diss., City University of New York, 1982], 175–76). Jones tried unsuccessfully for three years to raise money to produce the play. Other producers and agents rejected the play due to its "eccentric" structure and lack of star turns for a leading actress (William James Fadiman to Arthur Hopkins, 12 December 1935, UALSC, Box 13), or because of their inability to find a fresh, unknown actress capable of performing effectively the complex emotional characterization of Lily (Arthur Hopkins to Sophie Treadwell, n.d., UALSC, Box 13). Treadwell's agent, Richard Madden, discouraged a production of the play by a West Coast unit of the Federal Theatre Project while hoping for Jones to produce it (Richard Madden to Sophie Treadwell, 2 April 1937, UALSC, Box 13). Constant frustrations with Broadway producers had previously led Treadwell to begin producing her own plays, beginning with her 1925 drama, *The Love Lady*.

7. Luce Irigaray, "This Sex Which Is Not One," in *New French Feminisms*, ed. Elaine Marks and Isabelle de Courtivron (New York: Schocken, 1981), quoted in Sue-Ellen Case, *Feminism and Theatre* (New York: Routledge, 1988), 129.

8. Case, 129. Case also notes that the concept of a separate feminine morphology has not met with complete approval by feminist theorists, some of whom feel it implies that "gender has been biologised—the notions of the female body and the male body have been used to recreate the dominant cultural systems of representations" (130). Other theorists believe women should be free to create within a wide variety of forms without fear of censure.

9. Hélène Cixous, "The Laugh of the Medusa," in Marks and de Courtivron, quoted in Case, 129.

10. Treadwell continued to revise *For Saxophone* for at least eight years in the hopes of getting a commercial theatrical producer to take a chance on its innovative form. In a 1941 version, Treadwell altered the ending to provide less of a sense of closure. In this version, the final scene remains in the Kur Platz after the English woman has left Lily alone. A young man joins Lily at her table and provides solace to her lack of individuation. He delivers the advice of "defiance" offered by the novelist in the earlier version, and the play ends as Lily and the young man dance together. In many respects, this ending provides more satisfaction because it hints at the possiblility for Lily's self-realization, and the sense of anticlosure remains true to the contiguous narrative structure developed throughout the play.

11. Not all critics were unanimous in their enthusiasm for the ambiguous and elu-

sive style of *Machinal*. For example, most of the male critics viewing the London production in 1931 (retitled *The Life Machine*) found the deck stacked against the male characters in the play and responded on a literal level to allusions and images. W. A. Darlington of the *Telegraph* (4 August 1931) provided one such reaction: "Throughout the play, the author throws all the sympathy, and tries to attract ours, onto the side of the girl. The husband has damp hands. It is enough. He must die. . . . The moral balance of this play is all wrong."

Selves and "Other Shadows"

Grace Paley's Ironic Fictions

VICTORIA AARONS

A character in Grace Paley's short story "Listening" chastises the apparent narrator of the piece by saying, "You don't have to tell stories to me in which I'm a character."[1] The narrator need not because, as is typically the case, Paley's characters invent themselves by and in the stories they tell. Character, for Paley, is a dialectical process; characters are made and revised through the telling of their stories, stories that frame and define our perceptions of them and that make the story's narrator an accomplice to the invention. Conventional distinctions among narrator, character, and author are blurred in Paley's short fiction, where the unfolding of character becomes centrally and essentially a matter of self-invention, reflecting Paley's dual concerns with modern feminism and with post–World War II American Jewish life.[2] In particular, Paley's unswerving commitment to feminism creates finally the inviolate voice in all her fiction, for surely self-invention, a process of self-affirmation and conscious assessment of possibilities, of "openings," is central to feminism in the broadest sense. The making of character, its range and capacity for renewal and reinvention, not surprisingly remains the most consistent narrative activity in Paley's stories, as an assorted array of characters compete for narrative and ethical authority. They make and remake themselves, constantly in the process of revision, a bemused and often parodic process of self-construction and transformation that reveals a humorous self-consciousness about their function as characters "in a book," all the while defining what it means to *be* a character.[3]

What it means to be a character and what it means to be a story are concerns no less central to Paley's self-conscious narrators than they are to Paley's characters, who often seize narrative control, talking about themselves as "characters." Her short stories are compressed, often confessional, metafictional reflections on the making and status of character in fiction and, perhaps most interestingly, on the making and status of character in the delicately balanced complexities of daily ethical life. "Certain facts may become useful" the narrator of "Faith in the Afternoon" warns us, but in the telling of stories, Paley's characters can be counted on, as does the narrator in "Enormous Changes At the Last Minute," to "[place] between them a barrier of truthful information," always a verbal sparring, "part of the dance, a couple of awkward, critical steps from theory to practice."[4] This gap between "theory," for Paley's characters a humorous assessment of the way in which the world should work, and "practice," the often faltering and unpredictable ways in which her characters actually play out their lives, is the primary ironic conceit of the stories. Plots, then, conventionally understood as developing actions and events given meaning by the authorial rhetoric that defines and describes them, are related with terseness and minimal authorial "stage directions" in Paley's short stories, are only openings for stories, for stories where description is made subservient to dialogue and individual reflection and self-assessment, sometimes judged to be successful by Paley and sometimes not.

Paley's fiction thus is guided by indeterminacy, reflexivity, temporal ambiguity and rearrangement, and fragmentation of both character and plot. Her fiction seems often to discard the principle of a central guiding narrative voice, focusing instead on the competing voices of insistent characters, the role of whom in the unfolding of a given story is often indeterminate. That is, characters are often their own narrators as well as the controlling voices of the story line, the plot. There is a clear absence of unidirectional plot development in Paley's short fiction. Instead of linear movement, of beginning, middle, and end, we find a wash of time, wrinkles and waves of time, where what happens is far less important than how a particular character describes and judges events, other characters, and his or her own motives and decisions.

This central focus on character was made clear to me again in a conversation I had with Grace Paley in November 1991. When talking about storytelling as part of the tradition of bearing witness in Jewish literature, Paley made clear her perspectival conception of character: "Technically you really can't see a character unless other characters are looking at her or him. . . . It's sort of like in painting. In painting you have light moving in and other shadows; if you have a tree next to a person, the person looks different than if he is standing on a bare plain. And if there are three people in the rooms they each look different because of the other two. Or they each look more full almost. So, I mean, characters illuminate each other, densify each other."[5] It's these "other shadows" that provide the depth that we've come to associate with Paley's fiction, a deceptively simple telling or "reading" of lives, deepened by the multiple ironies that encircle both method and content.[6] One is compelled to read between the lines of her character's words in an attempt to locate the envisioning "eye," the lens through which we are asked, for a moment at least, to view the world. And true to form, to "theory," Paley's characters by their very presence inform and define one another, as much as any self-revelation that comes from a particular character herself. "I like your paragraphs better than your sentences," one of her characters announces to the narrator of the piece ("Listening," 205). What this character prefers is the "dance," the movement of defining words, the fluidity, changeability, and multiplicity of vision that mediates Paley's characters.

We experience Paley's narrative "movement," then, as a chorus of voices, characters who give way to narrators, narrators who relinquish their control over the narrative midway through the telling—in short, characters who step aside for the intrusion of other narrating voices, other stories, other lives. They may step aside, but they do not step out of the stories to which they have a deep and unswerving commitment: "From now on," one of Paley's disgruntled characters tells the narrator (whom she has just chastised for her choice of material), "I'll watch you like a hawk" ("Listening," 211).

Characters very quickly become competing narrators and self-appointed editors in Paley's fiction, one sometimes "standing in" for another, both equally committed to the story, to its method of presentation, its "truth," but also to its faithfulness to "character."[7] In the midst of responding to Jack's seemingly innocuous, "What did you do today with your year off?" the narrator of "The Story Hearer," typically disrupts her narrative, although she did agree to "begin at the beginning," to make room for the character of the butcher, whose shop was the direction of her literal route, if not her metaphorical or cerebral one. When asked by the butcher, "What'll you have, young lady?" the narrator "[refuses] to tell him." Jack, her intrepid listener, does not need to ask why: "Oh God, no! You didn't do that again," he futilely admonishes. But with easily an equal share of outrage and admonishment, the narrator, delighted at the opportunity for a brief but no less didactic digression, facilely picks up a subject that clearly is part of her narrative repertoire: "I did, I said. It's an insult. You do not say to a woman of my age who looks my age, What'll you have, young lady? I did not answer him. If you say that to someone like me, it really means, What do you want, you pathetic old hag?"[8]

In telling the story of the events of her day, the narrator constructs, defines, and interprets characters and their motives. And she, herself, in the ensuing description of the dialogue with the butcher, gives herself the "best lines," as it were. She is the not-unanticipated heroine of her own story. The self-conscious reaffirmation of their own characters becomes the lens through which they view other characters and events, the lens through which Paley shows us their struggles for self-awareness.

"Don't judge the world by yourself," one character cautions Faith, the recurring narrator in many of Paley's stories.[9] Such caution is based on the notion of the potentially restricting confines of the subjective perspective, limiting one's own capacity for change and self-invention as well as that of others. The limitations of the invented self are at once recognized—by narrators who desire what they know to be impossible and which is desired all the more for that very reason: "Don't you wish you could rise powerfully above your time and name? I'm sure we all try, but here we are, always slipping and falling down into them, speaking their narrow language, though the subject . . . is immense" ("Hearer," 140). The narrator here reminds herself of the limits of language and thus of created fictions.

Such narrative disjunctions and self-reflexive commentary, often abrupt and unexpected, seem to have a clear, or at least consistent, rhetorical function. In Paley's narratives, the making of fictions, which becomes, in effect, the making of character, forms the central thematic action by separating the narrative act from its pretensions to omniscience. Her narrators and characters, often indistinguishable in dialogue from one another and from the author herself, in the midst of telling stories of their lives and the lives of families and friends, explicitly refer to the very act in which they are engaged, storytelling.

Part of the fiction is their seeing themselves and others as fictional possibilities. After telling Jack about "two little stories," the narrator of "Listening" informs him that "one of those men was you" ("Listening," 202). So the character of Jack, like that of the narrator herself, is both in and out of the story, part of the story and adjacent to it, but nonetheless subjected to the narrator's placement of him. Story and life become inexplicably intertwined. And the characters who narrate these lives envision the world and thus themselves through acts of storytelling.

"What does he want? I should tell him the story of my life?" ironically asks one character of the story's implied listener.[10] Of course, this is exactly what Paley's characters do; they tell the stories of their lives. And they do it with conscious self-reflection, self-parody, and with a "critics eye" for the whole business, since, finally, they recognize the limits of fiction (and thus the limits of character): "She's a character in a book. She's not even a person," admits the narrator of "Love."[11] Of course, we are brought up short with this ironically summative proclamation (and we should be suspicious whenever one of Paley's characters makes a definitive remark), since in this particular story the "character" in question is, within the "real" world of the story, indeed a "real" person: "She was this crazy kid who hung around the bars. But she didn't drink" ("Love," 4). She has a history and thus is at least as "real" as the character about whom the narrator herself has a history and with whom the narrator is speaking: "I used to be in love with a guy who was a shrub buyer," reveals the narrator. "'No kidding,' said my husband. 'How come I don't know the guy?'" to which she can only, in exasperation, reply, "'Ugh, the stupidity of the beloved. It's you,' I said" ("Love," 4).

Ironically, then, the character in the story fails to recognize himself as a character in the "real" life of the storyteller. But this, too, is facetious because he is made for the moment not to recognize himself by the narrator, who in a futile attempt to control the whole process of reinventing the past, says of her husband's ex-lover, "That's not true. She was made up, just plain invented in the late fifties" ("Love," 5), just as we all, I suspect, are "invented" by our times, history defining our own individual histories. So we, like Paley's characters, are both invented and "real," existing in the time in which it takes to "construct" (in the sense, that is, of "live" or "tell") a story.

In this way, Paley good-naturedly relates the activity of fiction-making to that of love: "all because of love. . . . How interesting the way it glides to solid invented figures from true remembered wraiths. By God, I thought, the lover is real. The heart of the lover continues; it has been propagandized from birth" ("Love"—whose title is, by now, clearly ironic—5–6). Inasmuch as invented shadows or essences, "wraiths," can be "true," "remembered" because invented, so too can fictions, stories, have been lived and contain the possibility to be lived—loved because lived, lived because loved.

Thus, telling stories is always a reflective telling, a self-referential but limited assessment of the process of storytelling in which the teller never quite controls her own story or her own invention; characters evaluate themselves as both storytellers and members of an often humorously contentious community, and they do the one through the other.

There is thus in Paley's fiction a constant building-up of interpretive possibilities, as characters become the stories they tell: "She was imagination-minded," the narrator of "A Woman, Young and Old" ironically recalls of her grandmother, "read stories all day and sighed all night, till my grandpa, to get near her at all, had to use that particular medium."[12] It is "that particular medium," stories, storytelling in any form, that becomes the defining act in Paley's fiction, defining not only the "action" of her stories but also the self-perception and self-deception of her characters. Stories are thus ways *in* and ways *out* of potentially precarious situations.

Such metafictional narratives reveal Paley's playfulness with the literary conventions of the short story as artifact. For Paley, stories seem always in the making, both for Paley as author and for the chorus of characters who tell their own tales "within" her narratives. Her framing stories yield, more often than not, to other stories in her texts—characters who take over the telling. Thus we find not so much a layering of stories (the story within the story), but rather one story giving way to another, becoming and informing another, but in a metonymic chain of opened variation. No single story seems to be privileged over another, no controlling narrative authority guides the reader's response. Such elasticity defies stasis; it is the *process* of storytelling, not "the story" itself, that defines and controls Paley's fiction.

And it is through this process that character, understood as "character in the making," emerges in Paley's fiction and should be recognized as an ethical concept. For Paley, the status of character is always being assessed in the midst of the telling of a story. And characters make claims, not only for the primacy of their individual stories, but for the ways in which those stories are told. Paley constantly and humorously reminds us that characters, after all, are fictional inventions, but they are their own invention as much as the author's. They are the story; they take on a life of their own as a response to the moment of their own fictionalization.

"A Conversation with My Father," a paradigm case for Paley's method, is a story about the making of fiction and its "double," the making of lives. In it, Paley stages a dialogue between the narrator and her eighty-six-year-old father. It is a story about her attempts to "please him," to make good his request of her, "to write a simple story just once more." [13] It is a story ultimately about the narrator's inability to tell the kind of story her father wants to hear, just as it is about her inability to accept the inevitability of his dying. The first inability, of course, resides in the other. Keeping alive the story she constructs, manipulates, and reinvents as the narrative progresses is the means by which she attempts to stave off the predictability of his death. But, as I've suggested, to say that this story, or any of Paley's stories, is *about* anything is potentially to undercut the very design and conceit of her texts. Indeed, perhaps we need to conceive the critically metaphorical "about" in Paley's dislocating fiction as precisely that, what seems to fall to the side of an unapprehendable, or at least well-disguised, center.

In constructing a story for her father, the narrator, in effect, constructs herself, makes herself a character. To do so is at once to legitimize and delegitimize the telling voice. The invention of stories and the invention of selves are suggestive of an ongoing feminist narrative that is both self-interpreting and self-revealing. In "A Conversation with My Father," Paley's narrator invents a story about a woman, "a story that had been happening for a couple of years right across the street" (162) and, as such, immediately suggests the precarious distinction between what is invented and what is real. That is, Paley invites us to remove the frame, to take the quotation marks off the story, in order to see the depth of the relation between narrative and self-invention and the tenuous, fragmenting potential of each.

The story she tells is a story whose ending changes in the course of the verbal sparring between the narrator and her father, who, "still interested in details, craft, technique" (164), wants what his daughter will not, in fact cannot, give him: character and plot both well-defined and consistent, the internally coherent movement from beginning to end, which suggests closure to the relationship. The narrator, however, refuses to give closure to her story, but instead posits unwritten possibilities for her protagonist's life, possibilities outside and beyond the confines of her self-defining cathexis with her father's life and death: "She could be a hundred different things in this world as time goes on" (166). "Could be," here, is a way of preventing closure, but not without the humorous self-knowledge with which the narrator admits to her conscious manipulation of what she perhaps knows to be the case, but artistically wills to be otherwise: "In real life, yes. But in my stories, no" (163).

For both Paley and her narrators, stories provide openings, spaces in which to move, or to think about moving, beyond the confines of convention and history, whether explicitly or implicitly gendered. And although the narrator would like to comply with her father's request, "*would* like to try to tell such a story," she is quick to qualify her authorial prerogative with the unwavering conviction that "everyone, real or invented, deserves the open destiny of life" (162). Of his daughter's story, the father draws his own pessimistic and ironically unimaginative conclusion: "'Poor woman. Poor girl, to be born in a time of fools, to live among fools. The end. The end. . . . You don't want to recognize it. Tragedy! Plain tragedy! Historical tragedy! No hope. The end. . . . A person must have character. She does not'" (166–67).

As is so often the case in Paley's fiction, the main character of the story, or rather, of the frame story, here the father, steps into the narrator's role and takes over the telling, attempts to make the story his own, fights, even, for its narrative authority. In this instance, he demands from his daughter a stability of character, a stable character, which he himself both is and is not. His hold on narrative authority is as tenuous as his hold on his masculinist, centered, static notion of history and of his failed projection of his daughter's place in it.

This ambiguity, created by the flux of narrator(s), character(s), and story (stories), *is* the story for Paley, and the father's insistence on conventional, historical notions of character and plot parallel his desire to author and authorize her story, her self, a desire that Paley's narrator, the daughter, the "I" of this particular story, rejects. In her rejection, however, we hear spoken its hold on her, as she comes to admit her character's ever-increasing control of her story. As the narrator finally acknowledges, "you just have to let the story lie around till some agreement can be reached between you and the stubborn hero" ("Conversation," 164). And so, we are offered no clear protagonist, no definitive character with whom we might identify a moral center, a telling authority, save for the telling authority of self-invention, an open-ended authorization that both "tells," that is, invents narratives and selves, and is "told on," that is, revealed in ways it can't always control.[14]

Paley's characters and narrators all participate in the storytelling, an inadvertent rhetoric of collaboration. They are equally omniscient, which is, of course, to say that the notion of omniscience is playfully discarded for what I would like to call a rhetoric of voices. With character manifested only as voice, plot becomes rhetoric, a progressive elaboration of voices amid fragments of plot. Paley's stories are moved by voices, by people talking, talking through each other, over each other, around each other. The voices compete with each other, vying for authorial control, each pushing its way into the foreground of the developing narrative, each revealed as partial in its bid for control, thus casting doubt on the possibility and desirability of controlling interpretation.

When we experience Paley's texts as voices, as verbal acts given structural meaning in dialogue by the interplay of multiple telling voices, we hear her own idiosyncratic rhetorical inventiveness, the quick ironic reversals and distortions, the hyperbolized and understated account of subtle conversational orderings of experience. What we often experience is a rupture in the narrative patterning, a disjunctive interplay of stories and voices that produce an ironic tension that governs the unfolding of Paley's stories. This tension, moreover, is inseparably a gendered issue of who controls interpretation in these stories, the questions of who gets to define whom and of whether such struggles are eliminable.

Yet, with striking consistency, these stories seem less to conclude and more to open, to begin again or to allow for the possibility of more beginnings, more revisions. "I want . . . to be a different person," the narrator of the short story "Wants" contends. Of course, as she humorously makes clear, such self-invention is finally impossible: "I had promised my children to end the war before they grew up," she reveals. "I wanted to have been married forever to one person, my ex-husband or my present one. Either has enough character for a whole life, which as it turns out is really not such a long time."[15] Self-determining self-invention is perhaps as impossible as escaping the desire for it, yet such an imposition does not daunt these characters. And the self-conscious struggle to change and to bring about change is as fundamental to feminism as it is to Judaism. In the short story "Friends," Faith refers to "an old discussion about feminism and Judaism," by insisting that "on the prism of isms, both of those do have to be looked at together once in a while," the one refracted through and in the other, both occasions for interpretive possibilities.[16]

"The Immigrant Story" speaks perhaps most persuasively to this complex relation between storytelling and the act of legitimating a life. This particular story, not uncharacteristically, appears initially to be constructed around a conversation between two people, a woman narrator and Jack, a conversation from which one speaker, the one presumably not the initial narrator of the frame story, emerges to take over the narrative. His is the story that concludes the story; he, uncharacteristically (but true to Paley's liberal feminism), gets the final word. For the narrative, seemingly at the point of closure, opens up, takes on a new course: "Do you mind?" Jack demands. "Just listen." [17]

The "new" story, the story that "concludes" the narrative, is now solely Jack's story, or rather his story of his parents, told with rapidly apparent detachment, through the lens of Jack's strongly invested but less than definitive vision of their lives and his place within the makings of their world. And just when we seem to be given closure to Jack's self-legitimating story of his parents' wrenching experience as immigrants and the morally defining characteristics of their life in America, this story too gives way, opens itself up to another story, to Jack's story, told in present tense although about the past, a story that seems to "conclude" with Jack, now both "author" and "character" in his own story: "They are sitting at the edge of their chairs. He's leaning forward reading to her in that old bulb light. . . . Just beyond the table and their heads, there is the darkness of the kitchen, the bedroom, the dining room, the shadowy darkness where as a child I ate my supper, did my homework and went to bed" (175). But this is no more a conclusion than any of the other stories within the piece. Indeed, it subverts closure because it opens the question of Jack's own motives in telling it and in putting himself in "the shadowy darkness," right when we realize he has arrogated narrative authority to himself. The ending is thus abrupt, the final narrative disjunctive, as if it stops in mid-thought, just as it began, between self-knowledge and self-delusion.

Is this the "immigrant's" story, a story that ends with Jack's parents "sitting at the edge of their chairs"? Or is it Jack's story, the story of his childhood, a story that, although closer in proximity to the time of his telling it than his parent's story, shifts into the past tense, "ate my supper, did my homework and went to bed"? Or is it finally Paley's story, a story about a conversation, seemingly anchored to nothing, between Jack and the "I"? No doubt it is, but, in being so, it raises more questions about the relation of narrative, self-disclosure, self-concealment, and stable irony than it answers; raising such questions is the heart of Paley's fictional method.

If all of this seems mercilessly complicated, it necessarily and intentionally is meant to be so, because, finally, all these stories are really the same story of the struggle for identity in the post–World War II mix of feminism, liberal politics, and vestigial old-world Jewishness that forms the shadowy setting of

Paley's stories. The lack of traditional quotation marks to designate dialogue suggests exactly such shadowy, undefined possibilities, as does the lack of closure. We are not offered an answer to the question of whose story governs the text, nor to the question of whose point of view controls the narrative, exactly because the story is only important or only exists inasmuch as it reveals anxiety over possession of a guiding character for one's life narrative. Thus, by offering a variety of elastic, fluid, multi-realizable perspectives, Paley denies that self-invention is somehow a centered, or even a centering process. For example, in the short story "Listening," one character steps into the narrative in order to demand her own characterization, in other words, to demand invention: "Listen, Faith," she argues, "why don't you tell my story? . . . Where is my life?" ("Listening," 210).

Paley thus captures extraordinary attempts at self-invention, all the more extraordinary in their persistence in the face of failure. In the midst of seemingly ordinary situations, the remarkable is willed to happen; the quotidian is transformed by the talk that describes it.[18] Her characters are capable of great feats of transformation, redefinition, and denial. "Reality? A lesson in reality? Am I a cabdriver? No. I drive a cab but I am not a cabdriver" ("Changes," 124). Here, as in other places, one of Paley's characters, through a deft rhetorical maneuver, attempts to redefine himself, reconstructs, reconceptualizes, and transforms himself through language. Here, the character would be his own author, and the linguistic turn, the chiastic reversal from verb to noun, gives him a kind of authority both denied in "real life" and common to the reality of self-defining subjective life. It is a kind of metaphorical reevaluation that is itself a metaphor for the complex motives of self-invention.

Such metaphors, however, as Paley makes clear, are only fictions. But their fictions, for Paley, are never "mere" fictions. Such rhetorical inventiveness allows Paley and her host of ordinary people to reinvent and restructure their real circumstances, if only for the space of a single narrative.[19] They do so through Paley's conviction of language's malleability. "It's what you do with the word," one of her characters triumphantly reveals. "The language and the idea, they work it out together" ("Changes," 129). And in doing so they form the persistent idea of self-formation in her work.

For Paley, self is a made thing, an artifact that becomes the measure by which the voices that are her characters are able to leave, if only temporarily, the confines of their own limited perspectives and make themselves a part of a history they themselves invent. In this way, an ideology of deeply felt, urgent participation in the gendered power relations of ordinary life emerges from Paley's short fiction. It is inscribed so deeply, however, in the indeterminacies of Paley's fictional methods that it is inseparable from them. The various pressures and requirements that grow from the convoluted, ironic gestures of self-determination that I've discussed are themselves evidence both of their necessity and of their impossibility. And so Paley's narrator in the short story "The Loudest Voice" can, with absolute conviction, proclaim that "every window is a mother's mouth."[20] Voices, like windows, are openings, beckoning, inviting, and admitting. But, like mother's mouths, Paley's voices are also defining, limiting, organizing of a desire whose struggle for fulfillment is as preposterous as it is believable.

NOTES

1. Grace Paley, "Listening," in *Later the Same Day* (New York: Penguin, 1985), 203. Subsequent references are given in the text.

2. Elsewhere I argue that storytelling serves Paley's characters primarily as a process of self-invention, a continual reinvention of the self in relation to a community, typically a community of women (since women's voices tend to control her narratives) or a community of Jews, in either case people marginalized by history or by their sense of their shared historical context, a context of struggle, of suffering, of the will to maintain both continuity and change. See Victoria Aarons, "Talking Lives: Storytelling and Renewal in Grace Paley's Short Fiction," *Studies in American-Jewish Literature* 9 (Spring 1990): 20–35.

3. In this way, as in others, Paley strikes one as a characteristically postmodern writer: fixed notions of plot and character development subordinate themselves to "voice" or competing or controlling voices, and plot and character give way, in Jerome Klinkowitz's terms, to "one seamless text of narrative . . . something to be played with rather than played by" (Jerome Klinlowitz, *Structuring the Void: The Struggle for Subject in Contemporary American Fiction* [Durham: Duke University Press, 1992], 4).

4. Grace Paley, "Faith in the Afternoon," in *Later the Same Day*, 33; "Enormous Changes at the Last Minute," in *Enormous Changes at the Last Minute* (1960; New York: Farrar, Straus, Giroux, 1983), 119; "Listening," 205. Subsequent references to "Enormous Changes" are given in the text. For a discussion of Paley's recurring character-narrator, Faith, and her evolving role in the short fiction, see Minako Baba, "Faith Darwin as Writer-Heroine: A Study of Grace Paley's Short Stories," *Studies in American-Jewish Literature* 7 (Spring 1988): 40–54.

5. Victoria Aarons, "'The Tune of the Language': An Interview with Grace Paley," *Studies in American-Jewish Literature* 12 (1993): 50–61. Paley also speaks eloquently in this interview to her commitment to both Judaism and feminism.

6. In this way, Paley's postmodern sense of fragmentation is qualified by an underlying liberal ethics of self-formation, generally understood through the specifics of feminism, post–World War II "cultural" Judaism, and the potential of the two for intersection. For a succinct and provocative discussion of the tensions between liberalism and feminism, and of possibilities for their reconciliation, see Mary Dietz, "Context Is All: Feminism and Theories of Citizenship," in *Dimensions of Radical Democracy: Plural-*

ism, Citizenship, Community, ed. Chantal Mouffe (London: Verso, 1992), 63–85. Paley thus seems to understand that radicalization through feminism is not mitigated by a commitment to some of the abiding principles of liberal humanism, that liberal humanism, if not a sufficient condition for social justice, is perhaps a necessary one. As Terry Eagleton has put it recently, "a true liberal must be liberal enough to suspect his own liberalism. Ideology, in short, is not always the utterly self-blinded, self-deluded straw target its theorists occasionally make it out to be—not least in the cynical, infinitely regressive self-ironizing of a postmodernist age" (Terry Eagleton, *Ideology: An Introduction* [London: Verso, 1991], 61).

7. For a complete account of character as an ethical construct, see Wayne Booth, *The Company We Keep: An Ethics of Fiction* (Berkeley and Los Angeles: University of California Press, 1988).

8. Grace Paley, "The Story Hearer," in *Later the Same Day*, 133, 138–37. Subsequent references are given in the text.

9. Grace Paley, "Dreamer in a Dead Language," in *Later the Same Day*, 33.

10. Grace Paley, "Zagrowsky Tells," in *Later the Same Day*, 174.

11. Grace Paley, "Love," in *Later the Same Day*, 31. Subsequent references are given in the text.

12. Grace Paley, "A Woman Young and Old," in *The Little Disturbances of Man: Stories of Men and Women at Love* (1959; New York: Penguin, 1985), 25.

13. Grace Paley, "A Conversation with My Father," in *Enormous Changes at the Last Minute*, 161. Subsequent references are given in the text.

14. Over the last decade or so, "post-Marxist" writers like Ernesto Laclau and Chantal Mouffe have become increasingly influential in attempting to show how the postmodern commitment to a dislocating "logic of the signifier" can be consistent with self-inventing narratives of social autonomy. Thus, Laclau and Mouffe state that "the autonomization of certain [social] spheres is not the necessary structural effect of anything, but rather the result of precise articulatory practices constructing that autonomy. Autonomy, far from being incompatible with hegemony, is a form of hegemonic construction" (*Hegemony and Socialist Strategy: Towards a Radical Democratic Politics* [London: Verso, 1985], 140). Andrew Ross, in response to the kind of psychoanalytic determinism that one might mistakenly attribute to Paley's representation of the transferential chaos of ordinary speaking subjects in her fiction, echoes this projected reconciliation of socially determined identity with a mobility of self-invention in the following way: "Social transference, then, far from being seen as a relatively fixed and universal network of psycho-social relations, over-written by a master-code of necessary domination, could instead be viewed according to a logic of contingency whereby different subject positions are articulated from moment to moment, depending on the changing, and I suppose we could say, hegemonic configuration of transferences that are operative at any one time" ("The Politics of Impossibility," in *Psychoanalysis and . . .* , ed. Richard Feldstein and Henry Sussman [New York: Routledge, 1990], 125).

15. Grace Paley, "Wants," in *Enormous Changes at the Last Minute*, 5.

16. Grace Paley, "Friends," in *Later the Same Day*, 81.

17. Grace Paley, "The Immigrant Story," in *Enormous Changes at the Last Minute*, 174. Subsequent references are given in the text.

18. For a detailed discussion of the ways in which Paley transforms her ordinary characters and ordinary situations into the extraordinary, a transformative process that takes place through talk, through storytelling, and through the establishment of a "community of memory," see Victoria Aarons, "A Perfect Marginality: Public and Private Telling in the Stories of Grace Paley," *Studies in Short Fiction* 27 (Winter 1990): 35–43.

19. For a discussion of Paley's "ordinary" host of characters and their relation to the tradition of secular Jewish literature, see Bonnie Lyons, "Grace Paley's Jewish Miniatures," in *Studies in American-Jewish Literature* 8 (1989): 26–33.

20. Grace Paley, "The Loudest Voice," in *The Little Disturbances of Man*, 55.

From Warrior to Womanist

The Development of June Jordan's Poetry

JACQUELINE VAUGHT BROGAN

While no single essay could begin to represent fairly the full range of June Jordan's work (writing, as she does, in so many different genres), nor even the full range of voices and styles she moves among in her poetry alone, it is fair to say that at its best Jordan's verse combines the personal, the political, and the aesthetic in an act of sustained "resistance" to the world.[1] Hers is a resistance ultimately grounded in an appeal to the "ethical not-yet" or the possibility of a redemptive future, global in its magnitude, if we but have the courage to name (or re-name) our destiny.[2] Here I am, of course, adapting the title of Jordan's most important collection thus far—*Naming Our Destiny*.[3] And in the last half of this essay I wish to take a close look at the most important poem in that volume, the concluding suite entitled "War and Memory." However, I begin this essay in something of a predicament. For readers already thoroughly familiar with Jordan's extensive corpus, much of what I say in the first half may be quite obvious. Yet, placing her work within the broad strokes of its own terms and development seems to me crucial, for it remains quite true that many people do not know her work at all.

There is, of course, a politics to this fact. Despite her productivity and prominence in contemporary writing, she is notably not in Gilbert and Gubar's *Norton Anthology of Literature by Women*, a fact I continue to find baffling.[4] Nor does she appear in Harris and Aguero's *An Ear to the Ground*, an anthology of contemporary ethnic poetries in America.[5] Nor does Jordan's work appear in the first *Heath Anthology of American Literature*, an anthology self-consciously as inclusive as possible, though three of her poems have been added to the second edition.[6] And yet Jordan has authored over a dozen different books, and her work has influenced any number of contemporary writers, including Adrienne Rich, Audre Lorde, and Alice Walker—to name only a few. In this sense what follows in the first part of this essay is intended not only to give an overview of June Jordan's work but also to encourage a more widespread knowledge and appreciation of this remarkable and important poet.

Born in 1936, June Jordan is a playwright, novelist, essayist, professor, and political activist, as well as one of our nation's leading poets. From her earliest work, such as the novel *His Own Where* (1971), through such powerful collections as *New Days* (1974), *Things That I Do in the Dark: Selected Poetry* (1977), and *Civil Wars* (essays, 1981), to her most recent work, *Naming Our Destiny* (poetry, 1989) and *Technical Difficulties* (essays, 1992), Jordan's various writings have been marked by an increasing inclusiveness (ranging from the early focus on blacks in America to concern with other countries, other ethnic groups, and women everywhere) and a consistent faith in the power of language to create nothing short of a redemptive world.[7] At the same time, this idealism, which we find repeated again and again in whatever genre within which she is working, is consistently tempered by an intensity that at time borders on militant ferocity. There is always something of the warrior in Jordan, no matter what the form. As she notes in "White English/Black English: The Politics of Translation" (1972), "As a poet and writer, I deeply love and I deeply hate words" (*CW*, 68), the love stemming from human communication, even communion, the hate from the conscription that language inevitably means to individuals, groups, races who are not members of the "majority" who control, quite literally, the dominating sentence.

Jordan underscores this nearly irreconcilable division in her poetry later in the same essay: "As a human being, I delight in this miraculous, universal means of communion," by which she means language, and yet, she continues, "as a Black poet and writer, I hate words that cancel my name and my history and the freedom of my future: I hate the words that condemn and refuse the language of my people in America" (*CW*, 69). She has given much attention, both in poetry and prose, to this internal, external, and seemingly eternal fight. To give but one example from her earliest poetry, a poem admittedly more complex in tone than I can discuss here,

> Teach me to sing
> Blackman Blacklove
> sing when the cops break your head
> full of song
> sing when the bullets explode in the back
> you bend over me
> Blacklove Blackman . . .
> ("Poem: For My Brother," *NDays*, 109)

Despite such a critical division, Jordan's work is also marked by a certain thematic consistency, one might even say, integrity. As she notes in "Poem: From an Uprooted Condition," "sometimes the poem tends to repeat itself"

(*NDays*, 70), a remark that could well apply to her entire corpus. Thus, we find throughout her work the recurring themes and motifs of love and desire (see *Passion: New Poems, 1977–1980*), of family, of social injustice, of suffering, and of joy.[8] Fittingly, several of these themes coalesce in the poem (first called "Poem against a Conclusion") that concludes *New Days* and that becomes the title and opening poem for her selected poems, *Things I Do in the Dark*:

> These poems
> they are things that I do
> in the dark
> reaching for you
> whoever you are
> and
> are you ready?
> These words
> they are stones in the water
> running away
> These skeletal lines
> they are desperate arms for my longing and love.
> I am a stranger
> learning to worship the strangers
> around me
> whoever you are
> whoever I may become.
> (*NDays*, 131)

However, given what I have said thus far, it is perhaps not surprising that her attention to the suffering of blacks and later to the suffering of other ethnic groups, and especially of women, often results in a "scream" (both in tone and language), while her attention to the possibility of creative redemption modulates toward a visionary faith.[9] It is quite to the point that recently Adrienne Rich includes Jordan in an article on poetic/political activism entitled "The Hermit's Scream."[10] Here, I offer a brief example from Jordan's prose:

> I choose to exist unafraid of my enemies. . . . I choose to believe that my enemies can either be vanquished or else converted into allies, into Brothers. And I choose to disregard the death-obsessed, extravagantly depressed and depressing doom-sayers around. As a woman, as a Black woman, as a Black woman poet and writer, I choose to believe that we, women and Third World peoples, will in fact succeed in saving ourselves, *and* our tra-

ditional assassins, from the meaning of their fear and hatred. Even more deeply, I believe we can save ourselves from the power of our own fear and our own self-hatred.

This is my perspective, and this is my faith. (*CW*, 129)

As may be obvious, Jordan's vision strikes a middle ground between those of Toni Morrison and Alice Walker (other Black writers who have much in common with Jordan), as well as between those of Malcolm X and Dr. Martin Luther King Jr. (The latter comparison she makes herself in an essay appropriately entitled "Notes toward Balancing Black Love and Hatred" [*CW*, 85].) However, I would also like to stress the fact that despite certain generalities we can make about her poetry, Jordan's work has proven neither stagnant nor predictable. As implied earlier, her work has evolved from a fairly tight focus on the predicaments of blacks (the "dream of the fourteenth amendment," as she calls it in "War and Memory") to an increasingly inclusive embrace of all marginalized people (including, for example, Native Americans, Palestinians, Nicaraguans, people of the Third World, women, children, and most recently lesbians) and even of white men. As she notes in "Thinking about My Poetry," "At this point in time, I refuse nothing" (*CW*, 129), a remark that, although made in 1977, seems increasingly true of her poetry. She even goes so far as to say, given her first "warriorist" tendencies in verse, "I do read and I do indeed listen to the poetry of white male poets" (*CW*, 129), no small achievement given her own vision and the actual political realities within which she is having to write and which, of course, she is trying to "right."

My last general remark is that despite this "catholicity of interest" (*CW*, 129), Jordan's most recent work moves into emphatically feminist, or perhaps more accurately, "womanist" concerns.[11] Hence the strength of the concluding line of "War and Memory," the poem we shall look at momentarily, in which she imagines not simply a feminist but specifically a womanist invention of language, a language that clearly would not only sanction Jordan herself but possibly the world as well: "and I / invent the mother of the courage I require not to quit" (*ND*, 211). I should note that such an idea of invention, now feministically conceived as a new "mother tongue," may be traced (however ironically) to Jordan's early childhood attraction to the creative power of words, as in the biblical passage, "In the beginning was the Word." In the foreword to *Civil Wars* she explains this fascination: "Early on, the scriptural concept that 'in the beginning was the Word and the Word was with God and the Word was God'—the idea that the word could represent and then deliver into reality what the word symbolized—this possibility of language, of writing, seemed to me magical and basic and irresistible" (x). This "thesis of John" (to

quote a poem by Wallace Stevens) continually fuels Jordan's inherent optimism—if we are paying attention—an optimism or vision all the more courageous given the actual facts of life she so scrupulously notes, in poem after
poem. Consider, for example, the following lines from her 1982 "Moving
Home," a poem that in style and theme notably anticipates some of the strategies in Adrienne Rich's *An Atlas of the Difficult World*: [12]

> Nor do I wish to speak about the nurse again and
> again raped
> before they murdered her on the hospital floor
> Nor do I wish to speak about the rattling bullets that
> did not
> halt on that keening trajectory
> Nor do I wish to speak about the pounding on the
> doors and
> the breaking of windows and the hauling of families into
> the world of the dead
> I do not wish to speak about the bulldozer and the
> red dirt
> not quite covering all of the arms and legs. . . .
>
> <div align="center">(<i>LR</i>, 142)</div>

It is almost impossible, yet certainly consistent with Jordan's work, that she
concludes such a difficult and painful poem with this remarkable line, "It is
time to make our way home" (*LR*, 143). It is truly "re-markable," in both
senses of the word, being both courageous in context and committed to a
redemptive revision of the world.

As she clarifies in "Thinking about My Poetry," and as may have been suggested by the preceding section, June Jordan has gone through several aesthetic stages and stances. She describes, for example, the stage between age
seven and her mid-twenties as the stage when "poetry was the inside dictator"
to which she "submitted" herself. Next was her commitment to craft, writing
in the "manner of Herrick, Shelley, Eliot, or whoever" (*CW*, 123). Next came
her decision to make her poetry of interest to others, necessitating the choosing of subjects of general and substantive consequence (largely the recurring
motifs noted above). Later came the stage in which she decided "to aim for
the achievement of a collective voice" (125), of which "Gettin Down to Get
Over: Dedicated to My Mother" remains the finest example. I cite the opening lines:

MOMMA MOMMA MOMMA
momma momma
mammy
nanny
granny
woman
mistress
sista
luv

    (*NDays*, 118)

However, the last stage Jordan describes is for my purposes both the most important and the most successful. In this stage, the best of her work demonstrates in praxis what has become almost idiomatic in feminist cultural theory: that is, the personal *really is* political. The triumph of "War and Memory," the particular poem I wish to focus on for the remainder of this essay, is that Jordan makes this fact so compellingly clear while thematically and aesthetically evoking an evolution, a possible redemption, for a newly created world. It is a visionary poem, even as it is deeply historicized both in content and style.

However, I should first reiterate that in addition to her deep and obvious involvement with contemporary African American writers, Jordan is deeply involved with literary/linguistic history. To mention three obvious and relatively modern examples, one must have the mind of Elizabeth Bishop, or at least have her *North and South* in mind, to fully appreciate Jordan's poem "Problems of Translation" (*LR*, 37–41), or have Yeats's "Leda and the Swan" in mind to appreciate her alternative sonnet (both in form and content) such as "The Female and the Silence of Man" (*ND*, 190–91), or Robert Frost's "Mending Wall" in mind when reading her "War Verse," which begins, quite ironically, with "Something there is that sure must love a plane" (*LR*, 112).[13] The same is even more true of "War and Memory" (*ND*, 204–11), where the aesthetic, the political, and the personal modulate from a saturated past (including the personal violence in her family) to a redemptive, reconstituted lineage. As such, this poem encapsulates the entire development of Jordan's work so far.

Consider the first few lines of section 1, a section that is at once deeply personal, autobiographical, while stylistically anticipating the structural move to follow in the poem toward the larger polis, the political, even cosmos-polis:

Daddy at the stove or sink. Large
knife nearby or artfully

suspended by his clean hand handsome
even in its menace
slamming the silverware drawer
open and shut / the spoons
suddenly loud as the yelling
at my mother
no (she would say) no
Granville no
about: would he
be late / had she
hidden away the Chinese laundry shirts
again / did she think
it right that he (a man in his own house)
should serve himself a cup of tea a plate
of food / perhaps she thought that he
should cook the cabbage and the pot roast
for himself as well?

In addition to the influence of alliteration and rhythm from African American sources of various kinds (including perhaps even rap), my ear at least finds a subversive flirtation with Anglo-Saxon alliteration, rhythm, and assonance. Such lines as "handsome / even in its menace / slamming the silverware drawer" and, of course, is it "right that he (a man in his own house)" owe their success in part to their ability to evoke a literary and patriarchal legacy at odds with the action and tone of the poem. That is, the patriarchal legacy is certainly not venerated here, although just how culturally normalized this domineering patriarchy may be is made painfully clear through the nearly predictable phrases constituting these literal power lines.

There is simultaneously in the passage cited above an evocation of the kind of experimental writing characteristic of *How/(ever)* (an experimental feminist journal of poetry), as in the quasi-line breaks of lines 6, 12, 14, and 17. These self-consciously demarcated breaks complicate or defy the "normal" line ends, making them, by the way, very difficult to quote out of context. That, of course, is *the point*, as it is in much feminist and experimental poetry.

Section 2 works almost by way of medieval interlacing; the personal and gendered violence of the scene at home becomes both metynom and metaphor for a world at war, in much the same way that Elizabeth Bishop's "In the Waiting Room" relates a personal experience to the violence of World War I.[14] I cite the last several lines of this section:

"The camps?" I asked them, eagerly: "The Nazis?"
I was quite confused, "But in this picture,
Daddy, I can't see nobody."
"*Any*body," he corrected me: "You can't see
anybody!" "Yes, but what," I persevered, "what

is this a

picture of?"
"That's the trail of blood left by the Jewish girls
and women on the snow because the Germans
make them march so long."
"Does the snow make feet bleed, Momma?
Where does the bleeding come from?"

My mother told me I should put away
the papers and not continue to upset myself
about these things I could not understand
and I remember
wondering if my family was a war
going on
and if
there would soon be blood
someplace in the house
and where
the blood of my family would come from

Section 3 ["The Spanish Civil War: / I think I read about that one"] seems
not-so-humorously indebted to the well-known Hemingway device of "omission," and appropriately so, both in theme and aesthetics, given the fact that
omission (the difference between being an anybody and a nobody) is both the
linguistic and the political argument of the preceding section just cited. Sections 4–6 work more like a collage than interlacing, moving from personal
witnessing of North Korea, the Vietnam protest, and Kent State to the personal
and painful choices necessitated by the now-twin subjects of personal betrayal
and economic deprivation. I cite from the poem again at the point that a new,
important stylistic trait enters:

Plump during The War on Poverty
I remember making pretty good
money (6 bucks an hour)
as a city planner and my former

husband married my best
friend and I was never positive
about the next month's rent but
once I left my son sitting
on his lunchbox in the early rain
waiting for a day-care pickup and I went
to redesign low-income housing for the Lower
East Side of Manhattan and three hours after that
I got a phone call from my neighbors
that the pickup never came
that Christopher was waiting
on the sidewalk
in his yellow slicker
on his lunchbox
in the rain.

Period. As opposed to the staccato-like snippets of section 5—"It was very exciting. The tear gas burned like crazy" (lines that sound much like Gertrude Stein when she is collapsing our notion of the hierarchy of foreground and background, of hierarchy in any form)—section 6 is also stylistically of necessity one sentence with multiple "lines," as it were, in which everything bears on everything else. This point is made at a terrible risk to the poem, for it is in such horrible contrast to the acute isolation of Christopher, whose neighbors presumably leave him in the rain (a synecdochic symbol of the breakdown of society's ethical memory that we all bear on one another).

At this point the poem is almost unbearably painful. However, in the section appropriately numbered "#VII" (here I appeal, however ironically, to the traditional numerological reading of "7" as creation, just as Jordan appealed to the feminist sense of the possibilities latent in the phrase, "In the beginning was the Word"), African American literary devices of rhythm and repetition and even spiritual evangelism build to an incantatory evocation of a future, an expressly womanist world to come, that does not necessarily invert but rather redeems the obviously fallen patriarchal world (personally and politically) with which she began. Worried always about her mother, her father, this society, others, she creates an incantation that mesmerizes (in the old sense of the word):

And from the freedom days
that blazed outside my mind
I fell in love

I fell in love with Black men White
men Black
women White women
and I
dared myself to say The Palestinians
and I
worried about unilateral words like Lesbian or
                              Nationalist
and I tried to speak Spanish when I travelled
                              to Managua

and I
dreamed about The Fourteenth Amendment
and I
defied the hatred of the hateful everywhere
as best I could
I mean
I took long nightly walks to emulate the Chinese
          Revolutionaries
and I
always wore one sweater less than absolutely
                              necessary to
          keep warm
and I wrote everything I know how to write
                              against apartheid
and I thought I was a warrior growing up
and I
buried my father with all of the ceremony all of the
                              music
          I could piece together
and I
lust for justice
and I
make that quest arthritic/pigeon-toed/however
and I invent the mother of the courage I require
                              not to quit

I suspect that these words, which conclude the volume entitled *Naming Our Destiny*, summarize the efforts of many other women writers we discussed at the Women Writers Symposium in San Antonio and, I hope, the efforts we make as critics as well. We should note that the poem ends without any concluding punctuation. The "sentence," as it were, is open. . . .

NOTES

1. Since I have used the word "resistance" on numerous occasions to describe a political and ethical response to violence (especially to World War II), I should clarify that, first, Jordan's "resistance" is fundamentally more activist than anything someone like Wallace Stevens wrote and that, second, their shared sense of the power of the word to create a world in which we can live is uncannily similar. See, for example, my "Wallace Stevens: Poems against His Climate," *Wallace Stevens Journal* 11.2 (1987): 75–93. For Stevens's sense of "resistance," see his "The Irrational Element in Poetry," in *Opus Posthumous*, ed. Samuel French Morse (New York: Alfred A. Knopf, 1972), 225.

2. Here I am paraphrasing Drucilla Cornell, "From the Lighthouse: The Promise of Redemption and the Possibility of Legal Interpretation," *Cardozo Law Review* 11 (1990): 1689. It is quite fitting, given how politically activist Jordan's verse is, to find such discourse circulating among legal activists.

3. *Naming Our Destiny: New and Selected Poems* (New York: Thunder's Mouth Press, 1989); hereafter abbreviated as ND. By way of an aside, I'm always tempted to call this book *Naming Our Destinies*, with emphasis on the plural, which is in a way very keeping with her vision. But the singularity she finds in the title she did choose is, in fact, finally more in keeping with what we might call her—now—fundamental sense of solidarity, far more in keeping with Adrienne Rich's *An Atlas of the Difficult World* (New York: W. W. Norton, 1991) than with Wallace Stevens's World War II volume, *Parts of a World* (New York: Alfred A. Knopf, 1945). Other works to be cited in the text include *Civil Wars* (Boston: Beacon Press, 1981; abbreviated as CW); *Living Room* (New York: Thunder's Mouth Press, 1985; abbreviated as LR); and *New Days* (New York: Emerson Hall, 1974; abbreviated as NDays).

4. Sandra M. Gilbert and Susan Gubar, eds., *The Norton Anthology of Literature by Women: The Tradition in English* (New York: W. W. Norton, 1985).

5. Marie Harris and Kathleen Aguero, eds., *An Ear to the Ground: An Anthology of Contemporary Poetry* (Athens: University of Georgia Press, 1989).

6. The first edition of *The Heath Anthology of American Literature*, ed. Paul Lauter et al. (Lexington, Mass.: D. C. Heath, 1990) includes no mention of June Jordan. This omission has been partially rectified in the recent second edition (1994), vol. 2, which prints three of Jordan's poems: "Poem about My Rights," "To Free Nelson Mandela," and "Moving towards Home."

7. *His Own Where* (New York: Thomas Crowell, 1971); *Things That I Do in the Dark: Selected Poetry* (New York: Random House, 1977); *Technical Difficulties: African-American Notes on the State of the Union* (New York: Pantheon, 1992).

8. *Passion: New Poems, 1977–1980* (Boston: Beacon Press, 1980).

9. See "Thinking about My Poetry" (1977), in *Civil Wars*, 122–25.

10. See Adrienne Rich, "The Hermit's Scream," *PMLA* (October 1983): 1157–64.

It is worth noting, for points both made above and to follow, that Rich includes in this article, among others, Stevens, Walker, Lorde, and Bishop (as well as Jordan); the title of the article is borrowed from Bishop's "Chemin de Fer," a poem that has also figured in Drucilla Cornell's writings on legal jurisdiction.

11. Compare the following lines from the opening poem of Rich's *Atlas* with the lines cited from Jordan's work in the text above:

> I don't want to hear how he beat her after
>   the earthquake,
> tore up her writing, threw the kerosene
> lantern into her face waiting
> like an unbearable mirror of his own. I don't
> want to hear how she finally ran from the trailer
> how he tore the keys from her hands, jumped into
>   the truck
> and backed it into her. (p. 4)

12. The parallels between Jordan's verse and that of Yeats and Frost are quite obvious, the first noted by herself (we are told to compare Jordan's subversive sonnet with "Leda and the Swan" in a postscript below the title), the second so ironic in its allusory stance. However, the similarity between Bishop and Jordan (not just in the instance mentioned in the text above) cannot be stressed enough. Not only does "Problems of Translation" refer directly to Bishop's poems "Roosters" and "The Map" from *North and South*, it also emulates strategies of Bishop's subsequent volumes *Questions of Travel* and *Geography III*.

13. Section 2 of "War and Memory" is so indebted to Bishop's "In the Waiting Room" that the subject is itself worthy of an article. However, in both, pictures taken or looked at during a time of war evoke in rather naive and "eager" young girls' profound questionings of personal identity, of the relationship between linguistic objectification and actual violence. For the child Elizabeth in "In the Waiting Room," the horror is learning that she is "one of *them*," a linguistic subtlety much in keeping with that evoked by the difference between "anybody" and "nobody" in Jordan's poem.

14. See Joy Harjo, "An Interview with June Jordan," *High Plains Literary Review* 3.2 (1988): 60–76.

Part 4   Revising Tradition

Lost Boundaries

The Use of the Carnivalesque in Tabitha Tenney's *Female Quixotism*

SHARON M. HARRIS

When Tabitha Gilman Tenney's novel *Female Quixotism* was published in 1801, it joined a national voice of lament over the dangers of novel reading. The typical antinovel argument was that the genre's romantic allurements would lead women away from the realities of their domestic responsibilities. In *Female Quixotism*, however, Tenney used a comic, anti-romantic stance in relation to novel reading to demonstrate the failed sense of democracy in the new republic. No element of the citizenry escapes her comic examination; as the editors of the recent Oxford edition of *Female Quixotism* note, "The novel's cutting wit spares hardly any segment of society: droll servants, earnest merchants, scheming scholars, and self-deluding gentry all get their fair share of ribbing."[1] The argument I am presenting examines Tenney's novelistic use of the carnivalesque as a means of exposing the realities of the new nation's social order, especially as it oppressed and segregated its citizens by race, class, and gender. But I also want to address the bifurcated argument embedded in this text, an argument that both exposes the failed sense of democracy in the new republic and simultaneously perpetuates the dominant culture's encoding of racial and ethnic difference.

The concept of the carnivalesque was made available to critical studies by Mikhail Bakhtin. The historical significance of carnival is that it has always been linked to moments of social or political crisis. Thus, it is not surprising that carnivalesque images reemerge in post-Revolutionary U.S. literatures as the nation begins to define not only its role in international affairs but equally the roles of its various citizens. In denoting the carnivalesque as a mode aligned with "the peculiar culture of the marketplace and of folk laughter with all its wealth of manifestations," Bakhtin outlines three distinct forms these manifestations take: first, ritual spectacles, such as carnival pageants and comic marketplace shows; second, parodies, both oral and written, either in the vernacular or with an invocation of classical standards; third, the use of curses and oaths as a means of explicitly challenging classical language standards.[2] Most prevalent in medieval and Renaissance literatures, the carnival-esque exposes the "two-world condition" of those cultures: officialdom and a world outside that officialdom, that is, a world of the people. It is important to note that, while carnival resembles the spectacle, it is different in one important way. As Bakhtin reminds us, "carnival . . . does not acknowledge any distinction between actors and spectators. . . . Carnival is not a spectacle seen by the people; they live in it. . . . During carnival time life is subject only to its laws" (7). Freedom is embraced and all hierarchies are suspended; in its way, then, carnival is intended to constitute a true democratic moment.

Central to an understanding of the carnivalesque is its engagement with grotesque imagery, and Tabitha Tenney's main character in *Female Quixotism* may certainly, within her culture, be defined as a grotesque. She immerses herself in novel reading, deludes herself about a series of doomed romances, and at the novel's conclusion opts for spinsterhood and contrition. She may be wiser, but she is still single, and for women, in the new nation's emphasis on republican motherhood, that is a form of grotesque. Yet it is crucial to our understanding of how Tabitha Tenney employs the carnivalesque to recognize an important point, emphasized by Bakhtin but too often overlooked in subsequent analyses, namely, the historically evolving nature of the carnival-grotesque form. In the era of Molière and Swift, this form functioned "to consecrate inventive freedom, . . . to liberate from the prevailing point of view of the world, from conventions and established truths." In the late eighteenth century, however, a radical change took place. It began as a German literary controversy over the character of Harlequin but soon became "a wider problem of [aesthetic] principle: could manifestations such as the grotesque, which did not respond to the demands of the sublime, be considered art?" What evolved was a movement away from the broader concepts of Rabelais and Cervantes to what Bakhtin terms "the new subjective grotesque"; he cites *Tristram Shandy* as the "first important example" of this evolution (34–36).

Tabitha Tenney was well aware of the changes in the carnival-grotesque and contributed to its transformation. In the late eighteenth century the carnival-grotesque became not a festival of all the people but rather "a private 'chamber' character. It became, as it were, an individual carnival, marked by a vivid sense of isolation" (Bakhtin, 37). In the years leading up to publication of *Female Quixotism*, the United States, under Federalist rule, pursued an extreme isolationist ideology; the carnivalesque not only fit Tenney's artistic needs but also engaged her political inclinations, as will be outlined in detail below. What is critical in this transformation of the genre is that the "principle of laughter which permeates the grotesque" (especially in relation to the bodily life) lost its regenerative power; the grotesque becomes an object of fear to be relayed by the author and assumed by the reader. One example of this change is the mask: originally, the mask was "connected with the joy of change and reincarnation"; it celebrated difference rather than uniformity. In the late eighteenth century, however, the mask was "stripped of its original richness and acquire[d] other meanings alien to its primitive nature" (37–40). It became an instrument of deceit and secretiveness. The carnival-grotesque evolved into a noctural event, evoking themes of darkness rather than embracing the symbolic implications of sunrise and morning as the original carnival had.

This latter sense of the carnivalesque is explored by Julia Kristeva. "Carnivalesque discourse," she observes, "breaks through the laws of a language censored by grammar and semantics and, at the same time, is a social and political protest. There is no equivalence, but rather, identity between challenging official linguistic codes and challenging official law."[3] As Mary Russo has argued, we must embrace the carnivalesque with caution, since it can be employed as a panacea by a dominant culture rather than as a truly liberating vehicle.[4] Yet it is a tool of authorities only when the carnival is a ritual sanctioned by them. In *Female Quixotism*, it is precisely when Dorcasina Sheldon, the "private 'chamber' character," stops reading and breaks with officialdom (literally, with her father's house) that Tenney depicts her as secretly engaging in the carnivalesque as a means of moving from the role of the subjected to that of the subject, of reinscribing her world on her own terms. It is in the episodes that occur outside Mr. Sheldon's house that Tenney interjects the issues of gender, race, and class, leading the reader into a recognition of how limited the so-called democratic reforms of the eighteenth century had actually been.

In *Revolution and the Word*, Cathy N. Davidson recognizes *Female Quixotism* as a picaresque novel. Typically, Davidson notes, the picaresque's loose narrative form "allows a central character . . . to wander the margins of an emerging American landscape [and] to survey it in all its incipient diversity," but since women's mobility was severely restricted in the early federal period, the female picara cannot meet these narrative criteria. Davidson asserts, therefore, that Dorcasina's story does not challenge the status quo until the novel's conclusion, when she questions the nature of matrimony.[5] I would argue, however, that the status quo for Anglo American women is challenged throughout the novel; first, because the picaresque is itself a carnivalization of the novel's form, and second, because Dorcasina takes many "journeys" outside her domicile. Granted, these journeys may be only to an isolated grove or to a nearby town, but distance itself is insignificant in relation to the alternative experiences she encounters. In these journeys, the upper-class Dorcasina engages in relationships with members of every class of U.S. society, including her own Anglo American household servants, African American servants whose domain lies within the Sheldon estate but not within the household itself, an Irish rogue, an enterprising prostitute, schoolteachers, and a barber. It seems to me far more radical to assert that this diversity lies within one's own neighborhood than to assume an audience will translate so-called "foreign" experiences to a sense of the American polis.

In some respects, *Female Quixotism* foreshadows feminist and postmodern challenges to Enlightenment philosophies, especially the Enlightenment privileging of reason and science. In an era deemed the "Age of Reason," Tabitha Tenney's employment of the carnivalesque challenges cultural definitions of rationality itself, not only by depicting the chaos that surrounds the aristocratic Sheldon domicile but equally by exposing the class biases internalized in the celebration of "reason," as defined by the dominant culture. In the United States at the turn of the century, the voice of rationality was always deemed that of the white male aristocrat. Mr. Sheldon personifies this voice and Dorcasina's first love, Lysander, represents its perpetuation in the next generation of young, privileged males: "His person was noble and commanding . . . and his address manly and pleasing. . . . His ideas of domestic happiness were just and rational" (7). Tenney depicts Lysander as the ideal of absolute patriarchy. The gendering of reason by Enlightenment philosophies is also satirized by Tenney. In contrast to Lysander, Tenney presents an alternative voice of reason in that of the Anglo American servant Betty, Dorcasina's lifelong companion. Throughout the novel, Betty's intellectual, reasoning abilities are not aligned with issues of philosophy or overt politics but rather with her power to penetrate beneath the actions and the masks of propriety displayed by various characters in the novel; it is neither Dorcasina nor Mr. Sheldon but rather Betty who discerns individuals' "unmasked" natures and their degrees of reliability. It is Betty's voice, far more than Mr. Sheldon's, that Dorcasina needs to hear in order to escape her repeated cycle of misapplied love that results in emotional abuse and trauma. While the comic spirit of the carnival prevails, the pathos of Dorcasina's repeated traumatic experiences suggests the very real consequences of the gendering of reason and the marginalization of women, even in their own homes and their own country.

Mr. Sheldon is never fully aware of his daughter's beliefs and not aware at all of her adventures, while Betty not only knows of Dorcasina's experiences but also attempts to guide her away from self-defeating actions into a better sense of social reality. Tenney pushes the boundaries of rationality further, however, when she exposes the class-based consequences of Betty's knowledge. The prevailing ideology of the Age of Reason held that rational thought and action will lead to the best possible political and social orders; yet in spite of her wisdom and social astuteness, Betty's social class does not allow her to conquer prevailing misconceptions. The automatic devaluation of any expression by a person of her class is rendered both through her employers' lack of adherence to her cautionary voice and, more explicitly, through a physical (bodily) suppression of Betty herself. In episode after episode, when Betty cautions her against a particular action, Dorcasina pursues her own desires—to her detriment, surely, but it is almost always Betty who must endure physical abuse for Dorcasina's foolish actions. This abuse is rendered most explicitly when Dorcasina insists that Betty dress in Mr. Sheldon's clothing and pretend to be Dorcasina's lover. Betty has barely begun her impersonation when "she was interrupted . . . by the sudden appearance of Scipio, the gardener, Patrick, the boy, a white servant, and two or three labourers from the field," all of whom chase her about the grounds, believing that she is "some evil minded person" who intended to steal Mr. Sheldon's belongings (99). The episode ends when Dorcasina herself appears and exposes Betty's identity, but Betty is left as the mortified object of her peers' mirth, and she is seen at the end of the scene "sinking with shame and vexation" (99). In other, similar episodes, Betty is repeatedly abandoned by Dorcasina in moments of physical combat that Dorcasina's actions have created: several times Betty is beaten; in one episode her upper garments are stripped off of her; and in another, the servant of Dorcasina's latest lover "laid violent hands upon [Betty], pulled her hair, shook her, pinched her, and mauled her" (132). While there is always supposed to be a comic element to such scenes in the novel, the carnivalesque nature of these scenes exposes real consequences for the servant class due to antics perpetuated by the upper-class. Dorcasina may be humiliated when she loses lover after lover, but it is Betty whose body is mauled and appropriated for her mistress's use.

These episodes lead us to one of the most significant aspects of Tenney's engagement with the carnivalesque in *Female Quixotism*. In an era of denial and suppression of female sexuality, the carnivalesque by its very nature allows for its exploration. It is on this avenue of sexual exploration, too, that class and race distinctions are momentarily lost. The carnival is the time for cross-dressing and masquerading, and *Female Quixotism* is rife with instances of both activities, which allow Tenney to explore themes of sexuality that are banned in the father's house and by the father's law. The scenes that allow the issue of sexuality to be raised most often depend upon the eighteenth century's shift from open, daylight carnival celebrations to dark, surreptitious couplings, and this shadow culture, as it were, allows Tenney to explore racial and class "crossings" as well. In one instance, Dorcasina finds herself in the summer house and in the arms of Scipio, the African American gardener, whose own partner, the African American servant Miss Violet, is at the same moment being embraced by Dorcasina's white Irish lover, Patrick O'Connor. Both couples are quite delighted in their sexual explorations—until their true identities are exposed and their recognition of racial difference forces them to consider the false strictures of their usual "intercourse."

In another instance of masquerade, a prostitute presents herself as Dorcasina and rather than the expected narrative suggestion that no one could mistake a prostitute for an upper-class white woman, the women are easily mistaken for each other by people in the neighborhood. Other scenes of cross-dressing titillate the reader with images of women loving other women, not in the culturally sanctioned mode of female loving that Carroll Smith-Rosenberg has described, but in overt sexual play.[6] For instance, Dorcasina insists that Betty dress as Patrick O'Connor and imitate his sexual play with her, and later the very proper Miss Harriot Stanly dresses as a young officer, Captain Montague, and secretly takes on the part of Dorcasina's lover. This cross-dressing episode is especially significant for its exposure of women's sexual desires and equally so for its breaches of gender stereotypes. Harriot dresses as a captain, and one of Dorcasina's later lovers is also a captain, who has his servant masquerade as himself; the servant/captain is accepted by Dorcasina as her lover; the cycle of this episode is completed when Harriot later marries the captain whom the servant was imitating. If the reader becomes lost in this chain of masqueradings, that is precisely the point. The failure of language to distinguish the cyclical recasting of characters here exposes the false bases of social hierarchies and of gender stereotypes.

What the carnivalesque allows Tabitha Tenney to do, ultimately, is twofold: to expose the gender biases and prejudices still rampant in a nation that depicts itself as the ideal of democracy, and to address the suppression of (white) female desire. This is decidedly the late-eighteenth-century version of the carnivalesque, however, for the ending of this novel does not depict radical social or political change; in many ways Dorcasina is left in the dark, as it were, in the final chapter of *Female Quixotism*. Although she chooses to remain single and, importantly, to reclaim her nonromanticized name, Dorcas, she is left at the novel's conclusion a self-described isolate: "I am now, in the midst of the wide world, solitary, neglected, and despised" (324). She is, by her culture's standards, a grotesque. As a single woman, her experiences cannot lead her to the regenerative power once linked to carnival participation. No social freedom has been attained; all of officialdom's laws remain intact. Dorcas Sheldon thus represents the woman who has turned from romantic visions to reason, but her fate is not that of her male compatriots who make the same journey.

Like Betty, she is not elevated to the realm of philosopher or statesman. Yet Tenney's conclusion emphasizes the fact that Dorcas has gained two important features: self-knowledge and an ability to inscribe herself as subject. These features are rendered through carnivalesque discourse as Kristeva defined it, acting as a social and political protest through its damning indictment of the American republic's falsified representations of equality.

The challenges to the Anglo American woman's pattern of marital servitude should not be ignored or belittled. Such challenges were necessary steps in the prelude to the women's rights movements of the nineteenth and twentieth centuries. Nor should we ignore the fact that Dorcas Sheldon's carnivalesque conversion is dependent upon hierarchical structures and acts of racial and ethnic oppression. While Betty manifests the figure of the wise woman throughout the novel, and we see Dorcasina transformed from the fool into the isolate-sage, no such status or transformation is afforded the African American characters in the novel.

The carnivalesque is a means of disrupting the symbolic order, the production and representation of reality according to the Law of the Father. Tenney's narrative achieves that disruption and exposes "reality" as an ideology that must be perpetuated in order to sustain the realm (here, quite literally, the house) of the Father. While *Female Quixotism* succeeds in its disruptive practices in relation to the central white female character, it in fact reinscribes the dominant ideology in terms of class and race and does so especially with *women* characters. What appears to be a "feminization" in fact aids in the perpetuation of patriarchal hierarchies by dividing women (rather than articulating difference), by creating class and race conflicts, and thereby limiting resistence to the real source of domination, patriarchy itself. That Tabitha Tenney cannot fully write Dorcasina into a "happy ending" suggests her recognition of this dilemma.

Tzvetan Todorov's study of the colonization of the Americas emphasizes the significance of predetermined conceptualizations in the colonizer's interpretation and representation of the "Other."[7] This process is not, of course, limited to fifteenth-century cultural encodings of race. For all that Dorcasina is willing to experience the world anew, to discover "new worlds" for herself, her prior conceptualizations of class and race privilege are never abandoned. As she seeks to de-colonize herself from the control of her father and from patriarchal conventions, she does so through a process that re-colonizes all non-white, non-upperclass individuals. That Betty and Miss Violet are most forcefully re-colonized suggests the privileged woman's preconception of "other" women as dangerous. Mary-Louise Pratt has exposed the processes by which "frontier" propoganda literature acts as a "normalizing force . . . [that] serves, in part, to mediate the shock of contact on the frontier."[8] For Dorcasina, the novels she has been reading are the normalizing force through which she (mis)represents *to herself* her adventures in the grove-frontier. Every experience she has outside her father's house is read through her preconceived expectations formed from novel reading. Thus, ironically, while Tenney presents novel reading as dangerous, she elides the normalizing force not only of the texts Dorcasina reads but of her own imaginative text as well. The power of preconceptualization is evident in its subsequent and multifold misrepresentations in *Female Quixotism*. On the one hand, preconceived ideas lead Dorcasina to misinterpret her own demeaning experiences as romances while, on the other hand, it allows her to continue to read herself into a position of privilege, what Edward Said terms "positional superiority," over white servants and all people of color in spite of her own repeated foolish actions and subsequent humiliations. Indeed, the recovery of her sense of self against the normalizing forces surrounding gender in a patriarchal society is dependent upon her learned conceptions of race and class.

An examination of the masquerade, an integral feature in the production of the carnival, exposes Tenney's disruption of the patriarchal symbolic order as a disruption accessible only to the upper-class white woman. Unlike Bakhtin and Kristeva, Luce Irigaray is able to see beyond the phallocentric discourse of psychoanalysis and in that process exposes the vast plain of female desire behind "the *masquerade of femininity*." And desire with no adequate means of expression drives, shall we say, Dorcasina's life. As Irigaray observes, "The masquerade has to be understood as what women do in order to recuperate some element of desire, to participate in man's desire, but at the price of renouncing their own. In the masquerade, they submit to the dominant economy of desire in an attempt to remain "on the market" in spite of everything. But they are there as objects for sexual enjoyment, not as those who enjoy."[9] Ultimately, the masquerade (like the dominant culture itself) cannot posit viable difference, and Tenney's apparent discomfort is exposed at a crucial point in the narrative, the summer-house escapade.

The scene in the summer house is an example of the bifurcated argument Tenney presents. Early in the text, Tenney has Dorcasina mouth an antislavery position that reflects the changing attitudes in the northern United States. Although Dorcasina desperately desires marriage to Lysander, she laments that "what gives me the greatest pain, is, that I shall be obliged to live in Virginia, be served by slaves, and be supported by the sweat, toil, and blood of that unfortunate and miserable part of mankind. . . . Slavery and happiness are, in my opinion, totally incompatible; 'disguise thyself as thou wilt, still, slavery, thou art a bitter pill'" (8). As noted above, Tenney challenges many cultural assumptions about race and gender in the summer-house scene, yet her representations of African Americans, especially of African American women, are often complicit in those assumptions. As Dana Nelson has pointed out, in this era the dominant culture racially encoded the African in specific ways that helped to perpetuate and justify a slave society.[10] To unpack the complexities of this encoding is to understand its cultural tenacity as well. Africans were depicted as at the bottom of the human evolutionary chain, indeed as only partially human (the "founding fathers" registered Africans as only three-fifths human). Thus Africans were represented as "primitive" in all facets of their lives—emotional development, social institutions, religious practices—and this primitivism was joined with the assertion that Africans were sexually uninhibited. It is important, too, to realize that, in this "Age of Reason," reason itself was absolutely linked with written discursive abilities; therefore, the African's oral rather than written traditions were deemed evidence of an inability to reason. Further, reason was equated with selfhood and since, as the perverted syllogistic reasoning unfolded, Africans could not reason, they were not therefore individuals and could not have status as self or exert agency. It is not difficult to comprehend the necessity of such reasoning in order to perpetuate the extraordinary *system* of abuse against African Americans inherent in slavery. While Tabitha Tenney exposes the presence of African Americans in U.S. society, something that few of her contemporary novelists acknowledged, she perpetuates a discourse of racial difference that elides the necessity of addressing change in the characterizations of Scipio and Miss Violet and, indeed, that erases their presence from the end of the novel.

Tenney's depiction of Scipio as a careful and talented servant/gardener is diminished by her depiction of Miss Violet as the stereotypic lazy and promiscuous person of color. The latter characterization, however, also reveals the Anglo American woman's fear of disruptions to assumed race and class superiority. The rendering of that fear through the female figure (literally and representatively) further reveals and complicates her text's embodiment (em/ "body"/ment) of cultural difference.

As in any good carnival, all characters in the novel play the fool at some point. It is when the masks are removed and the carnival ends that we note Tenney's process of differentiation. During the scene in the summer house, Scipio is comically rendered, but his depiction is less characterization than simply a tool necessary to forward the narrative transformation of Dorcasina Sheldon. Scipio has fallen asleep; when Dorcasina enters the darkened summer house, she assumes he is her Irish lover, O'Connor, and is able to realize her desire for physical contact before he awakens: "[Dorcasina] approached him softly, sat down by his side, and, putting one arm round his neck and resting her cheek against his, resolved to enjoy the sweet satisfaction which this situation afforded her, till he should of himself awake. This liberty, in his waking hours, her modesty would have prevented her from taking; but, with a heart thrilling with transport, she blessed the accident, which, without wounding her delicacy, afforded her such ravishing delight" (53). The comedy of the scene is dependent upon the reader's shock at the contact between a white woman and a black man, as Tenney explicitly records their racial difference: "with her snowy arms, she encircled Scipio's ebony neck" (59). Tenney also makes explicit Dorcasina's shame at such contact when she discovers the truth: "Mortified and disappointed beyond measure, she crept into the house, and got to bed undiscovered: where, between her own personal chagrin, and distress for her lover, she lay the whole night in sleepless agitation. . . . Her delicate mind could hardly bear to reflect on her familiarity with her father's servant" (54–55).

When Scipio awoke and discovered O'Connor sneaking into the summer house, he immediately darted forth and cuffed the intruder several times; that is, he performed his legitimate duty of protecting the grounds from intruders. In Tenney's description of Miss Violet, however, we are exposed to an extended representation of uninhibited sexuality and "primitiveness" that encapsulates the racial coding of those white men whose inscriptions of white women's lives Dorcasina is supposed to reject in order to effect her own transformation from fool to sage. When O'Connor sees Miss Violet enter the garden and head for the summer house, he assumes it is Dorcasina. A reader's initial reaction is probably that this failure to distinguish identity is intended to expose race biases in the same manner that biases surrounding class and female sexuality were exposed through the confusion of identity between Dorcasina and the prostitute. However, we are told that "O'Connor, seeing a person *in white* advancing towards him, thought, *naturally enough*, that it could be no other than his mistress" (53, emphasis added). The racial coding here is evident: whiteness signifies sexual purity, the primary trait of womanhood in True Woman ideology, which was identified solely with white women and indeed, as Sidonie Smith has observed, was dependent upon "keeping black women in their place."[11] Tenney's purpose in this construction has less to do, at this point, with Miss Violet than it does with the exposure of O'Connor as a fool. (As will be noted more fully below, all of the Irish characters in this novel are as unredeemed as are the African American characters.)

A careful examination of the encounter of Miss Violet and O'Connor, however, will reveal how deeply internalized are Tenney's concepts of racial difference. When O'Connor met Miss Violet and mistakenly assumed she was Dorcasina, "he dropped on one knee, and poured forth a torrent of words in the usual style, blessing his supposed angelic mistress, for her goodness and condescension, in thus favouring him with an interview. Miss Violet was at first struck with astonishment, and could not divine the meaning of those fine compliments; but, perceiving by his manner and address, that it was a gentleman who thus humbled himself before her, and having a spice of the coquette in her disposition, she had not objection to obtaining a new lover; but, being totally at a loss what to reply to such a profusion of compliments, delivered in a style so new to her, she very prudently remained silent" (53). This passage exemplifies the racial encoding of the era. In spite of Tenney's previous satirization of Dorcasina as a foolish and easily duped woman, she is depicted here as "angelic" in contrast with Miss Violet's sexual indiscrimination ("a spice of the coquette"). Further, the failure of language is predominant. Because, as an African American, Miss Violet is assumed to have no reasoning ability, she cannot "divine the meaning" of O'Connor's compliments; his words constitute "a style so new to her" that she is rendered silent.

It is not enough that Miss Violet be rendered mute; her sexuality is explored and implicated in this scene again and again. We are told, for example, that after Scipio tosses O'Connor out of the garden, Miss Violet does not lament the loss of her new admirer. She simply excuses her behavior to Scipio so she may regain his attention, because she "could as easily change a white lover for a black, as receive the addresses of a new one" (53). Thus while Dorcasina is in her room, giving "herself up to sighs, tears and lamentations" (55) over her mistaken liaison with Scipio, Miss Violet is depicted as promiscuity personified. Indeed, as the figure of *willful* sexual discovery in the garden, Miss Violet becomes the body onto which the blame for Eve's indiscretions is transferred. Since Eve was the figure most often cited by religious and civil leaders in this period as the reason that women were to be subjected to men, it is a significant transformation: the blame for womankind's fate is now placed on the black woman while the white woman is exonerated through her shame and repentance.

Tenney's intent that we note this sexual and racial difference between Dorcasina Sheldon and Miss Violet is made even more pointed by her use of the masquerade to break the silence about female desire in a *positive* manner, through her characterization of Dorcasina's young white contemporary, Harriot Stanly. Whereas Miss Violet becomes the racially stereotyped figure of sexual promiscuity, Miss Stanly becomes the female figure in control of her sexuality, who can use it to her benefit and who is rewarded (to some extent) with marriage at the novel's conclusion.

Dorcasina's lack of a mother's influence is designated in the opening pages of *Female Quixotism* as the cause of her near-fatal attraction to novels: "At the age of three years, this child had the misfortune to lose an excellent mother, whose advice would have pointed out to her the plain rational path of life; and prevented her imagination from being filled with the airy delusions and visionary dreams of love and raptures, darts, fire and flames, with which the indiscreet writers of that fascinating kind of books, denominated Novels, fill the heads of artless young girls, to their great injury, and sometimes to their utter ruin" (4–5). In contrast, Harriot is not an "artless" young woman. Not only did she have an attentive mother but—an act that also reveals the very grave failure of the Mr. Sheldons of the world—she was afforded a proper female education that guided her away from Dorcasina's failings. Tenney's introduction of issues of desire into the characterization of a young woman is to be commended. Through masquerade, Harriot can express sexual longings under the guise of teaching Dorcasina a lesson about the folly of romanticizing relationships. Harriot's "play" goes far beyond mere titillation, and it recalls Irigaray's notion that the masquerade is necessary because, for women to "recuperate some element of desire, [they must] participate in man's desire, but at the price of renouncing their own." Thus, in order to express desire, Harriot must masquerade as a male. Dressed as a captain, she may take on aggressive (masculine) sexual behavior; notably, she directs her amorous acts toward another female: "She then threw her arms round Dorcasina's neck, and almost stopped her breath with kisses, and concluded by biting her cheek so hard as to make her scream aloud" (278). Significantly, this scene occurs at night, observing the transformation of the carnival in the late eighteenth century to a noctural event. When Harriot later marries a real-life captain, we might be tempted to see this alliance as both a comic moment, a (masked) captain marrying another captain, and as a regenerative one; but whereas Tenney is unable to inscribe racial difference, she is able to challenge the idea that heterosexual couplings are any more transformative than was the embrace between the masked Harriot and the duped Dorcasina. When Dorcasina visits Harriot (now Mrs. Barry) at the novel's end, the novel shifts from carnival time back to "real" time. After having observed Harriot's married life for a few days, Dorcasina addresses her friend:

> "I find that, in my ideas of matrimony, I have been totally wrong. I imagined that, in a happy union, all was transport, joy, and felicity; but in you I find a demonstration that the most agreeable connection is not unattended with cares and anxieties." "Indeed, Miss Sheldon," replied Mrs. Barry, "your observation is just. I have been married a twelvemonth, to the man whom of all the world I should have chosen. He is everything I wish him to be; and in the connection I have enjoyed great felicity. Yet, strange to

tell, I have suffered more than I ever did before, in the whole course of my life." (320–21)

Thus Tabitha Tenney exposes the disenfranchised status even of upper-class white women in the new republic. In important ways, Tenney critiques the gendered nature of existence in the new democracy and condemns the nation's failure to properly educate and employ its female members.

Yet at the same time, she exposes her own ironic alliance with class and racial prejudices. Her contemporary Thomas Jefferson also struggled with such issues, ultimately arguing in *Notes on the State of Virginia* for the creation of laws supporting a combination of slave emancipation and "distant colonization." Similarly, Tenney casts Betty as the privileged Dorcas's supportive and wise but naturally (read: by class) inferior servant-friend, and she follows Jefferson's ideal to its "logical" conclusion by removing the African American characters from the last portion of the novel: that act of removal/erasure is, of course, the very real effect of "distant colonization." As Dana Nelson observes, the failure of Jefferson's text to accomplish "'rational management' of the issue of slavery is a signpost to the Enlightenment philosophers' profound inability to master the incongruity between slave system and legal contract, between arbitrary power and 'natural' authority." [12] Similarly, for Tenney, her inability to create a narrative that fully allows the disruption of the social order intended through the depiction of carnival or to rationally manage the reining in of carnival by the privileged class (as Mary Russo cautioned) leads to her own text's failed conclusion. Tenney cannot write into her own text a full vision of democracy.

That she is (perhaps unwittingly) aligned with Jeffersonian ideologies concerning race is particularly ironic, since Tenney's political alliances were distinctly opposed to Jefferson's in most ways. As noted above, all the Irish characters in this novel are as unredeemed as the African American characters. Tenney's political views are rendered through her depiction of immigrants in the novel, most notably in the characterization of the disreputable and dangerous Irishman Patrick O'Connor, who wants to marry Dorcasina only to have access to her wealth and privilege. In the years during which Tabitha Tenney wrote *Female Quixotism*, her spouse, Samuel Tenney, was a Federalist senator in Washington, D.C., representing their home state of New Hampshire. During the volatile election of 1800, the extraordinary power of the Federalists was diminished under charges of unconstitutional use of their powers and, most notably, of the intentional suppression of political dissent. Of special concern to the party was "foreign subversion." In 1798 alone, the Federalists enacted the Naturalization Act, the Alien Enemies Act, and the Sedition Act. These enactments are of special significance in relation to *Female Quixotism*. The Federalist position was bluntly clarified by Harrison Gray Otis, who cautioned that the United States should not "invite hordes of Wild Irishmen, nor the turbulent and disorderly parts of the world, to come here with a view to distract our tranquility."[13]

Two famous New England trials of 1799 may also have influenced Tenney's class and ethnic characterizations, those of David Brown and Luther Baldwin. Both men were working-class individuals who dared to criticize the Federalist government. Opposed to the centralized government established by the new constitution, Brown asserted that the only goal of government was to steal from its citizens and to claim the new nation's western lands for the Federalist leaders' personal wealth. Brown was tried under the newly established Sedition Act, found guilty, fined $480, and sentenced to eighteen months in jail. Since it was impossible for a working-class individual to pay such a fine, the sentence inevitably resulted in continued imprisonment for speaking against the government. It was only after the Federalists were defeated in the election of 1800 that Brown was freed. A satiric comment against President John Adams by Luther Baldwin (rendered orally, unlike Brown's pamphleteering) also resulted in a conviction for sedition, with fines and imprisonment. The Jeffersonians picked up Baldwin's case and used it to expose what they saw as the Federalists' abuse of power and antidemocratic actions.

It is precisely such nationalistic and classist attitudes that pervade Tenney's depictions of the characters surrounding Dorcasina. At the point in the novel in which O'Connor appears, we are told of the power of her father's word: "It had always been her pleasure to conform, in every instance, to the wishes of her parent, whose mild commands had ever been to her a law" (48). And the law of the father, as with the Federalists, is isolationist. When Dorcasina persists in her love of O'Connor, the Irishman, over Lysander, an American and her father's preferred mate for his daughter, Mr. Sheldon admonishes her, "Alas, my dear! I grieve to see you thus infatuated. Will you persist in giving less credit to one of your own countrymen, whose character for probity is well known and acknowledged, than to a foreigner, whom nobody knows, and who has nothing to recommend him but his own bare assertions?" (76).

That Tenney aligns nationalism with patriarchal values is evident when Dorcasina finally accepts her father's views and rejects the "foreigner": her father's reward is expressed explicitly in terms that return her to the father's house, "Thank you, my dear, you are now again my daughter" (95). That is, she is given the only means of "enfranchisement" available to women: the protection of the "fathers." This is the issue that Tenney cannot reconcile in *Female Quixotism*. She seeks to challenge the erasure of difference in the new republic, but she depends upon difference—and acceptance of difference—in order to effect what changes do occur in Dorcasina Sheldon's struggle for subjectivity.

It is in the juxtaposition of Dorcasina, Miss Violet, and Harriot Stanly that Tenney most overtly reveals her own complicity with certain elements of patriarchy. If she characterizes Dorcas at the end of the novel as rejecting the limited role of the True Woman in turn-of-the-century America, Tenney maintains most heartily the encoding of racial difference. In fact, there is a necessary hierarchy of women in her vision. Harriot may not have a perfect life, but she does have significant status as conveyed by the title of "Mrs." Dorcas, in comparison, "found herself alone, as it were, on the earth. The pleasing delusion which she had all her life fondly cherished, of experiencing the sweets of connubial love, had now entirely vanished, and she became pensive, silent and melancholy" (322). She has rejected her former ways and turned from romance to realism, but she is self-condemning: "I have not charms sufficient to engage the heart of any man" (322). Her transformation is, at best, one of repentance. Yet Dorcas Sheldon's ostensible transformation at the novel's conclusion is, in turn, dependent upon a contrast not only with Harriot but also with Miss Violet. Whereas the African American woman has been depicted as indiscriminately gliding from man to man and is ultimately silenced by her status, and thereby easily erased from the text itself, Dorcas Sheldon has risen above the dominant culture's expectations of her as a woman. Because she remains single, she may be considered a grotesque by her culture, but she can still claim a certain status in the community because of her wealth. She uses her money for "acts of benevolence and charity" (323), thus gaining the status of Good Woman if not of Married Woman. It is Miss Violet who is cast as the inherently and unredeemed grotesque figure through the negative depiction of her sexuality and ultimately through her textual elision. What began as a novel notable for its exposure of the diverse nature of difference in eighteenth-century U.S. culture descends into an unresolved fracturing of narrative perspective. Ironically, when the carnival ends and Tenney seeks narrative closure, she cannot put all the pieces back together again. She cannot manage to fully liberate Dorcas from patriarchal strictures precisely because the decolonization process meant to be effected by the instigation of carnival has been predicated upon a return to colonialist measures.

NOTES

1. Jean Nienkamp and Andrea Collins, introduction to Tabitha Gilman Tenney, *Female Quixotism: Exhibited in the Romantic Opinions and Extravagant Adventures of*

Dorcasina Sheldon, ed. Nienkamp and Collins (New York: Oxford University Press, 1992), xiv–xv. Subsequent references to *Female Quixotism* will be given in the text.

2. Mikhail Bakhtin, *Rabelais and His World*, trans. Helene Iswolsky (Cambridge: MIT Press, 1968), 4–5. Subsequent references to this work will be given parenthetically in the text.

3. Julia Kristeva, "Word, Dialogue and Novel," in *The Kristeva Reader*, ed. Toril Moi (New York: Columbia University Press, 1986), 36.

4. Mary Russo, "Female Grotesques: Carnival and Theory," *Feminist Studies/Critical Studies*, ed. Teresa de Lauretis (Bloomington: Indiana University Press, 1986), 213–29.

5. Cathy N. Davidson, *Revolution and the Word: The Rise of the Novel in America* (New York: Oxford University Press, 1986), 132, 188.

6. See Carroll Smith-Rosenberg, "The Female World of Love and Ritual," *Disorderly Conduct: Visions of Gender in Victorian America* (New York: Oxford University Press, 1985), 53–76.

7. See Tzvetan Todorov, *The Conquest of America*, trans. Richard Howard (New York: Harper and Row, 1984).

8. Mary-Louise Pratt, *Imperial Eyes: Travel Writing and Transculturation* (New York: Routledge, 1992), 121.

9. Luce Irigaray, *This Sex Which Is Not One*, trans. Catherine Porter with Carolyn Burke (Ithaca: Cornell University Press, 1985), 133–34.

10. Dana D. Nelson, *The Word in Black and White: Reading "Race" in American Literature 1638–1867* (New York: Oxford University Press, 1993).

11. Sidonie Smith, *Subjectivity, Identity, and the Body: Women's Autobiographical Practices in the Twentieth Century* (Bloomington: Indiana University Press, 1993), 39. Barbara Welter's important essay casts its dates as 1820 to 1860 (see "The Cult of True Womanhood: 1820–1860," *American Quarterly* 18 [Summer 1966]: 57–70); texts such as *The Coquette* (1797) and *Female Quixotism* (1801) suggest that the ideology emerged in the late eighteenth century.

12. Nelson, 18.

13. Quoted in Gary B. Nash, et al., eds., *The American People: Creating a Nation and a Society* (New York: Harper and Row, 1986), 1: 254.

Engendered Nature/Denatured History

"The Yares of Black Mountain" by Rebecca Harding Davis

JEAN PFAELZER

By 1875 it was clear that radical reconstruction was coming to an end. To justify abandoning the post–Civil War goal of political equality for freed slaves, the North needed to reinvent southern history, indeed, to reinvent the South. Cultural representations of Southerners in plantation novels, vernacular fiction, and minstrelsy would constitute one way northern readers could ignore lynchings, allow racist voting restrictions, and anticipate the withdrawal of northern troops from the South. Another way was in representations of the South itself. Depictions of the American landscape have always been a trope for cultural nationalism. In the mid-nineteenth century, images of nature, writes Angela Miller, "proffered a sense of national identity in the absence of shared race history."[1] Traditionally, however, the invented harmonious landscape is devoid of artifacts of human life, human labor, and human history, and any landscape that appears "empty" allows for social definition, invites political intervention, and promises passivity.

In "The Yares of Black Mountain" (1875), however, Rebecca Harding Davis populates and politicizes Southern landscape, exposing aesthetic constructs which invited either hegemonic or solipsistic reactions to the South.[2] "Yares" is a tale of a young northern Civil War widow, Mrs. Denby, who travels into the Cumberland mountains in North Carolina, hoping to heal her sickly baby in the high balsam forests, only to discover, once there, a matriarchal family of resistance fighters. In this story Davis suggests that, like the widow, the industrial North is dependent on the rural South for healing and political renewal. Yet Davis's literary strategy only works because she has erased slavery as the source of American sectionalism. Reunion and reconciliation, she suggests, will arise from a new understanding of southern place and from a recognition of southern women as rebellious, matriarchal, communitarian, natural, and pro-North.

The story begins as a group of northern tourists arrive at the end of a railroad line, thirty miles from Asheville, North Carolina. "Civilization stops here, it appears," observes an industrialist from Detroit (35). This appearance is false, however, as the travelers are immediately welcomed into a generous rural community. Even so, most of the tourists are disappointed with what they see. The mountains, they find, offer neither inspiration nor industry. The cloud effects "lack the element of grandeur" of the White Mountains, and a speculator from Detroit—a postlapsarian industrialist, to be sure—finds the balsam lumber so spongy that "a snake couldn't get his living out of ten acres of it" (36). Even the travelers' fantasy of venison cooked over an open campfire is frustrated by the "civilized beastliness" of greasy fried meals in a local barroom, where a fly-covered print of the "Death of Robert E. Lee" hangs on the wall; insistently, the Civil War brackets this study of the role of the picturesque.

In "The Yares of Black Mountain" Davis explores cultural archetypes that convert the wilderness into economic and cultural raw material. One of the tourists, a female journalist sardonically named Miss Cook, has come to the Cumberlands to collect material for her book, *The Causes of Decadence in the Old South*. Miss Cook represents Davis's pointed (and perhaps self-reflexive) critique of the female local colorist, an outsider who reduces the complexity of Southern history to the sketch or tall tale. After Miss Cook makes a quick tour of the four local "emporiums," the village jail, the "quaint decaying houses," and "the swarming blacks," she purchases a package of photographic postcards from which to draw the sketches for her book. Perhaps echoing James Fenimore Cooper, Miss Cook concludes that the villagers "would be picturesque, dirt and all, under a Norman peasant's coif and red umbrella, but in a dirty calico wrapper—bah!" (37). Satisfied that in one morning she has "done the mountains and mountaineers" and has found nothing to write about, she announces that she is moving on to Georgia (40). Through this figure of the female writer, Davis writes about the act of writing about nature. Unlike Davis, who closely observed and researched details of the geological, botanical, and social life in the mountains, the fictional journalist claims, "I can evolve the whole state of society from a half a dozen items. I have the faculty of generalizing" (40). There is no doubt that Miss Cook will produce a manufactured, mythologized landscape that will confirm aesthetic conventions, in part because she confesses that she has quite forgotten to ask about the Civil War, a portentous omission.[3]

Interestingly, none of these middle class visitors has come south to indulge in the conspicuous consumption of landscape for its own sake, what critic Robert Bredeson calls the era's aesthetic "badge of status," because, as Davis would suggest in her own Southern travel studies "By-Paths in the Mountains" and "Here and There In the Old South," the postwar southern landscape had not regained the status of other emerging tourist destinations.[4] Yosemite, for example, was "discovered" in 1851 after the Mariposa Battalion pursued a group of Miwok and Piute Native Americans into the valley. Sensing the commercial possibilities in its "wild and sublime grandeur," writer and publisher James Mason Hutchings quickly recruited artist Thomas Ayres and photographer Charles Leander Weed to attract groups of tourists and promptly publish their conditioned observations, such as "What! . . . have we come to the end of all things? . . . Can this be the opening of the Seventh Seal?"[5] "The Yares of Black Mountain" was the first of a series of studies in which Davis called attention to the economic and tourist possibilities of the South.

Davis sought to recapture the aesthetic and moral sympathies of northern readers through the description of a northern woman's discovery of the power of southern female voice and female activity. For Davis, the allure of the Cumberlands was not the enchantment of the sublime. Mrs. Denby rejects the voyeuristic gaze of the overwhelmed tourists as she locates the social in the natural, a cultural recovery that emphasizes human actions over spiritual resolutions. She dismisses Miss Cook's fearful rumor that the Ku Klux Klan is terrorizing the area and her warning that the "mountains are inaccessible to women," and leaves the village of Asheville to go deeper into the mountains in the ox cart of the trapper, Jonathan Yare (36).[6] Parodying the lone male traveler of literary convention who leaves civilization (read women) behind in his quest for adventure in an eroticized frontier, Mrs. Denby too enters the high wilderness with a guide, and Jonathan, true to mythic convention, turns out to be more than what he seems. However, unlike a panoramist, who, as John Sears observes, looks at nature from a high place in order to "take in a large stretch of open country and remain outside of nature, master of what he observes," Mrs. Denby rejects the perspective of a master/hunter and sees herself as a domestic intruder who believes she has come "unbidden into Nature's household and interrupted the inmates talking together" (42)[7] Nature, she discovers, is a site of verbal domesticity.

As Mrs. Denby and her baby travel in the ox cart higher into the mountains, Davis explores a series of cultural tropes of nature: romantic perceptions of nature as the eroticized female, sublime and masculine visions of nature's dangerous wildness, and, ultimately, allegorical images of nature as female sanctuary. Leaving the village behind, the widow first sees the mountain as a beckoning virgin: "the very earth seemed to blush . . . the tupelo thrust its white fingers out of the shadow like a maiden's hand" (42), the flowers reminiscent of the sensual orchids and hummingbirds of contemporary colorist Martin Johnson Heade. These erotic tupelo flowers define the sensual appeal of southern botany as female. But as Mrs. Denby "penetrates" the higher summits of the Appalachians, nature as seductress evolves into nature as mother figure; the enticing heights become the "the nursery or breeding-place" of all the mountains that wall the eastern coast (42). At mid-day Jonathan, the rugged trapper, finds fresh milk for the baby by catching and milking a wild cow because the urban mother's milk has run dry.

Paralleling the shift in Mrs. Denby's perception from nature as sexual to nature as maternal, enclosing, and protective is the deconstructive shift from nature as luminous and sublime to nature as companionable and familiar.[8] Initially, the widow sees that "the sun was out of sight in a covered, foreboding sky, and black ragged fragments of cloud from some approaching thunderstorm were driven now and then across the horizon" (41). The sublime, quite typically, dislocates Mrs. Denby from her worldly affiliation, defamiliarizes her, and makes her receptive to a female story of the symbiosis of land and politics. Yet Davis immediately subverts the romantic sublimity of the panoramic of such painters as Thomas Cole, Frederick E. Church, and Albert Bierstadt, who, in the tradition of Washington Irving and James Fenimore Cooper, depicted the sublime as a frightening lesson in cosmic moralism, what Howard Mumford Jones called "the majesty of deity, the wildness of nature, the littleness of man, and the future of the republic."[9] Davis usurps the high romantic iconography of the sublime landscape to feminize it: "The road, if road you chose to call it, crept along beside the little crystal-clear Swannanoa River, and persisted in staying beside it, sliding over hills of boulders, fording rushing mountain-streams and dank snaky swamps, digging its way along the side of sheer precipices, rather than desert its companion. The baby's mother suddenly became conscious that the river was a companion to whom she had been talking and listening for an hour or two" (41). Mrs. Denby, the figure in the foreground, repudiates the overwhelming wrath of the Burkean sublime, which, as critic David Miller suggests, conventionally emphasized the terror of nature, the helplessness of humanity, and the precariousness of civilization in a world in which traditional meanings are jeopardized.[10] The widow's trip up the mountain involves not a male quest for absolute meaning but a female quest for a communal animism that is both material and psychological.[11] In this more mundane view of nature, Davis is closer to the realism of Winslow Homer, who frequently places a large female figure at work in the wilderness, than to the romanticism of Frederic Church, who typically pictures a tiny male traveler dwarfed at the pictorial edge of magnificent and symbolic wildness.

Through Mrs. Denby's trip into the higher peaks of the Cumberlands, Davis punctures a romantic moment of awe and melancholy to rescript the Oedipal plot, to foreshadow the movement from isolation to maternal community, from solitary adulthood to childlike dependence, from loneliness to intimacy, hence, from male to female way of viewing nature. During the 1870s, contemporary landscape emphasized the distant prospect, with a natural hierarchy of elements moving from an inhabited foreground to heaven, signifying either a topos of harmony (picturesque) or an expression of divinely instituted authority (sublime).[12] By contrast, through the image of the loquacious river, Davis deconstructs the figure of the lone tourist dwarfed by the glorious silence of nature. The companionable river, traditionally a feminized symbol in any case, leads Mrs. Denby to a filthy and rugged hut, the inhabited domestic space of Jonathan's mother, who warmly welcomes the widow and her baby. The widow's voyage into the wilderness is, in essence, a trip home, back to mother and her landscape of gendered political resistance.

At this point, Mistress Yare takes over the narration to tell Mrs. Denby the real story behind the legend of the "terrible history" of the Yare family. The linearity and chronology of Mrs. Denby's quest and her assumption that "human nature could reach no lower depths of squalor and ignorance" than she first perceives in the filthy cabin (42–43), collapses as Mistress Yare, rather like Mrs. Todd, the narrator in Sara Orne Jewett's "The Foreigner" (1900), relates her family saga to her guest. While old Mr. Yare tells Mrs. Denby stories of bear and panther hunts, that is, of his own heroism, Mistress Yare tells of a woman's courageous loyalty to the North during the Civil War. The Yare sons, she explains, had refused to serve the Army of the Confederacy. Along with her daughter Nancy, they spent the war years as mountain guides, leading both southern deserters and Union soldiers who had escaped from the brutal prisons at Andersonville and Salisbury across icy mountain gorges to the safety of the Federal lines in Tennessee. Northern readers would well remember the brutality of Andersonville and Salisbury, the Confederate prison in North Carolina where, by 1864, ten thousand destitute prisoners huddled in tents or burrowed into the earth in mud huts, and where, between October 1864 and February 1865, thirty-five hundred prisoners died.

As Nancy participates in the liberation of northern men, possibly including Mrs. Denby's late husband, she takes on the traditionally male capacity to move widely in geographical space. Yet these deeds are not at the expense of her domestic role, as she also works with her mother to maintain the Yare hut as a refuge for deserters headed north. Most heroically, when one of Nancy's brothers is wounded on the mountain, she evades the Confederate soldiers and on her own builds a log cabin to hide and shelter him in the frozen woods, thereby reappropriating the image of the house as a political space. Eventually Nancy is captured and held in jail in Asheville (ironically, the brutal prison

Miss Cook plans to expose) where the rebels threaten to hang her unless she discloses her brother's whereabouts. Only the announcement of General Lee's surrender and the end of the war save her.

Through the story of Nancy Yare, Davis liberates nature from the discourses of the Ideal, the discourses of Northern domination, and the discourses of female irrationality. By appropriating nature as a sign for female resistance and orality, Davis peoples and historicizes the Southern landscape. "The Yares of Black Mountain" resists what Howard Mumford Jones calls the inference "that American writing cannot be rich and full because the American landscape lacks historical, feudal, medieval . . . or family associations."[13] In "The Yares of Black Mountain" the vernacular is no longer, in Sandra Zagarell's insightful phrase, a "metonymy for a folk culture," but rather a realistic, accurate, and detailed construction of a particularized moment of national reconciliation situated domestically and geographically.[14]

In the end, overwhelmed by the Yareses' rural poverty and the story of their postwar ostracism, Mrs. Denby urges the family to move to the North, where they will be rewarded for their loyalty and service. Mrs. Yare, however, refuses: "It must be powerful lonesome in them flat countries, with nothing but people about you. The mountings [mountains] is company always, you see" (46). Thus Mrs. Denby discovers that the true intimacy of nature transcends social relations. She also comes to understand that nature and female speech transcend class: "These were the first human beings whom she had ever met between whom and herself there came absolutely no bar of accident—no circumstance of social position or clothes or education: they were the first who could go straight to something in her beneath all these things" (43).

Yet, for Davis, nature cannot transcend race. In the 1860s Davis had published several powerful antislavery stories, such as "John Lamar" (1862), in which a slave murders his unthinking master; "Blind Tom" (1862), the study of a blind slave who is a musical genius and autistic savant; and the early Reconstruction novel *Waiting for the Verdict* (1867), the story of a mulatto surgeon who finally acknowledges his African American identity and volunteers as an officer in the Union Army, only to die in Andersonville prison.[15] In "The Yares of Black Mountain," by contrast, written during the demise of Reconstruction in the 1870s, the telos of community hinges on the repudiation of race. While Mrs. Denby, "a violent abolitionist in her day," insists that the Yares should have gone into the Federal army to help free the slaves, Mistress Yare explains that her sons simply could not "turn agen the old flag." She then adds, "We never put much vally [value] on the blacks, that's the truth. We couldn't argy [argue] or jedge whether slavery war wholesomest for them or not. It was out of our sight" (44). Such racial indifference and invisibility would soon contribute to the end of Reconstruction in the North. Indeed, given the enduring political and economic inequality of African Americans in the South, this erasure of race became the unspoken terms for national reconciliation.

Through the figures of Jenny and Nancy, Davis reconfigures the romantic hero. As Harold Bloom suggests, although the intent of the quest is to widen consciousness as well as to intensify it, the romantic journey is inevitably "shadowed by a spirit that tends to narrow consciousness to an acute preoccupation with self." In the conventional Romantic resolution the Promethean hero finally stands "quite alone, upon a tower that is only himself, and his stance is all the fire there is." [16] Mrs. Denby, by contrast, in forging political, female, and verbal reconciliation, locates the unity of the self in the social. Ending her story inside a female house rather than upon a phallic tower, Davis claims engagement rather than solipsism as identity.

Like many women authors writing in the mid-nineteenth century, Rebecca Harding Davis inherited the sentimental critique of America's passage from a decentralized, agrarian life to an industrial, capitalistic one. Davis, however, rejects sentiment's generalized and nostalgic view, a view aligned with contemporary romanticism, that the pre- or non-industrial world offers a natural home in an earlier moment of economic development. Unlike popular domestic images that sever rural life from urban life, Davis's fiction deconstructs evocations of nature as the space where women can find meaning and where men can avoid society. Nature is not the safe spot that Annette Kolodny finds in the fictions of Alice Cary, where Eve may cultivate her New England garden. [17] Instead, Davis pictures the rural dangers hidden under ideologies of nostalgia, romantic, sentimental, or southern: the growth of industries in mountain towns in West Virginia, hardships in fishing villages on the New Jersey coast, or brutal mountain battles of the Civil War. Davis's stories of isolated Delaware fishermen, of "wrakers" who scrounge for the salvage from wrecked sailing ships, of impoverished women in coastal villages compelled to take in rude tourists as boarders, suggest that life close to nature promises neither nurture, abundance, nor unalienated labor. At times her lonely female characters succumb to the fantasies Kolodny has located in women's journals, records of visions of a harmonious natural space where they might find a maternal and feminine presence, an enclosing receptive environment that will offer painless satisfaction. [18] Davis, by contrast, deconstructs images of nature as a female respite from adult responsibility and questions voyages that recapture the primal warmth of womb or breast in an abundant, tempting, if vulnerable landscape of filial homage and erotic desire.[19] Nature is not a simple pastoral "home" for Davis; neither are her rural women unauthorized presences in landscapes to which they do not belong.[20]

In the famous conclusion to *Nature* Emerson observes, "Know then, that the world exists for you."[21] Davis, by contrast, rejects the masculinity of transcendentalism, which saw nature as an occasion for the individual mind to discover a reflection of itself and, ultimately, God. She also rejects the mechanistic masculinity of the Enlightenment, which saw the wilderness as a repugnant space wherein human beings lived mean and savage lives, a primitive space needing urban intervention and control.[22] Instead, Rebecca Harding Davis saw in nature the dialectic of matter and consciousness, the dialectic of matter and social history. In "The Yares of Black Mountain," she distrusts the modernist task, the Protestant duty, the rational responsibility, to understand and harness nature, to transform the wilderness, in particular the southern wilderness, into another industrialized northern civilization from whose lonely apartment Mrs. Denby has recently fled. Questioning the Cumberlands as a topos for aesthetic reassurance or psychological domination, Davis confronts the era's profound androcentrism, stimulated on the one hand by transcendentalism and on the other by the discoveries and demands of industrial capitalism.[23] Emerging ideologies of territorial and economic conquest encouraged Northerners to think that nature had a duty to satisfy their financial aspirations, political disillusion, and aesthetic hunger. If New York is the place where, as Mrs. Denby observed, "we came strangers, and were always strangers" (39), Black Mountain, read through the hermeneutics of female community and pictured through the acts of female storytelling, reveals nature as a space of female interdependence, communication, and balanced reciprocity rather than a site of man's dominion over all living things.

In "Life in the Iron Mills" (1861), Davis's first published story, the narrator, a middle-class spinster, suggests "the dream of green fields and sunshine is a very old dream—almost worn out, I think."[24] Almost. The narrator identifies her arid intellectual and sexual life with the suffocation of urban poverty in a raw factory town. To condemn a culture of urban/male individualism, she blends a sentimental appeal to feminine sympathy with images of industrial pollution. The narrator ends her story focused on Deb, a hunchback spinner in a textile mill, who serves three years in jail for theft and then flees into the hills to live with the Quakers, "pure and meek . . . more silent than they, more humble, more loving." Like the lonely narrator, Deb is "waiting: with her eyes turned to hills higher and purer than these on which she lives."[25] A silent woman in gray, she suggests the ultimate failure of industrial desire. In one sense, rural life implies ascetic self-denial to these two women, both figures of female endurance; it subsumes the story's political thrust by emerging as a metaphor for eternal life. Only nature is regenerative and available as a fantasized abandonment of urban history. Even so, Davis often praised the Quakers as engaged social activists in the movements for abolition and prison reform and wrote of their rural communities as stations on the underground railroad. Hence, the ending of "Life in the Iron Mills" also anticipates Davis's suggestion in "The Yares of Black Mountain" that a life lived in nature offers the possibility of attachment, continuity, and fusion. From the outset of her literary career, environment would be a determining and feminist element in her social vision. Region—its flora and fauna, weather, local history, landscape, dialect, dress, and the economics of place—would join class and gender to shape character and consciousness in her fiction.

Rooted in Davis's childhood in the mountains of West Virginia, her frequent trips to a farm in Manasquan on the barren New Jersey coast, and her travels in the South are other compelling stories of rural life, mostly written in the 1870s, which also challenge the romantic idea that through intuition and reflection, one can participate in an organic encounter with nature. Davis's informed intelligence about botany, geology, and climate does not lead to descriptions of plants or storms that exemplify Emersonian universals. Instead, her stories are much closer in intention to the writing of Henry David Thoreau, who argued that a "true man of science . . . will know nature better by his finer organization; he will smell, taste, see, hear, feel, better than other men. His will be a deeper and finer experience." [26] Davis similarly sought to reintegrate industrial consciousness through contact with the knowable natural world. Informed yet unmediated experiences in nature encourage social and political understandings—and feminist understandings. For Davis, the urban visitor to the wilderness is neither scientist, naturalist, proto-Indian, nor aesthete, but one who learns to understand that the cultural impositions on the natural world are polluting, hegemonic, anthrocentric, masculinist, and ultimately antisocial.

Thus Davis refused to divorce nature from society. She explored the economic and technological links between the country and the city, always grounding her rural tales in local history. In "David Gaunt" (1862) she pictures the ravishment of the land during the Civil War; "Out of the Sea" (1865) refers to the role of insurance companies in shaping the moral meaning of shipwrecks; *Dallas Galbraith* (1868) describes how mining has despoiled the land; in "Earthen Pitchers" (1873–74) land emerges both as a female property right and also as a dangerous symbol of desire that women must conquer and domesticate; "The House on the Beach" (1876) describes financial pressures to build lighthouses along the New Jersey shore and explains how inventions for predicting the weather united rural communities across the country; and in a late essay, "In the Grey Cabins of New England" (1895), Davis describes how men have abandoned the barren land, leaving the women similarly forsaken.[27]

Davis rejected the equation *nature:culture::female:male*, because she believed that the female telos resides in culture as well as nature.[28] In this she anticipates and shapes American regionalism. Nature to Davis is not presocial or oceanic. Rather, images of the city and the country, civilization and wilderness, mind and body, expose how culture has shaped our perception of nature as simple, static, and continuous. Political, economic, and cultural relationships between city and country do signify relationships between men and women, but Davis resists the essentialist view that nature and woman are mutually vulnerable and available to human intervention, control, or even definition.

As L. J. Jordanova reminds us, any distinction that poses woman as natural and man as cultural inevitably appeals to ideas about women's biology.[29] Davis's stories of rural life challenge an essentialist analogy in which women and nature are seen as fertile, backward, ignorant, and innocent. Neither woman nor nature are repositories of morality. Not even a rural woman, such as Mistress Yare, can completely transcend or escape culture. Nonetheless, because for Davis civilization is rational, exploitative, dominating, and competitive, it is often a metaphor for masculinity. As early as "Life in the Iron Mills" in Davis's opus, the struggle between the sexes takes on a historical dimension; the power and pollution of the industrial North exemplifies the rise of American civilization through domination over nature and at the same time represents the realization of masculine ways of being that women should resist.[30]

Thus Davis's stories undermine the widespread view in American literary criticism that women's regional writings of the late nineteenth century were emasculated tales produced by "'New England spinsters . . . driven to extremes of nostalgic fantasy' about 'imaginary pasts.'"[31] Caroline Gebhard traces how, as early as 1919, *The Nation* announced that women's local color stories revealed a "triviality of observation . . . connected with [a] strongly, often stiflingly domestic atmosphere," immured, Santayana would add, from the "rough passions of life."[32] Robert Spiller, in his influential *Literary History of the United States*, similarly observed, "As a group [female local colorists] avoided the commonplace, concerned themselves chiefly with the unusual, were incurably romantic, obsessed with the picturesque, and accurate only to the superficial aspects of their chosen materials."[33] More recently, Annette Kolodny has suggested that if a woman writer who lived on or visited the frontier saw it as the metaphorical landscape of someone else's imagination, she could not locate herself in nature. To feminize the frontier, she would confine herself to an "innocent amusement of a garden's narrow space" and, with equanimity, welcome the disappearance of primal wild spaces. Ann Douglas likewise finds women's local colorists "paranoid and claustrophobic."[34]

Rebecca Harding Davis, however, projected onto nature a vast imaginative landscape of gendered values. She seems to have avoided not only the colonizing female tropes that Kolodny locates, but also several recurrent male constructions of nature: as the place of a brutal exodus to an unpromising land, as the eroticized site of violent conquest, and as the source of guilt for its destruction. Surely she holds a unique spot in the tradition of female regionalists who were urged on by a series of editors of *The Atlantic* who, between 1857–1898, promoted a realist aesthetic that could depict authentic local details. Men such as Davis's early mentor, James Fields, and later James Russell Lowell, William Dean Howells, Thomas Bailey Aldrich, and Horace Scudder sought an American literature that would debunk overgeneralized descriptions, essentialist characterizations, and the pastoral nostalgia of sentiment, and they called this new prose "local color."[35] Among the authors of this emerging literature, Davis shares the grim antipatriarchal indictments of Rose Terry Cooke, the ironic ambivalence about matriarchal pastoralism of Mary E. Wilkins Freeman, the early class consciousness of Elizabeth Stuart Phelps, and the close observation of southern botany, geology, and language of such later regional writers as Mary Murphy and Constance Fenimore Woolson.

As a realist, Davis alters the pastoral landscape (which is not to say, as critic Roger Stein wryly reminds us, that nature doesn't still "mean").[36] She repopulates Arcadia with intelligent and competent female figures, empiricists who survive through their knowledge of tides, herbs, clouds, rock formations, and the dangers of storms, quicksand, and rural marriage. Her heroines can track a horse, build a log cabin in a blizzard, rescue a wounded lover in a blinding snowstorm, and row out to sea in a gale to save a shipwrecked son. Abandoning the "heroine's text" of seduction, betrayal, and marriage, Davis describes the realities of rural relationships, at times comfortable, caring, and mutually involved in the projects of agrarian work and rural survival, and at other times lonely, sexually repressed, and intellectually barren.

In order to portray rural life, and nature itself, as a female community, Davis recasts the rhetorics of romanticism. In her stories of the New Jersey shore, the Cumberland Mountains, and barren New England farms, nature emerges through images of dependence rather than autonomy, intimacy rather than isolation, speech rather than the silent awe of the sublime. The female traveler cannot remain a voyeur or outsider and finds, through whatever natural epiphany the plot provides, an organicism in nature. She also finds a voice. To the degree Davis pictures nature as maternal, it motivates her heroines not through quest to conquest but through quest to transcendent recognition of their own identity.

Simone de Beauvoir observed, "For the woman [writer] who has not fully abdicated, nature represents what woman herself represents for man: herself and her negation, a kingdom and a place of exile: the whole in the guise of the other." [37] It is in this feminist sense of transcendence that Davis builds on the narcissism of romanticism. By submission to natural law and the growth of a friendship with a rural woman, her urban female character recognizes the possibility of intimacy and allows the dissolution of ego.

Thus, through the voice of Mistress Yare, Davis shifts the story of "The Yares of Black Mountain" from an emblematic to a realist social narrative, undercutting the widow's early impressions that equate women with nature. While in the narrator's text, Mrs. Denby identifies with nature as female, immanent, communal, and available, in Mistress Yare's text nature refuses to constitute itself as an object of tourism, moral instruction, isolation, or even inspiration. Nancy emerges as an autonomous rural subject who lives within and works on nature to shape her rebellious deeds. In this matriarchal text, nature is populated and politicized. Mistress Yare's rural narrative thus signifies the mediation of a woman rather than the representation of a woman as nature. Although Mrs. Denby at first reminds her northern compatriots that they must understand why contemporary southerners are still "churlish and bitter" (39), ultimately, as much as the balsam air, it is Mistress Yare's story of heroism and compassion that heals the female traveler.

The "Yares of Black Mountain" opens as the northern travelers debate how to experience and interpret nature, for amusement, profit, instruction, inspiration, or healing. Parodying the picturesque conventions through her portrait of Miss Cook and then deconstructing the grandiose subjectivity of the sublime in Mrs. Denby's cart ride up the mountain, Davis suggests that the real meaning of nature is its connection with history and its role in forming true communities. Mistress Yare debunks the rumors of the untold tale of the "terrible history of the Yares" and tells Mrs. Denby a story of complex actions of rural people who are defined in and through the land as political territory. Romance with one of the rugged mountain sons is never an issue. Instead, Mrs. Denby is rewarded with the female grail, an intimate relationship with a mother figure who can tell a great story. Her passage into the Cumberland Mountains from her lonely apartment in New York suggests a daughter's return, but Black Mountain would not qualify for Gail David's female pastoral: "a place out of time associated with recollections of edenic childhood and fantasies of eternal paradise . . . nurturant, festive, and leisurely."[38] Instead, Mrs. Denby's quest for healing has led her to sympathetic engagement with a woman who teaches her the priority of history over allegory, struggle over escape, and the intimacy of women's narrative. Hence, the telos of her quest into the wilderness is not the inscription of the heroic and indomitable self, but the discovery of female community achieved through female orality, which is, in itself, about community.[39]

In "The Yares of Black Mountain," Davis has described the disjunction between the perceived images and the historical meanings of the South. As a geographic metaphor for the realization of freedom, she has replaced the traditional cultural drive from east to west with an analogous movement from north to south. Through the representation of the southern wilderness, of the rural communities in North Carolina, and in particular of southern womanhood, Davis erodes the patriarchal/industrial assumption that nature, like the South itself, is primitive, knowable, and separate from culture. "The Yares of Black Mountain" repudiates the emerging view through which the North sentimentalized southern history in order to force a premature reconciliation between the defeated Confederacy and the Union. By including the story of resistance on Black Mountain, the Cumberland Mountains join the Connecticut and Hudson River valleys as natural sites which characterize America.[40] "The Yares of Black Mountain" thereby resists the literary politics of appeasement, which was emerging in such journals as *Lippincott's*, *Harpers*, and the *Atlantic Monthly*.

In this story, the radical role of nature thus counters the hegemonic view of landscape that we see, for example, in Frederic Church's *Rainy Season in the Tropics* (1866), which Angela Miller calls "adamantly national, employing an imagery of plunging spaces, grandly scaled distances, and scenery aglow with the light of the spirit, [whose] central event is the rainbow, symbol of the renewed national covenant interrupted by the war."[41] In contrast to Church's archetypal conventions, Davis roots her narrative of reconciliation in detailed particularities of place and region. In "The Yares of Black Mountain," nature suggests neither the utopian telos of Church's national covenant nor the pastoral regression of William Dean Howells's anti-industrial Altruria.

Finally, nature for Davis belongs in the discourse of realism. If we compare the titles alone of Emerson's "Nature," Thoreau's *Walden*, and Davis's "The Yares of Black Mountain," the names themselves bespeak the movement I am delineating: from the abstract to the particular to the dialectical communal. Rather like Winslow Homer's representations of fisherwomen, Davis's story deconstructs the American sublime by inserting the feminized hut and inscribing the rebellious story of Nancy Yare. Yet paradoxically, Davis's representation of nature also supports those cultural representations—humorous tales, local-color stories, sentimental fictions, plantation novels, and transcendental landscapes—that offered reasons to abandon Radical Reconstruction and restore the national bond with the South. In a story written as Radical Reconstruction was about to fall apart, Davis's unifying cultural symbol is the figure of the southern mother. Reconciliation need not hinge on repression, nostalgia, romanticism, or the collapse of localism, nor need it rely on the acceptance of racial equality. Instead, nature will provide a realm of power that can, through female sympathy and orality, stimulate affection, nationalism, and social responsibility.

NOTES

1. Angela Miller, "Everywhere and Nowhere: The Making of the National Landscape," *American Literary History* 4.2 (Summer 1992): 213.

2. Rebecca Harding Davis, "The Yares of Black Mountain," *Lippincott's Magazine*, July 1875, 35–47. I cite this version parenthetically in the text. The story was reprinted in Davis, *Silhouettes in American Life* (New York: Charles Scribner's Sons, 1892), and is available in Jean Pfaelzer, ed., *A Rebecca Harding Davis Reader* (Pittsburgh: University of Pittsburgh Press, 1995).

3. See Max Oelschlaeger, *The Idea of Wilderness: From Prehistory to the Age of Ecology* (New Haven: Yale University Press, 1991), 149–52, for a discussion of development of Thoreau's quest to elucidate the relations between human consciousness and nature and his sense of how the material world, "brute facticity," could be seen as alien, even as he continued to explore humankind's absolute dependence on nature.

4. Robert Bredeson, "Landscape Description in Nineteenth-Century American Travel Literature," *American Quarterly* 20.1 (Spring 1968): 89; Rebecca Harding Davis, "By-Paths in the Mountains," *Harper's New Monthly*, July 1880, 167–85; August 1880, 353–69, September 1880, 532–47; and "Here and There in the Old South," *Harper's New Monthly*, July 1887, 235–46; August 1887, 431–43; September 1887, 593–606; October 1887, 747–60; November 1887, 914–25.

5. Quoted in John Sears, *Sacred Places: American Tourist Attractions in the Nineteenth Century* (New York: Oxford University Press, 1989), 122, 124–27.

6. The Ku Klux Klan was founded in 1866 in Pulaski, Tennessee, and initially used intimidation and terror to prevent newly enfranchised African Americans from voting. The Klan was active throughout the South by the time of this story.

7. Sears, 54.

8. By contrast, Angela Miller, in *The Empire of the Eye: Landscape Representation and American Cultural Politics, 1825–1875* (Ithaca: Cornell University Press, 1993), 243–88, sees luminosity in paintings by male artists as an automatic sign for feminine fluidity.

9. Howard Mumford Jones, *O Strange New World: American Culture in the Formative Years* (1964; Westport, Conn.: Greenwood Press, 1982), 361–62. Jones goes on to

observe that through the sublime representations of wild mountain passes, stunning clouds, Wagnerian rainbows, gigantic storms, nature is allegorized. Diminutive figures raise the question, "How was pygmy man not merely to subdue the wilderness but also found an enduring republic? Landscape could teach him that he might be, and frequently was, at the mercy of great natural forces, yet if he would but penetrate into the beauty and harmony of the whole, if he would set himself to understand the dynamism of the world, all, under God, might go well."

10. This definition of the sublime is indebted to the astute studies of David Miller, in particular *Dark Eden: The Swamp in Nineteenth-Century American Culture* (New York: Cambridge University Press, 1989), and "The Iconology of Wrecked or Stranded Boats in Mid to Late Nineteenth-Century American Culture," in *American Iconology: New Approaches to Nineteenth-Century Art and Literature*, ed. Miller (New Haven: Yale University Press, 1993), 186–208; see in particular 186–87.

11. David Miller, *Dark Eden*, 16.

12. Angela Miller, *Empire*, 244–49.

13. Jones, 351.

14. Sandra Zagarell, "Narrative of Community: The Identification of a Genre," *Signs* 13.3 (Spring 1988): 500.

15. Rebecca Harding Davis, "John Lamar," *Atlantic Monthly*, April 1862, 411–23; "Blind Tom," *Atlantic Monthly*, November 1862, 580–85; *Waiting for the Verdict* (New York: Sheldon, 1867).

16. Harold Bloom, "The Internalization of Quest Romance," in *Romanticism and Consciousness: Essays in Criticism*, ed. Bloom (New York: W. W. Norton, 1970), 6, 9.

17. Annette Kolodny describes how women migrating westward claimed the frontier as a potential sanctuary for an idealized domesticity, a site where they could relocate a home. The metaphor of the garden planted on the frontier resists associations of privatized erotic mastery. See *The Land before Her: Fantasy and Experience of the American Frontiers, 1630–1860* (Chapel Hill: University of North Carolina Press, 1984).

18. See Annette Kolodny, *The Lay of the Land: Metaphor as Experience and History in American Life and Letters* (Chapel Hill: University of North Carolina Press, 1975), 4.

19. Kolodny defines the "maternal landscape" in *The Lay of the Land*, 6, 22.

20. Kolodny locates such alien figures in the tales of E. D. E. N. Southworth and Maria Cummins in *The Land before Her*, 202.

21. Ralph Waldo Emerson, *Selected Writings of Ralph Waldo Emerson*, ed. William H. Gilman (New York: New American Library, 1965), 217.

22. Oelschalaeger, 93.

23. Ibid., 69.

24. Rebecca Harding Davis, "Life in the Iron Mills," *The Atlantic Monthly*, April 1861, 430–51. Rpt. Tillie Olsen, ed. (Old Westbury, N.Y.: Feminist Press, 1972), 12.

25. Ibid., 63–64.

26. Henry David Thoreau, "The Natural History of Massachusetts," in *Excursions and Poems*, vol. 5 of *The Writings of Henry David Thoreau* (Boston: Houghton Mifflin, 1906), 131.

27. "David Gaunt," "Out of the Sea," "Earthen Pitchers," "The House on the

Beach," and "In the Grey Cabins of New England" are all reprinted in *A Rebecca Harding Davis Reader*.

28. Carol MacCormack has observed, "When women are defined as 'natural,' a high prestige or moral 'goodness' is attached to men's domination over women, analogous to the 'goodness' of human domination of natural energy sources or the libidinal energy of individuals" ("Nature, Culture, and Gender: A Critique," in *Nature, Culture and Gender*, ed. MacCormack and Marilyn Strathern [Cambridge: Cambridge University Press, 1980], 6).

29. L. J. Jordanova. "Natural Facts: A Historical Perspective on Science and Sexuality," in MacCormack and Strathern, 42.

30. See ibid., 44–61; and Raymond Williams, *The City and the Country* (London: Chatto and Windus, 1973), 1–8.

31. Louis J. Renza's *"A White Heron" and the Question of Minor Literature* (Madison: Univ of Wisconsin Press, 1984), 44–45, quoting Warner Berthoff's summation of mainstream views of local color, cited by Caroline Gebhard "The Spinster in the House of American Criticism," *Tulsa Studies in Women's Literature* 10.1 (Spring 1991): 79–91. Gebhard astutely surveys the critical attack on local color literatures as trivial, senile, and sterile narratives written by unmarried women. Originating with the wave of masculinist nationalism around the turn of the century, this charge, according to Gebhard, appears to have been first popularized by George Santayana in "The Genteel Tradition in American Philosophy" (1911), passing through reviews in *The Nation*, then on through Henry Adams, Van Wyck Brooks, V. L. Parrington, up through Ann Douglas's *The Feminization of American Culture* (New York: Alfred A. Knopf, 1977).

32. *The Nation*, cited in Gebhard, 79; 27 September 1919, George Santayana, "The Academic Environment," *Character and Opinion in the United States* (New York: Charles Scribner's Sons, 1920), 44, cited in Gebhard, 81.

33. Robert Spiller et al., *A Literary History of the United States*, 4th rev. ed. (New York: Macmillan, 1974), cited in Gebhard, 83.

34. Kolodny, *The Land before Her*, 6–7; Ann Douglas [Wood], "The Literature of Impoverishment: The Women Local Colorists in America, 1865–1914," *Women's Studies* 1.1 (1972): 14.

35. See Josephine Donovan, *New England Local Color Literature: A Woman's Tradition* (New York: Frederick Ungar, 1983), for an astute discussion of American literary sources of local color, the relationship between local color and realism, and the connections among women local colorists that define them as a self-identified group. Jean Fagan Yellin, in her "Afterword" to Rebecca Harding Davis's *Margret Howth: A Story of Today* (New York: The Feminist Press, 1990; originally 1862), 271–302, argues that Davis generally acquiesced to James Fields's editorial suggestions, thereby diffusing some of the radical thrust of her first novel and establishing a pattern of "feminization" through which she would thereafter more strictly conform to narrative conventions.

36. Roger Stein, *The View and the Vision: Landscape Painting in Nineteenth-Century America* (Seattle: University of Washington Press, 1968), 8–9.

37. Simone de Beauvoir, *The Second Sex* (New York: Alfred A. Knopf, 1953), 710–11. For an analysis along these lines of twentieth-century fiction, see Annis Pratt,

"Women and Nature in Modern Fiction," *Contemporary Literature* 13.4 (Autumn, 1972): 477–90.

38. Gail David, *Female Heroism in the Pastoral* (New York: Garland, 1991), xvii–xviii.

39. See Zagarell, 499.

40. See Sears, 52; Angela Miller, "Everywhere," 214.

41. Angela Miller, "Everywhere," 224.

Whitman, Wharton, and the Sexuality in *Summer*

ABBY H. P. WERLOCK

There is a fine line," said Edith Wharton after writing a poem in 1902, "between prose and poetry, and I do not yet think I have ever crossed it." In fact, as R. W. B. Lewis has noted, she was an unusually astute critic of her own work, and this self-admission was correct: she was not to cross that line until some six years later with the publication of *Artemis to Actaeon and Other Verse* when she was forty years old.[1] By then she had spent years studying poetry, particularly that of Walt Whitman.

Wharton's critical appreciation of and emotional feelings for the poetry of Whitman, whom she and Henry James considered "the greatest American poet," have been well documented by Lewis, Cynthia Griffin Wolff, and Candace Waid.[2] By 1897 Wharton had developed "a reverential love for the poetry of Walt Whitman"; in 1898 Wharton inscribed extensively in her commonplace book from "Song of Myself" and "Life"; and in 1899 she and James delighted themselves by reading aloud from *Leaves of Grass*, exchanging favorite passages.[3] In 1906, commenting on a critical essay on Whitman, Wharton emphasized "his rhythms. It seems to me on *that* side that he was the great and conscious artist, and the great Originator."[4] And in 1908, a self-declared "Whitmanite," she made incisive notes for her own appraisal of Whitman.[5] In these copious notes for an unpublished critique, she discusses at length Whitman's power of description. Incorporating Whitman's own words, she writes: "Of some of his adjectives it might be said who touches this touches a man."[6] This illuminating statement suggests that Whitman's themes as well as his techniques fascinated Wharton: "Who touches this touches a man," a line from Whitman's "So Long" in "Songs of Parting," which Wharton singled out and committed to memory, provides a key to understanding not only her poetry but also her prose fiction, particularly her novel *Summer*.[7]

Not surprisingly, Wharton's own major poetic achievement, *Artemis to Actaeon*, a collection of twenty-five poems appearing in 1909, has been called Whitmanesque. "Life," for example, Lewis calls a "Whitmanian flight across the universe."[8] If the poem does not borrow its name from Whitman's

"Life," it, along with several others, undoubtedly echoes Whitman's "erotically charged and often ecstatic" language and imagery.[9] With *Artemis to Actaeon* Wharton not only "crossed the poetry line" but, in Lewis's words, "further confirmed Wharton's position as a woman of letters: she was alone among living American novelists in being capable of such genuine if modest poetic accomplishment."[10]

During the years leading to the writing and publication of this volume, Wharton not only read and reread Whitman, but also engaged in the now celebrated love affair with Morton Fullerton. And while critics are beginning to focus seriously on the poetry of *Artemis to Actaeon*, Wharton's most widely known poem is one she wrote during the still ecstatic but fast waning days of the affair: "Terminus," unpublished in Wharton's lifetime, surely (if ironically) owes its title to Whitman's "Terminus" in the "Drum Taps" section of *Leaves of Grass*. Although no one has yet demonstrated the earlier poem as a specific source, both Lewis and Wolff clearly acknowledge Whitman as the general inspiration. Lewis notes in Wharton's poem "the expanding rhythms and long lines of Walt Whitman. . . . 'Terminus' can remind one as well of Whitman's expression of union with all of suffering humanity"; and Wolff sees Whitman as "the ultimate authority" in the poem.[11] "Terminus" describes the passionate night Wharton and Fullerton spent at London's Charing Cross Hotel before Fullerton's departure for the United States the next day. Wolff, agreeing with Lewis that the title "Terminus" signifies both the railroad station hotel and the temporary end to their union, adds to these two meanings a third: Wharton's "conscious conclusion of the rhapsodic stage of the affair" evident in "an almost playful adaptation of [Fullerton's] transcendent 'religion' of passion." Citing the inadequacy of Fullerton's romantically charged language, Wolff believes that "even Whitman's magnificent invocation of transcendent affection could not manage the problems she faced" in 1911.[12]

"Terminus" was not her last poem, but it does seem to mark a departure from her earlier work. Indeed, although Wharton would write more poetry, including an elegy on the death of her friend Theodore Roosevelt, she was in fact to publish only one more book of verse, a slim volume containing a mere twelve poems, published in London but never in the United States.[13] Arguably, then, "Terminus" marks the end of her serious attempts to write and publish poetry, but marks the beginning of her use of Walt Whitman, its major inspiration, in various novelistic ways. If, as Waid has suggested, Wharton frequently turned to poetry "when she was profoundly unsettled," then it follows that, as she surmounted the emotional turmoil of her break with Fullerton and divorce from her husband Teddy, Wharton turned away from poetry and moved back to prose fiction.[14]

That Wharton continued to read American poetry and to critique it is clear not only in the myriad references in her letters, but also in the prose fiction she continued to publish until her death in 1937.[15] One of her last novels, *Hudson River Bracketed*, includes a long scene derived from Whitman's "Out of the Cradle, Endlessly Rocking," while its sequel, *The Gods Arrive*, borrows its title from an Emerson poem, "Give all to Love." The title of her memoir *A Backward Glance*, published in 1934, derives directly from Whitman's *A Backward Glance o'er Travel'd Roads*. Moreover, her 1924 novel *The Spark* actually includes a playfully adapted character named Walt Whitman.

"Quirky" or "playful" or "ironic" are operative words when reading Wharton, for, as recent studies of her novels indicate, her genius devised numerous literary techniques for veiling a feminist subtext that we are only now beginning to reveal and understand. Her lifelong love of Whitman's poetry and her extensive reading of it, especially during the years 1909–16, when the novel *Summer* was germinating, is a case in point. In fact, just as she had finished *Summer* she "devoured" Horace Traubel's gossipy account of Whitman's last days in Camden, calling herself "insatiable" in her "thirst" for the next volume.[16]

Before discussing *Summer* from a Whitmanian perspective, however, I must stress two points that, despite abundant evidence to the contrary, inexplicably continue to haunt Wharton. The first regards her so-called prudery about sexual matters, the second her alleged lack of a sense of humor.[17] Neither perception could be further from the truth. Not only did Wharton write lyrically of sexual passion and realistically of its demise, but she could—and did—write humorously about it. To her friends her ability to laugh was unparalleled; to Wharton herself, "a good joke" constituted one of her "ruling passions."[18] Recalling her capacity for laughter, Gaillard Lapsley wrote: "She never failed to rise to a fly that was fantastic or absurd. She would laugh with the sincerity of complete surrender to every paroxysm that followed a fresh vision of the ludicrous, with shoulders shaking and the tears running down her cheeks, lift a deprecating hand that bade you spare her another turn of the screw, or at least to 'give her ribs of steel.' . . . What she loved above all was *Fun*—the farce of life in its wildest and subtlest surprises, and how wild they could be, and how subtle, how blandly disguised, there was none like her to discover." Further, Lapsley recalls that he and Wharton "used to rock with laughter over chosen extracts from the *Journal of Abnormal Psychology*"; and she once jokingly suggested to Lapsley that he send their friend Sara Norton "a book she had seen advertised: 'La nouvelle *initiation sexuelle* . . . Le plus complet dans le genre, le *plus libere*'—underlinings by Edith—'illustrations dans le texte.'"[19]

Apparently *Summer* was at least partially inspired by a memorable but hot July week with Lapsley, Henry James, and John Hugh Smith at The Mount, Wharton's home in Massachusetts. Wrote Edith to Lapsley on July 18, 1911, "Were ever such splendours poured out on mortal heads as descended on ours during that fiery week?—" Although no one knows the exact nature of these "splendours," they apparently constituted a private joke that remained memorable to Wharton; we do know that in a subsequent letter dated December 21, 1916, Wharton urged Lapsley to read her new novel, saying that certain scenes from *Summer* would "amuse" him in a way that only they can "fully appreciate."[20]

In the writing of *Summer* Wharton not only seemed fully recovered from her romantic liaison with Morton Fullerton, but also prepared to use her familiarity with Whitman to continue distancing herself from idealistic representations of romantic love. In depicting Charity Royall, the discontented but self-assured young woman who mistakenly thinks she has the freedom and power to escape her emphatically male-dominated world, Wharton, I believe, draws on particular poems from *Leaves of Grass*—"Children of Adam," "Song of Myself," "When Lilacs Last in the Dooryard Bloom'd," "America," among others—and ironically reverses the general scheme of Whitman's philosophic optimism, demonstrating that neither a true "Song of Myself" nor real "Democratic Vistas" exist for American women. As Wharton sees it, the female sexuality Whitman so gloriously celebrates proves ephemeral and ultimately imprisoning, whereas the male sexuality remains potent, powerful, and permanent, an integral part of American historic and social fabric whose "warp and woof" Whitman so positively extols. According to Wharton, the United States was democratic only for men, and by incorporating Whitman's themes and techniques along with some of his most typical subjects—George Washington, Abraham Lincoln, American holidays, and a fierce sense of individuality and independence—she illuminated the impossibility of a woman's participation in that world.

Summer, set in Massachusetts near Wharton's old home, may be divided into three parts. In the first, Charity Royall, an adopted young girl, outspokenly rebels against education (embodied in Honorious Hatchard and Lucius Harney), religion (embodied in Mr. Miles), and the law (embodied in her guardian Lawyer Royall). Charity meets Harney in the library and believes that his youth and obvious interest in her render him different from the other men in her life who, by comparison, seem old and grotesque. Charity is wrong, of course: Harney shares with them an egotistical lust for power and for sex, differing from them only in method—and he is a determinedly methodical man, an architect who measures and calculates and defines houses, those male-owned and male-dominated homes that constitute the prescribed enclosures for their women. In this section of *Summer* Wharton draws liberally from *Leaves of Grass*, particularly from "Song of Myself" and "Children of Adam."

The second part, occupying the exact center of the book, occurs on Independence Day. In one of her cleverest and funniest and most overlooked scenes, Wharton describes the Fourth of July fireworks as a Freudian field day. Its humor temporarily disguises, mitigates, and postpones the message, that the male principle is historically dominant and that Independence Day is for men only. Charity's bid for freedom ends abruptly and appropriately at a "terminus," and without understanding its significance she is aligned with all the powerless women in the novel, prostitutes, wives, and mothers dominated by the men in the novel, against lovers, husbands, and fathers who remain secure in their memberships in "secret societies" or clubs. In this section Wharton draws from Whitman's patriotic descriptions of national heroes and celebrations and from her own "Terminus."

In the third part, Charity moves from house to house, trying to find the home where she belongs. Living at her stepfather's house, she meets daily at an abandoned house with her lover Harney, attends the "Old Home Week" celebration, which she discovers is for men only, and discovers Lucius's secret engagement to another woman. Finally the now pregnant Charity ascends the mountain in search of her mother only to find her dead, lying "like a dead dog in a ditch" with neither home nor possessions to bequeath her daughter.[21] Taken up to the mountain by Minister Miles and taken down by Lawyer Royall, the once-spirited Charity passively descends to yet another minister who marries her to her guardian. They return together to his house. The End. Terminus. In this last section Wharton draws from numerous Whitman poems, particularly "When Lilacs Last in the Dooryard Bloom'd" and verses in "Autumn Rivulets," "Songs of Parting," and "Sands at Seventy."

Of the astonishing number of Wharton's uses of Whitman in *Summer*, several key scenes in the novel serve to illustrate her ironic use of Whitmanesque themes and language. Early in the novel, depicting Charity's ripeness for sexual awakening, Wharton displays her gift for lyricism and rhythm, the qualities she most admired in Whitman; however, she also shows an uncanny knack for incorporating some of Whitman's key images. Here is Whitman in "Song of Myself":

I loafe and invite my soul,
I lean and loafe at my ease observing a spear of summer grass, . . .

Creeds and schools in abeyance, . . .
I breathe the fragrance myself and know it and like it. . . .
I will go to the bank by the wood and become undisguised and naked, . . .
I am mad for it to be in contact with me. . . .
And limitless are leaves stiff or drooping in the fields. . . .
And mossy scabs of the worm fence, heap'd stones, elder, mullein and
     pokeweed. (26–28)

In a similarly inspired scene, Wharton describes Charity escaping her guardian's house and her librarian's job to

a knoll where a clump of larches shook out their fresh tassels to the wind.
There she lay down on the slope, tossed off her hat and hid her face in
the grass.

She was blind and insensible to many things, and dimly knew it; but to
all that was light and air, perfume and colour, every drop of blood in her
responded. She loved the roughness of the dry mountain grass under her
palm, the smell of the thyme into which she crushed her face, the fingering of the wind in her hair and through her cotton blouse, and the creak of
the larches as they swayed to it.

She often climbed up the hill and lay there alone for the mere pleasure
of feeling the wind and of rubbing her cheeks in the grass.

And, shortly afterward:

Directly in her line of vision a blackberry branch laid its frail white flowers
and blue-green leaves against the sky. Just beyond, a tuft of sweet-fern uncurled between the beaded shoots of the grass, and a small yellow butterfly
vibrated over them like a fleck of sunshine. . . . All this bubbling of sap and
slipping of sheaths and bursting of calyxes was carried to her on mingled
currents of fragrance. Every leaf and bud and blade seemed to contribute
its exhalation to the pervading sweetness in which the pungency of pinesap prevailed over the spice of thyme and the subtle perfume of fern, and
all were merged in a moist earth-smell that was like the breath of some
huge sun-warmed animal. (53–54)

Again here is Whitman's well-known image in "Song":

I bequeath myself to the dirt to grow from the grass I love,
If you want me again look for me under your boot-soles. (68)

Now Wharton:

> Charity had lain there a long time, passive and sun-warmed as the slope on which she lay, when there came between her eyes and the dancing butterfly the sight of a man's foot in a large worn boot covered with red mud.
>
> "Oh, don't!" she exclaimed, raising herself on her elbow and stretching out a warning hand. (54)

Whitman's use of grass and boot imagery is here transposed into an ominous threat to Charity's natural and innocent inclinations. The grassy place in which Charity communes with both nature and herself is rudely intruded upon; throughout the rest of the novel Wharton uses images of dark masculine shapes which loom in doorways and obstruct Charity's view of the stars.[22]

In this same scene Charity looks up to see the "face of a slouching man with a thin sunburnt beard, and white arms" (55). The imagery strikingly echoes that in Whitman's "Song" when the persona describes

> The beards of the young men glist'n[ing] with wet. . . .
> The young men float[ing] on their backs, their white bellies bulge[ing] to the sun. (32)

The intrusion of this man, Liff Hyatt, obscurely related to Charity through her parents, introduces the themes of "family" and "houses" in this novel rife with Wharton's ironic insights into the relationships of sons and fathers with daughters, wives, and mothers, and the homes which house them. More immediately, the intrusion adumbrates the image of male sexuality to which Charity will shortly be introduced. In a brilliant scene depicting Charity on the threshold of sexual awakening, Wharton presents her as an innocently timid voyeur gazing through the window at Lucius Harney: "she saw the vigorous lines of his young throat, and the root of the muscles where they joined the chest" (103). As Charity watches Harney lying on his back on the bed in a scene rife with masturbatory images, she is aware of the unmasked sexuality emanating from him. Here is Whitman in "Children of Adam":

> From my own voice resonant, singing the phallus,
> Singing the song of procreation . . .
> Singing the muscular urge and the blending,
> Singing the bedfellow's song. . . .
> The female form approaching, I pensive, love-flesh tremulous aching, . . .
> The face, the limbs, the index from head to foot, and what it arouses,
> The mystic deliria, the madness amorous, the utter abandonment. . . .
> (69–70)

Charity, inarticulately aware of Harney's blatant masculinity, "suddenly understood what would happen" if she entered the bedroom. "It was the thing that *did* happen between young men and girls, and that North Dormer ignored in public and snickered over on the sly" (105, Wharton's emphasis). Shortly afterward, Harney writes Charity a note asking her to meet with him. The scene, including the freckled boy who delivers the message to Charity while looking "hard" at her window (122), echoes that in Whitman's "To A Common Prostitute" in "Autumn Rivulets":

> My girl I appoint you with an appointment, and I charge you that
> > you make preparation to be worthy to meet me,
> And I charge you that you be patient and perfect till I come.
> Till then I salute you with a significant look that you do not forget me. (273)

The unconsummated but sexually charged relationship is well on its way, ironically, just as Charity decides she will liberate herself by leaving North Dormer with Harney to celebrate Independence Day in Nettleton. A good deal happens to undermine Charity's false sense of independence, but all culminates in the description of the fireworks display. Wharton's intent in this scene—perhaps the most implicitly humorous she ever wrote—is suggested in her comment to Lapsley about her new novel. She writes, "There's a Fourth of July at Pittsfield [Massachusetts] that few people but you & I are capable of appreciating! . . . Anyhow, the setting will amuse you" (*Letters*, 385). Almost certainly, Wharton transformed the fireworks display at Pittsfield into the fireworks display at Nettleton in *Summer*.

But first, here is Whitman, writing in "Song of Myself" and "Drum Taps" of

> Landscapes projected masculine, full-sized and golden, . . .
> I am an old artillerist, I tell of my fort's bombardment,
> I am there again. (46, 52)

Especially significant in verses from "Drum Taps" describing "bombs bursting in air, and at night the vari-color'd rockets" (227) is Whitman's description of General George Washington:

> By his staff surrounded the General stood in the middle, he held up his
> > unsheath'd sword,
> It glitter'd in the sun in full sight of the army. . . .
> But when my General pass'd me,
> As he stood in his boat and look'd toward the coming sun,
> I saw something different from capitulation. (212, 214)

In *Summer*, Wharton uses the phallic potential of both fireworks and uniformed, sword-bearing men. On their way to the fireworks, Charity and Harney pass "a big omnibus groaning with Knights of Pythias in cocked hats and
swords" (140). Seating herself in front of Harney on the lakeshore, Charity
looks up amid the shooting of "pale Roman candles" and "fire-haired rock-
et[s]" and then

> the whole night broke into flower. From every point of the horizon, gold
> and silver arches sprang up and crossed each other, sky-orchards broke into
> blossom, shed their flaming petals and hung their branches with golden
> fruit; and all the while the air was filled with a soft supernatural hum, as
> though great birds were building their nests in those invisible tree tops. . . .
>
> Charity's heart throbbed with delight. It was as if all the latent beauty of
> things had been unveiled to her. She could not imagine that the world
> held anything more wonderful; but near her she heard someone say, "You
> wait till you see the set piece." . . .
>
> At last, just as it was beginning to seem as though the whole arch of the
> sky were one great lid pressed against her dazzled eye-balls, and striking
> out of them continuous jets of jewelled light, . . . a murmur of expectation
> ran through the crowd.
>
> "Now—now!" the same voice said excitedly; and Charity, grasping the
> hat on her knee, crushed it tight in the effort to restrain her rapture.
>
> For a moment the night seemed to grow more impenetrably black; then
> a great picture stood out against it like a constellation. It was surmounted
> by a golden scroll bearing the inscription, "Washington crossing the Dela-
> ware," and across a flood of motionless golden ripples the National Hero
> passed, erect, solemn and gigantic, standing with folded arms in the stern
> of a slowly moving golden boat.
>
> A long "oh-h-h" burst from the spectators: the stand creaked and shook
> with their blissful trepidations. "Oh-h-h," Charity gasped. . . .
>
> The picture vanished and darkness came down. In the obscurity she felt
> her head clasped by two hands: her face was drawn backward, and Har-
> ney's lips were pressed on hers. With sudden vehemence he wound his
> arms about her. . . . (146–149)

The transforming of Whitman's poetic description of the military bombard-
ment and General Washington in the boat, unsheathed sword held aloft, into
Wharton's prose description of the fireworks and General Washington in the
boat, "erect, solemn and gigantic" is, quite simply, hilarious. Wharton adroitly
emphasizes both sexual excitement and sexual climax in her uncharacteristic

use of "oh-h-h"'s, gasps, creakings and shakings, and exclamations of the words "Now—now!" Moreover, the "erect" stance of the "National Hero" echoes the stiffness of the "groaning" Knights of Pythias in their "cocked hats" and phallic swords.

The sexual joke loses its humor very shortly, however. Charity and Harney walk away together "isolated in ecstasy," but Wharton pointedly describes their reaching "the terminus" only to find they have missed their train, and "the throng about the terminus was so dense that it seemed hopeless to struggle for a place" (149–50). Minutes later on the lakeshore they encounter her drunken guardian: "in a desperate effort at erectness, Mr. Royall stepped stiffly ashore. Like the young men of the party, he wore a secret society emblem in the buttonhole of his black frock-coat" (150–51). Old or young, the men Charity encounters enjoy membership in male fraternities and clubs forever barred to her. The double standard quickly reveals itself as Lawyer Royall, drawing himself up "with the tremulous majesty of drunkenness," apostrophizes his adopted daughter: "You whore—you damn —bare-headed whore, you!" (151). Although Royall is with the "fallen" Julia Hawes who, after her disgraceful pregnancy and abortion, left North Dormer and turned to prostitution, he displays no qualms about denouncing his stepdaughter. Harney defends Royall's humiliating insult, telling Charity, "You must try to forget. And you must try to understand that men . . . men sometimes. . . . You must know one has to make allowances. . . . He'd been drinking—" (168, ellipses in original). Wharton reiterates the sympathetic connection among men in this novel through Harney's deference to Royall and through his membership in a New York "club with a long name in Fifth Avenue," information that "frighten[s]" Charity (213).

Employing a barrage of masculine allusions and demonstrations of force, as well as repeated use of the words "man" or "men," Wharton's insistent emphasis on forceful masculinity recalls the most explicit imagery of Whitman's "Children of Adam":

It is I, you women, I make my way,
I am stern, acrid, large, undissuadable, but I love you,
I do not hurt you any more than is necessary for you,
I pour the stuff to start sons and daughters fit for these States, I press with
    slow rude muscle,
I brace myself effectually, I listen to no entreaties,
I dare not withdraw till I deposit what has so long accumulated within
    me. . . .
On you I graft the grafts of the best-beloved of me and America. (77)

In much the same mode, the "towering and powerful" Royall is "much too big" (117, 22) for the town; he typically seeks companionship in "the store where he was always sure to find one or two *selectmen* leaning on the long counter, in an atmosphere of rope, leather, tar and coffee-beans" (36–37, my emphasis). Similarly, the pressing "vehemence" of Harney's kissing of Charity reiterates that of Whitman's persona in "Children of Adam":

O bashful and feminine!
O to draw you to me, to plant on you for the first time the lips of a determin'd man. (80)

Harney's Whitmanesque self-absorption, accompanied by its own phallic instrument, appears early in his meetings with Charity: "The architect's passion for improvement had already made him lose sight of her grievance, and he lifted his stick instructively toward the cornice" (50–51). Again he recalls the "Children of Adam" narrator:

The oath of procreation I have sworn, my Adamic and fresh daughters, . . .
till I saturate what shall produce boys to fill my place when I am
    through, . . .
and this bunch pluck'd at random from myself,
It has done its work—I toss it carelessly to fall where it may. (79)

Not only is Harney "utterly careless of what [Charity] was thinking or feeling" (164), but Charity is aware of the "hard beat of his heart" and the "hard" glances of Royall (111) and even of the little freckled boy whom Harney sends as his messenger (122). Moreover, like Whitman's masculine personae, careless of "whom they souse with spray" (32), Harney "carelessly" sows his seed, and Charity becomes pregnant with his child.

Harney is further connected with Whitman's male persona in "When I heard the Learn'd Astronomer." The speaker here sounds strikingly like Charity as she watches Harney:

When I heard the learn'd astronomer, . . .
When I was shown the charts and diagrams, to add, divide, and measure
    them, . . .
How soon unaccountable I became tired and sick,
Till rising and gliding out I wander'd off by myself,
In the mystical moist night air, and from time to time,
Look'd up in perfect silence at the stars. (196)

Whitman's "learn'd" astronomer appears the prototype of the educated architect Harney, whom Wharton portrays "bending over his sketch-book, frowning, calculating, measuring" (60), and "drawing and measuring all the old houses between Nettleton and the New Hampshire border" (68–69) as he meets Charity in house after house. "When he was drawing and measuring one of 'his houses,' as she called them, [Charity] often strayed away by herself into the woods or up on the hillside" (60).

A notable conflation of the themes of forceful masculinity and houses, as well as a reference to "charity," occurs in the following passage from Whitman's "Children of Adam":

> Behold, I do not give lectures or a little charity,
> When I give I give myself. . . .
> I do not ask who you are, that is not important to me,
> You can do nothing and be nothing but what I will infold you.
> on women fit for conception I start bigger and nimbler babes,
> (this day I am jetting the stuff of far more arrogant republics.). . .
> Every room of the house do I fill with an arm'd force. (57)

Earlier, Julia Hawes, in a shrewd aside to her male companions who, like Royall, wear "badges of secret societies," identifies her encounter with Charity and Harney as "Old Home Week" (145). In *Summer*, the relation of men to houses is nowhere more carefully constructed than during the "Old Home Week" celebration of American values, featuring Lawyer Royall's speech with its "allusions to illustrious men" (192), to "young men" (193, 194) and to "gentlemen" (194, 195). Replete with references to home, eminent men, and bygone national male heroes, Royall's speech underscores the major themes of the novel and, once again, echoes the Whitman line that Wharton knew well, "who touches this touches a man" (348). In a remarkable parallel, Wharton's Reverend Miles sums up his reaction to Royall's speech with the words "that was a *man* talking" (195, Wharton's emphasis). Old Home Week, like Independence Day, is clearly for men only. Charity, who at the opening ceremony had sung with "joy" (191), after Royall's speech loses consciousness as she dimly realizes that the songs and her stepfather's words are not for her and that her lover Harney is betraying her with Annabelle Balch, the woman he has intended to marry all along.

Her fainting is likely the first sign of her pregnancy as well. Understanding that she has no real home, Charity decides to search for her mother. Once again, however, her attempt at independent action fails as, weakened by her pregnant state, she is conducted up to the mountain by Minister Miles and Liff Hyatt, only to find that her mother cannot help her: she lies dead on the floor of a rude house. Charity's mother, who dies "like a dead dog in a ditch," is strikingly similar to Whitman's "poor dead prostitute" in "The City Dead-

House" in "Autumn Rivulets." Significantly, Whitman describes the unfortunate woman with the metaphor "that delicate fair house—that ruin!":

> Fair, fearful wreck—tenement of a soul—itself a soul,
> Unclaim'd, avoided house . . .
> Dead house of love—house of madness and sin, crumbled, crush'd.
> House of life, erewhile talking and laughing—but ah, poor house, dead
>   even then,
> Months, years, an echoing garnish'd house—but dead, dead, dead. (260)

At Charity's mother Mary's grim funeral, Wharton seems to be drawing partly on Whitman's "When Lilacs Last in the Dooryard Bloom'd." Indeed, her funeral service ironically reverses Whitman's homage to the assassinated Lincoln, another National Hero. Whereas in life Lincoln freed those in bondage and in death attracted mourners with much admiration, pomp, and circumstance, in life Charity's mother remained a slave to poverty, alcohol, and promiscuity, and in death her "vile body" (255) lies ignored by bystanders squabbling over her possessions. Whereas Whitman describes the flag-draped coffin, the "countless torches," and "the silent sea of faces and the unbared heads" (234), Wharton describes the absence of even the rudest coffin, a "candle stuck in a bottle" (247), and impoverished and uncaring bareheaded mourners with "pale aguish heads" (248). And whereas Whitman's funeral scene exudes images of spring, lilacs, and green grass, Wharton's occurs in a "wintry world" (260) of snow and harsh wind, "fawn-coloured stubble" (263), "dead grass" (254), and "an immensity of blackness" (254).

In "Lilacs," Whitman uses the image of mother as a metaphor for death:

> *Dark mother always gliding near with soft feet,*
> *Have none chanted for thee a chant of fullest welcome?*
> *Then I chant it for thee, I glorify thee above all,*
> *I bring thee a song that when thou must indeed come, come unfalteringly.*
>   (237)

His persona's chanting and singing is accompanied by

> The gray-brown bird . . .
> [Who] sang the carol of death, and a verse for him I love.
> From deep secluded recesses,
> From the fragrant cedars and the ghostly pines so still,
> Came the carol of the bird. (237)

Masterfully blending imagery from Whitman's funeral homage to Lincoln, Wharton demonstrates that Charity can neither celebrate her mother nor sing her a song. Nor can she reconcile Minister Miles's Christian burial service with reality. Miles's "mighty words" have the effect of "mastering" Charity (253–54), who realizes that he seems "to speak out of another world" (256). As the minister buries Charity's mother in the name of the "Father," her "bewildered brain" fails to relate her mother's life "in any way to the designs of a just but merciful God" (256, 259). Her mother has remained a dark and mysterious figure until the end; at best Charity can consign Mary to the earth, ponder her grave, and listen to the song of a Whitmanesque brown bird: "As she approached [her mother's grave] she heard a bird's note in the still air, and looking up she saw a brown song-sparrow perched in an upper branch of the thorn above the grave. She stood a minute listening to his small solitary song; then she rejoined the trail and began to mount the hill to the pine-wood" (263).

Not surprisingly, after quietly viewing her mother's grave, Charity sees her stepfather, recognizing "the heavy bulk of the man who held the reins" (265), who will bring her down from the mountain and make her his wife. The justice who presides over their marriage reads "out of the same book" Mr. Miles has used to sanctify her mother's death, and Charity notes "the same dread sound of finality" in both ceremonies (278). Regardless of circumstances or ceremonies, Charity has no more freedom than her mother.

Indeed, at the funeral, a young, nameless, female bystander names Charity as "another" one of "Mary's daughters." Just as Wharton links all the men with the stiff, erect phallic imagery and their memberships in "secret societies," for the remainder of the novel she links Charity more and more clearly with all the other women. Charity becomes uncomfortably aware of her "secret affinity" with this girl (260). They are not "Children of Adam," but of that suffering Mother, whether earthly or spiritual, whom Charity's mother Mary evokes. In Wharton's version of Whitman, Charity, trying to sing a song of herself, is outmaneuvered at every turn, partly by men and partly by the consequent dilemma of Motherhood. Indeed, pondering the alternatives of different women she knows, Charity learns that "in the established order of things, there is no place for her individual adventure" (234). Departed are her dreams of independence: in marrying her stepfather, Charity frees not herself, but Harney, writing to him to absolve him of his responsibility to her. By linking all the women in the novel, regardless of situation, Wharton exposes their destinies as powerless daughters moving volitionlessly into motherhood and into the houses of fathers, lovers, or husbands.

In Whitman's "The Sleepers," the persona apostrophizes "love and summer":

O love and summer, you are in the dreams and in me. . . .
I too pass from the night,
I stay a while away O night, but I return to you again and love you. . . .
I will duly pass the day O my mother, and duly return to you. (303)

At the end of the novel, bidding adieu to love, summer, and heroic dreams of independence, Charity has seen the fate of her mother and other women, and she acquiesces in the proscriptions of her gender and her pregnancy. With Whitman's persona in "The Sleepers" she may well agree: on the walls of Mrs. Charity Royall's hotel room is a picture of a young man and girl in a scene "full of a drowsy midsummer radiance" (280). Charity's summer has reached its terminus, however, and after passing a long dark night in the hotel room, she and Royall return "late the next evening, in the cold autumn moonlight, to the door of the red house" (291).

In her male/female, father/daughter, and husband/wife dichotomy, Wharton's ironic reversal of Whitman's "America" appears startlingly clear: for Whitman, the United States is a

Centre of equal daughters, equal sons,
All, all alike, . . .
Perennial with the Earth, with Freedom, Law and Love,
A grand, sane, towering, seated Mother,
Chair'd in the adamant of time. (353)

In "Democratic Vistas," Whitman calls for independence and freedom for men and women.[23] Yet in this same essay he paradoxically calls for a "new-founded literature" whose "most precious" outcome will be to insure "to the States a strong and sweet Female Race, a race of perfect Mothers—" (463).[24] Wharton surely understood the ramifications of the motherhood Whitman celebrates, and she wrote a whole novel echoing the lyricism of *Leaves of Grass* and ironically undercutting its sexual thematics. As a poetically gifted woman novelist, she might well echo these lines from Whitman's "To a Certain Civilian" in "Drum Taps":

Did you ask dulcet rhymes from me?
Did you seek the civilian's peaceful and languishing rhymes?
Did you find what I sang erewhile so hard to follow?
Why I was not singing erewhile for you to follow, to understand—nor am I
    now . . .

What to such as you anyhow such a poet as I? therefore leave my works,
And go lull yourself with what you can understand, and with piano-tunes,
For I lull nobody, and you will never understand me. (231)

Summer is a brilliant prose response to the masculine confidence and sexuality found in *Leaves of Grass*. In writing this remarkable novel Edith Wharton did not merely "cross the poetry line," she compounded, complicated, and transcended it. Paraphrasing the Whitman verse she liked to quote, Wharton could have truthfully proclaimed at the end of *Summer*,

Camerado, this is no book,
Who touches this touches a *woman!*

NOTES

1. R. W. B. Lewis, *Edith Wharton: A Biography* (New York: Harper and Row, 1975), 234. *Artemis to Actaeon and Other Verse* (New York: Charles Scribner's Sons, 1909).

2. Ibid., 140; Cynthia Griffin Wolff, *A Feast of Words: The Triumph of Edith Wharton* (New York: Oxford University Press, 1977); Candace Waid, *Edith Wharton's Letters from the Underworld* (Chapel Hill: The University of North Carolina Press, 1991).

3. Lewis, 81; Wolff, 90; Lewis, 140. In 1898, just before the publication of her first collection of stories, *The Greater Inclination*, she listed her favorite writers and poets, including all the poetry of Walt Whitman (Lewis, 86).

4. Quoted in Lewis, 237.

5. Lewis, 193.

6. Quoted in Waid, 132.

7. Walt Whitman, *Complete Poetry and Selected Prose*, ed. James E. Miller Jr. (Boston: Houghton Mifflin, 1959), 348. References to Whitman are from this edition and will be cited parenthetically in the text.

8. Lewis, 234.

9. Waid, 53.

10. According to Lewis, with "Mortal Lease" Wharton crossed the "poetry line" she mentions in her letter to William Crary Brownell, her editor at Scribners (Lewis, 234, 236).

11. Lewis, 260; Wolff, 198.

12. Wolff, 198, 204.

13. Edith Wharton, *Twelve Poems* (London: The Medici Society, 1926).

14. Waid, 53.

15. Wharton remarked to William Brownell that Poe and Whitman, together with Emerson, "are the best we have—in fact, the all we have" (quoted in Lewis, 236).

16. Lewis, 393.

17. Recent examples may be found in Lev Raphael, *Edith Wharton's Prisoners of Shame: A New Perspective on Her Neglected Fiction* (New York: St. Martin's, 1991), who believes that "sexuality was for Wharton a deeply shameful subject never to be

discussed" and that even "sexual liberation" with Morton Fullerton was "inextricably bound in shame" (300); and in David Holbrook, *Edith Wharton and the Unsatisfactory Man* (New York: St. Martin's, 1991), who concludes that "Wharton herself failed to make a lasting relationship, and this was felt deeply by her, as we may discover from her work, in all its bearing on her philosophy of being" (9). A survey of the growing number of fine studies on Edith Wharton and her fiction reveals valuable analyses of her anxieties, fears, humiliations, and other problems, but little to no mention of her sense of humor. The word "humor" appears in the indices of no book-length works except Lewis's biography.

18. Quoted in Lewis, 160.

19. Quoted in Lewis, 324, 520. "These unimaginative and learned writers, she continued, 'take that glorious and ignoble, that magical and mysterious Ark, the human body, and scramble over it with their goggles and their geological hammers,' as boring and irrelevant as an academic commentary on Faust" (Lewis, 520).

20. *Letters of Edith Wharton*, ed. R. W. B. Lewis and Nancy Lewis (New York: Charles Scribner's Sons, 1988), 244, 385. Hereafter cited in the text.

21. Edith Wharton, *Summer* (New York: Harper and Row, 1979), 250. References are hereafter given parenthetically in the text.

22. See, for example, 117, 119, 185, 203, 204, 206, 211.

23. In "Democratic Vistas," Whitman asks, "What is independence? Freedom from all laws or bonds except those of one's own being, control'd by the universal ones. To lands, to man, to woman, what is there at last to each, but the inherent soul, nativity, indiosyncrasy [*sic*], free, highest poised, soaring its own flight, following out itself?" (490). Yet that Charity cannot possibly soar is amply indicated by Wharton's description of her living in Eagle County, but ending "with a broken wing" (280).

24. Whitman in his prose merely reinforces the views of his persona in "Children of Adam," who says "there is nothing greater than the mother of men" (39).

Rewriting the "Rose and Lavender Pages"

Ethan Frome and Women's Local Color Fiction

DONNA M. CAMPBELL

As a writer of realistic fiction at the turn of the century, the young Edith Wharton faced a plethora of discursive modes and genres, including Jamesian realism, the novel of manners, local color, and naturalism. Despite these choices, in a 1904 letter to William Crary Brownell, her editor at Scribner's, an exasperated Wharton rejected the critics' attempts to "place" her among her contemporaries: "I have never before been discouraged by criticism . . . but the continued cry that I am an echo of Mr. James (whose books of the last ten years I can't read, much as I delight in the man), and the assumption that the people I write about are not 'real' because they are not navvies and char-women, makes me feel rather hopeless. I write about what I see, what I happen to be nearest to, which is surely better than doing cowboys *de chic*." [1] Wharton resisted the placement of her fiction in such "movements and trends" throughout her career. However, her determined efforts at such exclusion themselves suggest at least one type of inclusion: Wharton, like her male contemporaries Frank Norris, Stephen Crane, Theodore Dreiser, and Jack London, may profitably be viewed within the context of the shift in literary dominance away from women's local color and toward naturalistic fiction. As an ambitious woman writer responding to the 1890s transition between these two movements, she in fact provides a test case, an example of how the literary alliances of a strongly feminine, gender-linked tradition gave way before the imperatives of a predominantly masculine and generation-based rebellion against established forms.

In her response to women's local color fiction, Wharton showed that her desire for literary independence contained more than the junior author's customary chafing for recognition. She seems to have recognized early the pitfalls that awaited her if she followed the conventional route to success as a female author. The first is the danger, which her talent and wealth narrowly enabled her to avoid, of being a woman so closely identified with a great male author— in her case, Henry James—that her work becomes perpetually overshadowed by his. In her introduction to *Patrons and Protegées*, Shirley Marchalonis describes this type of literary sponsorship as consisting of "the important male author and the aspiring lady writer, he using his talent and intelligence to create literature, she a 'sweet singer'—an empty vessel through which the winds, or perhaps breezes, of inspiration might blow."[2] The second and potentially more serious threat, as Amy Kaplan has shown, was to risk identification with the "the same tradition of women's fiction that her aunts and grandmother devoured" or with their successors, the "society" novelists: "To become a woman novelist involved the further risk of being devoured as well as rejected, of being trivialized and absorbed into the category of the forbidden yet the consumable. If the upper-class lady was treated as a conspicuous commodity—a unique objet d'art, the sentimentalist produced inconspicuous commodities—mass-produced novels."[3] Further, Wharton's coming-of-age as an author, like that of her male naturalist contemporaries, coincided with a cultural shift in perceptions of local color fiction. Denounced as "limited" and "feminine" in its vision by James Lane Allen's 1897 *Atlantic* essay "Two Principles in American Fiction," local color or the "feminine principle" lost ground to the "vigorous" fiction of the "masculine principle" and suffered a subsequent decline.[4]

Wharton employed several strategies to combat these threats. The first, according to Kaplan, was to embrace an "ethos of professionalism" that opposes the domestic realm and "imagines a way of entering a cluttered literary marketplace while transcending its vagaries and dependence upon public taste."[5] Wharton also appropriated certain stylistic features for this purpose; as Katherine Joslin observes, "In order to tell the story of the individual within society and to tell it without the sentimentality of female domestic novelists, Wharton sought and borrowed the 'objective' tone and jargon of the male scientific discourse of her day."[6] Finally, Wharton's most central means of establishing her authority was to resist being judged as a "woman" author at all, as this passage from *A Backward Glance* demonstrates: "For years I had wanted to draw life as it really was in the derelict mountain villages of New England, a life even in my time, and a thousandfold more a generation earlier, utterly unlike that seen through the rose-coloured spectacles of my predecessors, Mary Wilkins and Sarah Orne Jewett. . . . Emily Brontë would have found as savage tragedies in our remoter valleys as on her Yorkshire moors."[7] Identifying local colorists Jewett and Freeman rather than the previous generation of sentimentalists as her "predecessors," Wharton defines herself as a rebel against the tradition of women's local color fiction rather than as a practitioner of it.[8] Significantly, she refers to herself as an "author" in the introduction to *Ethan Frome*, but she damns the local colorists by their very femininity, attributing the uproar over her portrait of the outlaw mountain folk in *Summer* to the New Englanders having "for years sought the reflection of local life in the rose-and-lavender pages of their favorite authoresses."[9] Wharton saw that, even if they hid their identity behind a masculine alias (as did Mary N. Murfree and Alice French), women writing in a female tradition like local color were obsolete. To survive in the increasingly professionalized world of fiction writing, as Josephine Donovan points out, "Wharton needed to distance herself from 'authoresses' in order to establish herself as an 'author,' to reject their view as feminine and 'unrealistic' in order to legitimate her masculine view as the serious, adult one."[10] An examination of *Ethan Frome* reveals Wharton's attempts to confront the genre of local color fiction on its own terms, and, using the same settings and characters as her predecessors, particularly those of Sarah Orne Jewett's *The Country of the Pointed Firs*, to disrupt and transform its narrative conventions, the assumptions underlying its iconographic and symbolic structures such as storytelling, preserving, and healing, and its insistence on the value of self-denial.[11]

The structure of *Ethan Frome* actually comprises two stories, both involving the initiation of the main character into a kind of truth: the frame story, which involves the narrator's quest to solve the puzzle of Ethan's life and his own initiation into the community of suffering that is Starkfield, and the inner story, the tragedy of Ethan, Zeena, and Mattie as the narrator imaginatively reconstructs it. Wharton further divides the frame story into two parts, a device that fulfills several functions in the novel. The distancing of the main story, suggestive perhaps of the "doubly distanced" narratives common to local color fiction, reinforces the thematic significance of the novel's threshold scenes; as Cynthia Griffin Wolff explains, narrator and character alike spend a "timeless eternity of hesitation on the threshold" that signifies opportunities lost and discarded.[12] The flow of narrative is additionally disrupted by Wharton's use of a series of witnesses from whom the narrator must glean the story. Besides increasing the suspense, the fragmentation of reality into a series of half-interpreted snippets demonstrates forcefully Wharton's stated unwillingness to resort to the artifice of having a know-all, tell-all village gossip give a single version of the events. To interpret such a purposefully refracted vision is the task of her much-maligned narrator.[13]

Although he has frequently been treated as an impediment to the "real" story of the Zeena-Ethan-Mattie triangle, the seemingly ordinary narrator exists as the frame story's most powerful and irreducibly ambiguous character. As Wharton's introduction makes clear, he is to be the traditional local color "sophisticated" onlooker who will act as the "sympathizing intermediary between his rudimentary characters and the more complicated minds to whom he is trying to present them."[14] In this way he becomes, like his counterpart in *The Country of the Pointed Firs*, the outside observer's or reader's representative whose initiation into the community depends upon his ability to reconstruct and relate the story that he hears. He is the sort of man who, as Wharton's reference to Emily Brontë suggests, will visit an isolated spot, experience some puzzling phenomena, receive some facts from a longtime resident (Nellie Dean/Mrs. Hale), and present to a sophisticated audience a sympathetic version of the tragic story he hears. The literary reference, however, scarcely hints at the complexities surrounding the narrator's position. For one thing, Wharton chooses a male rather than a female narrator to construct the story from the "small incidental effects" supplied by Mrs. Hale, a choice that reflects her own composing processes: "I conceive my subjects like a man—that is, rather more architectonically and dramatically than most women—& then execute them like a woman; or rather, I sacrifice, to my desire for construction & breadth, the small incidental effects that women have always excelled in."[15] Blake Nevius defends her use of the male narrator on grounds of practicality and consistency: a male engineer might more plausibly linger at Starkfield and be invited into Ethan's house; also, "The narrators employed in the framework of Edith Wharton's early stories are *always* men."[16] Equally important in Wharton's choice of this male narrator, however, is her determination to contrast her own modern (masculine) perspective with that of the local color "authoresses" who used female interpreters. Toward that end she gives him a hardheaded masculine profession, engineering, and creates an observer whose forte is objectivity rather than sympathy.

Wharton further distances herself from the local color use of the female narrator by emphatically rejecting a convention common to local color fiction and forming a good portion of *Wuthering Heights*: "I might have sat him down before a village gossip who would have poured out the whole affair to him in a breath" (ix). The engineer thus exists in a peculiarly temporary sort of powerlessness: because he must become a supplicant, dependent upon the villagers for scraps of knowledge, he seems at first to exist as a village parasite. The also unnamed narrator in *The Country of the Pointed Firs*, for example, spends her time with Mrs. Todd in a kind of Wordsworthian wise passiveness. Hearing the tale of Poor Joanna, itself a tale of pride, lost love, and self-imposed isolation not unlike that of Ethan Frome, she forms her own opinions but "did not like to interrupt" the flow of narrative between Mrs. Todd and Mrs. Fosdick.[17] Her rare questions are sympathetic and tactful, for "tact is after all a kind of mind-reading" (46). Far more frequent are the occasions when she is able to comment, as she does of her relationship with Mrs. Todd's mother Mrs. Blackett, that "we understood each other without speaking" (52). But as the existence of the frame story itself makes clear, the narrator of *Ethan Frome* is not a parasite or even a recorder, but a creator; it is his "vision," after all, that grants unity, stability, and decipherability to the fragmentary mutterings of his informants. He controls the vision imaginatively in two important senses, formulating it from the scraps of what he learns and presenting it to an audience that it would otherwise never reach. He is thus responsible for its unity, for he rivets the disparate elements that he hears and experiences into the form of classic tragedy, rendering the substance of Ethan's tale intelligible by enclosing it in a coherent form. Since Wharton implicitly forswears the traditional companionship of local color author and eager outside auditor in her introduction, the narrator also opens out the story to a variety of interpretive communities potentially scornful as well as sympathetic.

From the beginning, the narrator does not wait and watch like Jewett's female narrators; a modern man of action, he begins immediately and directly to investigate his characters.[18] After sensing a mystery surrounding Ethan, one of the strange folk of Starkfield from whom he feels himself distanced, the narrator pursues his quarry relentlessly, well past the bounds of simple politeness he might offer to one of his own class. Even the mail is not sacrosanct: he watches Ethan openly, noticing that Ethan "seldom received anything but a copy of the *Bettsbridge Eagle*" (4); nor does he scruple to read the return addresses on Zeena's mail from the patent-medicine manufacturers. After failing to glean information first from Harmon Gow, he hesitates with Mrs. Hale: "So marked was the change in her manner, such depths of sad initiation did it imply, that, with some doubts as to my delicacy, I put the case anew to my village oracle, Harmon Gow; but got for my pains only an uncomprehending grunt" (11). Presumably his "doubts" are meant to assure us of his sensitivity, but he immediately puts any delicacy aside, along with the memory of Mrs. Hale's "sad depths of initiation," in favor of renewed pursuit. The "uncomprehending grunt" turns out to be a paragraph of explanation about Mrs. Hale, including the useful information that she was "the first one to see 'em after they was picked up" and an admonitory hint that "she just can't bear to talk about it" (11). Despite sensing that "the deeper meaning of the stories was in the gaps" (7), the impatient narrator does not as yet realize how much information is contained in such laconic utterances.

Ironically, for he does not yet recognize the power of this local color method for getting at the story, the narrator gains the most information when he ceases to seek it. For a while he learns to keep still and accept information as a kind of community currency of exchange rather than as an ore to be extracted from the "granite outcroppings" of the villagers; his one-sided prying and interrogation give way to reciprocal social exchanges, as when he acknowledges his social indebtedness for Ethan's offer to drive him through heavy snow to the Junction. Like Jewett's narrator, who travels with Mrs. Todd to the secret pennyroyal field and "felt that we were friends now since she had brought me to this place" (49), Wharton's narrator believes that "the mere sight of the house had let me too deeply into his confidence for any farther pretence of reserve" (21). Indeed, Ethan does subsequently reveal himself obliquely, describing the isolation that caused his mother's slow decline and the reasons for the house's missing "L." Slowly learning to interpret the villagers' language metaphorically, the narrator, knowing that the "L" is "the center, the actual hearth-stone of the New England farm" (21), understands that Ethan is hinting at both the absence of life and love at the house and the demolition of his own dreams of romance with Mattie. The narrator further gains Ethan's trust when he symbolically descends to the older man's level, getting out of the sleigh "to walk along through the snow at the bay's side" (23) in order to "struggle on for another mile or two" beside, rather than above, his subject.

This lulling sense of communion does not last, however, for while Jewett's narrator, preferring companionship, turns back to her writing like a "reluctant child" (114), Wharton's narrator breaks off the story of growing friendship abruptly and, with a dramatic flourish and three rows of ellipses, announces, "It was that night that I found the clue to Ethan Frome, and began to put together this vision of his story. . . ." (25).[19] Unlike the pleasurable sharing of deferred experience common to local color fiction, the narrator's refusal to reveal the solution until a proper time teases his audience with heightened suspense as it reinforces his own control over the story. He relinquishes this control only reluctantly and clearly values his fictional art above humanity, Ethan's story over Ethan himself. At this point he still insists on maintaining a (masculine) linear mode of storytelling over a circular, digressive (feminine) one, unable as yet to reconcile twentieth-century technique with nineteenth-century sympathy.[20]

The second part of the frame story, occurring after the "vision" of Ethan's life, marks a change in the narrator, since he has become initiated into Ethan's community of suffering. Understanding now that his modern, masculine, detective-style questioning served rather to exclude than include him in the life of Starkfield, he embarks on a new strategy for eliciting information from his uncommunicative sources: "Beneath [the townspeople's] wondering exclamations I felt a secret curiosity to know what impressions I had received from my night in the Frome household, and *divined that the best way of breaking down their reserve was to let them try to penetrate mine*" (176, emphasis mine). He has, in fact, learned their language, or more correctly, to trust his perception that their language consists not in speech but in gaps and indeterminacies. More significantly, he has accepted the advantages of the feminine passivity he had hitherto ignored; as his language suggests, he will stop trying to invade their privacy and will instead allow his defenses to be "penetrated." Seeking confirmation from Mrs. Hale that the voice behind the "querulous drone" is Mattie's, not Zeena's, he comments, "I waited to let her trust in me gather strength" before his own understated observation that "it's pretty bad, seeing all three of them there together" (177), again employing passivity as a tactic. Mrs. Hale then pours forth the story of the day after the accident, of the village's response, and of the actions of Zeena, Mattie, and Ethan. Thus rewarded, the narrator becomes increasingly aware of the inverse relation between the strength of feelings and their ability to be articulated.

By the end of the frame story, the narrator is able not only to understand Ethan's story but to accept its gaps. He initially looks to Mrs. Hale to provide a final answer, but as she scrupulously reports the aftermath of the sledding accident, she can add only, "I never knew myself what Zeena thought—I don't to this day. Nobody knows Zeena's thoughts" (178). If "nobody knows Zeena's thoughts," and Ethan remains uncommunicative, then only Mattie's perspective can grant the narrator the closure that he seeks; yet even here his quest is frustrated. Mrs. Hale, Mattie's childhood friend, tells the narrator about the events of the next day: "'[Mattie] woke up just like herself, and looked straight at me out of her big eyes, and said . . . Oh, I don't know why I'm telling you all this,' Mrs. Hale broke off, crying" (178, ellipsis Wharton's). Like the unspoken word that passes between Lawrence Selden and Lily Bart at the end of *The House of Mirth*, the word here is never made concrete but remains a mystery to reader and narrator alike. The narrator has sought the word that would make his story perfect, confirming his vision and ending his search, but he is never to find it, for the situation remains finally unknowable. What he has learned is that he must, in effect, resign his quest, relinquishing his modern interest in facts and the "real story" in favor of a more fluid, emotion-based method of discerning truth. In contrast to his earlier probing, the narrator now cedes control over the story to Mrs. Hale. Occurring several paragraphs before the end of the story, his final words in the novel, "It's horrible for them all" (180), confirm and intensify his allegiance to the language of sympathy, a language to which Mrs. Hale responds reciprocally by echoing his words: "Yes, it's pretty bad" (180). Now that he feels himself a part of Starkfield, an initiate of the villagers' inner lives as well as of their customs, the narrator completes the tale by recording Mrs. Hale's version, bridging indeterminacies by means of the emotional rightness of his vision. The feminine passivity and sympathy he has learned complement the objectivity with which he relates the tale, rendering both his "vision" and his initiation into the world of emotion complete.

The inner story, the tale of Ethan's life, remains tragic whether one accepts the traditional view that the narrator's "vision" is a true one or believes instead with Cynthia Griffin Wolff and John Crowe Ransom that "we are forced to conclude that he did not gather it really; that, mostly, he made it up." [21] The inner story is one of the most extensively analyzed pieces in all of Wharton's fiction, with its imagery, symbolism, structure, and presentation of ethical choices receiving a great deal of attention. What needs to be explored further is the way in which the modern perspective of Wharton's narrator interrogates and implicitly condemns such standard local color myths as those of cohesive community, of healing, and of preserving and self-denial.

The myth of cohesive community is the first element exposed by the narrator's gaze. Despite Michael Eady's prosperous store and its railway station, Starkfield is one of the impoverished, dying villages common to local color fiction. In analyzing the isolation of Ethan's mother, Marlene Springer cites the motif of the railroad as an example of Wharton's "brilliant irony," since she "turns the coming of the railroad, historically the advent of mobility and expansion, into a catalyst for isolation and despair." [22] As Wharton was doubtless aware, however, the irony really resides within the conventions of local color fiction, where the coming of railroads often signals a town's increasing isolation. By facilitating escape for the "smart ones" that "get away," as Harmon Gow tells the narrator, and by providing a conduit for outside ideas that threaten to destroy the village's integrity as a community, the railroad drains vitality from the local color village. [23] The dances and sledding parties Mattie attends show that even Starkfield inhabitants do not lack for social life, but the community life of the village takes place off-stage, whereas the drama of its three self-willed isolates unfolds before the reader. Ironically, in refusing to join the community, all three become crystallized images of its people, frozen in time as virtual caricatures of New England types. For example, Ethan, who consistently refuses to interact with his fellow villagers, leans toward caricature in his taciturnity, which after the accident exceeds even that of legendarily close-lipped New Englanders like the isolate Nicholas Gunn of Mary Wilkins Freeman's "A Solitary." Trapped by Starkfield, all three main characters are nonetheless outsiders literally and figuratively. Zeena, whose "native village was slightly larger and nearer to the railway than Starkfield" (71), insulates herself from the town with a fierce pride that allows her to express a longing for human companionship only in her "sickly spells."[24] Set apart even in his youth by a superior intellect and a vision of other worlds, Ethan shares her pride, answering his neighbors in monosyllables and allowing few visitors to visit his bare house. Mattie Silver comes from Stamford, Connecticut, but after her father dies, she has nowhere to go except Starkfield. The compensations of the local color village, Wharton implies, fail to outweigh its limitations for characters such as these, particularly when their dearth of choices is compounded by "the hard compulsions of the poor" (179).

The motif of illness and healers also becomes transformed in the inner story. Although the characters' ailments have a physical basis, Ethan's deformed spine and Mattie's diseased one suggest Freeman's metaphor of spinal disease to indicate excessive Puritan will and frustrated lives in *Pembroke*, a disease of self-willed isolation curable only through a reintegration into the community.[25] Zeena's psychogenic illness, which "had since made her notable even in a community rich in pathological instances" (72), together with her constant "doctoring" of herself with patent medicines, recalls the many female healers and herb-women in local color fiction. As embodied in Zeena, however, the concept of women as healers and servers has been warped into a monstrous parody of itself. Her ineffective patent medicines, unlike herbs, are as unnatural as her clicking upper plate of false teeth.[26] Further, Zeena acts as both healer and patient, collapsing the distinction between the two roles and negating the possibility of human sharing in the process. Her illnesses provide a sort of homeopathic remedy for the boredom of her life, an antidote or pharmakon, by way of small repeated doses of "complications," to the death-in-life that she shares with Ethan, who, in another role reversal, is "the one who always done the caring."

Wharton also borrows from local color tradition in her choice of situation and themes. Ethan's story is more than a classic love triangle; it recalls the tales of self-sacrifice and renunciation, of elderly lovers and unspoken, inchoate longings that pervade the works of Freeman and Jewett. Ethan's situation with Zeena is also a nightmare version of the crotchety mother / patient child theme prevalent in local color fiction. Wharton even alludes to the tradition when, in the second part of the frame story, Mrs. Hale relaxes once her exacting elderly mother Mrs. Varnum goes up to bed. Indeed, Mrs. Hale serves as more than a witness here. She represents the unspoken alternative story to Ethan's: the traditional local color tale *not* told of a middle-aged woman's domestic troubles and forbearance with an elderly parent. Generations of readers, culturally conditioned to praise self-denial and stoic endurance in local color heroines, have been frustrated when a man like Ethan chooses to exercise these same virtues, seeing his self-sacrifice as evidence of a wasted, tragic life. By telling instead the man's story, as the local colorists seldom did, Wharton simultaneously breaks with her "predecessors" and uses this change in gender to demonstrate not the nobility of self-denial but the dreadful consequences of a life ruled by what Wharton in "Bunner Sisters" calls "the inutility of self-sacrifice."[27]

Like Rose Terry Cooke's and Mary Wilkins Freeman's characters, Ethan ultimately chooses resignation, despite his awareness that, as Elizabeth Shepley Sergeant puts it, "the real New England tragedy . . . is not that something happens but that nothing does."[28] Only once does he make an attempt to break out of his imprisonment: in making the suicide attempt, he chooses the ultimate renunciation—of life itself—and the ultimate extravagant gesture, to die with his beloved.[29] However, the earlier episode of Zeena's pickle dish has warned us that Ethan's self-denial will yield no satisfaction. Sent from Philadelphia as a wedding present, the red glass pickle dish is Zeena's pride and joy, so precious to her that she keeps it on the top shelf of the china closet and never uses it. On the night when Zeena is away, Mattie puts it on the supper table, but when Ethan's and Mattie's hands meet over the milk jug, Zeena's cat backs into the dish and knocks it off the table. Joseph X. Brennan sees the wedding gift, unused by Zeena but taken up and destroyed by Mattie, as a symbolic representation of "the pleasure and passion that Ethan had sought and Zeena had thwarted in their marriage"; when Zeena carries out the pickle dish "as if she carried a dead body" (128), it is, as Kenneth Bernard comments, the "corpse of her marriage" that she carries.[30] Another significance, though, can be attached to the incident. The seldom-used pickle dish, like the medicine jar that, Zeena tells Mattie, will "do for pickles" if she can "get the taste out" (66), refers obliquely to local color fiction's preserving of food and stories, of the continual urge to postpone the savoring of experience. But preserving here is futile: all Zeena's careful saving comes to naught when her precious possession is smashed by a chance occurrence, just as Ethan's constancy in the face of adversity fails to gain him happiness or to protect him against the accident of living through his suicide attempt. In presenting the utter bleakness of Ethan's life, the futility of his self-denial, and the impossibility of any change for the better, Wharton forges local color virtues into instruments of terror that sustain and prolong the torturous process of Ethan's life. It is a terror that, combined with the pity, transforms the elements of local color into New England tragedy.

Viewed in this context, Wharton's much-maligned device of the male narrator in *Ethan Frome* becomes not only comprehensible but essential, for through her (re)vision of the local color world through his fact-obsessed, masculine sensibility, Wharton seeks to reclaim for her own mainstream fiction the marginal territories occupied by the local colorists. Like Jewett and other local color writers, Wharton employs a sympathetic, well-educated outsider/observer as her narrator; like Jewett's, her narrator undergoes an initiation of sorts into the secrets of the village, but his aggressive seeking after facts, his horror at the self-denial that freezes Ethan's life, and even his choice of Ethan's story over that of Mrs. Hale mark him as an alien—modern, masculine—sensibility in this local color community. Yet he does learn to decode the villagers' digressive, fragmentary attempts at storytelling and, in effect, he does resign his quest, relinquishing his modern interest in facts and the "real story" in favor of a more fluid, emotion-based method of discerning truth.

As the end of the story indicates, however, only the narrator, the modern man, escapes this frozen vision of wasted lives. Maintaining his objectivity allows him to sympathize with the Starkfield villagers without becoming enraptured by their world as Jewett's narrator is in *The Country of the Pointed Firs*. Considered as the corrective rewriting of what Wharton saw as the bleak rural landscapes, grotesquely extended love affairs, excessive preserving, and masochistic renunciations and self-denial of local color fiction, *Ethan Frome* almost becomes Wharton's blackly comic joke, a vision of the genre so extreme as to border on private parody. *Ethan Frome* argues that the type of local color renunciation practiced by Ethan and his kind suggests not spiritual nobility but spiritual impoverishment; their habitual denial of healthy appetite for emotion recalls not the *anorexia mirabilis* of the saints but the *anorexia nervosa* of the cultural victim.

Hence, although Wharton clearly encouraged the image of herself as a self-created artist, the evidence of her fiction suggests that, far from remaining aloof from literary trends, she developed into the kind of writer she became in part because of the complicated influences and pressures that women's local color fiction exerted upon her. She tried to reinvent herself as a writer free from the constraints of local color, and critics have generally followed her wishes by downplaying her literary antecedents. As an upper-class woman vacationing genteelly in the impoverished communities of New England, she might have followed Jewett and represented herself as an eager postulant and sympathetic feminine recorder of the rituals of community life (Jewett's stance in *Deephaven* and *The Country of the Pointed Firs*). However, Wharton realized that to be taken seriously as an author, not an "authoress," she would have to repudiate the local colorists thoroughly and unmistakably. In *Ethan Frome* she achieves this victory over "the authoresses," and the literary power of its bleak vision has until recently all but obliterated their "rose and lavender pages."

NOTES

Some material in this essay appears in a different form in Donna Campbell, *Resisting Regionalism: Gender and Naturalism in American Fiction* (Columbus: Ohio University Press, 1997).

1. *Letters of Edith Wharton*, ed. R. W. B. Lewis and Nancy Lewis (New York: Charles Scribner's Sons, 1988), 91.

2. Shirley Marchalonis, introduction to *Patrons and Protegeés: Gender, Friendship, and Writing in Nineteenth-Century America*, ed. Marchalonis (New Brunswick: Rutgers University Press, 1988), xi. In "The Traditions of Gender," another essay in the same volume, Cheryl B. Torsney demonstrates that Constance Fenimore Woolson was not so fortunate in escaping the stereotype of being "the ash from which the Jamesian phoenix rises" (170).

3. Amy Kaplan, *The Social Construction of American Realism* (Chicago: University of Chicago Press, 1988), 73, 71.

4. Recent scholarship has revived the critical reputation of local color fiction. Even before the work of Josephine Donovan, Candace Waid, and Barbara White, however, critics noted parallels between Wharton and her "predecessors." Tracing Wharton's debt to local color fiction in three of her unpublished New England novels, Nancy R. Leach ("New England in the Stories of Edith Wharton," *New England Quarterly* 30 [1957]: 90–98) argued that she "is certainly not a New England writer in the sense that Sarah Orne Jewett and Mary E. Wilkins Freeman are," concluding that her vision "can best be compared to Eugene O'Neill's" (97). More critical of Wharton's regional fiction than Leach, Abigail Ann Hamblen, "Edith Wharton in New England" (*New England Quarterly* 38 [1965]: 239–244), contended that "Edith Wharton's approach to the Massachusetts 'hill country' savors decidedly of the air of an aristocrat going slumming among the lower orders" (240). Alan Henry Rose showed that the "void" or "absence of experiential possibilities in Wharton's New England" ("'Such Depths of Sad Initiation,'" *New England Quarterly* 50 [1977]: 423–39) prevents her characters from becoming initiated into "a sound sense of self" (424).

5. Kaplan, 74.

6. Katherine Joslin, *Edith Wharton* (New York: St. Martin's, 1991), 39.

7. Edith Wharton, *A Backward Glance* (New York: Charles Scribner's Sons, 1934), 293–94.

8. In *Edith Wharton's Letters from the Underworld: Fictions of Women and Writing* (Chapel Hill: University of North Carolina Press, 1991), Candace Waid comments that throughout her life Wharton "made no distinctions between local colorists and sentimentalists" (8).

9. Wharton, *A Backward Glance*, 294.

10. Josephine Donovan, *After the Fall: The Demeter-Persephone Myth in Wharton, Cather, and Glasgow* (University Park: Pennsylvania State University Press, 1989), 48.

11. Donovan prefaces her discussion of the mother-daughter estrangement theme in *Ethan Frome* by connecting it in passing with *The Country of the Pointed Firs*: "The barren, frozen world of Starkfield, an obviously symbolic name, could not be farther from the green-world bower of the local-color matriarchs. To read *Ethan Frome* in tandem with Jewett's *Country of the Pointed Firs* (1896) is to realize a study in contrast" (66).

12. Cynthia Griffin Wolff, *A Feast of Words: The Triumph of Edith Wharton* (New York: Oxford University Press, 1977), 172. In addition to Wolff's psychobiographical approach to the novel's thresholds, see Candace Waid's *Edith Wharton's Letters from the Underground*, a perceptive examination of Wharton's use of frames and interiors ("the woman behind the door") as a key to reading the novel's pervasive images of silence and infertility.

13. In "Gender and First-Person Narration in Edith Wharton's Short Fiction," Elsa Nettels notes that of the twenty-three male narrators in Wharton's short fiction, "only the first-person narrator of Ethan Frome has been criticized as unconvincingly masculine" (*Edith Wharton: New Critical Essays*, ed. Alfred Bendixen and Annette Zilversmit [New York: Garland, 1992], 246).

14. Edith Wharton, introduction to the Modern Student's Library Edition of *Ethan Frome* (New York: Charles Scribner's Sons, 1922), viii. Subsequent references to the introduction and the novel proper will be cited parenthetically in the text.

15. Wharton, *Letters*, 124.

16. Blake Nevius, *Edith Wharton: A Study of Her Fiction* (Berkeley and Los Angeles: University of California Press, 1953), 123. Elsa Nettels further notes that Wharton's male narrators are "equal or superior to the other characters in social position" (247) and are identified primarily with other men in groups. She distinguishes several reasons for Wharton's use of male narrators, among them Wharton's "persistent view of literary creation as a man's vocation" (248), the implicit sanction of tradition, and above all a need to adopt the objectivity and power associated with the male perspective, lest the women's stories they tell be lost.

17. Sarah Orne Jewett, *The Country of the Pointed Firs and Other Stories* (New York: Doubleday, 1956), 60. Subsequent references are to this edition and will be given parenthetically in the text.

18. In "Characters and Character: A Note on Fiction" (*American Review* 6 [1936]: 271–88), John Crowe Ransom comments that Wharton's reporter makes "slight detective motions at gathering [the story]" (273).

19. In "Edith Wharton's Art of Ellipsis" (*Journal of Narrative Technique* 17 [1987]: 145–62), Jean Frantz Blackall rejects the readings of Cynthia Griffin Wolff, who argues that the blank is "the author's personal absorption in the narrator's fearful vision," and of Elizabeth Ammons, who claims that "the ellipses signify a change in genre, from the realistic outer narrative to the fairy tale within." Blackall contends rather that Wharton uses ellipses here to mark the shift from narrative to drama and back: "The augmented ellipses mark this transition into the critical moment and out of it into enduring time" (154–55).

20. Elizabeth Ammons identifies these two narrative patterns in "Going in Circles: The Female Geography of Jewett's *The Country of the Pointed Firs*," *Studies in the Literary Imagination* 16.2 (Fall 1983): 83–92; revised and included as chapter 4 of *Conflicting Stories: American Women Writers at the Turn into the Twentieth Century* (New York: Oxford University Press, 1992).

21. Ransom, 273.

22. Marlene Springer, *Ethan Frome: A Nightmare of Need* (New York: Twayne, 1993), 81.

23. The latter point is made by Jay Martin in *Harvests of Change* (Englewood Cliffs, N.J.: Prentice-Hall, 1967) quoting a passage from Thomas Bailey Aldrich's *An Old Town by the Sea* (1893): "The running of the first train over the Eastern Road from Boston to Portsmouth—it took place more than forty years ago . . . was attended by a serious accident. . . . [This] initial train, freighted by many hopes and the Directors of the Road, ran over and killed—Local Character" (135).

24. The extent to which Zeena is seen as an evil force in Ethan's life varies. In *Edith Wharton's Argument with America* (Athens: University of Georgia Press, 1980), Elizabeth Ammons sees Zeena as a fairy-tale wicked witch (complete with cat) to Mattie Silver's Snow White (63). R. B. Hovey, in "Ethan Frome: A Controversy about Modernizing It," *American Literary Realism* 19 (1986): 4–20, describes Zeena as another kind of villain, one who wields her psychosomatic illness as a weapon in the power struggle against Ethan that ends when "Neurosis conquers all" (17). Susan Goodman, on the other hand, argues that the narrator, blinded by male preconceptions, lacks sympathy for Zeena in what is obviously an untenable situation for her. In *Edith Wharton's Women: Friends and Rivals* (Hanover, N.H.: University Press of New England, 1990), she reads Zeena as an unfairly maligned figure whose story the narrator ignores because of "what he has been primed to see culturally and literarily. . . . By undercutting his authority and reliability, [Wharton] dissociates herself from his error: telling the wrong story" (68).

25. Diane Price Herndl interprets Ethan's case differently, viewing his lameness as a metaphoric castration and Ethan himself as "stuck at home tending an ill parent . . . feminized, and therefore ill" (*Invalid Women: Figuring Feminine Illness in American Fiction and Culture, 1840–1940* [Chapel Hill: University of North Carolina Press, 1993], 181).

26. The same perversion of "woman as (natural) healer" occurs in the "false hair, the false teeth, the false murderous smile" of Dr. Merkle in Wharton's *Summer*.

27. Edith Wharton, "Bunner Sisters," *Xingu and Other Stories* (New York: Charles Scribner's Sons, 1916); reprinted in *The Best Short Stories of Edith Wharton*, ed. Wayne Andrews (New York: Charles Scribner's Sons, 1958), 254.

28. Elizabeth Shepley Sergeant, "Idealized New England," *New Republic* 3 (1915): 20. In "Cold Ethan and 'Hot Ethan,'" Cynthia Griffin Wolff sees this resignation as a different sort of antiheroic act, the consequence of Ethan's own ineffectual, unrealistic romanticizing about his situation: "he explores no avenues that might give their love the adult, social context it requires for survival" (Bendixen and Zilversmit, 108).

29. The sledding incident itself, although drawn from contemporary sources, suggests also the fatal, forbidden sledding incident in Freeman's *Pembroke*, where Deborah

Thayer believes her son Ephraim's death to be due to his forbidden sledding, not to a severe beating that she administered. As it does for Ethan Frome, sledding becomes for Ephraim the only symbol of male freedom from his domination by an all-powerful woman. In "The Sledding Accident in Ethan Frome," *Studies in Short Fiction* 21 (1984): 145–46, Jean Frantz Blackall discusses Wharton's sources for this incident and concludes that Ethan's wish to sit in the front of the sled signifies his desire to protect Mattie by hitting the elm tree first.

30. Joseph X. Brennan, "*Ethan Frome*: Structure and Metaphor," *Modern Fiction Studies* 7 (Winter 1961–62): 352; Kenneth Bernard, "Imagery and Symbolism in *Ethan Frome*," *College English* 23 (December 1961): 183.

Fairy Tales and Opera

The Fate of the Heroine in the Work of Sandra Cisneros

LAURA GUTIERREZ SPENCER

Take away the mantillas, the golden colors, the cigars—take away
Egypt and the memory of Isis—and the tale you will hear is about any
woman at all.

Catherine Clément, Opera, or the Undoing of Women

Within the Western narrative tradition, female characters are commonly presented within the narrow confines of polarized roles limited to either madonna or whore, villain or victim. In a similar fashion, the fate of these characters also tends to fall to extremes. Depending upon the narrative form, the female protagonist all too often finds either an early end in death or an equally premature, if metaphorical, "demise" as she conveniently disappears into a cloud of anonymity after the hero has come to the rescue and married her. In so many plots, the appropriate denouement of dramatic tension is the death of the heroine. Female characters who are adventurous, inquisitive, active, or otherwise rebel against patriarchal rules of female comportment are often killed in punishment for their disobedience. Unfortunately, the passive, pliant heroine often meets the same fate. Her death is portrayed as a valiant sacrifice for the life or comfort of the male hero. More simply stated, female protagonists, whether they are "good girls" or "bad girls" still die, in literal and metaphoric terms. Catherine Clément, in *Opera, or the Undoing of Women*, documents this tradition. Among the most famous operas for instance, the death toll includes "nine by knife, two of them suicides; three by fire; two who jump; two consumptives; three who drown; three poisoned; two of fright; and a few unclassifiable, thank god for them, dying without anyone knowing why or how. Still, that is just the first sorting. And with my nice clean slate in my hands, I examine all those dream names in their pigeon-holes, like butterflies spread out on boards. All that is left is to write their names above them: Violetta, Mimi, Gilda, Norma, Brunhilde, Senta, Antonia, Marfa. . . ."[1] The misogynistic effect of these plots, of course, is not limited to the world of opera. This tendency comes from the very wellspring of literature, myth.

The most common example of myth in modern times and the form that has had the most impact upon our society is the fairy tale. Many of the tales that we tell our children before they sleep include plots in which male heroes are rewarded for their audacity, courage, and curiosity. Demure princesses are praised for their beauty and kindness, while other female characters, like Goldilocks, are punished for their curiosity and active natures. The active female character in fairy tales is either vilified as a figure of evil or is punished for her audacity.

Throughout her work, Sandra Cisneros has critiqued the fate of the heroine in Western patriarchal literature. She accomplishes this, in part, through reference to popular fairy tales. Cisneros's first book includes a feminist analysis of the social and personal consequences for women who believe in fairy tales and wait for Prince Charming to fulfill their existence. In *The House on Mango Street*, Cisneros draws attention to the messages that fairy tales impart to females about the roles they should play, or not play, in life. This book contains glimpses of the lives of various women and the social, cultural, and economic forces that have entrapped them in stultifying circumstances. Although individual stories in *The House on Mango Street* include examinations of prejudice, poverty, domestic abuse, sexual harassment, sexual assault, and sexism, one of the central themes of the book is that the women of Mango Street have been limited in the opportunities available to them to develop their own agendas and talents. This repression serves to subordinate these women's lives to husband and home. The theme of limitation and restriction is represented by many images of trapped women. In these stories women lean out of windows, stand in doorways, stare at the seams between ceiling and walls, and envy other women who "throw green eyes easily like dice and open homes with keys." [2]

The stories in *The House on Mango Street* that take the form of revisionist fairy tales feature characteristic elements of the classic children's stories but are set within a different context and have more specific outcomes for the female characters. They oppose the traditional marriage to the hero and "happily-ever-after" conclusion. Cisneros's version of these fables reveal the truer-to-life consequences for women who are socialized to live their lives waiting for the happy ending. The stories "Rafaela Who Drinks Papaya and Coconut Juice on Tuesdays" and "The Family of Little Feet" allude respectively to "Rapunzel" and "Cinderella." Cisneros's heroines are young girls and women in the housing projects of Chicago. They do *not* live happily ever after. Beautiful Rafaela, for instance, is locked in her own house by a jealous husband. She "leans out the window and leans on her elbow and dreams her hair is like Rapunzel's. On the corner there is music from the bar and Rafaela wishes she could go there and dance before she gets old" (*House*, 76). In "The Family of Little Feet" the little-girl protagonist and her friends are given a bag of used high-heeled shoes. The girls try on heels for the first time in their life and marvel at how the shoes make their legs look beautiful and long. They walk, dance, and strut around the neighborhood until they realize the power of the shoes. On this sojourn, the girls become the objects of leering glances, an angry rebuke, and the offer of a dollar for a kiss from a drunken bum. As if by magic, the shoes have drawn unwanted attention to the budding sexuality of the young girls. As opposed to the blushing Cinderella whose symbol of salvation is a shoe, these young heroines learn that high-heeled shoes "are dangerous" (*House*, 38). They learn that the power their sexuality holds in attracting attention from males often has negative consequences.

Cisneros's portrayals of fairy-tale heroines are revisionist only in the sense that she applies a feminist analysis to the underlying messages that fairy tales convey to women. In drawing attention to how male domination, denial of personal ambition, lack of education, abuse, and low expectations affect women's lives, Cisneros attacks the weak heroine of the fairy tale who is "unable to act independently or self-assertively; she relies on external agents for rescue; she restricts her ambitions to hearth and nursery."[3] By revealing the concrete effects of waiting for someone to keep us "on a silver string," the author reveals the other side of the fate of the fairy-tale heroine.

Sandra Cisneros's use of operatic themes dates also to *The House on Mango Street*. Here, in a manner similar to her use of fairy tales, the author calls attention to the misogyny of patriarchal literature by way of reference to Puccini's *Madama Butterfly*. In a vignette entitled "A Smart Cookie," the protagonist's mother laments her own lack of education and the life it might have brought her: "I could've been somebody, you know? my mother says and sighs. She has lived in this city her whole life. She can speak two languages. She can sing an opera. She can fix a T.V." (*House*, 83). In this quote, the mother's knowledge of opera serves as confirmation of her intelligence. However, as the story continues, it becomes evident that the author has featured the protagonist of Puccini's opera in the story to represent the patriarchal archetype of feminine virtue and sacrifice. The narrator talks about her mother, saying, "Today while cooking oatmeal she is Madame Butterfly until she sighs and points the wooden spoon at me. I could've been somebody, you know? Esperanza, you go to school. Study hard. That Madame Butterfly was a fool. She stirs the oatmeal. Look at my comadres. She means Izaura whose husband left and Yolanda whose husband is dead. Got to take care all your own, she says shaking her head" (*House*, 83). The mother in "A Smart Cookie" has seen through the sentimentalization of the heroine's sacrifice. The lives of her sisters and comadres serve as evidence of the foolishness of relegating the direction of one's life to another. The mother's disgust with Butterfly's sacrifice mirrors the disgust she feels over her own self-destruction: "Shame is a bad thing, you know. It keeps you down. You want to know why I quit school? Because I didn't have nice clothes. No clothes, but I had brains. Yup, she says disgusted, stirring again. I was a smart cookie then" (*House*, 84). Again, Cisneros reveals the danger for women of being more concerned with the opinions and impressions of others and allowing these concerns to dominate one's life. The mother does not perceive poverty but a lack of internal authority to be the source of her loss.

Even though the stories in *The House on Mango Street* fail to rewrite the tragic fate of the heroine, there is a foreshadowing of the desire to do so. For instance, in the story "Beautiful and Cruel," the narrator claims as a role model a type of woman that she has seen in the movies. This woman is free, powerful, beautiful, and defiant:

> In the movies there is always one with red red lips who is beautiful and cruel. She is the one who drives the men crazy and laughs them all away. Her power is her own. She will not give it away.
>
> I have begun my own quiet war. Simple. Sure. I am one who leaves the table like a man, without putting back the chair or picking up the plate.
> (*House*, 82)

The narrator's gesture of defiance, leaving the table "like a man," signifies that she refuses to become a domesticated female. The heroine that Cisneros has created in this story will not self-destruct, nor will she give up control of her life. In the operatic realm, this character is most easily identified as Carmen. According to Catherine Clément's analysis of the ill-fated heroines of opera, the most feminist of these is "Carmen the Gypsy, Carmen the damned."[4] Carmen indeed is an operatic manifestation of Cisneros's "one with red, red lips," for Carmen "drives the men crazy and laughs them all away." Carmen, like the Medusa, the Sphinx, and the Minotaur, is a figure of paradox. The mere fact that she is a woman who acts like a man proves it, for within the symbolic order, the male occupies a position of active supremacy over the passivity of the female. To oppose that order is to invite disaster. Yet, what else could Carmen do? What Cisneros does not mention in "Beautiful and Cruel" is that according to the patriarchal literary tradition, the powerful and defiant female figure is inevitably punished for her audacity. That is why Clément refers to her as "Carmen the damned." The hierarchical structure upon which patriarchal societies are based cannot allow this carnivalesque figure to upset the social apple cart in which men are allowed more power and choices than women. According to Elisabeth Bronfen, the death of the female protagonist functions to eliminate a threat to the patriarchal order: "Countless examples could be given to illustrate how the death of a woman helps to regenerate the order of society, to eliminate destructive forces or serves to reaggregate the protagonist into her or his community."[5] The defiant Carmen must be suppressed or die, and since she will never give her power away, she is killed.

The story "La Fabulosa: A Texas Operetta" appears in the collection by Sandra Cisneros entitled *Woman Hollering Creek and Other Stories*. This story at first reading is notable because of one salient and surprising element: the heroine does not die. Not only is she *not* punished for her freewheeling ways, but she flourishes and thrives. In this incongruous tale, the active, independent, and defiant woman is the one who "lives happily ever after." Upon closer examination, the reader discovers the subtext of this story. This is a revision of *Carmen*. The first clue Cisneros allows the reader is the title: "La Fabulosa: A Texas Operetta." The author gives an adulatory nickname to her protagonist, changes the context of the story from Spain to Texas, and calls the work an "operetta," a small opera.

In the first paragraph of the story Cisneros makes a tongue-in-cheek reference to the Spanish heritage of the original Carmen: "She likes to say she's 'Spanish,' but she's from Laredo like the rest of us—or 'Lardo,' as we call it. Her name is Berriozábal. Carmen."[6] On one level, the narrator appears to be ridiculing this character, who, like many Mexican Americans, attempts to "whitewash" herself by ignoring her Indian heritage and eschewing the word "Mexican" in exchange for "Spanish." On another level, of course, Cisneros is associating her protagonist with the operatic figure.

The narrator continues with a description of the protagonist. Her most salient physical trait is her large breasts: "big *chichis*, I mean big" (*Woman*, 61). Carmen's other characteristic trait is her independent nature. "Carmen was a take-it-or-leave-it type of woman. If you don't like it, there's the door. Like that. She was something" (*Woman*, 61). While in some ways Cisneros's heroine is a quintessential feminist, unlike many authors, Cisneros avoids an idealization of her heroine. The narrator describes her as "not smart. I mean, she didn't know enough to get her teeth cleaned every year, or to buy herself a duplex" (*Woman*, 62). Although the protagonist is portrayed as a woman of limited attributes, this does not detract from her status as a heroine worthy of a happy end.

Cisneros's plot mirrors the opera in many ways. At the beginning of the Prosper Merimée plot, Carmen has taken as her lover a brigadier named Don

José. The Chicana Carmen becomes involved with a corporal at Fort Sam Houston named José Arrambide. The Spanish Don José is engaged to a sweet young thing named Micaela who is waiting for him to marry her. In Cisneros's version, José's high school sweetheart "sold nachos at the mall, still waiting for him to come back to Harlingen, marry her, and buy that three-piece bedroom set on layaway" (*Woman*, 61). In the figure of Micaela, both plots include a reference to the classic fairy-tale heroine, the demure and passive one who waits for her prince to take charge of her life. She is often used in literature as the virtuous foil of the lecherous, adventurous "witches and bitches." According to Karen Rowe's analysis of fairy-tale figures, "Because cleverness, will-power, and manipulative skill are allied with vanity, shrewishness, and ugliness, and because of their gruesome fates, odious females hardly recommend themselves as models for young readers. And because they surround alternative roles as life-long maidens or fiendish stepmothers with opprobrium, romantic tales effectively sabotage female assertiveness."[7] Another Micaela-like figure in opera is Alfredo's sister in *La Traviata*. This virginal character provides the motivation for the courtesan's sacrifice of her own happiness, in order that the other woman may make a financially and socially profitable marriage. Carmen, however, makes no sacrifice and fearlessly confronts her announced fate.

Again, according to Merrimée's story, Carmen entices Don José to abandon the army and join a group of smugglers, then leaves him for a toreador named Escamillo. Cisneros, on the other hand, has Carmen leave José for an ambitious Texas senator named Camilo Escamilla (*Woman*, 62). In both stories, the besotted José is overcome with rejection and the realization that he has no control over Carmen. The opera ends as José confronts Carmen outside the bullring. Carmen defiantly proclaims her love for Escamillo before she is stabbed to death by her former lover. The violent death of the rebellious heroine is deemed as necessary in a symbolic system where the existence of a free and enterprising female is viewed as seditious and damaging to the social order. This tendency is as common, Rowe observes, in mythic tales as much as opera libretti: "By punishing exhibitions of feminine force, tales admonish, moreover, that any disruptive nonconformity will result in annihilation or social ostracism."[8] While Western literature provides few examples of the rebellious feminine, these characters are necessarily punished in order to serve as an example to potential Carmens.

Catherine Clément has made an intriguing analysis of how Georges Bizet's score musically represents the conflict between the unfettered feminine versus the hierarchical rigidity of the patriarchal order. She identifies Bizet's use of tonality as a technique of representing the patriarchal social order in which the masculine has dominion over the feminine.[9] Within this context, the term "tonality" refers to music written in a key according to the paradigm of a seven-tone scale.[10] In its linear quality and the rigidity with which the tonal scale differentiates between notes considered harmonious and dissonant in each key, tonality could be said to correspond to the oppositional qualities of symbolic texts.

As Julia Kristeva has emphasized, in Western thought the "symbolic" is based upon the definition of elements of reality by means of restriction. These elements, then, are oriented according to mutual opposition, a system of opposition hierarchically organized in such a manner that good occupies a position superior to evil, light to dark, and male to female. It might be argued that the importance of the symbolic in patriarchal society is to maintain this hierarchical paradigm. The "semiotic" modality, on the other hand, is perceived to be seditious in its ignorance of phallocentric paradigms and traditions. It does not operate upon an epistemology of opposition and heirarchy. One of the primary characteristics of the semiotic modality is the figure of paradox. In its unification of disparate entities, the figure of paradox by definition defies the oppositional structure of the symbolic. The unclassifiable nature of paradox is, at the very least, threatening to the rational order of the symbolic, represented by mythic figures of opposition such as the male hero and the passive heroine.[11] When paradox does enter into the realm of myth it is considered to be disruptive, even evil. In Western mythology at least, when a male hero confronts a figure of paradox, the hero inevitably prevails. This pattern is evident when one notes that in classical mythology Theseus slew the Minotaur and defeated an army of Amazons, Perseus beheaded the Medusa, and Hercules took the golden girdle of Ares from Hippolyte, the queen of the Amazons.

According to Clément, Bizet's use of chromaticism serves to challenge the supremacy of the tonal scale just as the semiotic modality challenges the patriarchal authority of the symbolic. Chromaticism, which came into common use in Western music during the end of the Romantic period, was used to stretch and blur the authoritative and restrictive quality of tonal music.[12] Clément describes chromaticism as "the sultry, slippery, seductive female who taunts and entraps, who needs to be brought back under tonal domination and absorbed."[13] The correlations between tonality and the symbolic order compared to those of chromaticism and the semiotic are remarkable. Within the domains of language and music, these modalities serve, respectively, to sustain and repudiate patriarchal epistemologies.

Within the text-score of *Carmen* we can see that chromaticism serves to disrupt a strict sense of tonality, just as the heroine diverts José from his militaristic discipline: as Clément remarks, "Carmen makes her first appearance with the slippery descent of her 'Habanera' and it is her harmonic promiscuity—which threatens to undermine Don José's drive for absolute tonal closure at the conclusion of the opera—that finally renders her death *musically necessary*."[14] The predominance of the symbolic over the semiotic is made manifest by the defeat of the paradoxical figure of the active woman. Although Bizet's opera includes one of the most powerful of operatic heroines, her demise is as ignominious and inevitable as the rest. The Amazon is conquered again.

In her "Texas Operetta," Sandra Cisneros acknowledges the literary tradition that punishes audacious heroines, yet she chooses to defy that tradition by rewriting millennia of literary history. Instead of imposing a finite conclusion upon the reader, Cisneros offers three possible endings from which to choose. The elective nature of the conclusion is created by the testimonial form of the narration: "According to who you talk to, you hear different" (*Woman*, 62). The first conclusion is similar to that of the opera in that José attacks Carmen with a knife: "José's friends say he left his initials across those famous chichis with a knife." The violence of this ending is mitigated by the skeptical attitude of the narrator: "but that sure sounds like talk, don't it?" (*Woman*, 62).

The second conclusion focuses on the male protagonist's pain: "*I* heard he went AWOL. Became a bullfighter in Matamoros, just so he could die like a man" (*Woman*, 62). The figure of Escamillo is alluded to with the reference to bullfighting. The expressed desire to "die like a man" represents the deleterious effect that Carmen's strength has upon the masculinity of the hero. This version of the conclusion turns the narrative violence of self-destructive tendencies toward the male figure. Of course, this particular twist is quite rare in the operatic tradition, as women in opera are forever dying for, or because of, men. This option is provided in the following sentence: "Somebody else said *she's* the one who wants to die" (*Woman*, 62).

The first two conclusions provided in "La Fabulosa: A Texas Operetta" fall into the register of the symbolic, under which only one of two opposing forces can prevail. Hélène Cixous deems it inappropriate for feminists to follow this traditional "rational" system in their writing. She observes: "Opposition, hierarchizing exchange, the struggle for mastery which can end only in at least one death (one master–one slave, or two nonmasters = two dead)—all that comes from a period in time governed by phallocentric values."[15] In an effort to provide a literary space where resolution is not based upon unilateral annihilation, Cisneros provides another possible conclusion. Despite the discretionary quality presented by the inclusion of alternate endings, Cisneros uses

the voice of the female narrator to give authority to the last and most felici-
tous conclusion. The narrator begins by denying the veracity of the first two
denouements: "Don't you believe it. She ran off with King Kong Cárdenas,
a professional wrestler from Crystal City and a sweetie. I know her cousin
Lerma, and we saw her just last week at the Floore Country Store in Helotes.
Hell, she bought us a beer, two-stepped and twirled away to 'Hey Baby Qué
Pasó'" (*Woman*, 62). Cisneros refuses to allow the suppression of the rebellious, chromatic feminine. This Carmen not only is not punished, but continues upon her adventurous path, finding love with a nurturing, masculine
partner. The Tex-Mex hit "Hey Baby Qué Pasó" includes the only reference
to the fate of José in this last version of "La Fabulosa's" conclusion. The lyrics
include the phrases: "Hey baby, ¿qué pasó? / Porque me tienes el loco / No
me dejes de ese modo."[16] Cisneros uses this musical reference to create the
background for Carmen's joyous exit from the story. Instead of the righteous
and apocalyptic climax created by Bizet for the death of the heroine, the Chicana author employs a joyous polka by the Texas Tornados, appropriate for
triumphant Carmen. In spite of the celebratory quality of the song, one can
hear the echoes of José's incredulity in the chorus: "Hey baby, ¿qué pasó?"

Sandra Cisneros is indeed skillful in utilizing long-established literary traditions for revolutionary purposes. Her versions of Cinderella and Rapunzel
turn the classic versions inside-out to disclose the real consequences for
women of patriarchal socialization. Within her stories, Cisneros reveals the
metaphoric death of the fairy-tale heroine. Although the princesses of the
classic fairy tales supposedly go on to live "happily ever after," we never hear
of their lives or paths of growth after the nuptials to the handsome prince.
Cisneros picks up the tale and tells the *real* fate of the heroine who lives in
patriarchy.

Within the operatic tradition there is no need to uncover the propensity for
misogyny. On the contrary, scenes of women murdered at the hands of men
or who commit suicide on behalf of men number among the most glorified
moments in opera. In one salient characteristic, however, opera differs from
the fairy tale. In the classic children's stories, the sweet, pliant princesses are
rewarded by marriage to the prince, while the only active characters, witches
and wicked stepmothers, are vilified and often punished with gruesome
deaths. Opera libretti, on the other hand, tend to punish with remarkable
regularity the passive heroine as well as the active, rebellious one. Sandra Cisneros defies this tradition in opera and other narrative forms by recreating the
powerful female figure of Carmen and allowing her to live and thrive. Just as
she retells the fairy tale in a more realistic light, Cisneros changes the context
of the opera *Carmen* from nineteenth-century Seville to modern-day Texas.

However, by altering the standard denouement of the tragedy in a way that contradicts the patriarchal necessity of opposition and the ultimate domination of the male, Cisneros dismisses the tradition of eliminating the paradoxical figure of a powerful woman. Through her revisions of fairy tales and *Carmen*, Sandra Cisneros's works demonstrate how literature can challenge deeply inculcated values and change the ways in which we perceive the world. Consequently, she tells stories that shake the roots of a literary tradition as old as the fairy tale.

NOTES

1. Catherine Clément, *Opera, or the Undoing of Women*, trans. Betsy Wing (Minneapolis: University of Minnesota Press, 1988), 47.

2. Sandra Cisneros, *The House on Mango Street* (Houston: Arte Público Press, 1985), 76. Subsequent references will be cited in the text as *House*.

3. Karen E. Rowe, "Feminism and Fairy Tales," in *Don't Bet on the Prince: Contemporary Feminist Fairy Tales in North America and England*, ed. Jack E. Zipes (New York: Methuen, 1986), 211.

4. Clément, 48.

5. Elisabeth Bronfen, *Over Her Dead Body: Death, Femininity and the Aesthetic* (New York: Routledge, 1992), 219.

6. Sandra Cisneros, *Woman Hollering Creek and Other Stories* (New York: Random House, 1991), 61. Subsequent references will be cited in the text as *Woman*.

7. Rowe, 218.

8. Ibid.

9. Clément, xiii.

10. "Tonality," *The New Harvard Dictionary of Music*, ed. Don Michael Randel (Cambridge: Harvard University Press, 1986).

11. Julia Kristeva, *Desire in Language: A Semiotic Approach to Literature and Art*, ed. Leon S. Roudiez, trans. Thomas Gora, Alice Jardine, and Roudiez (New York: Columbia University Press, 1980), 38–39.

12. "Chromaticism," *The New Harvard Dictionary of Music*.

13. Clément, iii.

14. Ibid., xiii.

15. Hélène Cixous, "The Laugh of the Medusa," *Signs* 1.4 (Summer 1976): 893.

16. Augie Myers and Bill Sheffield, "(Hey Baby) Qué Pasó" (San Marcos, Tex.: Brujo Music), *Los Texas Tornados*, compact disc, Reprise Records, 1990.

Amy Lowell and Cultural Borders

PAUL LAUTER

I began thinking about Amy Lowell in connection with a book I have been writing on the construction of cultural authority, and particularly academic cultural authority, in the 1920s and thereafter. The hegemony of New Critical and Cold War cultural paradigms in which I had been trained in the 1950s at Indiana and Yale had long troubled me, even as I had to acknowledge their continuing power. Work on the book led me to ask what alternatives had been in the field when Eliot, Pound, and their academic successors developed the literary canon I had initially learned and shaped accounts of literary history and poetic value so determinative of later pedagogical and critical practice. Since history, including cultural history, is, if not written by the winners, certainly written about them, it is easy to forget the conflicted nature of social and cultural change. Yet any historical moment, looked at closely, will display a contest for authority, among differing—and generally antagonistic—parties. The problem is to unearth those accounted as "losers" from the cultural debris heaped upon them by their opponents.

I followed Cary Nelson's proposal that, to know the real character of a culture, one should look most closely at what it scorns.[1] Apart from the working-class writers in whom I had long been interested, I was quickly drawn to writers of the New Negro Renaissance, marginalized in ways even a political activist like me found remarkable, and, odd choice at first glance, to Amy Lowell. What was striking to me as I read about her (to the extent that there was anything useful to read) was the degree to which she had been and continued to be marginalized, even in the midst of a feminist revival.[2] And, she was, moreover, the subject of a degree of vituperative comment that made some of the attacks on Kate Millett's *Sexual Politics* seem mild.

To fill out the first point with a few statistics: in the last twenty-five years, according to the MLA *Bibliography*, about 28 books and articles devoted to Lowell have been published. By way of comparison, 33 have been devoted to Nella Larsen, 44 each to Louise Bogan and Edna St. Vincent Millay, 112 to Djuna Barnes, 202 to Zora Neale Hurston, 318 each to H.D. and Marianne Moore. The champion, with a score of 426, is Gertrude Stein. Champion among the women, to be sure. Eliot's total of books and articles is 522—with many more in earlier decades—and the indefatigible Pound's an amazing 2,063. The figures register what we are mostly familiar with: that interest in Lowell declined sharply after her death in 1925 and that writers like Pound and Eliot, and even Stein and H.D., preoccupy the academics most likely to produce books and articles on literary subjects.

Indeed, the figures alone really do not tell us much that we did not know. The character of the writing about Lowell is much more indicative. By writing, I mean not only chapters, articles, or substantial units devoted to her work, but brief comments as well, a sentence or phrase here, a nasty crack there. For Lowell often provides an object of derision against which the virtues of other writers, especially male modernists like Pound, are constructed. In fact, I began to find it puzzling that critics should devote all the energy it takes to write a book to a person many of them seemed altogether to despise. Immediately after Lowell's death, for example, Clement Wood prepared a volume on her which attacks her poetry as, in its nature, an expression of her perverse desires.[3]

More characteristically, perhaps, Horace Gregory in 1958 published a two-hundred-page volume that concludes that Lowell was an "archetypical American clubwoman," a circus barker for poetry, a Leigh Hunt of her time. But, he writes, "one should not conclude that the 'barker' because of his activity is a poet."[4] Similarly, a decade later Cudworth Flint concludes his Minnesota pamphlet with, "She cannot be left out of any history of American poetry of her time" any more than the stage manager of a new company could be absent from its performance of *Hamlet*.[5] The operative tone of much of the writing on Lowell between her death and the last few years is represented by the questions posed in Horace Gregory and Marya Zaturenska: "Was she a great poet? Was Amy Lowell a poet at all?"[6] They go on to answer their questions, in the negative, by quoting Winfield Townley Scott: "Her poems are the work of a woman who would have shown as extraordinary in any career; they are, even at their most expert, remarkable in the very light of their weakness, for Amy Lowell was not a poet at all."[7]

More and more it came to seem to me that Lowell was peculiarly threatening to many of her critics, less personally engaged with her than the vituperative Pound had been. I wondered what it was in Lowell that so menaced, even at distances of a quarter century and more. I will return to this question shortly.

To be sure, there was much about Lowell's background and manner to antagonize opponents. From one of New England's most prominent, and wealthy, families, she lived much of her life in the family's Brookline mansion, Sevenels. Shy, overweight, and prefering the avocations of boys, she disliked schools, spending as little time as she could trapped in them. With her father's death in 1900, she came into possession of Sevenels, a prominent social position, and more money, but little sense of vocation. Sometime during the first decade of the century, however, she began to chart out a course for herself as a literary figure, and toward that goal she applied her talents, prodigious energy, and funds. She wrote poetry extensively (eleven books in fifteen years), including her funny and controversial take on her peers, A *Critical Fable* (1922). She also collected volumes and manuscripts of Keats; she was ultimately to publish an impressive two-volume study of the poet. She sought out the young movers and shakers of the new renaissance in American poetry and organized a number of them into imagist collections and other poetic ventures, read widely to great response (favorable and otherwise) at poetry societies and colleges across the country, and entered into well-publicized cultural brawls with poetry traditionalists as well as with figures like Pound. In 1914, she also persuaded Ada Dwyer Russell to share her life at Sevenels, where they were able to build a certain sanctuary within a life of activity and contest. In ill-health, to which her obesity contributed, through much of the last eight years of her life, Lowell died just after the Keats book was published in 1925, at age fifty-one.

In reading Lowell and her adversaries I was struck by the discrepancy between the considerable body of her critical writing and the virtual absence of discussion of it, even by commentators willing to examine her poetry. Gay Wilson Allen (later to be known as the biographer of Whitman) devoted considerable space to Lowell (and none to Pound, incidentally) in his 1935 book on *American Prosody*, but few have followed his lead and, so far as I know, none of Lowell's prose works has been in print for over thirty years.[8] I was reminded of the question: "What counts as theory?" For Lowell's critical work provides an interesting contrast to that of Eliot and Pound. Pound, it has seemed to me, is filled with negative prescriptions, poetic "don'ts," which is what he entitled a brief manifesto of the Imagist period. While he was obviously a significant force in encouraging and teaching some younger poets, and in editing Eliot, he somehow always evokes for me Blake's line from "The Garden of Love" about "binding with briars my joys & desires." He is concerned to differentiate the modern from the Victorian, the hard-edged from the "sentimental," the discipline of rhyme from the "prose kinema"—in short, to establish and ardently to police borders. Eliot, too, takes on such roles. His canon-establishing essay "The Metaphysical Poets" is primarily concerned to trace the true "main current" of English poetry, from the Elizabethan dramatists, through the Metaphysical poets, and, by way of certain French *symbolistes*, to the high modernism of . . . well, himself. And thus to distinguish the legitimate line of succession from the false alternatives of Milton and Dryden and, more particularly, from the dissipating ruminations of his Romantic predecessors. Eliot's project, after all, was not simply to validate tradition over against the lure of personal expressiveness, but to establish a *particular* tradition as central to what is nowadays talked about as "western civilization."

By contrast, Lowell's theoretical work, including the "Manifesto" she and Richard Aldington prepared for the first imagist collection she gathered, is more eclectic, inclusive, perhaps unsystematic.[9] Some have seen it as theoretically sloppy, even contradictory. Certainly Lowell's practice, as Flint, among others, points out, seems full of contradictions. While, for example, she proclaimed herself an Imagist, beginning with objects and suggesting significance for them, she as often practiced a form of symbolism, beginning with subjective states or "a significance" and finding images to express them.[10]

This kind of contradictory practice suggested to me that maybe it was precisely Lowell's boundary-dissolving qualities that have been the source of her threat, personal and poetic. She represents a sharp departure from late-Victorian and Pre-Raphaelite models, as the poetry societies of her time recognized. Yet neither did she fall into the high modernist camp, at least as its boundaries were constructed by Pound and Eliot, and walled higher by academic New Critics. She was a poet and a promoter of poetry (a "demon saleswoman" of poetry, Eliot called her), but she clearly saw these roles as integrated, not discontinuous, much less contradictory, as critics like Gregory supposed. In particular, she did not see opening venues for women to write poetry and writing it herself as separable enterprises. Similarly, she was unwilling to separate poetry as an object of study from poetry as a performed text. Indeed, she insisted—a point to which I will return—that "Imagism is presentation, not representation."[11] She was a woman, but—as many of her biographers have insisted on describing it—"masculine" in her demeanor, in her enterprise, as well as in the public persona she constructed with an acute, sometimes campy mix of humor and seriousness.

It is worth quoting at length Alfred Kreymborg's 1929 comment to get a sense of how contradictorily, and indignantly, she was often viewed:

Her own role was not the role of an artist, so much as a mummer's—an actress in male attire. One thought of her as a buccaneer scuttling the craft of conservatives and even going so far as to strip radical vessels of their best prizes. But the masculine Miss Lowell was more than a pirate. The one time I dined at the Brookline estate, I felt as if I were in audience with a late Roman emperor—possibly Nero fiddling among the flames. And yet,

I learned to know her a little more closely, perhaps more accurately. In unguarded moments, she seemed an intensely feminine person, not without innocence and wistfulness, and I decided—if one can ever decide anything—that her abnormal ambition and industry had obscured her true character. The role she played for the world was masculine, valiant, combatative—and the inner being, private, lonely susceptible to human fragility.[12]

And this, I need to emphasize, was a relatively sympathetic portrait.

Finally, as every male and many female writers about Lowell make it impossible to forget, she is insistently embodied: she read poetry about throwing off clothes, asserting in a culture increasingly mad for feminine thinness her corporeal self (about which, at the same time, she was intensely embarrassed—and very possibly proud, too). It was not, then, only her poetry that she conceived, and delivered, as "presentational," but her self.

It came to seem to me, then, that Lowell's boundary-challenging qualities were distinctively threatening, especially in times, like the 1920s and 1950s, of hysteria over boundary maintenance, indeed, in times when maintaining the borders became matters literally of life and death. One thinks of texts from Nella Larsen's *Passing* to Adolf Schicklgruber's *Mein Kampf*, in which the boundaries between black and white, Jew and Aryan take on lethal dimensions. For myself, I came to contemplate particularly the cold-war culture in which I was trained as a New Critic in the 1950s. One might view that time as a culminating moment of boundary hysteria, when the search for duplicitous Reds, hiding as democrats, obsessed even supposed political liberals, let alone traditionalists; when drawing and policing boundaries—the 38th Parallel, the Berlin Wall, the divide between the Vietnams—became a central goal of national elites, on both sides of the Iron Curtain.[13] It was a time, too, of often savage efforts to reinscribe gender boundaries, loosened by the movement and urban concentration brought on by World War II.[14] Rosie was to learn to be content at home, and Johnnie could learn to be cured of "homosexual tendencies" in the therapist's office. One turns to Ginsberg's "America"—"Go fuck yourself with your atom bomb / . . . I'm putting my queer shoulder to the wheel"—with a profound breath of relief.

I feel confirmed in this view of Lowell's threat by the recent turn toward serious interest in her. It comes precisely at the moment in which the dissolution of borders, the stance of liminality, is embraced by many cultural workers, even in the face of right-wing attacks on lesbian and gay studies in colleges, on the rights of homosexuals in the military, and on their bodies in the streets of American cities.[15] Suddenly Lowell seems to be emerging as a striking transitional figure in the work of Lillian Faderman, Cheryl Walker, and Betsy Erkkila, to name three of the most prominent critics. Faderman poses Lowell's grouping "Two Speak Together," a series of effective love poems from the 1919 volume *Pictures of the Floating World*, as the most fully articulated sequence of lesbian poetry between Sappho and the 1960s, so successfully coded that critics even within the past decade miss its point.[16] Walker presents Lowell as an archetype of the androgynous, desiring "to melt her categories, male and female." Walker takes her up precisely because her "contradictions are instructive."[17] Erkkila's brilliant reading of "The Sisters," one of Lowell's most important poems, opens the poet's altogether conflicted relationships both with the women writers she claims as her predecessors and those others Lowell herself ambivalently marginalizes.[18]

Lowell thus becomes interesting in our conflicted and tense cultural moment because she was not in any sense "free" either to express her sexuality or to police it. She could not have the confidence—or perhaps bravado—of overseas 1920s lesbian communities, or even of the more modest bohemianism of the Village. On the contrary, at the center of many of her most interesting poems, like "Venus Transiens," are painfully contradictory impulses toward revelation, display, or even a certain form of "flaunting," and hiding, a poetics of the closet, as I have suggested elsewhere.[19] A much less familiar, but excellent, poem may serve to focus this point, entitled "The On-Looker":

Suppose I plant you
Like wide-eyed Helen
On the battlements
Of weary Troy,
Clutching the parapet with desperate hands.
She, too, gazes at a battle-field
Where bright vermilion plumes and metal whiteness
Shock and sparkle and go down with groans.
Her glances strike the rocking battle,
Again—again—
Recoiling from it
Like baffled spear-heads fallen from a brazen shield.
The ancients at her elbow counsel patience and contingencies;
Such to a woman stretched upon a bed of battle,
Who bargained for this only in the whispering arras
Enclosed about a midnight of enchantment.[20]

Like many of Lowell's best poems, this one presents a speaker ambiguously gendered, a distinctly female "you," and a woman from history or myth (like

Botticelli's Venus in "Venus Transiens"). Unlike the lesbian sequence in *Pictures of the Floating World*, however, this poem is filled with combat, weariness, even desperation derived from a secretive "midnight of enchantment": the enclosed closet of passion has become a painfully public "bed of battle." Both the person addressed and Helen look down at "a battle-field," a too-brightly etched male domain of metal and contention, in which the weapons of the onlookers' gaze are ineffectual. Nor do traditional pieties offer comfort; on the contrary, the language of convention sounds insulting to the ear of such an embattled woman. All this the speaker knows. Yet is she warning, inviting, or perhaps both? The poem remains elusive at that level: on one hand, the speaker clearly wishes to connect the desperation of Helen—and potentially the woman addressed—with two familiar arenas of female literary experience: the enraptured bed and the on-looking parapet. On the other hand, did not Helen, does not the person addressed, "bargain" the consequences of a perhaps sado-masochistic and certainly closeted passion? Read in an orthodox way, hypothesizing a male speaker, this poem can be connected to Lowell's familiar "Patterns" and other poems of war-abandoned women. But read from within the framework of knowledge that the speaker, the addressed, and Helen seem to share—a woman's knowledge—the poem proposes a less literal set of events, a symbolic and direct engagement *in* battle rather than a reaction of isolation *from* it. One could, indeed, argue that battle is here posed both as the consequence of and the alternative to the closet of passion, the story of which is concealed and, it may be, simultaneously "whispered" abroad by Lowell's verbal tapestry.

Such different readings depend critically upon the construction of the speaker's gender, a matter, I would argue, decisive to far more of Lowell's better poems than has usually been accounted. One of Lowell's accomplishments, as Lillian Faderman has shown at length, was her clearly calculated strategy of using the conventions of amorous male poetry to encode lesbian desire. Not surprisingly, as I have tried briefly to suggest here, the reevaluation of Lowell derives in some measure from such an ambiguously gendered borderland, where traditional narratives of women as observers are converted into metaphors that construct and dismantle the closet.

Which suggests one further basis of the renewed interest in Lowell: her insistence, about which I commented briefly above, on "presentation" or performance as central to constructing poetry as well as identity. In poetry as in life, I think, Lowell struggled precisely with the contradictions between experienced and constructed sexual identities that preoccupy Queer theory today.[21] "The On-Looker" begins with "Suppose," an invitation to pretend, to don the mask of Helen, "stretched upon a bed of battle." Here a fourth participant, the reader, enters the poem's action: Toward what midnight masque are we being invited? In whose production are we being asked to join? Paris, of course, is nowhere to be found, only a conflicted writer invoking beauty and anguish, the bedroom and the battlefield, to create her possible identities. I would not wish to argue that Lowell anticipates the complex arguments of today's essentialists and social constructionists, only that her work embodies the lived experience of one who found herself "stretched upon a bed" of equivalent battle.

During and after her life, Amy Lowell was often the butt of male humor. Indeed, the more she rushed into literary combat, the more she was derided. Whether she ever sufficiently turned the joke while she lived we will probably never know. But there is a fine and pleasing irony in the fact that now, seventy-some years later, her work can become part of a cultural movement bringing into question the borders her antagonists struggled so hard to erect and maintain.

NOTES

1. "We also need to reevaluate precisely those texts we habitually mark as mediocre. A second axiom, then, can be stated baldly: we should always read what people assure us is no good. Finally, we need to rediscover poets whose work is no longer even mentioned in most literary histories" (*Repression and Recovery: Modern American Poetry and the Politics of Cultural Memory, 1910–1945* [Madison: University of Wisconsin Press, 1989], 51).

2. Useful information, including a selected and annotated bibliography, is contained in Ricard Benvenuto, *Amy Lowell* (Boston: Twayne, 1985). Jean Gould, *Amy: The World of Amy Lowell and the Imagist Movement* (New York: Dodd, Mead, 1975) is probably the most useful biography.

3. Clement Wood, *Amy Lowell* (New York: Harold Vinal, 1926). Ironically, perhaps, the publisher is the same fellow derided in e. e. cummings's "Poem, or Beauty Hurts Mr. Vinal."

4. Horace Gregory, *Amy Lowell* (New York: Thomas Nelson and Sons, 1958), 208, 206.

5. F. Cudworth Flint, *Amy Lowell* (Minneapolis: University of Minnesota Press, 1969), 44.

6. Horace Gregory and Marya Zaturenska, *A History of American Poetry, 1900–1940* (New York: Harcourt, Brace, 1942), 183.

7. The Scott quotation is from his "Amy Lowell after Ten Years," *New England Quarterly* 8 (September 1935).

8. Gay Wilson Allen, *American Prosody* (New York: American Book Company, 1935).

9. Amy Lowell and Richard Aldington, eds., *Some Imagist Poets (With a Preface on*

Imagism) (Boston: Houghton Mifflin, 1915). Lowell reproduces and comments interestingly on these tenets in "'H.D.' and John Gould Fletcher," *Tendencies in Modern American Poetry* (Boston: Houghton Mifflin, 1917), 239–47.

10. Flint, 25.

11. *Tendencies in Modern American Poetry*, 245.

12. Alfred Kreymborg, *Our Singing Strength* (New York: Coward-McCann, 1929), 354.

13. See, for example, William Epstein, "Counter-Intelligence: Cold-War Criticism and Eighteenth-Century Studies," *ELH* 57 (1990): 63–99.

14. See, for example, John D'Emilio, "Capitalism and Gay Identity," in *The Lesbian and Gay Studies Reader*, ed. Henry Abelove, Michèle Aina Barale, and David M. Halperin (New York: Routledge, 1993), 467–76; and Robert J. Corber, *In the Name of National Security: Hitchcock, Homophobia, and the Political Construction of Gender in Postwar America* (Durham: Duke University Press, 1993).

15. The widespread interest in Gloria Anzaldúa's *Borderlands/ La Frontera: The New Mestiza* (San Francisco: Spinsters/Aunt Lute, 1987) reflects such concerns.

16. Lillian Faderman, "'Which, Being Interpreted, Is As May Be, Or Otherwise': The Lesbian Poetry of Amy Lowell," ms. from forthcoming book on lesbian encoding. Cf. Faderman's earlier groundbreaking essay "Warding Off the Watch and Ward Society: Amy Lowell's Treatment of the Lesbian Theme," *Gay Books Bulletin* 1 (Summer 1979): 23–27.

17. Cheryl Walker, *Masks Outrageous and Austere* (Bloomington: Indiana University Press, 1991), 17, 43, and more generally, 16–43.

18. Betsy Erkkila, "Rethinking Women's Literary History," *The Wicked Sisters* (New York: Oxford, 1992), 8–14.

19. Paul Lauter, "Little White Sheep, or How I Learned to Dress Blue," *Yale Journal of Criticism* 8 (1995): 103–29, especially 113–20.

20. Amy Lowell, *What's O'Clock* (Boston: Houghton Mifflin, 1925), 66–67. The volume contains some of Lowell's best work, including "The Sisters," "Lilacs," "Purple Grackles," and "Which, Being Interpreted, Is as May Be, or Otherwise."

21. A useful summary of some of the arguments by, among others, Judith Butler, Sue-Ellen Case, and Mary Ann Doane is provided by Ruth D. Johnston in "Academic Voguing, or the Politics of Appropriation," *Concerns* 23 (Fall 1993): 17–24. On the issue of "performance" see, among other works, Sue-Ellen Case, ed., *Performing Feminisms: Feminist Critical Theory and Theater* (Baltimore: Johns Hopkins University Press, 1990); Lynda Hart, ed., *Making a Spectacle* (Ann Arbor: University of Michigan Press, 1989); and Alisa Solomon, "Not Just a Passing Fancy: Notes on Butch," *Theater* 24 (1993): 35–46.

Contributors

Victoria Aarons, professor of English at Trinity University, has published extensively on American Jewish writers, including Bernard Malamud, Delmore Schwartz, and Grace Paley. Aarons is the author of *The Measure of Memory: Storytelling and Identity in American-Jewish Fiction* (1996).

Jacqueline Vaught Brogan, professor of English at the University of Notre Dame, is a poet and critic. Among her numerous publications are *Stevens and Simile: A Theory of Language* (1986) and *Part of the Climate: American Cubist Poetry* (1991). She is currently coediting *Women Poets of the Americas*, as well as working on the conjunction of politics and poetics in the work of Elizabeth Bishop and on her own poetic sequence.

Donna M. Campbell is assistant professor of English at Gonzaga University. Her articles on Frank Norris and Mary Wilkins Freeman, Louisa May Alcott and Susan Warner, and Edith Wharton have appeared in *American Literary Realism*, *Legacy*, and *Studies in American Fiction*. Her book *Resisting Regionalism: Gender and Naturalism in American Fiction, 1885–1915* (1997), won the 1995 NEMLA–Ohio University Press Book Award.

Rae M. Carlton Colley is a Ph.D. candidate and instructor of English at Emory University. She has published on Katherine Anne Porter, Caroline Lee Hentz, Lydia Maria Child, part-time faculty, and pedagogical issues. She has served as Book Review editor for *Southern Lifestyles* magazine and editor of *Georgia On My Mind* magazine. She is at work on a dissertation on early southern women writers and their Native American subjects and influences.

Jerry Dickey is associate professor and director of Graduate Studies in Theatre Arts at the University of Arizona. His article on Sophie Treadwell's plagiarism lawsuit against John Barrymore appeared in the 1995 issue of *History of Theatre Studies*. Previous publications have appeared in *Theatre Journal*, *Theatre Topics*, the *New England Theatre Journal*, and *Old West-New West: Centennial Essays*. Dickey is a past-chair of ATHE's Theatre History Focus Group, and is author of a sourcebook on Sophie Treadwell.

Sharon M. Harris is associate professor in the Department of English at the University of Nebraska. She is the author of *Rebecca Harding Davis and American Realism* (1991) and editor of *Redefining the Political Novel: American Women Writers, 1797–1901* (1995), *Selected Writings of Judith Sargent Murray* (1995), and *American Women Writers to 1800* (1995). Harris is also vice president of the Society of Early Americanists, and coeditor of *Legacy: A Journal of American Women Writers*.

Trudier Harris is J. Carlyle Sitterson Professor of English at the University of North Carolina. She has lectured worldwide and published numerous works in her specialty areas of African American literature and folklore. She is the author of *From*

Mammies to Militants: Domestics in Black American Literature (1982), *Exorcising Blackness: Historical and Literary Lynching and Burning Rituals* (1984), *Black Women in the Fiction of James Baldwin* (1985), *Fiction and Folklore: The Novels of Toni Morrison* (1991), and *The Power of the Porch: The Storyteller's Craft in Zora Neale Hurston, Gloria Naylor, and Randall Kenan* (1996). She also coedited three volumes of the *Dictionary of Literary Biography* series on African American writers and edited three additional volumes. She has just completed coediting *The Oxford Companion to African American Literature*.

Ronna C. Johnson has taught American literature, American Studies, and Women's Studies at Tufts University, where she also directed the women's studies program. She writes on nineteenth- and twentieth-century U.S. literature and is currently completing a book on gender and narrative in Jack Kerouac.

Paul Lauter is Allen K. and Gwendolyn Miles Smith Professor of Literature at Trinity College (Hartford). He is the general editor of the revisionist *Heath Anthology of American Literature*, author of *Canons and Contexts*, among other books, and is president of the American Studies Association.

Lisa Marcus is assistant professor of English at Pacific Lutheran University in Tacoma, Washington, where she teaches American Ethnic Literature and Feminist Theory. With Elaine Hedges, she is editing a special project for *Signs* on feminism and generational conflict, and is completing a book on genealogies of slavery and national subjectivity in American women's narrative.

Elsa Nettels is professor of English at the College of William and Mary. Her publications include *James and Conrad* and *Language, Race, and Social Class in Howells's America* and also articles on Howells, James, Wharton, Cather, and Conrad. She has completed a book on language and gender in the work of Howells, James, Wharton, and Cather.

Jean Pfaelzer, professor of English at the University of Delaware, is the author of *The Utopian Novel in America* (1985–1988) and *Parlor Radical: Rebecca Harding Davis and the Origins of American Social Realism* (1995), and is editor of *A Rebecca Harding Davis Reader* (1995). She has also written on feminism and utopia, feminist theory, Tillie Olsen, Louisa May Alcott, Charlotte Perkins Gilman, and Edward Bellamy.

Tey Diana Rebolledo is professor of Spanish at the University of New Mexico, where she has been the recipient of numerous fellowships, grants, and awards for her work on Chicana writers, including awards from the National Endowment for the Humanities, the Rockefeller Foundation, the New Mexico Quincentennial Commission, and the Mexican American Women's National Association. She served on a Fulbright project in India and has been a Fellow at the Aspen Institute. She is the author of numerous articles on Mexican American women writers in books and journals, is the author of *Women Singing in the Snow: A Cultural Analysis of Chicana Literature* (1995), and has edited three volumes.

Jeanne Campbell Reesman is author of essays on the presentation of female characters by American writers as diverse as Jack London and Djuna Barnes, Henry James and Flannery O'Connor. She has published four books: *American Designs: The Late Novels of James and Faulkner* (1991); *A Handbook of Critical Approaches to Litera-*

ture, 3d edition, with Wilfred Guerin, et al. (1992); *Jack London: Revised Edition*, with Earle Labor (1994); and *Rereading Jack London*, coedited with Leonard Cassuto (1996). She is professor of English and Division Director of English, Classics, Philosophy, and Communication at the University of Texas at San Antonio.

Shu-Mei Shih was born in Korea, raised and educated in Korea, Taiwan, China, and the United States. She teaches modern Chinese literature and Asian American literature at the University of California, Los Angeles, where she is assistant professor, and is presently working on a book-length study of Chinese literary modernism. Her articles can be found in *Positions, Journal of Asian Studies,* and *Public Culture.*

Laura Gutierrez Spencer studied at Agnes Scott College for two years, then transferred to the University of Colorado, where she received her B.A. in Spanish. After studying French and Spanish in Europe, she received her Masters degree in Spanish at New Mexico State University. Spencer completed her Ph.D. at the University of New Mexico. Her dissertation is entitled "A Feminist Analysis of the Poetry of Maria Eugenia Vaz Ferreira." She is director of Chicano Programs at New Mexico State University.

Susan Elizabeth Sweeney is associate professor of English and director of Women's Studies at Holy Cross College, and past president of the International Nabokov Society. In addition to her work on postmodernist fiction, detective fiction, narrative theory, and feminist narratology, she has coedited a book on women and language, *Anxious Power: Reading, Writing, and Ambivalence in Narrative by Women* (1993). Her other publications on Wharton include "Forbidden Reading and Ghostly Writing in Edith Wharton's 'Pomegranate Seed,'" a coauthored essay in *Anxious Power* (1993), and "Edith Wharton's Case of *Roman* Fever," in *Wretched Exotic: Essays on Edith Wharton in Europe* (1993). Her current project concerns twentieth-century revisions of the Gothic romance.

Daneen Wardrop has contributed to *AJQ, Texas Studies in Literature and Language,* the *Emily Dickinson Journal* and is the author of *Emily Dickinson's Gothic: Goblin with a Gauge* (1996). An associate professor of English, she teaches American literature at Western Michigan University.

Linda Wagner-Martin is Emerite Hanes Professor of English and Comparative Literature at the University of North Carolina. Recent books are *The Modern American Novel, 1914–1945; Telling Women's Lives: The New Biography*; and a biography of Gertrude Stein and her family. She is coeditor of *The Oxford Companion to Women's Writing in the United States* and its companion anthology, *The Oxford Book of Women's Writing in the United States.* Editor of the Contemporary section for the *D. C. Heath Anthology of American Literature,* she has written widely on such contemporary authors as Anne Tyler, Toni Morrison, Denise Levertov, Paul Bowles, Sylvia Plath, Joyce Carol Oates, Margaret Atwood, Anne Sexton, and others.

Abby H. P. Werlock, associate professor of English at St. Olaf College, received her doctorate in American Studies from the University of Sussex in England. The recipient of grants from the National Endowment for the Humanities, the Joyce Foundation of Chicago, and the Hemingway Foundation, she received the 1992 Bob Casey award for her article on Steinbeck and Faulkner published in *San Jose Studies.* She is coauthor of the book *Tillie Olsen* (1991) and editor of the forthcoming *A*

Reader's Companion to the American Short Story and *British Women Writing Fiction*, and she has published articles and reviews on numerous American authors, particularly Edith Wharton.

Cynthia Griffin Wolff holds the Class of 1992 Professorship of Humanities at the Massachusetts Institute of Technology, where she teaches American literature and the writing of autobiography and biography. She has published widely on women writers and issues concerning representation of women in literature. The author of *Emily Dickinson* (1986) and *A Feast of Words: The Triumph of Edith Wharton* (1977), she is currently working on Willa Cather.

Index

Aarons, Victoria, xxiv, 195 (n. 2), 197 (n. 18)

Abelmann, Nancy, 161 (n. 20)

Abolition, 4, 5, 6; women's sympathy for, 19 (n. 12); and Christianity, 20 (n. 14)

Adams, Henry, 244 (n. 31)

Adding Machine, The (Rice), 182

African American Women Writers, 90–94

Aguero, Kathleen, 198

Aldington, Richard, 42, 43, 44, 45, 46, 48, 49, 291

Aldrich, Thomas Bailey, 239

Alexander, Meena, 161 (n. 16)

Alice in Wonderland (Carroll), 49

Allen, Gay Wilson, 290

Allen, James Lane, 264

American Antislavery Society, 5

American Colonization Society, 10, 22 (n. 34)

American Literature Association: Symposium on Women Writers, ix–x, 85, 87, 207

Ammons, Elizabeth, 23 (n. 38), 73 (n. 15), 275 (n. 19), 276 (nn. 20, 24)

Anderson, Beatrice, 24 (n. 39)

Anderson, Benedict, 160 (n. 8), 161 (n. 9)

Anthias, Floya, 148

Anzaldúa, Gloria, 80

Aphrodite, 73 (n. 11)

Apthorp, Elaine Sargeant, xxviii (n. 1)

Asquith, Lady Cynthia, 50

Atlantic Monthly, 165, 239, 241, 264

Attlee, Clement Richard, 72 (n. 4)

Austenfeld, Thomas, xxviii (n. 3)

Ayres, Thomas, 231

Baba, Minako, 195 (n. 4)

Baker, Houston A., Jr., 91

Bakhtin, Mikhail, xvi, xxix (n. 5), 213–14, 220

Baldwin, Luther, 226

Bambara, Toni Cade, 90

Barker, Wendy, ix

Barnes, Djuna, 288

Barthes, Roland, 33

Baym, Nina, 18 (n. 6), 19 (n. 7)

Beardsall, Lydia, 47

Beecher, Henry Ward, 5–7, 11, 19 (n. 10)

Beecher-Tilton adultery trial, 3, 17 (n. 1), 19 (n. 10)

Befu, Harumi, 160 (n. 8)

Bennett, Gwendolyn, 93

Bennett, Mildred, 166, 174 (n. 5)

Benson, George, 20 (n. 21)

Berger, John, 59

Berggren, Paula, 69

Berlant, Lauren, 141 (n. 15)

Bibb, Henry, 10

Bierstadt, Albert, 232

Bishop, Elizabeth, x, 203, 209 (n. 12); *North and South*, 203, 209 (n. 12); "In the Waiting Room," 204, 209 (n. 13); "Chemin de Fer," 209 (n. 10); *Geography III*, 209 (n. 12); *Questions of Travel*, 209 (n. 12); "Roosters," 209 (n. 12)

Bizet, Georges, 283, 284; *Carmen*, xxv, 281, 283–86

Bizzell, Patricia, xviii

Black militancy, 8–10, 20 (n. 16), 21 (n. 23)

"Black is as Black Does" (Grimké), 118

"Black Valley" (Sand), 28

Blackall, Jean Frantz, 275 (n. 19), 276 (n. 29)

Bloom, Harold, 235

Bogan, Louise, 289

Booth, Wayne, 196 (n. 7)

Borders, ix–x, xiv–xv, xxi, xxvi, 291–92; and slavery, 130; as kinship, 130–31, 142 (n. 29); and race, 139, 148, 292; simultaneity of, 146; gender of, 148, 292; and nationhood, 148, 292; sexual, 292–93

Bredeson, Robert, 230

Brogan, Jacqueline Vaught, xxiv, 208 (n. 1)

Bronfen, Elisabeth, 282

Brontë, Emily, 264, 266–67, 271; *Wuthering Heights*, 266

Brooks, Gwendolyn, xxiii, 117–18, 119, 121, 127, 140 (n. 2)

Brooks, Van Wyck, 244 (n. 31)

Brown, David, 226

Brown, Gillian, 16, 18 (n. 7), 24 (n. 44)

Brown, Henry "Box," 24 (n. 45)

Brown, John, 21 (n. 25)

Brown, William Wells, 21 (n. 27), 22 (n. 34)

Brownell, William Crary, 261 (n. 10), 263

Bruner, Jerome, xvi

Burleigh, Charles, 5

Butler, Judith, 296 (n. 21)

Calhoun, William, 140 (n. 6)

Callander, Marilyn, 169

Campbell, Donna M., xxv

Canon, revision of, xx–xxi, xxii, 79–88, 90–94, 288–89, 290

Carby, Hazel V., 113 (n. 2), 125–26, 127, 136, 140 (n. 2), 141 (n. 16)

Carlin, Deborah, 172

Cary, Alice, 235

Case, Sue-Ellen, 178–83 (n. 8), 296 (n. 21)

Castillo, Ana, 80

Cather, Willa, x, xiii, xxviii (n. 1), 165–75; *My Ántonia*, xxiii, 165, 166, 168–72; *My Mortal Enemy*, xxiii–xxiv, 165, 168–72; use of male narrators by, xxiv, 165, 166–67, 168–72, 173; use of female narrators by, xxiv, 165, 167, 168–73; "The Novel Demeuble," xxiv, 165, 170; "Panther Cañon," 28; "Tom Outland's Story," 165; *The Professor's House*, 165; *Sapphira and the Slave Girl*, 165; "On the Gull's Road," 165–66, 168; assumption of male identity by, 166; as editor, 166; and S. S. McClure, 166; *Alexander's Bridge*, 166; "The Affair at Grove Station," 166; "The Willing Muse," 166, 167; "Behind the Singer Tower," 166, 168; "The Namesake," 166, 168; "Jack-a-Boy," 167; "A Wagner Matinee," 167; "The Diamond Mine," 167, 168; "Uncle Valentine," 167, 168; "The Joy of Nelly Deane," 168; "Two Friends," 174 (n. 1)

Century, 41

Cervantes Saavedra, Miguel de, 214

Cha, Theresa Hak Kyung, xiv, xxiii, 146–62; *Dictee*, xxiii, 149–60; hybridity of, 147; use of national history by, 147–48, 150–52, 153; multi-voicedness of, 149, 154–55, 159; use of personal history by, 151–52; on "blood-writing," 153–54, 158; on colonization, 153, 154–55, 159; on body-as-text, 154–55; on patriarchy, 154, 158–59; on mother-daughter bonding, 156, 157; on mother-as-self, 159; *Story of a Soul*, 159, 162 (n. 30)

Chatterjee, Partha, 148, 160 (n. 8), 162 (n. 29)

Chesnutt, Charles, 138: "The Wife of His Youth," 134–37, 142 (n. 35)

Chicana writers, 79, 80, 82; and the canon, 79–80, 82–83, 86–87; and the academy, 80–81, 83–86; as philosophers, 81, 82

Child, Lydia Maria, 19 (n. 8)

Chin, Frank, 144, 160 (n. 1)

Chopin, Kate, x, xiii; *The Awakening*, 141 (n. 20)

Christian, Barbara, xx, 99, 114 (n. 8)
Chung-hee, Park, 147, 152
Church, Frederick E., 232; *Rainy Season in the Tropics*, 241
"Cinderella," 279–80, 286
Cisneros, Sandra, x, xx, xxix (n. 4), 79–80, 270–87; "Down There," xx; use of fairy tale figures by, xxv, 279–80, 286; *House on Mango Street*, xxv, 279–81, 286; *Woman Hollering Creek*, xxv, 281–83, 285; use of operatic figures by, xxv, 280–83; "The Family of Little Feet," 279; "Rafaela Who Drinks Papaya Coconut Juice on Tuesdays," 279; and patriarchy, 279–82, 286; "A Smart Cookie," 280–81; "Beautiful and Cruel," 281; "La Fabulosa: A Texas Opera," 282, 286–87; use of female narrator by, 285–86
Cixous, Hélène, 28–29, 34, 35, 180, 285
Clarissa (Richardson), 97
Clark, Suzanne, xvii
Clay Walls (Ronyoung), 147
Clément, Catherine, 278–79, 281, 283–85
Cliff, Michelle, xxix (n. 4)
Clifton, Lucille, 93, 94
Cole, Thomas, 232
Colley, Rae M. Carlton, xxii
Collins, Kathleen, 94
Colored American Magazine, 118, 132, 136, 140 (n. 8), 141 (n. 13)
Colored Cooperative Publishing Company, 141 (n. 13)
Compromise of 1850, 9
Cooke, Rose Terry, 239, 272
Cooper, Anna Julia, 126–27, 141 (n. 22)
Cooper, J. California, 93
Cooper, James Fenimore, 230, 232
Cornell, Drucilla, 208 (n. 2), 209 (n. 10)
Crafts, Ellen, 24 (n. 41)
Crafts, William, 24 (n. 41)
Crane, Stephen, 263
Cress Delahanty (West), 59
Critical Inquiry, 80

Crummell, Alexander, 10, 13
Cummins, Maria, 243 (n. 20)

Dark Madonna Conference, 85
Darlington, W. A., 183 (n. 11)
David, Gail, 240
David Walker's Appeal, 8
Davidson, Cathy N., 92, 215
Davis, Angela, 112, 115 (n. 14), 141 (n. 14)
Davis, Rebecca Harding, xiii, xiv, xxv, 229–45; use of the sublime by, xxv, 241; "The Yares of Black Mountain," xxv, 229–42; use of picturesque by, xxv, 233; construct of female community of, xxv, 231–32, 239–41; on race, 229, 234–35; and Reconstruction, 229, 241–42; use of landscape by, 229–33, 239, 241; use of cultural archetypes by, 229–30; "By-Paths in the Mountains," 230; "Here and There in the Old South," 230; as female local colorist, 230, 238–39, 244 (n. 35); on nature-as-female, 231–33, 237–38, 240; on class, 234; "Waiting for the Verdict," 234; "John Lamar," 234; "Blind Tom," 234; and Enlightenment, 236; "Life in the Iron Mills," 236–38; "Out of the Sea," 237; *Dallas Galbraith*, 237; "David Gaunt," 237; "Earthen Pitchers," 237; "The House on the Beach," 237; "In the Grey Cabins of New England," 238
Davis, Thadious M., 93
de Hoyos, Angela, xxii, 80
D'Emilio, John, 296 (n. 14)
de Lauretis, Teresa, 72 (n. 6)
Delaney, Martin, 10–11, 16, 22 (n. 33), 25 (nn. 45, 48); *Search for a Place*, 15, 22 (n. 33); *Blake*, 21 (n. 24), 25 (n. 45); *The Political Destiny of the Colored Race*, 22 (n. 33)
Demeter/Persephone myth, 156–57, 159
Dialogics, xvi, xvii
Dickens, Charles, 13, 15, 18 (n. 4)

Dickey, Jerry, xxiv
√ Dickinson, Emily, x, xiii, xiv, 87
Dietz, Mary, 195 (n. 6)
Discourse: Asian American, 144,
    145–47; on Victorian sentiment
    and gender, 3–4; on slavery, 3; on
    nationalism, 147–48, 151–52; as
    "blood-writing," 153–54; and female
    irrationality, 234; of the ideal, 234; on
    Northern domination, 234
Doane, Mary Ann, 72 (n. 6), 296 (n. 21)
Donovan, Josephine, 244 (n. 35), 265,
    274 (n. 4), 275 (n. 11)
Douglas, Ann, 4, 18 (n. 6), 37 (n. 5),
    239, 244 (n. 31)
Douglass, Frederick, 8–9, 18 (n. 3),
    19 (n. 8), 21 (n. 25), 22 (n. 34), 96,
    109, 115 (n. 15); *Frederick Douglass's
    Papers*, 21 (n. 27), 25 (n. 45)
Douglass, Sarah M., 9
Dove, Rita, 90
Doyle, Laura, 131
Dreams of Two Yi-min, The (Pai), 147
Dreiser, Theodore, 263
Dryden, John, 291
Du Bois, W. E. B., 126–27, 134, 139,
    141 (n. 23)
duCille, Ann, 142 (n. 27)
Du-Hyun, Yi, 162 (n. 28)

Eagleton, Terry, 195 (n. 6)
Eliot, George, 50; "Red Deeps," 28, 202
Eliot, T. S., 288–91
Ellison, Ralph, 117, 118, 132, 134;
    Invisible Man, 118
Emerson, Ralph Waldo, 19 (n. 8), 27, 37
    (n. 11), 237; *Nature*, 236, 241; "Give
    all to Love," 248
Encounter, 48
Epstein, William, 296 (n. 13)
Erdrich, Louise, x
Erickson, Peter, xxix (n. 4)
Erkkila, Betsy, 293
Ernest, John, xxviii (n. 3)

Faderman, Lillian, 293, 294
Fee, John J., 22 (n. 36)
Felman, Shoshana, 67
Feminine, the, 12, 18 (n. 6); nineteenth-
    century construct of, 125; African
    American model of, 125–26, 127–28;
    and miscegenation, 126–27, 134–36;
    and morphology, 183 (n. 8)
Feminist film theory, 56, 72 (n. 6); "gaze
    theory," 56, 58–59, 66–67
Fernández, Roberta, 85
Fetterly, Judith, xxviii (n. 1)
Feux (Yourcenar), 62 (n. 24)
Fields, James, 239, 244 (n. 35)
Fields, Julia, xxiii, 93, 94
Fisher, Dorothy Canfield, 174 (n. 5)
Fisher, J. T., 10
Flint, Cudworth, 289, 291
Foucault, Michel, 56, 117, 120, 141
    (n. 24)
Fox, Richard Wrightman, 3, 4, 5, 17
    (n. 1), 19 (n. 10)
Fox-Genovese, Elizabeth, 98
Frantz, Marshall, 56, 66, 71
"Fraternal Love" movement, xxi, 4–9,
    19 (n. 10)
Freeman, Mary E. Wilkins, xxv, 239,
    264, 270–72, 274 (n. 4); "A Solitary,"
    270; *Pembroke*, 276 (n. 29)
French, Alice, 265
Freud, Sigmund, 56, 60, 62, 99
Frost, Robert, 203, 209 (n. 12); "Mend-
    ing Wall," 203
Fugitive Slave Act of 1850, 3, 9, 12, 22
    (n. 34)
Fullerton, Morton, 247, 261 (n. 17)

Gaines, Kevin, 142 (n. 37)
"Garden of Love, The" (Blake), 290
Garnet, Henry Highland, 8, 10
Garrison, William Lloyd, 5, 7, 8, 20
    (n. 21), 21 (n. 23), 22 (n. 34)
Gates, Henry Louis, Jr., 91, 92, 93, 96,
    101–2, 113 (n. 3), 114 (n. 9)

Gebhard, Caroline, 238
Gelfant, Blanche, 171
Genette, Gérard, 75 (n. 35)
Genovese, Eugene D., 115 (n. 17)
Gibson, P. J., 94
Gienapp, William E., 17 (n. 3)
Gilbert, Sandra M., xxviii (n. 4), 59, 167, 198
Gonzales-Berry, Erlinda, 85
Goodman, Susan, 276 (n. 24)
Gray, Judd, 176
Gregory, Horace, 289, 291
Gubar, Susan, xxviii (n. 4), 59, 167, 198

H. D. (Hilda Doolittle), 288–89
Hafen, Jane P., xxviii (n. 3)
Haizlip, Shirlee Taylor, 119–20
Haley, Alex, 118; *Roots*, 118
Hamblen, Abigail Ann, 274 (n. 4)
Hansberry, Lorraine, 90, 93
Hardy, Thomas, 45
Harjo, Joy, 209 (n. 14)
Harper's, 241
Harper's Ferry, raid on, 21 (n. 25)
Harper, Frances Ellen Watkins, 93
Harris, Marie, 198
Harris, Sharon M., xxiv
Harris, Trudier, xxii, 91
Hayes, C. J. H., 161 (n. 20)
Heade, Martin Johnson, 231
Hearst, William Randolph, 71 (n. 1)
Hearst's International-Cosmopolitan, 54, 56, 66, 71 (n. 1)
Heath, Stephen, 59, 62, 72 (n. 6)
Hedrick, Joan, 3
Helen of Troy, 293–94
Hemenway, Robert, 93
Hemingway, Ernest, 205
Henderson, Mae, 141 (n. 12)
Henry, Patrick, 24 (n. 45)
Herndl, Diane Price, 276 (n. 25)
Heroic Slave, The, 21 (n. 24)
Herrick, Robert, 202
Herteberg, Bruce, xviii

Higginbotham, Evelyn Brooks, 104
High Wind in Jamaica, A (Hughes), 40
Hine, Darlene Clark, 93
Hofstadter, Richard, 116 (n. 26)
Holly, James Theodore, 10
hooks, bell, 110, 115 (n. 17), 148
Hopkins, Pauline, x, xiv, xvi, xxiii, 117–43; concept of racial purity of, xxiii, 117–19, 128–31, 138, 142 (n. 31); *Contending Forces*, xxiii, xxviii (n. 3), 117–18, 119, 120–36, 139, 141 (n. 13); and assimilation, 117–18; editorial stance of, 117–18; use of language by, 117; *For My People*, 118; "Talma Gordon," 118, 135–39; *Hagar's Daughter: A Story of Southern Caste Prejudice*, 119, 140 (n. 8); *Of One Blood, or, The Hidden Self*, 119, 140 (n. 8), 142 (n. 31); *Winona: A Tale of Negro Life in the South and Southwest*, 119, 140 (n. 8); racialization of gender by, 120–21, 123, 124; gender constructs of, 127, 135–36
Hovey, R. B., 276 (n. 24)
Howard, Richard, 28
Howells, William Dean, 165, 239, 241
Huichol Indians, xxvi
Huo, Hyung Soon, 157, 158, 159
Hurston, Zora Neale, xiv, xxiii, 90, 92, 93, 288; *Their Eyes Were Watching God*, 91, 92
Hutchings, James Mason, 231
Hybridization of races (hybridity), 146–47. *See also* Miscegenation

Ibsen, Henrik, *A Doll's House*, 52
Infinite Divisions (Rebelledo and Rivero), xx
Inness, Sherrie A., 75 (n. 44)
Irigaray, Luce, 73 (n. 13), 220
Irving, Washington, 232

Jackson, Elaine, 94
Jackson, Helen Hunt, xiv, xxi, 27–38;

Jackson, Helen Hunt (*continued*)
critique of American acquisitiveness
by, xxi, 27, 35; *Ramona*, xxi, 27–38;
use of *jouissance* by, xxi, 28, 34, 36;
advocacy of, for Native American
rights, 27–29, 34, 36, 38 (n. 17);
use of quests by, 29–30; *A Century of
Dishonor*, 35, 37 (n. 1)
Jacobs, Harriet, 90, 96, 109, 114 (n. 6),
115 (n. 15); *Incidents in the Life of a
Slave Girl*, 114 (n. 6)
James, Henry, 39, 63, 67, 246, 249, 263;
"The Turn of the Screw," 67; *The
Princess Casamassima*, 74 (n. 27)
Jay, Gregory S., xxi
Jay, William, 6, 17, 24 (n. 43)
Jefferson, Thomas, 225–26
Jehlen, Myra, 3
Jewett, Sarah Orne, xxv, 165–66, 264,
273, 274 (n. 4); "Hallowell's Pretty
Sister," 165; "The Foreigner," 233;
The Country of the Pointed Firs, 265–
66, 273, 274 (n. 11); *Deephaven*, 273
Joan of Arc, 157, 158, 159
Johnson, Abby Arthur, 118
Johnson, Georgia Douglas, 93, 94
Johnson, Rhea, 48
Johnson, Ronald Maberry, 118
Johnson, Ronna C., xxiii
Jones, Howard Mumford, 232–34, 242
(n. 9)
Jones, Jennifer, xxviii (n. 3), 182 (n. 1)
Jones, Robert Edmond, 183 (n. 6)
Jones, Will Owen, 166
Jordan, June, x, xxiv, xxix (n. 4), 198–209;
"War and Memory," xxiv, 198–201,
203–8, 209 (n. 13); *Naming Our
Destiny*, 198, 203–8; and "creative
redemption," 198, 200, 203, 206;
inclusiveness of, 199, 201–3, 205;
views on language of, 199, 201, 204;
Civil Wars, 199–202; *His Own Where*,
199; *Technical Difficulties*, 199; *Things
That I Do in the Dark: Selected Poems*,
199–200; "Poem: For My Brother,

199; "Poem against a Conclusion,"
200; *New Days*, 200, 203; *Passion:
New Poems*, 200; as feminist, 201;
"Gettin Down to get Over: Dedicated
to My Mother," 202–3; "Moving
Home," 202; *Living Room*, 202–3;
"The Female and the Silence of
Man," 203; "Problems of Translation,"
203, 209 (n. 12); use of "medieval
interlacing," 204–5; "Moving Towards
Home," 208 (n. 6); "Poem about My
Rights," 208 (n. 6); "To Free Nelson
Mandela," 208 (n. 6)
Jordanova, L. J., 238
Joseph (of Genesis), 99–101, 103–4
Joslin, Katherine, 264
Jouissance, xxi, 28–29, 33, 34, 146
Journal of Black Male Studies, 90
Joyce, James, 39
Joyce, Joyce Ann, 92
Jubilee (Walker), 118

Kafka, Franz, 49
Kahlo, Frida, xv, xxvii
Kandiyoti, Deniz, 148
Kang, Hyun Yi, 161 (n. 17)
Kaplan, Amy, 264
Kaplan, E. Ann, 72 (n. 6)
Keats, John, 290
Keckley, Elizabeth, 96, 114 (n. 6); *Be-
hind the Scenes; Or, Thirty Years a
Slave and Four Years in the White
House*, 114 (n. 6)
Keng-huan, Yu, 162 (n. 22)
Kennedy, Adrienne, xxiii, 93, 94
Kim, Elaine, 160 (n. 3)
Kim, Myung M., 147–48, 160 (n. 7)
Kindred (Butler), 140 (n. 2)
King, Martin Luther, Jr., 201
Kingston, Maxine Hong, 87
Klinkowitz, Jerome, 195 (n. 3)
Kolodny, Annette, 235, 238–39, 243
(nn. 17, 18, 19, 20)
Korean nationalism, 147, 153–54;
masculinist views in, 147; and the

feminine, 147, 158; and gender, 148;
and the female body, 150, 152, 154;
and language, 151; and religion, 157–
59; and the "minjung" movement,
161 (n. 20)
Kramarae, Cheris, 88 (n. 4)
Kreymborg, Alfred, 291–92
Kristeva, Julia, xvi–xvii, xviii–xix, 73
(n. 13), 160 (n. 8), 215, 219, 220,
284
Ku Klux Klan, 231, 242
Kun, Ahn Joong, 154, 162 (n. 22)

"La Passion de Jeanne d'Arc" (Dreyer),
158
La Traviata (Giuseppe Fortunino
Francesco Verdi), 283
LaBelle, Jenijoy, 57–58, 59, 73 (nn. 8, 11)
Lacan, Jacques, 33, 56, 57, 74 (n. 23)
Laclau, Ernesto, 196 (n. 14)
Lapsley, Gaillard, 248–49
Larsen, Nella, 93; *Quicksand*, 142
(n. 40); *Passing*, 292
Last Lecture Series, 81
Lauter, Paul, xx, xxv, xxviii (n. 4)
Lawrence, D. H., xxii, 39–52; *Lady
Chatterley's Lover*, 39, 40, 48, 49; *The
Plumed Serpent*, 39–42, 46, 47, 49;
"The Daughters of the Vicar," 44;
"You Touched Me," 44; infidelities of,
46; relationship with children of, 47,
48, 50; and class, 47; *Sons and Lovers*,
47; *Aaron's Rod*, 47; *The Rainbow*, 48,
50, 51; *Women in Love*, 50, 51; "The
Captain's Doll," 51; *St. Mawr*, 51
Lawrence, Frieda, 42–46, 48
Leavis, F. R., 44, 47–50, 51–52
Lee, Hermione, 167, 170
Lewis, R. W. B., 71 (n. 1), 246–47, 261
(n. 10)
Liberator, 7, 22 (n. 34)
*Like One of the Family . . . Conversations
from a Domestic's Life* (Childress), 93
Lim, Shirley, 160 (n. 4)
Lincoln, Abraham, 249, 258–59

Lippincott's, 241
Literary World, 15
"Little Snow White" (Grimm and
Grimm), 58–60, 64–65, 73
(nn. 11, 15)
Little Women (Alcott), 27
London, Jack, 263
Lorde, Audre, 198, 209 (n. 10)
Lost Names (Kim), 147
Lowe, Lisa, 150
Lowell, Amy, x, xiv, xxv–xxvi, 288–96;
and borders, xxv–xxvi, 291–93; life of,
289–90; work on John Keats by, 290;
"A Critical Fable," 290; "Manifesto,"
291; sexuality of, 292–94; *Pictures
of the Floating World*, 292–93; "The
Sisters," 293; "Two Speak Together,"
293; "Venus Transiens," 293; use of
Helen of Troy by, 293–94; "The On-
Lookers," 293–95; "Potters," 294; and
gender, 294
Lowell, James Russell, 239
Lyons, Bonnie, 197 (n. 19)

MacCormack, Carol, 244 (n. 28)
Madame Butterfly (Puccini), 280
Madden, Richard, 183 (n. 6)
Magazine of Mexico, 41
Malcolm X, 201
*Man Sei: The Making of a Korean
American* (Hyun), 147
Mansfield, Katherine, 39, 173–74;
Journal, 173–74
Marchalonis, Shirley, 263, 264
Marcus, Lisa, xxiii
Marshall, Paule, 93
Marsh-Lockett, Carol P., 94
Martin, Jay, 276 (n. 23)
Martyred, The (Kim), 147
Masculinity, constructs of, xxi, 4–7, 18
(n. 6); and patriarchy, 6; and slavery, 6,
16; and nonviolence, 7, 9, 15; African
American, 8–9, 11, 15–16
Mather, Cotton, xxvii (n. 1)
May, Samuel J., 5, 7

McBride, Phyllis, xxviii (n. 1)
McClure, S. S., 166
McClure's Magazine, 166
McDowell, Deborah, 93
McDowell, Margaret B., 75 (n. 44)
McKay, Nellie Y., 91
McMillan, Terry, 93
Medusa, 62, 73 (n. 11)
Mein Kampf (Schicklgruber), 292
Melville, Herman, 24 (n. 45), 27; *Benito Cereno*, 21 (n. 24); *White-Jacket*, 27
Memoirs of Pancho Villa, The (Guzmán), 81
Mexican War, 6
Meyering, Sheryl L., xxviii (n. 1)
Millay, Edna St. Vincent, 87, 288
Miller, Angela, 229, 241, 242 (n. 8)
Miller, David, 243 (n. 10)
Miller, Floyd R., 25 (n. 45)
Millett, Kate, 288
Milton, John, 291
"Mirror" (Plath), 54, 64–65
Miscegenation, 119–20, 130–32, 134, 136, 136–37, 138, 140 (n. 6), 142 (n. 27)
Mitchell, Juliet, 73 (n. 13)
Moers, Ellen, 28, 34, 35
Moghadam, Valentine M., 148
Moi, Toril, xvi
Molière, 214
Monk, Janice, 88 (n. 4)
Moore, Harry T., 47, 48
Moore, Marianne, 288
Mora, Pat, xxii, xxvi, 80; *Nepantla: Essays from the Land in the Middle*, ix
Morrison, Toni, x, xiv, xx, xxiii, 90–92, 93, 201; *Beloved*, 91, 140 (n. 1); *Song of Solomon*, 91, 139 (n. 1)
Moses, Wilson Jeremiah, 11, 22 (n. 34), 140 (n. 9)
Mouffe, Chantal, 196 (n. 14)
Mujeres Grandes, ix
Mulvey, Laura, 56
Murfee, Mary N., 265

Nation, The, 238, 244 (n. 31)
National Association for Chicano Studies Conference, 84
Naylor, Gloria, 92; *Mama Day*, 91
Negro a Beast, The (Carroll), 138, 140 (n. 6)
Nelson, Cary, 288
Nelson, Dana, 221, 225
Nettels, Elsa, xxiii, 275 (nn. 13, 16)
Nevius, Blake, 266, 267, 275 (n. 16)
Newman, Beth, 56, 72 (n. 6)
Nichos, xv, xxvi–xxvii
"No More Cookies, Please" (Trujillo), 83
Norris, Frank, 263
North American Anti-Slavery Convention, 10
North Star, 26 (n. 48)
Northampton Association, 9, 20 (n. 21)
Norton, Sara, 248
Norwood, Vera, 88 (n. 4)
Nuernberg, Susan, xxviii (n. 1)
Nye, Naomi Shihab, ix

O'Brien, Sharon, 167
Obregón, Álvaro, 41, 176
Oelschlaeger, Max, 242 (n. 3)
Omolade, Barbara, 108, 114 (n. 14), 115 (n. 17), 116 (n. 26)
O'Neill, Eugene, 274 (n. 4)
Opening the American Mind (Sill, Chaplin, Ritzke, and Wilson), xx
Other, the, xv, 219; and construct of self, xvii, xx, 88; female as, 178
Otis, Harrison Gray, 226

Paley, Grace, xxiv, xxix (n. 4), 185–97; creation of character by, 185–86, 188–89, 191; invention of self by, 185–92, 193–94; and feminism, 185, 193; and Judaism, 185, 192–93; "Faith in the Afternoon," 185; "Listening," 185, 187–88, 194; "Enormous Changes at the Last Minute," 186; use of multivoiced narrators by, 186–87, 192, 194;

"The Story Healer," 187–88; "Love," 188–89; "A Conversation with My Father," 189–90; "A Woman Young and Old," 189; "Friends," 192; "Wants," 192; "The Immigrant Story," 192–93; "The Loudest Voice," 195

Pali, 156–57, 159, 162 (n. 25)

Parker, Andrew, 16 (n. 9)

Parrington, V. L., 244 (n. 31)

Passage to India, A (Forster), 40

Paul, Saint, 66, 74 (n. 32)

Peterson, Carla L., xxviii (n. 3)

Pfaelzer, Jean, xxv

Phelps, Elizabeth Stuart, 239

Phillips, John S., 166

Pierce, Edward L., 18 (n. 5)

Pinsker, Sanford, xxix (n. 4)

Plessy v. Ferguson, 134, 142 (n. 34)

PMLA, 80

Poe, Edgar Allan, 17, 261 (n. 15)

Porter, Katherine Anne, xiv, xxii, xxviii (n. 3), 39–53; search for order by, xxii, 40, 51; *Flowering Judas*, 39; "Quetzalcoatl," 39, 40, 42; "A Wreath for a Gamekeeper," 39, 40, 42, 44, 48; and D. H. Lawrence, 39–42; as feminist, 40; and Mexican primitivism, 40–42; "Flowering Judas," 41; views on obscenity of, 42, 49; attitude toward marriage of, 46–47; attitude toward maternity of, 47; and class, 47

Pound, Ezra, 288–91

Powell, William P., 21 (n. 23)

Pratt, Annis, 244 (n. 37)

Price, Kenneth M., xxviii (n. 1)

Purvise, Robert, 9

Quiet Odyssey (Lee), 147

Rabelais, François, 214

Radharkrishnan, R., 146, 153

Radicalism, nineteenth-century, 5, 7, 19 (n. 8)

Ransom, John Crowe, 270, 275 (n. 18)

Raphael, Lev, 261 (n. 17)

"Rapunzel," 279–80, 286

Rebelledo, Tey Diana, xxii; *The Memoirs of Panchita Villa*, xxii, 80–81, 88

Recolonization Movement, 9–11, 15, 16, 21 (n. 27), 22 (n. 34), 24 (n. 45)

Redefining American Literary History (Ruoff and Ward), xx

Redmond, Patricia, 91

Rees, David, 161 (n. 19)

Remond, Charles Lennox, 19 (n. 8)

Renza, Louis J., 244 (n. 31)

Rich, Adrienne, 198, 200, 202; *An Atlas of the Difficult World*, 202, 208 (n. 3), 209 (n. 10)

Rigney, Barbara, 91

Rolph, C. H., 48

Roosevelt, Theodore, 247

Rose, Alan Henry, 274 (n. 4)

Rose, Jacqueline, 33

Rosowski, Susan, 169, 172

Ross, Andrew, 196 (n. 14)

Roth, Moira, 162 (n. 30)

Rowe, Karen, 283

Russell, Ada Dwyer, 290

Russo, Mary, 215, 225

Said, Edward W., 160 (n. 8), 220

San Antonio de Padua, xv

Santayana, George, 238, 244 (n. 31)

Scott, Winfield Townley, 289

Scudder, Horace, 239

Sears, John, 231

Search for a Place (Campbell), 15, 22 (n. 33)

Self: constructs of, xiv–xvi; rhetoric of, xiv, xvi, xvii; semiotics of, xvi, xvii; and narration, xvi, xx, 155–56, 157, 158–59; and Other, xvii; and separation anxiety, xviii; Latina, xx; and gendered gaze, xxii; and race, 114 (n. 7), 116 (n. 26); and sexual exploitation, 114 (n. 6), 115 (nn. 15, 17), 116 (n. 26); masculinist, 144, 147; transnational,

Self (*continued*)
144–46, 152–53; Asian American, 145–46; borders of, 146; multivoicedness of, 149; as mother, xviii, 159; and blood-writings," 162 (n. 22); contiguity of, 178
Sergeant, Elizabeth Shepley, 272
Shakespeare, William, 174; *Hamlet*, 289
Shelley, Percy Bysshe, 202
Shih, Shu-mei, xiv, xxiii; 1.5 generation, xxiii
Siebers, Tobin, 62
Signs, 80
Simson, Rennie, 114 (n. 6)
Singley, Carol J., 72 (nn. 6, 7), 74 (n. 32), 75 (n. 39)
Slave Narratives, 139 (n. 2)
Slote, Bernice, 166
Smith, Gerrit, 5
Smith, Jessie Carney, 93
Smith, John Hugh, 249
Smith, Sidonie, 222
Smith, William Benjamin, 140 (n. 6)
Smith-Rosenberg, Carroll, 218, 228 (n. 6)
"Snow White," 58–60, 64–65, 73 (nn. 11, 15)
Sollers, Werner, 142 (n. 35)
Soon, Yu Guan, 149–50, 157, 158, 162 (n. 22)
Sor Juana Inés de la Cruz, xxii, xviii, 80, 87; *Carta Atenagórica*, 80
Southworth, E. D. E. N., 243 (n. 20)
Spencer, Laura Gutierrez, xxv
Spiller, Robert, 238
Spillers, Hortense, 114 (n. 7), 124–25, 127, 130–32, 139, 141 (n. 17), 142 (n. 29)
St. Thérèsa de Lisieux, 157–58, 159; *Story of a Soul*, 159, 162 (n. 30)
Stafford, Beth, 88
Stasi, Lawrence Di, 74 (n. 23)
Stein, Gertrude, 206, 289
Stein, Roger, 239
Stevens, Wallace, 202, 208 (n. 1), 209 (n. 10); *Parts of a World*, 208 (n. 3)

Stewart, James Brewer, 18 (n. 5)
Stout, Janis, xxviii (n. 3), 169
Stowe, Harriet Beecher, xiii, 11–17, 27, 30, 96; and "Fraternal Love" movement, xxi, 11–13; *Uncle Tom's Cabin*, xxi, 11–17, 27, 30, 115 (n. 20); construct of masculinity of, xxi, 11–17, 18 (n. 7), 23 (n. 39), 24 (nn. 41, 43); and Cotton Mather, xxvii (n. 1); and gynocentrism, xxviii (n. 1); construct of slavery of, 3, 18 (n. 7), 25 (n. 48); as political propagandist, 3, 4, 17 (n. 3), 18 (n. 7); use of sentimental fiction by, 4; *Dred: A Tale of the Great Dismal Swamp*, 11, 21 (n. 24); as racist, 23 (n. 37), 25 (n. 47)
Strand, Ginger, 182 (n. 1)
Street, The (Petry), 93
Sumner, Charles, 18 (n. 5)
Sundquist, Eric, 142 (n. 34)
Sweeney, Susan, xxii, 72 (nn. 6, 7), 74 (n. 21), 75 (nn. 37, 39)
Swift, Jonathan, 214
Synder, Ruth, 176, 177
Syngman, Rhee, 147, 152

Tan, Amy, 87
Tate, Claudia, 97, 101, 109, 113 (nn. 3, 5), 126, 128
Taylor, Anne Robinson, 167
Tenney, Tabitha, xiv, xxiv, xxviii (n. 3), 213–27; *Female Quixotism*, xxiv, xxviii (n. 3), 213–27; use of the carnivalesque by, xxiv, 213–14, 216–19; view on "anti-novel" of, 213, 223–24; grotesque imagery of, 214–15, 218; on class, 215–18, 219–23, 225, 227; on gender, 215–18, 222–23, 225–27; and the Enlightenment, 216, 221, 225; on sexuality, 217–18, 221–23; on race, 217–18, 220–23, 225, 227; and colonization, 219–20; on patriarchy, 219, 226–27; and isolationism, 225–26
Tennyson, Alfred, Lord, 134, 135

Terry, Ellen, 166, 174 (n. 5)
Terry, Lucy, 92
Texas Tornados, "(Hey Baby) Qué Pasó?,"
    xxv, 286
"There is Nothing" (Gonzales), 88
Thoreau, Henry David, 237, 242 (n. 3);
    Walden, 241
Tilton, Elizabeth, 6
Tilton, Theodore, 6, 19 (n. 10)
Todorov, Tzvetan, 219, 228 (n. 7)
Tompkins, Jane, 18 (n. 6), 19 (n. 7)
Torsney, Cheryl B., 274 (n. 2)
Traubel, Horace, 248
Treadwell, Sophie, xiv, xxiv, 176–84;
    Machinal, xxiv, xxviii (n. 3), 176–79,
    181–82, 183 (n. 11); *For Saxophone*,
    xxiv, 177–82, 183 (nn. 6, 10); use of
    expressionistic devices, xxiv, 176–77,
    182 (n. 3); use of Synder-Gray Case
    by, 176, 182 (n. 1); *Gringo*, 176; as
    reporter, 176; *Poe*, 176; *Rights*, 176;
    use of Mary Wollstonecraft by, 176;
    woman-as-subject in works of, 177–
    78, 180–82; use of introspective mono-
    logue by, 177–78; use of dramatic
    narrative by, 177, 181–82; *The Eyes
    of the Beholder*, 182 (n. 3); *Madame
    Bluff*, 182 (n. 3); *The Love Lady*, 183
    (n. 6)
Treichler, Paula A., 88
Tristram Shandy (Sterne), 214
Truth, Sojourner, 9

Ultraviolet Sky, The (Villanueva), 84, 89
    (n. 5)
Utopian Communities, 6

Vasquez, Arturo, xv, xxvi–xxvii; *Libro de
    las Santos de EneArt*, xxvi
Vasquez, Enedina Casarez, xv, xxvi–xxvii;
    Libro de las Santos de EneArt, xxvi
Virgen de Guadalupe, xxviii
Virgin, cult of, xvi–xvii
Voice of the Fugitive, 10
Vygotsky, Lev, xvi, xxix (n. 5)

Wagner-Martin, Linda, xxvi, 92
Waid, Candace, 246–47, 274 (nn. 4, 8),
    275 (n. 12)
Walker, Alice, xxiii, 90, 92, 93, 198, 201,
    209 (n. 10); *The Color Purple*, 91;
    Meridian, 139 (n. 1)
Walker, Cheryl, 293
Wardrop, Daneen, xxi
Warhol, Robyn, 72 (n. 6)
Washington, Booker T., 118
Washington, George, 249, 253–54
Weed, Charles Leander, 231
Welter, Barbara, 141 (n. 20), 228 (n. 11)
Welty, Eudora, x
Werlock, Abby, xxv
West, Dorothy, xxiii, 93
Wharton, Edith, x, xiii, xxii, xxv, xxviii
    (n. 1), 54–75, 166, 167, 246–61,
    263–77; "Looking Glass" ("The
    Mirror"), xxii, 54–72; *Summer*, xxv,
    73 (n. 8), 246–62, 264; *Ethan Frome*,
    xxv, 246–62, 264–74; influence of
    Walt Whitman on, xxv, 246–61; and
    local color, xxv, 263–66; use of theme
    of gaze by, 55–59, 62, 64–66, 67, 68,
    73 (n. 10); use of theme of identity by,
    55–59; "The Eyes," 62, 69, 74 (n. 24);
    use of Medusa by, 62, 74 (n. 24); *The
    Writing of Fiction*, 63; use of mascu-
    line discourse by, 69, 263–64; *Ghosts*,
    69, 71 (n. 1); and authorial identity,
    69–70, 264; "A Place of Perrier," 71
    (n. 1); *The Collected Stories of Edith
    Wharton*, 71 (n. 1); *The World Over*,
    71 (n. 1); "All Souls," 72 (n. 4); *The
    House of Mirth*, 72 (n. 8), 73 (n. 21),
    269; *The Custom of the Country*, 72
    (n. 8); *The Reef*, 72 (n. 8); Aphrodite,
    73 (n. 11); *The Mother's Recompense*,
    73 (n. 8); *Artemis to Actaeon and Other
    Verse*, 246–47; and Morton Fullerton,
    247, 261 (n. 17); *The Gods Arrive*, 248;
    The Spark, 248; *Hudson River Brack-
    eted*, 248; *A Backward Glance*, 248,
    264; sexuality of, 248, 252, 254–55,

Wharton, Edith (*continued*)
261 (n. 17); "Terminus," 250; importance of mother to, 257–59; "Mortal
Lease," 261 (n. 10); and naturalism,
263–64; "Bunner Sisters," 272
White, Barbara A., 274 (n. 4)
Whitman, Walt, xxv, 246–61, 290;
"Children of Adam," xxv, 249–50,
252, 255–59, 262 (n. 24); "Song of
Myself," xxv, 246, 249–53; "America,"
xxv, 249, 260; "When Lilacs Last in
the Dooryard Bloom'd," xxv, 249–50,
258–59; "So Long," 246; *Leaves of
Grass*, 246–47, 249–61; "Life," 246–
47; "Songs of Parting," 246, 250; "Terminus," 247; "Drum Taps," 247, 253,
260; "Out of the Cradle, Endlessly
Rocking," 248; *A Backward Glance
o'er Travel'd Roads*, 248; "Democratic
Vistas," 249, 260, 262 (n. 23); "Autumn Rivulets," 250, 253, 258; "Sands
at Seventy," 250; "To A Common
Prostitute," 253; "When I heard the
Learn'd Astronomer," 256–57; "The
City Dead-House," 257–58; "The
Sleeper," 260; "To a Certain Civilian," 260
Williams, Sherley Anne, 90; *Dessa Rose*,
140 (n. 1)
Wilson, Harriet E., x, xiv, xvi, xxiii, 96–
116; female self-representations of,
xxiii, 96, 98, 108, 115 (n. 14); narrative
interventions of, xxiii; *Our Nig: or
Sketches from the Life of a Free Black*,
xxiii, xxviii (n. 3), 96–116; sexual
exploitation as theme used by, 97–
98, 101, 103, 109–11, 115 (n. 14);
biblical metaphors used by, 99, 100,
101, 104; authority of, 102; authorial
motives of, 104
Wolff, Cynthia Griffin, xxi, 23 (n. 38),
246–47, 265, 270, 276 (n. 28)
Wollstonecraft, Mary, 176
Wood, Clement, 289
Woolf, Virginia, 39; *To the
Lighthouse*, 40
Woolson, Constance Fenimore, 239, 274
(n. 2)
Wright, Richard, 118, 140 (n. 2); *Native
Son*, 118

Yarborough, Richard, 23 (n. 37)
Yeats, William Butler, 203, 209 (n. 12);
"Leda and the Swan," 203, 209 (n. 12)
Yellin, Jean Fagan, 244 (n. 35)
"Yellow Wallpaper, The" (Gilman), 87
Yuval-Davis, Nira, 148

Zagarell, Sandra, 234
Zaturenska, Marya, 289
Ziolkowski, Theodore, 73 (n. 13)